D1711371

The Literature of Labor and the Labors of Literature juxtaposes representations of labor in fictional texts with representations of labor in nonfictional texts in order to trace the intersections between aesthetic and economic discourse in nineteenth-century America. This intersection is particularly evident in the debates about symbol and allegory, and the author contends that allegory during this period was critiqued on precisely the same grounds as mechanized labor. Despite the undeniable differences between literary characters and historical workers, the discursive possibilities for constructing the character of both fictional and nonfictional persons are strikingly similar. Both allegory and new forms of labor produced a version of personhood that seemed frighteningly flat, a flatness that attacked the substance of the work ethic and, indeed, the very foundations of American individualism.

Using this contextualized model of allegory, Weinstein goes on to argue that texts by Hawthorne, Melville, Twain, and Henry Adams are best understood as both allegories of labor (that is, the allegorical representations of the nature and cost of being a laboring being) and labors of allegory (that is, the visibility of the author's work of representation). In the course of completing a historical investigation, Weinstein revolutionizes the notion of allegorical narrative, which is exposed as a literary medium of greater complexity and consequence than has previously been implied – a working authorial vehicle for engaged and at times socially turbulent thought.

CAMBRIDGE STUDIES IN AMERICAN LITERATURE AND CULTURE

The Literature of Labor and the Labors of Literature

CAMBRIDGE STUDIES IN AMERICAN LITERATURE AND CULTURE

Editor:
ERIC SUNDQUIST, *University of California, Los Angeles*

Founding Editor:
ALBERT GELPI, *Stanford University*

Advisory Board:
Nina Baym, *University of Illinois, Champaign–Urbana*
Sacvan Bercovitch, *Harvard University*
Albert Gelpi, *Stanford University*
Myra Jehlen, *University of Pennsylvania*
Carolyn Porter, *University of California, Berkeley*
Robert Stepto, *Yale University*
Tony Tanner, *King's College, Cambridge University*

Continued on pages following the Index

D'YOUVILLE COLLEGE
LIBRARY

The Literature of Labor
and the Labors of Literature

Allegory in Nineteenth-Century American Fiction

CINDY WEINSTEIN

California Institute of Technology

CAMBRIDGE
UNIVERSITY PRESS

Published by the Press Syndicate of the University of Cambridge
The Pitt Building, Trumpington Street, Cambridge CB2 1RP
40 West 20th Street, New York, NY 10011-4211, USA
10 Stamford Road, Oakleigh, Melbourne 3166, Australia

© Cambridge University Press 1995

First published 1995

Printed in the United States of America

Library of Congress Cataloging-in-Publication Data
Weinstein, Cindy.
The literature of labor and the labors of literature : allegory in
nineteenth-century American fiction / Cindy Weinstein.
p.   cm. – (Cambridge studies in American literature and
culture : 89)
Includes bibliographical references and index.
ISBN 0-521-47054-4 (hc)
1. American fiction – 19th century – History and criticism.
2. Work – Social aspects – United States – History – 19th century.
3. Aesthetics, American – 19th century.   4. Working class in
literature.   5. Work in literature.   6. Allegory. – I. Title.
II. Series.
PS374.W64W45   1995
813'.409355 – dc20   94-12212

A catalog record for this book is available from the British Library.

ISBN 0–521–47054–4 hardback

Do your work, and I shall know you. Do your work, and you shall reinforce yourself.

Emerson, "Self-Reliance"

Contents

Acknowledgments

This work is the product of inspired and inspiring teachers. My deepest debt of gratitude goes to Eric Sundquist, who has always been supportive, generous, and kind. I am especially grateful to Martha Banta, Mitch Breitwieser, Lawrence Buell, Wai-chee Dimock, Michael Gilmore, Carolyn Porter, Michael Rogin, and John Sutherland. Jon Klancher, Mac Pigman, and W. J. T. Mitchell offered valuable advice. Ron Bush, Kevin Gilmartin, Larry Howe, and Jim Astorga have read this book almost as many times as I have written it, and I thank them for their time, energy, and endless support. Over the years, Dori Hale has tirelessly talked about these ideas and has critiqued more versions of this project than anyone has a right to ask. Her readings have immeasurably improved the argument. Thanks also to Jeffrey Knapp, master documenter. The Americanist reading group at Berkeley offered invaluable suggestions that have found their way onto many of these pages. Thank you to T. Susan Chang and the editorial staff, especially Jane Van Tassel, at Cambridge University Press for guidance all along the way. I would also like to thank Doreen Domb for her assistance. Stacey Byrnes, Mary Caraway, Jane Garrity, Annie Thrower, and Arlene Zuckerberg, as well as my siblings, Linda Madden and Lyle Weinstein, have given me the necessary intellectual and personal sustenance over the course of many years. My mother's full heart and my father's fine mind have been my inspirations. Finally, Jim Astorga's generosity, intelligence, and humor have made all of my labors endurable. I thank him for this and for Sarah, the reward for my labors.

The research for this book was made easier by many librarians. Thanks to Tess Legaspi in the Inter-Library Loan office at Caltech, Pat Rowe and Janine Whitcomb at the Center for Lowell History, Kathleen Leslie and Janet Heywood at the Mount Auburn Cemetery Archives, and Robert Hirst, Brenda Bailey, and Simon Hernandez of the Mark Twain Project at the University of California, Berkeley. I would also like to thank the Mark Twain Project for permission to use material from the collection.

Earlier versions of the Hawthorne and Melville chapters appeared as "The Calm Before the Storm: Laboring Through *Mardi*" (*American Literature*, 65 [June 1993]), "The Invisible Hand Made Visible: The Birthmark" (*Nineteenth-Century Literature*, 48 [June 1993]), and "Melville at the Machine of Allegory" (*Praxis*, Spring 1990).

Introduction

The narrator of Poe's "The Man That Was Used Up" is thoroughly capti-
vated by Brevet Brigadier-General John A. B. C. Smith, whose good
looks and fine physique make him "an especial favorite" with "the ladies"
as well as the gentlemen in the tale.[1] He lingers over each part of Smith's
body, from "the handsomest pair of whiskers under the sun," "a mouth
utterly unequalled," and "the most brilliantly white of all conceivable
teeth" to the "admirably modelled" arms and the "properly proportioned
calf" (405–6). But even as he delectates in Smith's "bodily endowments"
(406), the narrator begins to suspect that the sum of these endowments
does not equal its parts:

> There *was* a primness, not to say stiffness, in his carriage – a degree of
> measured and, if I may so express it, of rectangular precision attending
> his every movement, which, observed in a more diminutive figure,
> would have had the least little savor in the world of affectation, pompos-
> ity, or constraint, but which, noticed in a gentleman of his undoubted
> dimensions, was readily placed to the account of reserve, *hauteur* – of a
> commendable sense, in short, of what is due to the dignity of colossal
> proportion. (406)

Smith's dignity has nothing to do with his character and everything to do
with his size. The prim and precise way in which Smith carries his body
is initially understood by the narrator to be a sign of reserve appropriate
to such a well-proportioned body; yet the truth of the matter, as the
narrator eventually discovers after repeated and arduous attempts to
fathom Smith's secret, is that Smith's body carries *him*, and the sign of
reserve is no sign at all but rather the literal reserve of a body that is
affected, constrained, and made up of manufactured body parts. The
stiffness and primness of Smith's carriage, far from signifying the dignity
of his character, refer to a mechanical body that calls attention to itself as
an artifact or, more precisely, as a product of labor in a market economy.

1

In 1839, the same year that Poe published "The Man That Was Used Up," William Ellery Channing delivered a lecture to an audience of mechanics' apprentices entitled "On the Elevation of the Laboring Classes." His subject was the value of manual labor and the impact of labor on the development of character. Channing insists on the necessity of work, for "work we all must, if we mean to bring out and perfect our nature."[2] Only when comprehending and experiencing the transcendental quality of work do we realize that work is "one of our great preparations for another state of being" (39). But his concerns about certain less transcendental states of being produced by new kinds of work are evident early on, particularly "the division of labor" that "tends to dwarf the intellectual powers, by confining the activity of the individual to a narrow range, to a few details, perhaps to the heading of pins, the pointing of nails, or the tying together of broken strings" (39). These divisions transform work from an "essential foundation of improvement, exertion, and happiness in the world to come" to "a monotonous, stupefying round of unthinking toil" (39). Channing's adherence to an ideal of work begins to break down as his representation of labor splits into two: the first being a utopia of satisfying manual labor in the Jeffersonian tradition and the second being a more problematic vision of industrialized, mechanical labor. This development in Channing's address suggests that to talk about labor in this period, whether it be manual, mechanical, or literary, is inevitably to talk about mechanization, machines, and the market economy. To invoke one is to invoke the other. Channing's sanctification of labor is thus uneasily constrained by the reality of mechanization and specialization, which has the deleterious effect of narrowing, stupefying, and even flattening out individual character, until a man working may look more like a "machine than like a man" (46).

This is, of course, what the narrator of "The Man That Was Used Up" is worried about when he first meets John A. B. C. Smith and is unable to interpret satisfactorily his "rectangular precision." John A. B. C. Smith's body is understood by the narrator to be an allegory, but of what? His "primness" and "stiffness" are taken to be the signs of gentlemanly reserve, the signs of a well-developed, bourgeois character. But at the definitional heart of allegory, which comes from *allos* (other) and *agoreuein* (speak openly, speak in the assembly or market), is the possibility of disjunction or simulation. The disjunction between Smith's bodily movements and what those movements mean is first read in the context of gentlemanly behavior and thus explained (away). If disjunction is at the very core of allegory, so too is an injunction to contain it. This unambiguous, one-to-one correlation between allegorical characters and what they stand for is, of course, the starting point not only for Coleridge's critique of allegory but also (even after de Man) for our expectations of allegorical characters: "Now an allegory is but a translation of abstract notions into a picture-language which is itself nothing but an abstraction from objects of the senses."[3] Although the narrator of Poe's tale eventually learns the mistaken simplicity of this account of allegory, which posits a hermeneutic utopia where abstract notions and picture language exist in a mirror relation to one another, we, as readers, might have anticipated it right from the start, if only because of the protagonist's name – John A. B. C. Smith, a name that confuses as much as it clarifies the identity of the central character. On the one hand, "John Smith" refers to the famous seventeenth-century Indian fighter of Jamestown, and, on the other, "A. B. C." alludes to the letters of the alphabet, the beginning of language, and even the unavoidable fact of Smith's textual existence in a story by the nineteenth-century author Edgar Allan Poe. To be called John Smith is easily explicated, relatively speaking. To have A. B. C. as one's middle name(s) is less so. The name is both transparently and ambiguously referential. The name simultaneously says one thing and means another. The narrator is, however, less interested in Smith's name than in his body, which shares some of the subtleties of his name. Smith's body, it turns out, is transparently, indeed shockingly, referential (the "rectangular precision" exists because his body parts are quite literally rectangularly precise, having been made by workers) at the same time as his body ambiguously refers to his pomposity or dignity or size. But even as Smith's "primness" and "stiffness" are interpreted as the signs of a gentlemanly reserve, the narrator has the nagging sense that these signs might be signifying something else. Why the inkling of something else, and what might it be?

I take the moment of hermeneutic uncertainty, when the qualities of Smith's body that had first impressed the narrator as noble and ideal but now seem enigmatic and discomforting, as representative of a cultural disease with allegorical characters which was especially acute in nineteenth-century America. Smith's body is a text (and his status as text is further underscored by the A. B. C. of his middle name[s]) that the narrator wishes to but cannot confidently read. His "measured" and precise movements are the corporeal signs that seem to be particularly resonant, particularly confusing, particularly "remarkable" (405) – remarkable, it turns out, in ways similar to the bodily performances of Melville's Cadwallader Cuticle or the female mill workers in the "Tartarus of Maids" or the duplicates in Twain's *Mysterious Stranger, #44.* Allegorical characters, as Poe's tale makes clear, represent a perfection of the body (in all of its glorious precision and mechanicalness) while simultaneously problematizing the relation between that ideal body and other ideals axiomatic to the construction of American identity, such as the self-made man, individual agency, and the work ethic. Smith's "rectangular precision," for example, exists courtesy of the art of prosthetics. Having lost his arms, legs, scalp, and even voice in a battle against the Bugaboo and Kickapoo Indians, he has nevertheless managed to reconstitute himself by purchasing body parts from experts in the field – certainly an inversion/perversion of the self-made man.[4] The body of this self-made man has been assembled by the blood of Indians (even his name has been borrowed from another Indian fighter, John Smith), the toil of Smith's "black rascal" (412) servant Pompey who puts his body together each day, limb by limb, and the labor of the many workers who make those arms, legs, and even voices for a living. Furthermore, the communal and mechanical nature of this allegorical body, which can be witnessed by the narrator only in the privacy of Smith's home, powerfully undermines any faith in individual agency or, for that matter, in the individual at all. In fact, the title of the story includes a grammatical ambiguity suggesting that the man that was used up is not even a man; after all, how can a man be a "that"? But we need only think of Ahab or the boys in Hank Morgan's Man-factory or Henry Adams the manikin to realize that Smith takes his place in a long line of men who are also "thats" because of the work they do: work that unravels the distinction between organic and mechanical, between agent and instrument, between person and thing. Smith's allegorical body is, in part, a result of his work, his "rather hot work" (411), to use Smith's own phrase; moreover, his mechanical body is the clearest sign of his expertise in and dedication to the work of Indian killing.

John A. B. C. Smith also fits the profile of an allegorical character as defined in the twentieth-century tradition by Angus Fletcher and Charles Feidelson, whose critical debts to Coleridge are ubiquitous and will be elaborated on in the following chapter. This traditional account (and often dismissal) of allegorical characters alleges an overall simplicity at the core of such characters. Indeed, critics committed to a normative conception of fictional character based on progressive development, complex motivation, and human agency would have a difficult time knowing what to do with a character like Smith. First, he has an obsessive, though certainly understandable, focus on "mechanical invention" (407); in fact, while trying to solve the mystery of Smith's identity, the narrator complains, "Lead him where I would, this was a point to which he invariably came back" (407). Second, he has a constitutional inability to develop as a character, which is nicely illustrated by his repetitive speech ("The most wonderful – the most ingenious – and let me add, Mr. – Mr. – Thompson, I believe, is your name – let me add, I say the most *useful* – the most truly *useful* – mechanical contrivances are daily springing up like mushrooms, if I may so express myself, or, more figuratively, like – ah – grasshoppers – like grasshoppers, Mr. Thompson – about us and ah – ah – ah – around us!" [407]). And third, he radically problematizes the notion of individual agency, given his status as an assemblage of mechanical parts. Repetitive, undeveloped, and mechanical – Smith would certainly qualify as an allegorical character, only to be tautologically dismissed by virtue of his "mechanistic" behavior (both bodily and psychic) and his "air of contrivance," to use Fletcher's and Feidelson's words.[5]

The language used by Fletcher and Feidelson to describe and condemn allegory is the language of work. The mechanical and the contrived allude to the space of labor, whether it be the labor of machinery or the labor of authorship. This discursive intersection, it turns out, is no coincidence, given the fact that these twentieth-century theories of allegory derive from an antipathy to allegory that was most fully theorized and disseminated in the nineteenth century; an antipathy that was articulated in relation to and often in terms of the language of labor, particularly industrial labor. *The Literature of Labor and the Labors of Literature* thus links nineteenth-century American responses to allegory and mechanized labor and suggests that the discursive possibilities for constructing the character of fictional and nonfictional persons were, to borrow a word from Poe's narrator, "remarkably" (405) similar. Characters like John A. B. C. Smith are culturally significant because they strikingly foreground the fact of the body and of work – the literal work (like Smith who is an Indian fighter) that a fictional character does in a text, the authorial work that goes into making a fictional character, the narrator's/reader's work in solving the puzzle of Smith's identity, and last the relation between work in a literary text and work in a market economy.

The Literature of Labor and the Labors of Literature proposes that we can best understand allegorical characters by rethinking traditional, ahistorical formulations of allegory in order to see the powerful conjunction among the discourse of allegory in nineteenth-century America, the representation of persons as mechanical and undeveloped in the discourse of labor, and a burgeoning market economy.[6] I argue that allegory, as understood, practiced, and received during this period, was the literary mode that foregrounded its relation to labor, whether through allegorical characters who signified the nature or cost of being a laboring being or through authorial signs which made visible the author's work of representation. The first I will call the allegory of labor, the second the labor of allegory. Whereas one emphasizes the effect of labor on persons and the other the labor of producing persons, both manifestations of allegory refer to the multiple and problematic relations between labor and personhood. As a definitionally labor-intensive mode of producing personhood, allegory exceeds the bounds of both the literary and economic domains. Allegorical characters were being produced not only in the fictions of Susan Warner and Henry Adams but also in the factories at Fall River and the workshops of scientific manager Frederick

Winslow Taylor. Taylor's ideal workers correspond remarkably to characters in *A Connecticut Yankee* or *The Mysterious Stranger, #44*. Similarly, after reading *Moby-Dick*, descriptions of Lowell mill workers seem strangely familiar. Certainly there are incontrovertible differences between literary characters and workers; however, the significance of these differences diminishes once we realize that the discursive possibilities for constructing the character of persons, whether fictional or not, depend upon a set of shared (though often contested) assumptions about labor, agency, and the market.

Traditional accounts of allegorical characters often condemn them as simplistic or, to use E. M. Forster's language, "flat," in contrast to the complexity of "round" characters. "The test of a round character," Forster argues, "is whether it is capable of surprising in a convincing way. If it never surprises, it is flat. If it does not convince, it is a flat pretending to be round."[7] Would Smith pass the test? The narrator expends all of his energy in figuring out whether Smith is round or flat, and he turns out to be quite surprisingly, quite literally flat. Smith complicates Forster's model of character, because even though he surprises he is clearly not round. But might not the pretense of being round, even though one is flat, be the equivalent of being round? The complexity of Smith's flatness, a flatness which can best be explained in its antebellum context, would certainly problematize dismissive readings of seemingly simple characters like Smith. I want to reconfigure Forster's claims about round and flat characters to argue that the flatness of allegorical characters is itself a primary locus of meaning. Their flatness becomes the departure point for my reading of them. Poe's story suggests that flatness is itself allegorical, that flatness is itself an allegory of cultural anxieties about changing relations between labor and agency. The literal flatness of Smith might conclude the narrator's reading, but it begins another reading of Smith which situates allegorical characters in a cultural context.[8]

The flatness of allegorical characters might thus be taken as an occasion for a laborious reading not unlike the one undertaken by Poe's narrator. "Laborious" is indeed the word to describe the narrator's efforts, for it is only after four unsuccessful attempts, at church, at the theater, at a soiree, and in conversation with a friend, to figure out the enigma of Smith's character that he finally decides to go to Smith's home and learns the secret of the man that was used up. The results of this visit suggest that the home is not a space of recuperative leisure, à la domestic ideology, but rather a space where the signs of labor (the servants, the mechanical parts of the body) are most fully visible.[9] Reading allegorical characters, as the narrator's experience reminds us, requires that one spend one's leisure time doing a kind of hermeneutic work (in fact, the narrator gains access to Smith's bedroom by pleading "urgent business" [411]) which contests the boundaries defining leisure and labor. Many readers, as we shall see by looking at antebellum literary reviews and more general philosophical discussions of reading, were not at all pleased by the kind of laborious reading that allegorical characters required. The project of this book, though, like the task of our perseverant narrator, is to read John A. B. C. Smith and others like him, characters whose "remarkableness" resides in their bodies, in their status as allegorical characters and in their relation to work.

The notion of allegory that is being deployed might at first seem counterintuitive, especially if we have in mind an allegory like Bunyan's *Pilgrim's Progress*. Wouldn't Poe's John A. B. C. Smith, Hawthorne's Mr. Smooth-it-away, or Twain's mysterious stranger, #44, simply suggest a nostalgic return to the "simpler," more integrated seventeenth-century world of Mr. Worldly-Wiseman or Evangelist? Such satisfied nostalgia would seem to explain the popularity of *Pilgrim's Progress* (witness the centrality of Bunyan in *The Wide, Wide World*, the most popular work of fiction in America until *Uncle Tom's Cabin*), but it would not help us much in understanding why an 1852 *Harper's* review of Henry Cheever's *A Reel in the Bottle* warned, "Modern allegory is a dangerous species of composition" or why in his 1851 preface to *Twice-Told Tales*, Hawthorne worried that "in what purport to be pictures of actual life, we have allegory, not always so warmly dressed in its habiliments of flesh and blood as to be taken into the reader's mind without a shiver."[10] Both the reviewer's and Hawthorne's anxiety about allegory, an anxiety that Hawthorne articulates in the language of the insufficiently clothed or impoverished body, suggests that there is something unsettling or unstable about allegory itself which allows it to be both affirming and disturbing. Even Poe was caught between affirming the descriptive power of allegory in many of his short stories ("Thou Art the Man" and "How to Write a Blackwood Article") and viciously condemning allegory in his magazine reviews. His 1841 excoriation of Bulwer-Lytton's *Night and Morning*, for example, contains the following: "Pure allegory is at all times an abomination – a remnant of antique barbarism."[11] This barbarism, however, could assume a peculiarly modern form. When Poe complains that "the simplest noun becomes animate in his [Bulwer-Lytton's] hands," he is, in effect, objecting to a representational world in which attributes of personhood, such as animation or agency, might possibly inhere in "the common-place character of anything." Bulwer-Lytton's relentless use of allegory confounds the distinction between objects and persons as one threatens at any moment to become the other. To locate this confusion in antebellum America, we need only remind ourselves of the conversion of persons into objects in slavery or the alienation of labor(ers) in a market economy. Indeed, this ubiquitous and enigmatic animation of objects comprises the world of Marx's commodities, in which "the productions of the human brain appear as independent beings endowed with life."[12] As antique as allegory may be, then, Poe's review attests to the fact that allegory also functions in the specific context of his cultural milieu. John A. B. C. Smith is, of course, the best example of this disjunctive temporality in that he alludes at once to the historical John Smith of the seventeenth century and to the market economy of the nineteenth. Thus allegory is as motivated by the temporality of antiquity as it is by the temporality of antebellum America.[13]

Smith's "remarkable" body is, as has already been suggested, the product of workers in a nineteenth-century market economy that is represented in the text by characters like Pettit, who "makes the best shoulders" (411), or Thomas, who "is decidedly the best hand at a cork leg" (411). And as a product, his allegorical body does not, indeed cannot, exist outside of a market economy in which body parts are commodities and workers themselves are body parts (note that Thomas is referred to as a "hand," the synecdoche most often used in the nineteenth century to characterize laborers). In supplying him with artificial limbs, the market economy functions to cancel out any damages done to Smith in his job as Indian killer. Moreover, settling the frontier, killing Indians, and developing America's market economy were inextricable pursuits.[14] Smith's allegorical body, in other words, calls attention to itself as a product of labor that is made in a market economy.

Foremost among all the workers whose job it is to construct Smith in the image of a self-made man (in the style of Benjamin Franklin, for example) is Poe. But Poe's own status as worker ultimately motivates the tale to expose Smith as something other than a self-made man, as a character made by Poe, a "literary laborer" with a desire to sustain the relation between author and product.[15] Even John A. B. C. Smith's name foregrounds Poe's labor, as the presence of the alphabet alludes to the linguistic medium of authorship. But Poe's presence is, perhaps, even more evident in the narrator's opening description, in which, we remember, he "readily place[s]" Smith's affectation "to the account of reserve, *hauteur*." Here the term *hauteur* not only alludes to the arrogant or haughty or even upper-class persona of Smith, about which I shall have more to say, but also calls attention to the *auteur*, or author, of Smith's character, that is Poe. Thus, Smith capaciously functions as *hauteur/auteur*, character, and the materiality of writing (A. B. C.) and as such makes inescapably palpable Poe's literary labors. But it would not be quite accurate to say that Smith unambiguously stands in, as it were, for Poe, because Smith's *hauteur* is precisely what Poe as *auteur* ends up sabotaging. The ideal of the gentleman author, removed from the contexts of the market, technology, and labor, is "used up" once it is discovered that Smith's *hauteur* is the effect of a body produced in the market by a whole host of specialized laborers.[16] Unlike Jonathan Auerbach, who links Smith with Poe in order to argue that "the figure of the self-made man serves to image the writer's own status in society," I see Poe and Smith in a much more antagonistic relation; that is, Poe "uses up" Smith as a way of dispensing with a configuration of fictional character and authorship that depends upon false assumptions about agency, identity, and work, and replaces it with a model of allegorical personhood, in which those very assumptions are contested.[17] Furthermore, Poe's rivalrous relation to Smith suggests that the market economy is so powerful that a character created by an author possesses an agency potentially threatening to the agency of that author.

The reconfiguration of allegory proposed in *The Literature of Labor and the Labors of Literature* challenges some of our most basic assumptions about allegory: that allegory transcends history and that it is a purely textual phenomenon disengaged from its cultural context. However great the differences may be between a new critical conception of allegory, like Angus Fletcher's, and a deconstructive paradigm of allegory, like Paul de Man's, surely they are united by a turning away, indeed an erasure, of history. This inheritance has limited our use of the term allegory to the domain of literature, and yet new historicist criticism has shown that the category of the "literary" is constituted in relation to the discourse of economics, politics, race, and gender. It is in the spirit of contesting the boundaries between literary and nonliterary constructions of personhood that I undertake this contextualization and expansion of our understanding of allegory. My opening chapter traces the intersections between aesthetic and economic discourse – not so as to produce a traditionally historical argument that posits a cause–effect relation between allegory and economic transformation, or vice versa, but rather to present a critical analysis of narrative rhetoric, specifically relating to allegory and labor, in historical perspective. This historicization is meant, in other words, to map out a discursive landscape, one in which literary evaluations of allegory and cultural judgments about new forms of labor equally descry a model of personhood that interacts with the self-reliant world of Emerson and the religious world of Bunyan. The contextualizing functions to illustrate a discursive field rather than the force of historical evolution.

Allegorical characters in mid-nineteenth-century American fiction, it will be claimed, partook of a culture whose own investment in allegorical agency was inflicting severe damage on one of that culture's most powerful organizing myths – the work ethic.[18] While embodying an identity that conformed to a middle-class ideal of efficient workers in a market economy, allegorical figures contested a middle-class ideology based on the moral (and economic) sanctity of work. They suggested that work, far from inspiring laborers to greater economic and moral heights, was merely an exercise in mechanical repetition that had a corrosive effect on the work ethic's fundamental belief in individual progress through work. Furthermore, they foregrounded the fact that identity was constructed and, in doing so, registered a critical cultural moment in which relations between labor, bodies, and agency were being (re)invented, renegotiated, and reproduced. My reading of John A. B. C. Smith suggests that the unsettling quality of allegorical characters locates itself in their mechanical bodies, which possess a kind of agency that is never quite sure of itself – that is continually being possessed, repossessed, and dispossessed in a drama of constant circulation. This version of agency is historically specific and should therefore be read in the context of what Darko Suvin identifies as "historically possible *attitudes toward* animate and active entities."[19] It is, of course, impossible to outline all of these possible attitudes, and my inquiry is limited to those attitudes having to do with the problematics of work and personhood, with the understanding that the reconfiguration of allegory in nineteenth-century America was explicitly thematized and articulated in relation to those particular attitudes. Thus if characters like John A. B. C. Smith resonate with the spirit of Bunyanesque allegory, they also allude to a nineteenth-century reconfiguration of allegory with radically untraditional configurations of personhood that bear little relation to the religious world of Bunyan.

Poe's Smith presents us with a model of personhood that represents at once the perfection of identity as constructed by an industrialized market economy and the site at which that identity is most threatened. Allegorical characters and their mechanical bodies are, in fact, excellent subjects for the kind of genealogical reading proposed by Foucault, in which one's "task is to expose a body totally imprinted by history."[20] These allegorical bodies do not expose an uninterrupted history of monolithic power but rather a history of contest and intervention in which the relations between work and identity are being continually challenged and reshaped. Their contextual saturation does not silence them to a fate of passive reflection but rather ensures a sustained dialogue and dialectical relation with that context. Carolyn Porter has convincingly described this interpretative model as one which calls attention to the ways in which "both dominant and oppositional ideological strains are at work."[21] The echo of Raymond Williams is particularly pertinent here if we think of allegory in relation to the category of the "archaic," which he defines as "that which is wholly recognized as an element of the past." Archaic cultural formations, like allegory, are/should be safely stored in the past. Williams goes on to contrast the "archaic" with the "residual, which may have an alternative or even oppositional relation to the dominant culture."[22] As I have been suggesting, allegory, so clearly archaic on the one hand, is nevertheless simultaneously modern. It carries with it the safety of the archaic with the potential oppositionality of the residual. Thus the "harsh disturbance of the peace," to quote Benjamin, that characterizes allegory lies precisely in its blurring of the categories of archaic and residual in such a way as to make impossible those crucial temporal (and political) distinctions between archaic and residual, between contained and oppositional.[23] The example of Smith powerfully reveals how the allegorical body becomes the site of these potential confusions, where certain networks of power are most visible (dead Indians, black servants, workers) and where oppositionality (in the figure of Poe) is most possible.

It is in the texts of Hawthorne, Melville, Twain, and Henry Adams that these themes of allegory, the body, and labor are most strikingly conjoined. Chapter 1 broadly situates "an economics of allegory" in the context of nineteenth-century and contemporary debates about allegory as well as discussions about a market economy. Both discourses attempt to construe a stable relation between the body and identity which those very discourses reveal as always already unraveling. Hawthorne's pivotal role in establishing this paradox will be made clear in Chapter 2, which argues that Hawthorne's "The Celestial Rail-road," in particular, presents us with two different and ultimately incompatible versions of allegory. These competing approaches are presented in "The Celestial Rail-road" as alternative ways of configuring the relation between one's identity and one's name. In this heretofore marginalized tale, we can see a Bunyanesque model of allegory, grounded in a tradition of religious hermeneutics, transformed by the logic of America's developing market economy into an economics of allegory, which will be most fully articulated in "The Birth-mark." In this later tale and in *The Scarlet Letter* as well, Hawthorne finds himself in the Poe-like position of struggling against characters committed to the erasure of the signs of literary labor.

The shape of Hawthorne's career suggests that the practice and reception of allegory were undergoing substantial changes that, along with transformations in the market economy, created a space for allegory to circulate amid competing models of personhood. Hawthorne's work suggests that at least by the 1830s in America there existed an incompatibility between allegory as traditionally understood and an economics of allegory. The remaining chapters show how Melville, Twain, and Adams each practiced a version of this economics of allegory. Whereas Hawthorne's later efforts indicate that this new paradigm of allegory may have, in part, prevented him from completing his projects, texts by these other writers suggest that allegory could serve the political function of producing alternative relations among labor, agency, and the body. Allegory was reconfigured in fits and starts, and Melville's texts, in his self-conscious deployment of allegory, most vividly exemplify this rocky transformation. Chapter 3, "Melville's Operatives," charts the function of allegory in *Mardi*, *Moby-Dick*, and *Billy Budd* in order to argue that allegory at once undermines the traditional understanding of the relation between literature and labor and paves the way for Melville's alternative version of the work ethic.

"Twain in the Man-factory" argues that Twain finds the labor of producing fictional characters especially complicated and burdensome because of his allegiance to two antithetical notions of work, the first represented by engineers like the West Pointers in *Life on the Mississippi*, Hank in *A Connecticut Yankee in King Arthur's Court*, and #44 in *The Mysterious Stranger, #44*, and the second represented by conventional writers of literature. Torn between these competing versions of labor, Twain ends up combining them to create his own rather peculiar model in which the labor that goes into his production of fictional characters is offset by the labor that goes into their erasure, usually in the form of death – humorous, serious, or apocalyptic. Allegorical characters in these texts are sites upon which Twain's own anxieties about the inefficiency of his literary labors can be read.

Chapter 5, "The Manikin, the Machine, and the Virgin Mary," considers how the manikin in the preface to *The Education of Henry Adams* functions as an exemplary allegorical agent whose class and gender identities have been erased and whose legibility seems to be guaranteed by its absorptive passivity. The blank body of the manikin is, however, constructed by precisely those discourses of class and gender that have been erased – an erasure that, in turn, generates a surplus of meaning that cannot be fully contained. My closing remarks suggest that the muckraking texts of the early twentieth century may usefully be read as the culmination of this repoliticized, rehistoricized, and rematerialized conception of allegory.

1

The Problem with Labor and the Promise of Leisure

A censorious review of Melville's *Mardi* appeared in the April 1849 issue of the *Southern Literary Messenger*: there is "an effort constantly at fine writing, [and] a sacrifice of natural ease to artificial witticism."[1] Melville, according to dissatisfied critics, seemed to be continuing the assault against the gentlemanly figure of the (h)auteur that Poe had launched in "The Man That Was Used Up" by foregrounding the effort that went into the act of writing. Melville's talent is here assessed according to an aesthetic that uses the discourse of work, promoting those texts which display "natural ease" while dismissing others for their constant "effort." Thus it was not unusual to see the following kind of praise in literary reviews: "Mr. Bryant's style in these letters is an admirable model of descriptive prose. Without any appearance of labor, it is finished with an exquisite grace."[2] Writing was supposed to appear effortless, natural, and easy. Bryant's did and Melville's did not. Simply put, writing was not supposed to look like work, especially of the unnatural and artificial variety.[3] We can easily understand the many critics who pronounced *Mardi* a colossal failure because of its lack of organization or its disconnected flights into philosophical speculation, but to frame the attack against *Mardi* in the language of work seems especially problematic and interesting, given the fact that one of the dominant discourses of antebellum America, namely the work ethic, championed precisely the degree of effort evidenced throughout Melville's text. It is this compelling and, to my mind, most fruitful paradox that this chapter will explore. What might it mean for a culture to castigate literature for displaying characteristics which that very culture elsewhere valorizes? What might we say about a work ethic that increasingly called for an ideal of invisible labor?

I shall suggest that new techniques in the workplace and a developing market economy problematized the value of labor to such an extent that virtually any manifestation of labor seemed to resonate with the ambiguous status of industrial labor. Of particular interest is the relation between

13

reconfigurations of work and the work ethic and representations of labor in literary texts. It was not simply the case that nineteenth-century literary sensibilities prohibited literature from representing work (one need only think of the popularity of Warner's *The Wide, Wide World* or Fanny Fern's *Ruth Hall*, both of which go to great lengths to represent work). At stake in the relation between literature and the work ethic was not work as the subject matter of a narrative per se but rather how fictional texts erased or called attention to the literary labors that went into them, the visible signs of a fiction being made, and how the cost of being a laboring being, specifically a laboring being in an industrialized market economy, was foregrounded (or not) through fictional characters.[4] Literature registered the work ethic as both damaged and repaired; that is, literature had the impossible task of functioning as a haven from the damaged ideals of the work ethic while becoming the site where those ideals could be (and should be) repaired and disseminated.

This chapter thus begins with an analysis of the work ethic and the strains put upon it by new forms of production. Factory work, in particular, destabilized the work ethic to such an extent that work was no longer adequate to the task of upholding such basic principles of the work ethic as moral uplift, economic reward, and the spiritual development that should come from hard work. As a consequence of the breakdown of the work ethic, one's leisure time took on increased significance, because leisure was now required to fulfill those ideological duties that could no longer be effectively administered by work. Mount Auburn Cemetery ideally exemplifies the complex function of leisure in antebellum America, because this leisure space was constructed as both a world outside work and a world that promoted the ideals of the work ethic. A close reading of Mount Auburn illustrates how any manifestation of labor inevitably intersected with anxieties about a developing and industrializing market economy. Such intersections produced an aesthetic that called for the erasure of labor. This aesthetic of erasure is then read in the context of discussions of literature which called for a similar ideal of invisible labor on the part of literary laborers. The final section of the chapter offers a reading of the discourse of allegory in antebellum America and suggests that allegory can be read as a discursive site in which the fragility of the work ethic was most fully exemplified. The debate between symbol and allegory thus takes on new meaning when read as an attempt to stabilize the ideological inconsistencies of the work ethic as it applied to literature. If allegorical characters brought these discursive contradictions to the surface and demonstrated their insolubility, the symbol erased both the signs of work and the problems attendant upon an unstable work ethic. As new forms of work destabilized the work ethic, they also generated the two narratives which make up this chapter: the allegory of labor and the labor of allegory.

I. THE ALLEGORY OF LABOR: VERSIONS OF THE WORK ETHIC

Because the ideology of the work ethic structured any number of cultural activities, whether one's goal were religious salvation, economic improvement, or moral rectitude, versions of the work ethic can be found in a variety of sources from the antebellum period – from sermons to public lectures to newspaper editorials. These versions of the work ethic usually combined a belief in hard work with the promise of reward, sometimes economic, sometimes moral, and sometimes both. Although the inherent value of work almost always functioned as the rhetorical point of departure, the work ethic was not a monolithic discourse. It was being constructed and debated in a variety of different contexts for a variety of different audiences.

As a powerful and organizing discourse in nineteenth-century American culture, the work ethic cannot be overestimated. The ideal of self-sufficiency through meaningful work is dramatically articulated in the following passage from Emerson's "Self-Reliance": "There is a great responsible Thinker and Actor working wherever a man works . . . a true man belongs to no other time or place, but is the centre of things."[5] When he proclaims, "Do your work and you shall reinforce yourself" (34), the power of work not only to produce objects but to construct selves is made manifest. To focus on the individual as "the centre of things" is to suggest that the work ethic properly understood exists outside the realm of competition, of exchange, of the market. But in order to be at "the centre," there must be a context, and, as we shall see, the context in which the individual works and reinforces himself is the market. The market is, in other words, the invisible hand guiding the work ethic. The discourse of the work ethic, as Emerson's passage suggests, kept the instability of the market safely at a distance and focused attention on the uplifting principle that work was a means to economic and moral superiority. It trained young men to fear idleness and embrace industry, it educated young women in the science of domestic economy, and it held out the possibility of prosperity for all. The mythological premise of the work ethic was that America was a classless, endlessly mobile society. The work ethic, moreover, promulgated the notion that the perpetual motion of a classless society was far less threatening than the instabilities generated by a society in which citizens identified themselves according to class. To acknowledge the presence of class in America would imply that manifest destiny was visible in the dreaded factories of industrial England and that the "virgin land" of the West could no longer absorb the labor supply. Class, according to the ideology of the work ethic, could only be a part of American identity as an absence, because the existence of class presupposed a need to focus on work *as work* rather than on work *as a sign* of one's economic or spiritual success. The work ethic, in other words, gave work both an ontological and an epistemological status. People were the work they did. To know their work was to know them. If identity and work existed in a transparent relation to one another, class threatened to undermine this hermeneutic structure by suggesting that, far from being a sign of one's character, work only indicated work.

A complete adherence to the virtues of work is not uncommon in the writings of antebellum Americans, whether in the religious, moral, or economic domain. Let us briefly return to Channing's 1839 address, because it offers one of the most concise articulations of the work ethic: "I have great faith in hard work. The material world does much for the mind by its beauty and order; but it does more for our minds by the pains it inflicts; by its obstinate resistance, which nothing but patient toil can overcome; by its vast forces, which nothing but unremitting skill and effort can turn to our use."[6] Channing bases his utopian vision of American society on a correct understanding of work because, he claims, only through work can one become "one of God's nobility, no matter what place he holds in the social scale" (42). In a series of lectures delivered to members of the Westminster Church of Providence, Rhode Island, Augustus Woodbury had similar words of praise for the virtues of work: "[The house carpenter] would find that he was doing something more than driving nails, and hewing timbers, and wearily shoving the plane; that he was giving form to ideas; that he was growing into a love of the beautiful and true, and that every day's labor was aiding in the noiseless but certain work of building up the structure of a manly and noble character."[7] Only "by means of labor," writes Woodbury, do we "arrive at the development of our various faculties" (80). Labor, in other words, has the enormous responsibility of building and developing a person's character.

Horace Greeley, the popular reformer and editor of the *New York Tribune*, advocates a similar faith in the values of work, only this time the work ethic appears in the context of a discussion of immorality. In *Hints Toward Reform*, Greeley reminds his readers of the necessity for continual vigilance when entering upon adult life, a time when one is sure to encounter what he calls "the soft breezes of Temptation." "Truth and Goodness," he warns, find their staunchest opponent in "every hour of non-resistance [that] relaxes [one's] energies while it increases the power of the adversary."[8] Offering the rather standard fare, he prescribes hard work if one wishes to maintain the high moral ground. In Channing and Woodbury, the resistance of the material world fosters a sense of endless pursuit and heightened expectations; for Greeley, these expectations are thwarted by one's own nonresistance to temptation and, presumably, heightened by one's resistance. Although they proffer the work ethic as the solution to slightly different dilemmas, Channing, Woodbury, and Greeley similarly conclude that work is the defining and self-defining activity of American life.

The perilous temptations at which Greeley only hints are fully developed in Henry Ward Beecher's *Lectures to Young Men on Various Important Subjects*, a popular tract that never tires of singing the praises of hard labor, or what Beecher calls "industry," whether one is working at a job or doing battle with the assaulting passions of youth. In *Lectures*, Beecher reminds his audience that "in the ordinary business of life, Industry can do anything which Genius can do; and very many things which it cannot."[9] Industry prevails over genius in Beecher's formulation because the former entails a commitment to work, which develops individual character and promotes ethical behavior, whereas the latter is defined by virtue of its absence from labor. Industry not only functions to bring about pecuniary rewards but more importantly serves to stabilize and regulate the sexual impulses of young men. It acts as a moral fortress prohibiting the entry of idlers, gamblers, and prostitutes. The relation between labor and virtue (as well as idleness and depravity) determines one's success or failure in all cultural activities, whether business, politics, or aesthetics.

Lest we mistakenly think that the work ethic only came from the economic top down, we need only look at the *Voice of Industry*, one of the more radical newspapers published in Lowell, Massachusetts, during the antebellum years. The relation between labor and character formation is the subject of "Morale of Labor," a column that appeared in 1845: "We have before spoken of the *formation of a good character and of the necessity of energy* as all-important to the young man in laying the foundation of success in life. We need not say that, in addition to the adoption of good principles and the requisite resolution and perseverance to carry them out, it is equally important that industry should be constantly and cheerfully applied, if a young man would secure success."[10] In "A Call to the Members of the Legislature and the Mechanics and the Laborers of this Commonwealth," columnist Samuel Whitney denounced an economic state in which "the monopolising money-power is confined with all its profits to the comparatively *idle few*" such that "all the sources of wealth, all the instrumentality of life, and even the right and privilege of industry are taken away from the *people*."[11] Far from being an ideological critique of the work ethic, Whitney's address situates labor as the savior of a work ethic that has been grossly perverted. Indeed, "the privilege of industry" is precisely the founding principle of the work ethic. Such complaints about work would seem to have less to do with the work ethic itself or even with the conditions of work than with workers' not receiving the benefits of their labor. The fact that some of the same rhetorical formations appear in the *Voice of Industry* as in the texts of Woodbury, Greeley, and Beecher indicates the cultural commitment to the work ethic and its effectiveness in bringing together, at least on the level of discourse, members from different classes. For example, just as one must work against the power of the adversary in Greeley, labor must fight against "the monopolising money-power," and just as one must valorize Beecher's ideal of industry over genius, because genius excludes the constitutive category of value, that is labor, workers must fight against the *idle few*, those geniuses who have successfully taken away the rights and privileges of industrious laborers. And the inextricable relation between labor and character development appears in all of these texts. Thus the *Voice of Industry*, in its commitment to the work ethic rightly understood, voices many of the same positions promulgated in mainstream, middle-class texts.

These examples of the work ethic make clear that its power as a unifying discourse stemmed, in part, from its ability to reroute class anxieties about the work ethic, especially those directed toward the working class, into attacks against idleness. Although idleness cut across all classes (one could be a working-class, middle-class, or upper-class idler), it is clear that idleness was seen to be a particularly upper-class phenomenon. Thus we find Channing criticizing "the upper ranks of society" (40), for whom "fashion is a poor vocation . . . idleness is a privilege, and work a disgrace" (40). Similarly, Woodbury thinks more highly of the man whose "hands may be hard with toil" and whose "frame sturdy through his honest industry" (103) than the man who possesses "all the comforts of wealth, and the pomps of power, and the delicacies of fashion" (104). As one might expect, almost any page of the *Voice of Industry* includes an admonition against idleness: "How many there are . . . who are living in affluence and luxury without adding one farthing to [society's] wealth, and who are greedy to devour and monopolize the treasure of honest industry."[12] The invidious evil of idleness was strategically meant to disseminate the ideology of the work ethic across all of the classes. If the work ethic could restage potential class conflict as individual conflict, the problems described in the *Voice of Industry*, according to the logic of the work ethic, were not systemic but rather the result of individual lapses into idleness.

But the rhetoric of individualism, which interpreted idleness as an individual problem that compromised one's ability to pursue those economic and spiritual benefits guaranteed by an adherence to the work ethic, did not necessarily contain the element of class dissatisfaction, as is evident in the passages from the *Voice of Industry*. In contrast to Woodbury, Greeley, and Beecher and their emphasis on the individual, columnists for the *Voice of Industry* usually read idleness as a systemic problem to be cured by systemic solutions. One columnist, for example, complained about "the slavish 'twelve to fifteen hour' system which is making such inroads upon the health and happiness of our *'free, well paid'* operatives" and justified his complaint by saying, "We do not bring this before the public, as a crude, and undigested scheme – a partial fragmentary measure, based merely upon selfishness, the result of which shall be to personally aggrandize one class of our people at the expense of another; but one fully attested and theoretically acknowledged by all classes of society."[13] Another columnist for the *Voice of Industry* notes the "hords of unproducing exchangers, speculators, and idlers" who "are living upon the producing classes and oppressing the real workingmen of the country."[14] Some, in other words, saw the perversion of the work ethic as one more element in a larger system which was generating a class structure in which some people worked and other people remained idle. Thomas Skidmore's *The Rights of Man to Property*, written in 1829, launches a critique similar to the Lowell piece, though from a slightly more radical perspective: "Most of the indolence, now existing among mankind" stems from the "ease and indulgence [that] spring[s] from enormous fortunes, acquired without labor, and possessed without right. . . . By the introduction of a system of equal property, indolence itself would be banished also."[15] It was becoming painfully clear to certain segments of the American population that living and laboring according to the principles of the work ethic did not necessarily guarantee upward mobility and economic reward; in fact, William Heighton in his 1827 *Address to the Members of Trade Societies and the Working Classes* suggests that hard work and economic reward were often mutually exclusive. "Money is always most abundant in the hands of the rich, who never labour nor produce any thing."[16] Idleness and indolence, according to Heighton's and Skidmore's working-class perspective, were not only the results of wealth but, paradoxically, seemed to be the precondition for it.

As early as the 1820s, then, the gap between what the work ethic promised and what it delivered was apparent to many. What made this gap even more obvious, especially by the 1840s, were the visible changes in modes of production. It is important to keep in mind that although changing conditions in the workplace galvanized critiques of the work ethic and made the problems with the work ethic more obvious, critiques of the work ethic, at least in the early stages of industrialization, did not exclusively depend upon technological transformations in the workplace.

In fact, Heighton sang the praises of new machinery: "With the aid of it, the labour of a *single individual* will create as much wealth as the unassisted labour of *eighty* can without it. . . . Amazing power! happy nation, how superabounding in wealth must she be" (20). What destroys the promise of machinery is "*competition* which renders the invention of machinery a curse instead of a blessing to mankind" (21). Skidmore echoes these sentiments and urges workers not to waste their energies blaming machinery for their difficulties, but rather to go to the root of the problem – the unfair distribution of property. He issues the following call to arms: "LET THEM APPROPRIATE . . . THE COTTON FACTORIES, THE WOOLEN FACTORIES, THE IRON FOUNDERIES, THE ROLLING MILLS . . . AS IS THEIR RIGHT; and they will never have occasion any more to consider that as an evil which never deserved that character" (384).

II. FACTORING IN THE FACTORY: THE DESTABILIZATION OF THE WORK ETHIC

Although early critiques of the work ethic often had as much to do with the unfair distribution of property rights as with anxieties about new conditions of labor, these new conditions, particularly the introduction of labor-saving machinery and the division of labor, came to assume center stage and thus repositioned the terms of the debate.[17] The language of ownership and property remained, but it was more explicitly directed at industrialization and, in particular, the relation between machinery and the bodies of laborers, as new forms of labor appeared to be undermining the worker's proprietary relation to her own body. In his compelling discussion of the incipient dissolution of the work ethic in antebellum America, labor historian Daniel Rodgers notes that changes in production "create[d] not only new work relations but a new kind of work: specialized, repetitious, machine-paced, and, often, deadeningly simple."[18] The appearance of clocks in the factory, for example, best represents these new work relations and the new kind of work with which laborers in the early 1840s had to cope. When Henry Craig installed clocks at the Harper's Ferry armory, workers replied with the clock strike of 1842.[19] Many laborers refused to work when disciplinary techniques seemed outrageously restrictive. One worker, for instance, walked off the job when he discovered "regulations posted in his shop requiring all employees to be at their posts in their work clothes when the first bell rang, to remain there until the last bell, and to be prevented from leaving the works between those times by locked doors."[20] Clocks and locked doors were just some of the controversial techniques deployed in order to dispossess workers of their bodies. Such strategies as these were transforming the bodies of workers into territories upon which and over which they found themselves fighting to (re)own themselves.

Workers objected to what they experienced as a pernicious reconstruction and reterritorialization of their bodies. We need only turn to the controversy surrounding the Lowell mills, in which some female workers specifically complained about the negative effects of work on their bodies, others celebrated the salubrious environment of the mills, and visitors to the mills left with diametrically opposed opinions on the subject, in order to realize that the bodies of, in this case, female workers became a battleground upon which was waged a conflict about ownership and agency. Did a woman worker agree to disown herself once she entered "the Counting Room [and] receive[d] therefrom a Regulation paper, containing the rules by which she must be governed while in their employ?"[21] And if so, what aspect of themselves as agents had they consented to dispossess? The case of the women workers of Lowell is especially illuminating, because the mills were understood by many (including the workers) to be ideal work spaces and were the subject of intense scrutiny in the antebellum period.[22] Furthermore, because workers were exclusively women of childbearing age, special attention was given to the relation between factory labor and the body. The marks of labor on the female body alluded, as we shall see, to the potentially damaging effects of work on a woman's femininity and, by extension, her ability to reproduce.

In one of the Factory Tracts of 1845, a series of articles written by operatives in the Lowell mills, "Julianna" addresses some of these explosive issues and predicts a rather horrible future for America's labor force if the factory system continues unchanged: "What but ignorance, misery, and premature decay of both body and intellect? Our country will be but one great hospital filled with worn out operatives and colored slaves!"[23] "Julianna" points to the transformation of both body and mind experienced by female operatives and, most damagingly, conjoins it with slavery. This linkage appeared in many indictments of the northern factory system (from working-class to proslavery enthusiasts), and one need only look in the pages of the *Voice of Industry* to find statements such as the following: "They [those who believe in the inevitability of a poverty-stricken class of workers] hate, perhaps, black slavery, but must have forsooth a class of white slaves."[24] The conjunction of slaves and workers powerfully situates the issue of ownership in terms of one's own body and raises the emotional and ideological stakes of laborers' self-representations.

In stark contrast to "Julianna's" negative evaluation of factory life at Lowell, the *Lowell Offering* printed a series of articles and short stories written by workers themselves, all of whom attested to the healthy life they led. In an 1842 editorial entitled "Health," the writer observes:

> A favorable circumstance in connection with factory labor is its regularity; rising, sleeping, and eating, at the same hours on each successive day. . . . The appearance of the girls is generally that of health and cheerfulness; but yet there is sickness here, and far more than there need be. In many cases where health is lost the loser is greatly to blame, and yet it is spoken of as a necessary result of factory labor. The desire to lay upon others the blame of our own faults is "as old as Adam," and we see examples of it almost every day. There are thousands of girls in Lowell at that age when their constitutions are maturing, where girls are always most careless.[25]

If one turns to "professional" opinions to clarify what appear to be the mutually exclusive statements of workers at Lowell, the contradictions simply reappear. On the one hand, we have Dr. Elisha Bartlett's *A Vindication of the Character and Condition of the Females Employed in the Lowell Mills*, originally written in 1839, which claims that "*The manufacturing population of this city is the healthiest portion of the population*" because "their labor is sufficiently active and sufficiently light to avoid the evils arising from the two extremes of indolence and over-exertion."[26] Given Lowell's clean bill of health, it is difficult to know what to make of an anonymous pamphlet that appeared only two years later, entitled *Corporations and Operatives: Being an Exposition of the Condition [of] Factory Operatives, and a Review of the "Vindication," by Elisha Bartlett, M.D.*, which challenges all of Bartlett's observations. "They [the owners of the mills] regard them, but as mere parts of the machinery, with which they accumulate money, – and their greatest skill is used to keep that part of the machines, which is made of human *flesh, and blood, and bones*, in operation, the same number of hours, and at the same speed, as those parts, which are made of *iron and wood*."[27] Add to these the observations of the Reverend William Scoresby in *American Factories and Their Female Operatives*, and the situation seems impossible to figure out: "After a year or two they have to procure shoes of a size or two larger than before they came," and "the right hand, which is used in stopping and starting the loom, becomes larger than the left."[28] It would seem that these documents allow us to conclude that we cannot come to any conclusion about the "real" understanding of the effects of the factory system upon the health of the Lowell operatives.

This, however, does not mean that we cannot reach any conclusions. Indeed, what becomes obvious in this debate is the fact that the multiple communities of Lowell, whether its workers, its doctors, or its visitors, were deeply committed to understanding the problems posed by the

relation between factories and the health of the workers and to defending
their own versions of that relation. Furthermore, debates about Lowell
suggest that anxieties about mechanization in the workplace grounded
themselves in questions about the body and the problematic signs of
labor that made visible its effects on the body. If one could not see the
signs of factory labor, that is if the operatives wrote bucolic sketches for
the *Lowell Offering* and maintained their healthful vigor, then this new
kind of labor was innocent of the charges leveled against it. If, however,
the signs of factory labor were visible, that is if bodies were decaying or
changing in grotesque ways, as suggested by "Julianna" and Scoresby,
then this new kind of labor was guilty as charged. In the case of the
female body, new modes of production endangered female reproduction.
If hands and feet were metamorphosing, what about the other parts of
the female body? And last, at the very moment that the ideological
foundations of the work ethic were being called into question by new
conditions of labor, the best guarantee of a salutary work ethic was the
invisibility of work itself. The body, then, either became a marked (or
remarkable, to invoke John A. B. C. Smith) text upon which was written
the visible signs of labor gone amok or a blank page whose very invisibility was a kind of sign too, but one that referred to a much more salvific
version of labor. This ideal of invisible labor eventually functioned as an
aesthetic paradigm according to which readers assessed the merits and
demerits of literary texts.

Erasing the visible signs of labor became a cultural imperative, whether
in factories, in landscapes, or in fictions.[29] To conclude that these signs
needed erasure meant to admit that new kinds of labor, especially labor
that was mechanical, repetitive, and simple, were, at the very least, potentially damaging to both workers and the work ethic. All labor, whether
performed by men or women, becomes potentially damaging as anxieties
about the role of industrialization in the production of individual character
are reproduced in texts that not only have little to do with mechanical labor
but explicitly aim to celebrate work. Thus even someone as committed to
the work ethic as Woodbury made a plea on behalf of time spent away from
work: "We are accustomed to think of ourselves as a nation of plodders,
always and feverishly at work, with occasional remissions of toil, when we
either express our playfulness in the most unparalleled noise and overwhelming din – as on Independence day – or give ourselves up to the
worst indulgences, and call them relaxation and rest, instead of so combining the light with the heavy duties of life in such excellent and harmonious
proportion, that each may temper and relieve the other, and both combined produce a full, rounded, and complete character."[30] It is not simply
the case that labor leads to "the development of our various faculties" (80),
but "occasional remissions" from labor are now required to produce a

"complete character."[30] A similar point is made by Daniel Eddy in *The Young Man's Friend*, where he writes, "The body was not made for constant toil. . . . Had God designed man for ceaseless labor, he would not have given him such a body as he now possesses, he would have darkened the eye, deadened the ear, and blunted all the nicer sensibilities, and made the hand as hard as iron, and the foot as insensible as brass."[31] Here are John A. B. C. Smith and Ahab's mechanical man.

Worries about the tendency of factory work not to promote character development (or to promote the wrong kind) are evident in Edward Bruce's *The Century: Its Fruits and Its Festival,* in which at the very moment he tries to exonerate mechanical labor from the charge of aiding and abetting mental atrophy, he notes: "The dullest of factory-people are apt, as they observe the automatic movements of their senseless co-worker, to conceive points where this may be bettered and their condition improved. Should this aspiration take no shape and bear no perceptible fruit, the feeding and tending of their charge occupies the attention and keeps the mind more or less on the alert."[32] Although Bruce maintains that factory work requires some mental attention, his language reveals the dilemma presented to the work ethic by mechanization. Exactly whose condition will be improved? The "dullest of factory-people" or "their senseless co-worker"? While insisting upon the worker's humanity (a dull one at that) in contrast to the machine's senselessness, Bruce ends up blurring the distinctions between them, as "the automatic movements of the senseless co-worker," which require "feeding and tending," have taken on the characteristics of personhood. Moreover, if a worker's observations lead to the improved condition of neither worker nor machine, then at least the human qualities of the machine will "keep the mind more or less on the alert." The value of work has certainly diminished if now all one can expect is that work keep one somewhat alert.

If this were so, a new space was required to realize the moral values of the work ethic, and this was the space of leisure. This would certainly be the logic governing *The First Century of the Republic*, a homage to American progress, which nevertheless concedes that industrial progress has meant the breakdown of the work ethic and the inability of work to develop what Woodbury had earlier called "manly and noble" character: "Much of the necessary work of the laboring people fails to develop character . . . hence, as the labor of production becomes more and more a matter of machinery and apparatus rather than of individual exertion of brain and muscle, [the capability for enjoyment] . . . must come from culture and education outside their work, and not in the work itself."[33] In a society so committed to the ethical importance of labor, "the hardest wrench of values" writes Rodgers, "was to admit that work under modern industrial conditions was inherently harmful, its 'damage' to be undone only by leisure" (93). But it is important to note that these industrial conditions permeated the space of leisure as well; that is, the space of leisure not only had to provide a refuge from the damages done by work, but if the ideology of the work ethic could no longer function in the workplace because of changes in work, leisure had the additional task of disseminating the work ethic. Thus, at the same time that industrialized labor changed the physical contours of the workplace, leisure time took on an increasingly significant role in the dissemination and maintenance of the work ethic. The paradox, of course, was that the failure of the work ethic was proportionally related to the significance of leisure.

III. WORK AND LEISURE: THE CASE OF MOUNT AUBURN CEMETERY

The complicated relation between work and leisure is vividly illustrated in Edward Everett Hale's *Public Amusement for Poor and Rich*, a lecture delivered in 1857 to his congregation in Worcester's Church of the Unity. Hale rails against what he considers to be the naive assumption that work alone is good and "rest, or recreation" is bad, and criticizes the legacy left by the Puritans, who "educate the soul alone, and mortify body and mind together."[34] At first Hale sounds surprisingly like those factory workers who were complaining about assaults upon their bodies. His perspective, however, turns out to be radically different, as is evident in his definition of rest: "I say rest, or recreation, because recreation or amusement are but other names for rest. Such is the place which the hours of rest hold, in the subdivision of our time, – in our arrangements for it" (7). Although Hale begins by separating rest and work, his description of rest, with its "subdivision of time" and its "arrangements," sounds suspiciously like work. Hale, it turns out, is not nearly as concerned about rest for "the rich, the educated, who can supply, in their own homes, the necessity for entertainment," as for the "poor and the ignorant [who] are supplied by Public Amusements alone" (8). Of course, Hale's worries stem from the fact that he does not like those amusements, such as card playing, drinking, or concertgoing, with which the poor entertain themselves. Given the problematic amusements of the poor, leisure finds itself having a great deal of work to do: "In our gradual work for the improvement of public amusement . . . we need to undertake the management of the people's entertainment" (21–3). Hale, then, becomes a kind of scientific manager of the working-class leisure circuit.

Hale's lecture demonstrates that transformations in the workplace generated changes in cultural spaces outside work which, at the very moment that they were meant to mark their difference from work, reduplicated the rhetoric and structures of work (and for that matter, the industrialized labor of subdivision and management) in their purest form. Although Hale concerns himself in this instance with the amusements of the working class, analogous examples abound in the case of the middle class. In *Letters to the People on Health and Happiness*, domestic economist Catharine Beecher characterizes the health problems of those whom she calls "brain-workers": "One portion of the world weakens their muscular system, either by entire inaction of both brain and muscle, or by the excess of brainwork and the neglect of muscular exercise [while] another large portion . . . overwork their bodies and neglect their minds."[35] The mental muscles of these middle-class brainworkers are unnaturally overdeveloped compared with Hale's working-class carousers, whose brains have apparently not been well developed enough in the teachings of middle-class ideology. To combat this "overwork," Beecher proposes the construction of a building, a "Temple of Health," in which "a great variety of apparatus and accommodations for the in-door amusements that *exercise the muscles*" would be made available to those who experienced the symptoms of physical atrophy which might accompany a mentally demanding job.[36] By emphasizing the recuperative nature of leisure, Hale and Beecher indicate the extent to which all kinds of work had become vulnerable to attack.

Clearly, innovations in the workplace meant not only the importation of machines, though this was a significant component, to be sure, but also that the meanings of one's labor had to be reconceptualized and the relation between work and leisure to be reevaluated.[37] It is certainly the case that "the transition to industrial society entailed a severe restructuring of working habits – new disciplines, new incentives, and a new human nature upon which these incentives could bite effectively," as E. P. Thompson claims, but it is equally true that this transition brought with it a significant restructuring of leisure habits.[38] The discussion that follows looks at the changing expectations brought to the experience of leisure time, those elements that produced or denied pleasure whether one were strolling through a New England cemetery or reading a work of American fiction, and how those expectations and pleasures were inextricably grounded in the ideology of the work ethic.

One can only hope that death brings an end to work and inaugurates an eternity of leisure. It is hard to imagine a space more cut off from the world of work than a cemetery. But in this unlikeliest place of all, the logic of the work ethic is in full force. If death is the ultimate space of leisure, and that space is being reconstructed as an idealized image of work, then our reading of Mount Auburn Cemetery will exhume the (body of) work that is the underlying principle of the cemetery.

Mount Auburn is an especially interesting cemetery to examine because its founder, Jacob Bigelow, had a dual career as vocal proponent of the virtues of technology and industrialization and active participant in the cemetery reform movement, which Ann Douglas has described as a "transformation of death" that turned cemeteries into "places of resort, well suited to holiday excursions."[39] In other words, Bigelow covered his bases by simultaneously helping to refashion and destabilize the worlds of both work and leisure while attempting to keep the values of work firmly in place (even if that meant disseminating them in a cemetery). The reconstruction of leisure habits in Mount Auburn Cemetery suggests the somewhat bizarre lengths to which some Americans would go in order to satisfy what I have identified as a cultural imperative to conceal the signs of labor. Labor at Mount Auburn was inevitably linked to the corruptions of the market economy, and so a tremendous amount of pressure was exerted to preserve the illusion of naturalness and effortlessness. Although its founders intended to provide a leisure world outside the world of work, one soon discovers that work is in fact *the* constitutive category of Mount Auburn. Furthermore, this example seems especially relevant to our discussion, given the fact that Bigelow's Mount Auburn project includes some of the same players who were active in the construction and operation of the Lowell mills.

During the 1820s and 1830s, Bigelow not only occupied himself with spreading the gospel of technology but also became active in the reform movements of the day. Most attractive to him were the Massachusetts Horticultural Society, in which he served as an officer, and the crusade for the beautification of cemeteries. In his *History of the Mount Auburn Cemetery*, Bigelow boasts: "In the course of a few years, when the hand of Taste shall have passed over the luxuriance of Nature, we may challenge the rivalry of the world to produce another such abiding place for the spirit of beauty."[40] Whereas his activities in the field of technology promulgated the conversion of "natural agents into ministers of our pleasure and power," his participation in the campaign to reform Cambridge's Mount Auburn Cemetery reveals the seemingly contradictory desire to safeguard nature from technological conversion.[41] Ironically, Bigelow's attempts to protect nature from "the application of acquired knowledge" (4) depended upon technological artifice.

Upon reading Bigelow's *History*, we discover that his "hand of Taste" had a far more active role than Bigelow would have us at first believe. For example, General Charles Dearborn, an avid horticulturalist and one of the earliest members of the Mount Auburn planning committee, "zealously devoted himself nearly the whole of this time to the examination of the ground, the laying out of roads, and superintending the workmen" (20). Furthermore, contracts were made with various Cambridge entrepreneurs in order to procure the necessary fences, gates, and statuary.

Last, Bigelow informs us of a certain twenty-four acres of land, "belonging to David Stone and others, and to Ann Cutter," that were "deemed desirable to secure" (27) and were eventually obtained by the Corporation of Mount Auburn. Unfortunately, Bigelow never tells us what happened to the previous proprietors of the land, but we may safely conjecture that they did not benefit as much from the conversion of "natural agents into ministers" as did the Corporation. Presumably the activities of the Mount Auburn Corporation, some having to do with taste and others with money, made up at least a few of the fingers on Bigelow's "hand of Taste."

The crusades for cemetery improvement reflected the desire to preserve the beauty of nature against the intrusions of industrialization, where people were hands: "Where else shall we go with the musings of Sadness, or for the indulgence of Grief; where to cool the burning brow of Ambition, or relieve the swelling heart of Disappointment? We can find no better spot for the rambles of curiosity, health, or pleasure; none sweeter, for the whispers of affection among the living; none lovelier, for the last rest of our kindred" (14). The beauty of Mount Auburn promulgated family unity and moral discipline as well, precisely those values that many believed were being undermined by the world of work. Mount Auburn was not alone in promoting this utopia of middle-class ideology. In his guide to the Philadelphia Laurel Hill Cemetery, Nehemiah Cleveland echoes many of Bigelow's sentiments: "Here the man of business . . . would often reassure his hesitating virtue."[42] Rural cemeteries offered an escape from the worries of everyday life to the metaphysical worries of life and death. But even death itself could be left behind as "Nature thr[ew] an air of cheerfulness over the labors of Death" (13). The very idea of death was both transformed in Mount Auburn and erased by an act of exchange in which one could trade loss for cheerfulness and erase the "labors" of mournfulness. The power of Mount Auburn, or rather the reconstruction of nature by technology, was indeed awesome: it had managed to transcend death in the middle of a cemetery.

As a way of concluding this analysis of the cemetery, it is necessary to address the pleasure of this particular cultural text, because those in charge of Mount Auburn were convinced that the "cheerfulness" one derived from a cemetery was a direct result of how successfully they managed to erase any signs of the labor that went into its construction and how well they protected Mount Auburn from the world of labor outside its gates. Douglas maintains that the rural cemetery "functioned not like experience but like literature; it was in several senses a sentimental reader's paradise."[43] Mount Auburn, like the sentimental novel and like the antebellum home, offered its visitors "quiet, seclusion, and privacy" while also creating an appropriate context in which "the enduring strength of family ties" could be renewed.[44] Undoubtedly, visitors derived a great deal of comfort from Mount Auburn because it successfully provided an atmosphere in which one could escape the pressures of work and everyday annoyances. The rural cemetery, however, generated pleasure in a more subtle way as well. At the very moment that it provided a haven from the world of labor, Mount Auburn vigorously promoted an ideal of work that operated according to two basic principles: (1) the labor required to construct and maintain Mount Auburn existed outside the competitive and corrupt marketplace, and (2) the pleasure experienced by the visitors to the cemetery derived from the erasure of any signs of labor. Therefore, the extent to which labor was simultaneously expended and erased constituted the pleasure one got out of the cemetery, or to put the equation in Lukácsian terms, one's pleasure was determined by the degree to which "second nature" successfully imitated "first" nature.[45]

An 1860 collection of poems and prose entitled *Mount Auburn: Its Scenes, Its Beauties, Its Lessons* reflects in miniature the struggle between first and second nature that the entire institution of Mount Auburn represents. Wilson Flagg, the editor of the collection, includes a short piece of his own, "Flowers Around Graves," which is meant to distinguish between proper and improper displays of flowers upon graves:

> There is a very simple and practicable method by which flowers might be made to grow upon a new-made grave, without resorting to cultivation. This is to procure the turfs that are to be placed upon the surface of the mound, from some wild pasture that is sprinkled with violets, anemones, columbines, and other flowers, which are not too rank in their growth to injure the smooth appearance of the turf. The little wildings of the wood and the pasture are the evidence that we are in the presence of nature. We feel, while we behold them unmixed with the artificial flowers of the florist, that we are treading upon nature's own ground, and we are led to pleasing meditations, which the scenes of a voluptuous flower garden could never inspire.[46]

The someone who would not only have to "procure the turfs that are to be placed upon the surface of the mound" but also lay them without injuring its smooth appearance disappears in the passive-voice constructions. It is as if the flowers would simply be there. Both the absence of agency and the illusion of naturalness here work together to bring about the "pleasing meditations" experienced in a cemetery. Although the word "made" appears twice in the first sentence, Flagg insists that the flowers upon the grave exist "without resorting to cultivation." The pressure to maintain this absence of agency is truly astonishing in this sentence, as both the made and the newly made lack makers. The discourse of nature in Flagg's piece functions to mystify the artifice (and artificer) necessary to make this environment seemingly natural.

Flagg's concern about the importation of "the artificial flowers of the florist" into Mount Auburn was very much to the point; it illustrates how almost any issue related to the cemetery led to the problematization of the boundary between the natural and the artificial, between the realms of work and leisure. In fact, the history of Mount Auburn reveals that this "problem" existed from the very start. Alongside the rural cemetery that had been proposed by Bigelow and powerful New England industrialists Abbott Lawrence, Charles Lowell, and Samuel Appleton, other Mount Auburn activists, most notably Dearborn and Zebedee Cook, suggested that some of the cemetery land might be used for the purposes of horticulture. According to Blanche Linden-Ward's history of Mount Auburn, Dearborn wished to found an "institution for the Education of Scientific and Practical Gardeners," while Cook wanted to "domesticate foreign plants and develop new hybrids, with sections devoted to fruit trees, timber trees, ornamentals and shrubs, vegetables, flowers, orangeries, hotbeds, vineries, and greenhouses."[47] Although a horticultural center was never established because of economic and institutional difficulties, I would add that the enterprise was doomed to failure because it located itself on the wrong side of the natural–artificial dichotomy. Flagg's "Flowers Around Graves" illustrates the horticultural dilemma: "Affection, that loves to see the dead surrounded with images borrowed from nature and the skies, cannot be thus cheated by its own artifices" (56). Flagg recommends the "spontaneous wildings of nature, rather than the careful products of art and cultivation [because] wild flowers are more poetic than those of the florist, which always suggest the idea of art, and of something that is to be bought and sold," and concludes, "A wild rose would be more pleasing than a garden rose, as an ornament of a grave, because the former is a literal production of nature, while the latter is associated with the wreaths and bouquets of a confectionary store" (57). The roses of a florist do not belong in a rural cemetery, a place intended to mark the boundary between rural and urban, between the hectic round of work and the serene atmosphere of contemplation, because the imported roses bring both the world of artifice and the market economy, that locus of exchange, into an alleged refuge from exchange.

But this concern with mixing the natural and the cultivated came from both sides; that is, Flagg worried about the mixing from the position of one who wished to preserve the integrity of the naturalness of the flowers, whereas Dearborn worried about the mixing from the position of one who wished to maintain the integrity of the cultivated. The intense pressure for taxonomic clarity is evident in Dearborn's *Guide Through*

Mount Auburn, which includes a warning against mixing flowers from outside the cemetery gates with flowers from within: "Any person who shall be found in possession of flowers or shrubs, while in the grounds or before leaving them, will be deemed to have tortiously taken them in the grounds, and will be prosecuted accordingly. N. B. Persons carrying flowers INTO the Cemetery, to be placed on any lot or grave, as offerings or memorials, are requested to notify the Gatekeeper as they pass in; in every other case, flowers brought to the Cemetery must be left without the gate."[48] The importation of flowers from the florist had to be documented, since such activity threatened to unravel the already vulnerable distinction between the natural and artificial. This documentation functions, moreover, as part of a strategy to enforce the rights of ownership, or "possession." Persons failing to register their possessions will not only lose them but will be punished. Dearborn's rather disciplinary approach to infractions against the flower code was echoed in a poem by Mrs. C. W. Hunt entitled "Touch Not the Flowers," a maudlin and humorous verse which Dearborn printed on the back page of the 1858 edition of his guide, whose concluding lines read: "God speaks in every glorious hue, / Bright words of promise unto you; / O'er all his healing love he sheds: / Touch not the flowers. They are the dead's" (48). Interestingly, Hunt requests that visitors to the cemetery refrain from picking flowers not because they belong to the Corporation of Mount Auburn but because they belong to the dead. Those buried in this cemetery would be pleased to know that their rights as owners transcend even death. This suggests that the values of the market were safely ensconced in Mount Auburn.[49]

Although the flowers developed by the Mount Auburn horticulturalists did not find their way into the economy of exchange, they were, nevertheless, a far cry from the "literal production of nature" championed by Flagg. Like Mount Auburn, horticulture was constituted as an activity separate and apart from the damaging world of mechanical labor. Horticulture was, as historian Tamara Plakins Thornton reminds us, tasteful labor that was performed by persons of impeccable taste. But even though horticulture referred more to the Jeffersonian ideal of pastoral rather than factory labor, the stated relation between horticulture and labor resonated enough with the problematic status of labor at the time to make horticulture an unwelcome presence at Mount Auburn. Ultimately, horticulture took away from the pleasurable experience of going to the cemetery by calling attention to the fact of both its madeness and new-madeness. It undermined the dominant ideology of work at Mount Auburn.

The basic structure of this ideology appears in the figure of Bigelow's "hand of Taste," which conceded the necessity for labor while in the same breath calling for its invisibility. A logic of erasure governs Bigelow's metaphoric choice. In his formulation, taste is another word for the kind of unlaborious labor required to transform the beauty of nature into the beauty of Mount Auburn. The figure of the hand was, of course, a commonly used metonymy for the laborer. This figure, then, simultaneously conjoins two representations of labor as well as two classes of laborers: a distasteful kind of labor evoked by the term "hand" and the more satisfactory, more genteel, less visible kind, to which Mount Auburn is dedicated, suggested by the term "taste."[50] Here labor itself is not so much the problem as a particular type of labor which calls attention to itself as "effort" or as "artifice," to return to the terms of the *Mardi* review. This kind of labor bore the ambiguous signs of a developing industrial market economy in which workers were "hands" and work was defined according to its exchange value in the market. Bronson Alcott, transcendentalist and founder of Fruitlands, projects a utopian vision of "tasteful" labor like the hand of taste in Mount Auburn: "A race of more worthy artists shall take the place of our present vulgar artisans, and clean and tasteful products shall spring from their labours . . . [and] artists will not trade [their spirit] in the market or profane it by vulgar toil."[51]

IV. THE LABOR OF ALLEGORY: VERSIONS OF THE (LITERARY) WORK ETHIC

The ideology that informs Bigelow's hand of taste not only applies to the sphere of cemetery reform but serves as a representative figure for a nineteenth-century aesthetic that consistently acknowledged and denied the hand(s) of labor. This aesthetic appears in the general discussions of literature and the numerous literary reviews of the period, which often valorized those texts that most successfully camouflaged the labor that went into their making. In the June 1855 issue of the *Tribune*, for instance, one reviewer praised the writings of popular novelist Charles Reade because they successfully avoided "the conventionalities of fictitious writing, and often ha[d] a salient freshness which [went] far to account for their attractions, without referring to any skill in construction of plot, or the delineation of character."[52] No one denied the fact that writing fiction was hard work, but nineteenth-century taste was predicated on its absence. And no wonder. We have seen this language in discussions about the value of work and, in particular, the problematic relation between labor and character development. Literary versions of the work ethic make their presence felt in reviews which validated authors and texts to the extent that they exhibited, according to the *North American Review*, "the development of character";[53] in other words, to the extent that literature was safely insulated from difficult questions having to do with labor and character. The issues surrounding the production of workers' bodies and individual character in the Lowell mills were reappearing in debates about literary texts. The developing literary marketplace was formulating an aesthetic ideology in keeping with the ideology of the marketplace: did authors foreground or erase their labors? did the signs of labor uphold or undermine the work ethic? were their characters round or flat? Even though the scene of work was different (literary texts, unlike workers' bodies, were not produced in a factory), the requirements of invisible labor were, nevertheless, the same. The remainder of this chapter thus focuses on literary versions of the work ethic, or what will be identified as the discourse of literary labor. I will consider why this labor proved especially problematic for nineteenth-century readers and why allegory became the discursive locus around which the controversy surrounding authorial labor played itself out.

The discourse of literary labor applies the ideology of the work ethic to a fictional text and valorizes those fictions that most effectively erase the signs of labor that go into the making of those texts. Because this discourse was meant to mark the boundaries between aesthetics and work, between leisure and labor, an inherent paradox emerges. Once fictional texts are judged within the context of the work ethic, those discursive boundaries immediately break down. Although a detailed analysis of this discourse will be provided in this chapter, let us for a moment linger upon one example of it which appeared in an unsigned 1850 *Boston Post* review of *White-Jacket*. The reviewer, whom we know to be Charles Gordon Greene, raises the issue of Melville's competence to discuss the complexities of naval discipline and the Articles of War, and concludes that Melville was not, in fact, competent to do so. Of particular interest, however, is the way in which he formulates his objection: "The mind as well as the body is subject to the 'Division of Labor,' and, in most cases, those gifts and acquirements which enable one to produce a good romance unfit him for the calm, comprehensive and practical consideration of questions of jurisprudence or policy."[54] The division of labor invoked by Greene speaks rather directly to the point of *White-Jacket*, because the *Neversink*, like the *Pequod*, reproduces many of the same divisions of labor that exist on shore. More important, Greene's reference suggests that the divisions of labor pertaining to the body ought to pertain to the mind as well – the authorial mind of Melville. In the hands of Greene's review, then, Melville's literary labor would undergo precisely the kind of subdivision experienced by other laborers, like the women of the Lowell mills, whose work was being similarly subdivided.

This subdivision is cogently described in a letter from James Stubblefield, superintendent of the Harper's Ferry armory, to investor George

Bomford. After singing the praises of improved tools and machinery, which have increased factory output, Stubblefield discusses a new principle of production which has also increased worker productivity: "By this division of labor, a great deal of expense and trouble are saved, a great amount of tools is saved, and the work can be executed with infinitely more ease, more rapidly, as well as more perfectly and uniformly; and moreover, a hand can be taught, in one-tenth part of the time, to be a good workman when he has but one component part to work upon."[55] Stubblefield is not merely subdividing the time to perform a task (one-tenth) or the task itself (one component part), but the workman (a hand) as well. It is hard to imagine how the work ethic could incorporate this scene of work into its vision of the moral value of labor. The point is that it could not.

This division of labor, we recall, received mixed reviews among workers of all sorts, whether factory workers or literary laborers. Melville figures this subdivision of labor in one of *White-Jacket*'s most extraordinary scenes – the operation conducted by one of the *Neversink*'s most "professional" crew members, Cadwallader Cuticle, M.D.[56] The radical instability of this new kind of (subdivided) work is nowhere more pointedly and ghoulishly and comically figured than with this allegorical character, who incarnates the problematic relation between an allegorical character and work. His utter commitment to his "eminent vocation" (251), a vocation of amputation that he literally embodies and seeks to embody in others, is what leads him to stage such gruesome acts of violence. In one of the longest chapters of the book, the surgeon Cuticle, who "can drop a leg in one minute and ten seconds" (257), amputates the leg of a sailor, who, though forbidden to leave the ship, had attempted to escape and was shot. Instead of simply removing the piece of artillery, Cuticle insists that "amputation is the only resource" (253). Before commencing the ultimately fatal operation, Cuticle "snatched off [his] wig, placing it on the gun-deck capstan; then took out his set of false teeth, and placed it by the side of the wig; and, lastly, putting his forefinger to the inner angle of his blind eye, spirted out the glass optic with professional dexterity, and deposited that, also, next to the wig and false teeth" (258). Once Cuticle "divest[s] [himself] of nearly all inorganic appurtenances" (258), his lust for the organic emerges. The narrator emphasizes Cuticle's enjoyment of "an unusually beautiful" (261) amputation that did not need to occur except for the fact that he wanted to operate upon an unusually "splendid subject" (262). After amputating his helpless patient's leg, Cuticle, with "bloody" (262) and "ensanguined" (263) hands, passionately lectures his fellow surgeons on the procedure they have just witnessed. In the operating room, Cuticle both takes back the properties of the natural body, in the form of blood, and inflicts his own state of inorganicism

market and reinscribes that economy in his doctor–patient rela-
he connection between literary reviews and potential amputation
ccurs in an early chapter of *White-Jacket*, in which the narrator
he literary sensibility of the noble Captain Jack Chase, who "was
ualified to play the true part of a *Quarterly Review*; – which is, to
arter at last, however severe the critique"(41). Unlike reviewers
arles Greene, who play a false part and "quarter" (hence, the *Quar-
view*) authors like Melville, Jack Chase would instead "play the true
d "give quarter."

signs of Melville's literary labor as embodied by Cuticle were not
g, according to an aesthetic ideology that demanded the erasure of
gns. Cuticle is uncomfortably like those Lowell mill workers who,
ll, registered transformations in their bodies that seemed to be the
f new forms of labor. We might usefully compare the unsatisfying
experience generated by a character like Cuticle with a text like
Beecher Stowe's *Uncle Tom's Cabin* – one which antebellum read-
gined to be in keeping with the aesthetic logic of Mount Auburn
ery and one which naturalized work and sentimentalized death to
nt of their mutual invisibility. We need only quote a passage from
Eva's death scene to realize that the aesthetic informing Mount
n finds its literary counterpart in *Uncle Tom's Cabin*: "St. Clare
. . . For so bright and placid was the farewell voyage of the little
– by such sweet and fragrant breezes was the small bark borne
s the heavenly shores, – that it was impossible to realize that it was
hat was approaching."[58] The naturalizing, aestheticizing experience
e Eva's death scene is a far cry from the death-by-amputation scene
te-Jacket. Stowe's sentimental aesthetic anesthetizes Cuticle's pain.
Melville foregrounds, Stowe erases. A brief glance at *Uncle Tom's*
the most popular book in antebellum America, registers the
l opposition between Melville's adherence to the visibility and pal-
y of literary labor and Stowe's commitment to its erasure.

rly, it is not the case that Stowe's presence does not make itself felt
hout *Uncle Tom's Cabin*. We need only remind ourselves of the
uthorial intrusions that punctuate the narrative, such as when Mr.
rs. Bird decide to assist Eliza in her escape by giving her son Harry
thes of their dead son Henry: "And oh! mother that reads this, has
never been in your house a drawer, or a closet, the opening of
has been to you like the opening again of a little grave? Ah! happy
r that you are, if it has not been so" (153–4). Eliza's escape is
icated by difficulties encountered on a muddy road about which
has the following to say: "But we forbear, out of sympathy to our
s' bones. Western travellers, who have beguiled the midnight hour
interesting process of pulling down rail fences, to pry their car-

upon his patient's body; that is, he carves
organic body parts with prosthetic ones. Hi
a zest for death.

Cuticle illustrates the allegorical charact
particularly problematic configuration of a
ethic operates. Cuticle's work is both the
agency and the means by which he dispo
Whereas the "possessive individualism" o
Macpherson's phrase, produces a version o
agency depends upon the territorial appropi
ethic formulates agency as a matter of indi
constituted within but removed from the
place. The work ethic, though, fully cooper
vidualism of the market. Allegorical charac
of individual agency, as promised by the
dispossessed of individual agency, as requir
of the market. The agency of allegorical ch
complexities of the market – more often tha
of either possessing agency or not possessir
Cuticle suggests, they are most lacking age
they are most possessing it. Their agency i:
deeply discomforting, because even though
two positions in the network of power – ei
they do not have any at all – it is never clea

If Cuticle appeared in a Hawthorne story,
argument for Cuticle as the violent artist fig
identified and from whom he wished to distar
ent conclusion obtains when we consider M
especially in light of Melville's infamous rela
possible, in other words, to read Cuticle as M
ers like Greene who recommended the subd
labors. Clearly, Cuticle displaces the violenc
through violent acts against others. (The) Ci
the hands and fingers, the metonymies of lat
cle's violence dramatizes a last-ditch effort
labor, no matter how unsavory they may be.
of labor, itself a violent amputation of the aut
of violence committed by the laborer Cuticle.
berserk, the violence and power of Cuticle's
from his own experience of self-violation and
others. In occupying these seemingly mutuall
and the same time, Cuticle illustrates the divi
gorical agent who circulates within the econor

by the
tions.
even c
praises
not ill
give q
like C
terly R
part"
The
pleasir
those s
we rec
result
readin
Harrie
ers im
Ceme
the po
Little
Aubu
smilec
spirit,
towar
death
of Litt
in *Wh*
What
Cabin
mark
pabili
Cle
throu
many
and N
the ch
there
whicl
moth
comp
Stow
reade
in th

riages out of mud holes, will have a respectful and mournful sympathy with our unfortunate hero. We beg them to drop a silent tear, and pass on" (158). Stowe's continual appeals to the emotions direct her readers, according to Jane Tompkins, toward "salvation, communion, reconciliation" (132) and instruct them to "see to it [that] *they feel right*" (624). Although "feeling right" requires one to work at attaining "the sympathies of Christ" (624), this emotional labor, according to Stowe, is no labor at all but rather a matter of allowing one to be governed by the "natural" sympathies that are inherent in all persons. In a scene between Tom and another slave, John, who has just been separated from his wife, this sanctification of the "natural" is especially evident: "Poor John! It *was* rather natural; and the tears that fell, as he spoke, came as naturally as if he had been a white man" (199). The "natural" erases the differences between black and white, female and male, poor and rich, because it creates an invisible atmosphere where such oppositions are overcome, where "an atmosphere of sympathetic influence encircles every human being" (624). The power of this atmosphere is demonstrated when Mrs. Shelby must tell Aunt Chloe and Uncle Tom that they are to be separated. "For a few moments they all wept in company. And in those tears they all shed together, the high and the lowly, melted away all the heartburnings and anger of the oppressed" (167).

Not only does Stowe intervene in the narrative to instruct her readers in "real sympathy" (167), but she frequently calls attention to her own act of narrating, as in this account of a slave warehouse: "The reader may be curious to take a peep at the corresponding apartment allotted to the women" (470), or in this description of Aunt Chloe: "Just at present, however, Aunt Chloe is looking into the bake-pan; in which congenial operation we shall leave her till we finish our picture of the cottage" (67). Stowe's presence, unlike Melville's, is designed not so as to obtrude into the reading experience but rather to make that experience as straightforward and smooth as possible. These interventions, in other words, do not call attention to themselves as signs of the difficulties inherent in literary labor (as in the case of Cuticle) but rather successfully and gracefully propel the story forward. Stowe is continually anticipating her readers' needs: "There is danger that our humble friend Tom be neglected amid the adventures of the higher born; but, if our readers will accompany us up to a little loft over the stable, they may, perhaps, learn a little of his affairs" (348), or "Our readers may not be unwilling to glance back, for a brief interval, at Uncle Tom's Cabin, on the Kentucky farm, and see what has been transpiring among those whom he had left behind" (371). Passages like this foreground Stowe's capacity for sympathy because we see her worried not only about neglecting Tom and Chloe but about us readers, who may want to know what has been happening to them. Thus Stowe's authorial intrusions, whether they comment upon the subject matter or the actual act of narrating the subject matter, function to enlarge her readers' capacity for sympathy by showing readers in her own relation to them its powerfully unifying effect. Although Stowe's literary labors are indeed evident in the text, they do not become the sole object of our focus, because Stowe has naturalized them and made them insignificant by inserting them into a fictional world which values sympathy and feeling above all else.[59]

The popularity of *Uncle Tom's Cabin* and other sentimental novels, like the success of Mount Auburn Cemetery, can thus be understood from the point of view of antebellum aesthetic ideology and its adherence to an ideal of invisible labor. This ideal is especially clear in the "introduction to Miss Ophelia":

> Whoever has travelled in the New England States will remember, in some cool village, the large farmhouse, with its clean-swept grassy yard, shaded by the dense and massive foliage of the sugar maple; and remember the air of order and stillness, of perpetuity and unchanging repose, that seemed to breathe over the whole place. . . . There are no servants in the house, but the lady in the snowy cap, with the spectacles, who sits sewing every afternoon among her daughters, as if nothing ever had been done, or were to be done, – she and her girls, in some long-forgotten fore part of the day, *"did up the work,"* and for the rest of the time, probably, at all hours when you would see them, it is *"done up."* The old kitchen floor never seems stained or spotted; the tables, the chairs, and the various cooking utensils, never seem deranged or disordered; though three and sometimes four meals a day are got there, though the family washing and ironing is there performed, and though pounds of butter and cheese are in some silent and mysterious manner there brought into existence. (244–5)

The passage begins with an image of "unchanging repose" (and ahistoricism) which we have seen was concretized in Mount Auburn. More interesting, perhaps, is the discussion of work with which the passage concludes. The labor that the women "did up" has already been forgotten; so forgotten that it can be better thought of in the passive voice, or as having been "done up." The proliferation of passive-voice constructions suggests an ideal of labor in which the agent performing the labor disappears, thus creating the exceedingly pleasurable illusion that the family's dairy products "are in some silent and mysterious manner there brought into existence."[60]

Labor is not absent from *Uncle Tom's Cabin*, but the ideal of absent labor is everywhere present.[61] The image of the hand, which has been so pervasive in our discussion thus far, appears once again in Stowe's text and unfolds in ways which suggest this ideal of invisibility. The hand appears as early as the first chapter, "A Man of Humanity," in which a deal is made between Haley, the slave trader, and Mr. Shelby, who sadly says, "I don't like parting with any of my hands, that's a fact" (43). *Uncle Tom's Cabin* thus begins with the problem of hands, and not only the selling of hands but the fact that people are being identified as hands and that a slave's "hands," according to the logic of slavery, belong to someone else. Mr. Shelby can imagine selling his "hands" because at the level of corporeality his "hands" are not his hands. This sense of hands continues into the chapter "The Feelings of Living Property" as Mr. Shelby has the uncomfortable task of reporting this state of affairs to his wife: "I shall have to sell some of my hands" (82). But the figure of the hand undergoes significant transformations in the text first when Uncle Tom says, "I'm in the Lord's hands" (163) and later when St. Clare is reminded of one of his mother's favorite Bible passages: "It is true what she told me; if we want to give sight to the blind, we must be willing to do as Christ did, – call them to us, and *put our hands on them*" (410). As human hands become Christ's hands (or Christ-like), the proper relation between persons and hands is reestablished. Thus Little Eva's death leads to St. Clare's "turning away in agony, and wringing Tom's hand, scarce conscious of what he was doing," and to Tom's "ha[ving] his master's hands between his own" (427). The figure of the hand no longer operates as a synecdoche signifying the laborer as hand, as it did in the early chapter of *Uncle Tom's Cabin*, but rather the hand now signifies the irrefutable ownership one has over one's hands which has been made possible by Christ. Although this final passage culminates in the liberating moment in which Tom gets "his own" hands, it voices this liberation in a language that also suggests that Tom's hands are not entirely his own; that is, how can Tom have his own hands when St. Clare's hands are still imagined as "his master's hands"? The appeal to Christ's hands in Stowe is meant to avert the situation in which one's hands are never one's own, but it would seem that even Christ's hands cannot completely erase the vestigial sense of the hand as (slave) labor.

Even though Stowe's ideal of invisible labor does not function quite as seamlessly as she might have wished, her own representation of writing *Uncle Tom's Cabin* nevertheless confirms her commitment to an aesthetics of sentimentalism which denies the hands of literary labor as foregrounded by Melville. In fact, the creation myth of *Uncle Tom's Cabin* is right out of the annals of Romantic ideology, with the requisite amount of spontaneity and inspiration: "The first part of the book ever committed to writing was the death of Uncle Tom. This Scene presented itself almost as a tangible vision to her mind while sitting at the communion table in the little church in Brunswick. . . . Scenes, incidents, conversations, rushed upon her with a vividness and importunity that would not be denied. The book insisted upon getting itself into being, and would take no denial."[62] One might suspect that someone other than Stowe wrote these words, given the third-person identification of the author. But Stowe herself wrote them, attesting to an invisibility that fits with her depiction of the book as having its own being separate and apart from Stowe as author, and an invisibility with which Melville would have nothing to do. Stowe presents us with an image of writing in *Uncle Tom's Cabin* radically unlike the figure of writing suggested by Cuticle. It is the image of the dying Little Eva with "her little transparent fingers lying listlessly between the leaves" (413) of the Bible. In representing herself as a medium (of transparent fingers) through which the story of Uncle Tom tells itself, Stowe's sentimental aesthetic wholeheartedly validates the aesthetics of the literary marketplace, to which we now turn.

My general analysis of the discourse of literary labor begins with a consideration of what might best be described as advice literature for authors in training – those literary reviews and essays that claimed to represent the taste of middle-class antebellum readers. In a collection of essays entitled *Eyes and Ears*, Henry Ward Beecher provides an account of the function of literature in his essay "Reading." Reading permits one to see the world "so refashioned that we no longer know where we are, or what we are, but seem to ourselves carried back scores of years, and walking up and down again the ways of childhood."[63] The geographical, temporal, and historical displacements that should occur when we read, according to Beecher, are reiterated in an 1850 *Harper's* article depicting the ideal style of writing that would promote the ideal experience of reading: "[The author] is the invisible agent that moves the magic machinery by which you are transported into a region of illusory enchantments. . . . The moment you perceive the finger of a man the fond deception vanishes."[64] The pleasure of reading depends upon the fiction of an agency that invisibly controls the magic machinery of the text. Displeasure comes about when the reader detects the presence of agency, an agency that is metonymically figured as the author's finger (transparent fingers, I might add, are permissible). Bigelow's hand of taste has once again reappeared, but this time as a finger. The finger, though, is a metonymy on two levels. Not only does it synecdochically represent the author as laborer (in the same way that the hand represents the laborer in Mount Auburn Cemetery), but it also metonymically represents the author's actual labor in that the finger is the part of the author's body that holds the pen that transforms thoughts into language. In describing the relation between authorship and labor, then, this review fragments both the author's body and the authorial labor of writing itself.

The discourse of literary labor often acknowledged the author's labor, whether synecdochically in the *Harper's* article or more directly in the case of Beecher when he claims that "the masterpieces of antiquity, as well in literature, as in art, are known to have received their extreme finish, from an almost incredible continuance of labor upon them," only to urge its erasure.[65] The work ethic was alive and well in the production of literature, even though the traces of labor (and laborer) were better left out of the picture (or the text). Horace Bushnell, who along with Emerson was widely recognized as one of America's most important religious thinkers and philosophers of language, articulates a variant (he adds the weight of religious belief to the discourse) of this position in his 1848 oration "Work and Play": "The writer himself is hidden and can not even suggest his existence. Hence egotism, which also is a form of work, the dullest, most insipid, least inspiring of all kinds of endeavor, is nowhere allowed to obtrude itself."[66] By excising the traces of "labor," "historic results," and the writer's existence, the text "becomes to the cultivated reader a spring of the intensest and most captivating spiritual incitement" (22). The pleasure of this text, like the text of Mount Auburn, depended upon the erasure of work and, more radically, of agency.[67] In contrast to the satisfaction derived from an adherence to the ideal of invisible labor, the appearance of authorial labor often made the reviewer quite strident, as is evident in Bushnell's essay as well as in this 1850 *Harper's* review: "The scene, which is frequently shifted without sufficient regard to the locomotive faculties of the reader, betrays occasional inaccuracies and anachronisms, showing the hand of a writer who has not gained a perfect mastery of his materials. . . . Recourse is had to an awkward and improbable plot, many of the details of which are, in a high degree, unnatural, and often grossly revolting."[68]

The situation seems paradoxical. On the one hand, we find a culture representing and celebrating the valiant struggle to attain virtue through industrious behavior, while we find, on the other hand, that same culture disdaining a literary text because it represents its own labor. As the very idea of labor in antebellum America underwent radical transformations, literary critics called upon authors to keep their labor to themselves. This paradox begins to make sense, however, once we consider that at the same time that actual machinery gained visibility on a scale previously unknown, in factories like the textile mills of Fall River and Lowell, and reconfigured the modes (and means) of production, literary critics were advising authors to hide their own machinery. The discourse of literary labor marked the discomfort with this transformation; it defined literature as a self-contained sphere, invulnerable to the dilemmas being faced in the world of work while using the language of labor to make the point. The problem was that at the very moment that these critics wished to separate literature from labor, they themselves constructed a version of literature's relation to labor that looked remarkably like the problematic relation that seemed to exist between the new machinery in the workplace and laborers. The discourse of literary labor repeated the basic elements in the discourse of labor: ideals of invisible labor, subdivided labor, and absent agency. The invisibility of authorial agency and the synecdochic fragmentation of the author's body which we have seen in the discourse of literary labor are strikingly like workers' anxieties about their lack of agency and the corporeal changes brought about by new kinds of labor. The attempt to make authorial labor invisible so as to keep literature safely outside this debate paradoxically brought literature even further into the cultural fray. The discourse of literary labor thus collapsed the very distinction it meant to preserve.

The literary labor that seemed most fully to illustrate this destabilization of work and the work ethic was allegory and, in particular, the allegorical representation of fictional character. The discomfort that often accompanied the presence of allegorical characters in fiction went beyond the confined boundaries of literary taste. Although critics furnished their reviews with a variety of aesthetic reasons for the unacceptability of allegory, I shall make clear that the aesthetic headache brought on by allegory had some rather painful cultural and, in particular, economic sources. Allegorical characters foregrounded many of the most difficult and challenging issues being faced by nineteenth-century Americans: the problematic status of agency, the reconstruction of the body, and the changing nature of work, and that is why allegory was denounced. If allegory caused the dis-ease, the symbol provided the cure.

A brief overview of the expectations nineteenth-century readers brought to fictional texts reveals why allegory became a favorite target for reviewers. It will become evident that even though reviewers did not always use the term allegory, their language suggests that they leveled their criticism at the allegorical elements in the story. In her study of antebellum responses to fiction, Nina Baym convincingly demonstrates that most readers connected allegory to inadequate characterization and offers a persuasive account of why this kind of characterization proved so obnoxious to reviewers. An 1855 review in *Putnam's* criticized those incompetent writers who failed to spend enough time developing the complexity of human character and praised others who made "the nicest distinctions and shades of character with a keen, firm touch, and without those strong and exaggerated contrasts, which are too often evidences of confused conceptions, and imperfect execution."[69] Similarly, we find Poe castigating Bulwer-Lytton for his "absurd sacrifices of verisimilitude, as regards the connexion of his *dramatis personae*," or a review in the *Home Journal* congratulating a writer for her admirable depiction of "the progressive development of character."[70]

According to Baym, nineteenth-century readers expected "a change in the reader's knowledge of that character, an increasing discovery of what was already there."[71] Readers wanted to experience what E. M. Forster would later call surprise, but not the surprise that would come from the discovery that there was nothing more to know about a fictional character than had already been presented. Lack of character development was part of an even larger problem. Baym correctly identifies the problematic status of agency as the element of allegory that readers found especially difficult to accept: "Characters in fiction were devised as the agents of action, in allegory they were vehicles for concepts. . . . [Allegory] was not and could not be a popular form. Hence, much as our reviewers wanted better novels, they did not want them to become allegory."[72] In focusing attention on the problematics of agency and the related issue of character development in antebellum culture, we get to the heart of its objections about allegory. Once allegory was reconfigured as an attack on individual agency, an ideal of self-made and self-reliant agency that was being undermined in the workplace, the fundamental reason for its devaluation and marginalization becomes obvious. As the paradigm of individual agency through the work ethic came to seem more and more illusory, one could, presumably, always rescue agency in the space of leisure. But if allegorical agency occupied that space as well, the recuperation could not take place.

V. HISTORICIZING ALLEGORY: FROM COLERIDGE TO DE MAN

Allegory, it should be recalled, was not always negatively regarded. One need only think of Dante and Bunyan to realize that the antipathy toward allegory (whose currency has finally run out) was a product of the Romantic ideology which culminated in the writings of Samuel Taylor Coleridge. Thus, although the debate about allegory appears throughout the history of literary criticism, beginning as early as the fourth century B.C. with Philo and Origen, dominating the writings of Saint Augustine and Dante, and continuing through the Renaissance with Milton and Spenser, my own narrative will begin in the nineteenth century with Coleridge's attack on allegory in "The Statesman's Manual." After all, it was Coleridge's forceful articulation of his theory of symbol and allegory in this essay which had the greatest impact on antebellum theories of figurative language and has informed some of the most influential readings of American literature. The specific focus of this discussion will be the relation between allegory and history. My claim is that Benjamin's theory of allegory, in contrast to the theories of Coleridge, Fletcher, and de Man, most compellingly works out the relation between allegory and history and thus provides us with a model for reconfiguring allegory in the context of nineteenth-century American culture.

A symbol, according to Coleridge, "always partakes of the Reality which it renders intelligible; and while it enunciates the whole, abides itself as a living part in that Unity, of which it is the representative" (30). Allegories, by contrast, "are but empty echoes which the fancy arbitrarily associates with apparitions of matter" (30). One of Coleridge's most significant theoretical moves, which had a lasting impact on Emerson as well as on much American literary criticism in the twentieth century, was to hierarchize these figures according to an aesthetic framework that valorized symbols to the degree that they instantiated universal laws of nature and transcended history, and that debased allegories to the degree that they obeyed the laws of "mechanic philosophy" (28) and exemplified the "counterfeit product of the mechanical understanding" (30). The realm of allegory, according to Coleridge, is best characterized by a mechanical worldview consisting of "the depthless abstractions of fleeting phenomena, the shadows of sailing vapors, [and] the colorless repetitions of rain-bows" (23). Given his wish to move beyond "the hollowness of abstractions" (28), the abstract, mechanical, and depthless qualities of allegory will never be as aesthetically pleasing as what he deemed the organic, unifying quality of the symbol. But the aesthetics of symbol and allegory in this essay are conceptualized in relation to profoundly political and historical phenomena. Here Coleridge seeks to map the mechanical and abstract nature of allegory onto a political landscape, alluding to the politics of the French Revolution: "In periods of popular tumult and innovation the more abstract a notion is, the more readily has it been found to combine, the closer has appeared its affinity, with the feelings of a people and with all their immediate impulses to action" (15). In contrast, the symbolic order has the capacity to unify "the contradictory interests of ten millions," who can "be reconciled in the unity of the national interest" (21). It might be useful to remind ourselves that "The Statesman's Manual" was not addressed to "a promiscuous audience" of persons infected with "the general contagion of its mechanical philosophy" (28) (some of whom are presumably mechanics) but rather to "the higher classes of society."[73] Clearly, the aesthetics of allegory and symbol are conceived of in relation to labor and class, where allegory is aligned with the lower class of mechanics and symbol with the higher classes. Catherine Gallagher notes the continuity between Coleridge's political and literary theories of representation: "Although Coleridge hoped that all citizens would internalize the idea of the state and thus submit to its governance, most citizens, he claimed, are incapable of independently interpreting and representing the Idea."[74] Clearly, Coleridge's paradigm is not in itself ahistorical. Its privileging of the symbol is, however, a consequence of the (negative) historicity of allegory.

Coleridge's theory of the transcendent symbol offered Americans a powerful way out of the contradictions at the heart of the discourse of literary labor, and Emerson effectively deployed it. The Coleridgean preference for the symbol is borne out in any number of Emerson's essays, but "The Poet" offers an especially vivid illustration of the powers inherent in the symbol. In this 1844 essay, Emerson celebrates the poet's ability to absorb and "re-attach things to nature and the Whole, − re-attaching even artificial things, and violations of nature, to nature, by a deeper insight" and then goes on to explain the relation between literature and the world of work:

> Readers of poetry see the factory-village, and the railway, and fancy that the poetry of the landscape is broken up by these . . . the poet sees them fall within the greater Order not less than the bee-hive, or the spider's geometrical web. Nature adopts them very fast into her vital circles, and the gliding train of cars she loves like her own. Besides, in a centred mind, it signifies nothing how many mechanical inventions you exhibit. Though you add millions, and never so surprising, the fact of mechanics has not gained a grain's weight. The spiritual fact remains unalterable, by many or by few particulars; as no mountain is of any appreciable height to break the curve of the sphere.[75]

This is indeed the language of the Coleridgean symbol, with its valorization of the great order achieved by poetic vision and the centered mind that sees coherence where others, perhaps, might not. By the end of this passage, "the fact of mechanics" has lost all of its power to ruin the poetry of the landscape. Against the forces of unchanging "spiritual facts," these other facts, such as the factory village and the railway, have been reduced to utter irrelevance.[76] The natural language of the poet has appropriated the millions of mechanical inventions until they fail to signify at all. By nullifying the signs of labor, Emerson has effectively done away with the problematic relation between literature and labor. Simply put, labor no longer exists. Against the discourse of literary labor, which unsuccessfully attempts to preserve the distinction between literature and labor, Emerson's essay illustrates the proper understanding of the relation between literature and labor: the power of the symbolic imagination to unify these two seemingly separate spheres and in so doing to provide a model of literary labor that would keep at bay the problematics of labor foregrounded by allegory. The strategy here, of course, is that instead of erasing the agency of the poet, the Emersonian symbol wipes out everything in its path, except what he calls the one unalterable spiritual fact. Paradoxically, Emerson's American Scholar can only be complete by an imaginative act of erasure.[77]

In contrast to Emerson's full-scale appropriation of the Coleridgean distinction between symbol and allegory, contemporary theorists have challenged Coleridge on a number of issues. One of the most influential and powerful of these critiques appears in Angus Fletcher's *Allegory*, which seeks to repair the damaged reputation of allegory. At the end of his introductory chapter, Fletcher remarks: "Allegories are far less often the dull systems that they are reputed to be than they are symbolic power struggles. If they are often rigid, muscle-bound structures, that follows from their involvement with authoritarian conflict. If they are abstract, harsh, mechanistic, and remote from everyday life, that may sometimes answer a genuine need."[78] The first sentence of this passage marks Fletcher's strategy. By conflating allegory and symbol, he signals a departure from the Coleridgean model. Although he agrees with Coleridge's description of allegory as "abstract, harsh, [and] mechanistic," Fletcher distances himself from an evaluative use of such terms: "The word 'symbol' in particular has become a banner for confusion, since it lends itself to a falsely evaluative function whenever it is used to mean 'good' ('symbolic') poetry as opposed to 'bad' ('allegorical') poetry" (14).

Fletcher, however, recapitulates the value system he wishes to critique, because his analysis ultimately depends upon the Coleridgean model, whose premise is, of course, the opposition between symbol and allegory and, most important, the valorization of the former. Although Fletcher challenges this basic structure, one of its fundamental pillars remains solidly in place. This is the ahistoricism that results in Coleridge's devaluation of allegory. In his introduction to *Allegory*, Fletcher claims that he will validate allegory first by dismantling Coleridge's oppositional model and second by systematizing the "overall purposes [of allegory] . . . without damaging the minor subtleties" (23). This taxonomic clarity is achieved by excising "certain special historical confusions" (13) from the debate. While occasionally referring to an historical component of allegory, as in an early passage where he alludes to the "conflict between rival authorities" (22) or where he acknowledges the fact that "allegory is serving major social and spiritual needs" (23), Fletcher is uninterested in the difference between symbol and allegory, because "this unhappy controversy . . . is a primarily historical matter, since it concerns romantic conceptions of the mind, and of 'imagination' in particular" (13). Because he ultimately wishes to "formulate a theory cutting across historical lines," (13) he is more like Coleridge (and Emerson) than he might prefer to believe. According to this logic, the influence of history upon allegory must be contained in order to rescue allegory from its Coleridgean fate.

Unsurprisingly, this flight from history has significant consequences, none more important than the oppositions between allegory and realism and allegory and history. In explaining the first opposition, Fletcher claims that allegories must often be "abstract, harsh, mechanistic, and remote from everyday life" (23) because "the price of a lack of mimetic naturalness is what the allegorist . . . must pay in order to force his reader into an analytic frame of mind" (107). Allegory, the argument goes, grabs the reader's attention and forces her to contemplate that which she might otherwise read uncritically. The measure of allegory's success is the extent to which it remains separate from the banalities of everyday life. Although Fletcher's proposition might work for the Metaphysical poetry he discusses, the opposition between allegory and mimetic naturalness surely does not "cut across historical lines" – at least not in the case of allegory in nineteenth-century America. The example of Cuticle contradicts this logic, where allegory and realism gruesomely come together as Cuticle's allegorical (and allegorizing) body dramatizes the work ethic gone awry that might seem all too familiar to readers. Furthermore, Fletcher's opposition between allegory and mimesis does not permit an historical reading of "harsh, mechanistic" characters such as the Carpenter in *Moby-Dick* or the Duplicate workers in *The Mysterious Stranger, #44* or the "child of steam and the brother of the dynamo" in *The Education of Henry Adams*.[79] These allegorical figures force us to rethink the traditional dichotomy between allegory and realism; they demonstrate a new conception of realism in which what seems remote is in fact close, if not perilously close, to everyday life.

The theoretical move away from history (and the history of the everyday) is also a move away from the body in that the body bears upon it the marks of history. But even though Fletcher does not directly address the relation between allegory and the body (after all, his analysis of allegory is primarily a formal one), his language comes suggestively close to providing us with a corporeal model of allegory, as does Coleridge's.[80] In describing the kind of abstract thinking he had earlier linked to allegory, Coleridge notes that "the widest maxims of prudence are like arms without hearts, muscles without nerves" (17). Similarly, a number of passages in Fletcher's text use the language of the body to describe allegory: for example, in my first quotation above, he refers to its "rigid, musclebound structures"; elsewhere he accounts for the ability of allegory to evoke powerful responses in readers by pointing to its "surrealistic surface texture" (107); and in a lengthy footnote he claims, "There is a tendency for the ornamental image of clothing external to the body to merge with the body itself, and we find in fact an extensive use of the body-image in allegorical and mythopoeic poetry" (114). Fletcher's debt to Coleridge, and the fact that *Allegory* was written in the heyday of the new criticism, means that his suggestive allusions to the body will remain just that – suggestive.

Historicizing allegory permits us to "flesh out" these shadowy presences of the body and to give them their hermeneutic due. To dismiss the corporeal element of allegorical characters is to miss the ways in which the allegory of labor, as I have identified its contours in antebellum America, is inscribed upon the bodies of workers. And to dismiss the corporeal element in attacks on the labor of allegory is to miss the fact that literary labor was marginalized precisely because of the visible, bodily signs of authorial agency, whether they be an author's hand, finger, or cuticle. Erasures of the body, like erasures of history, prevent us from realizing the extent to which critiques of allegory were grounded in anxieties about the changing relations between workers, be they in fiction or factories, and their bodies.

Coleridge's (and by extension, Fletcher's) definition of allegory as "mechanical" and "abstract" and of the symbol as "living" and "real" has had drastic consequences for the interpretation of American texts and requirements for canonicity. We can find these assumptions about allegory and symbol in many of the earliest and most influential discussions of American literature. Richard Chase, for example, dichotomizes American texts according to their affinities with "the romance" or "the novel." Although his terms are different, the categories the romance and the novel recapitulate the distinctions made between allegory and symbol. Characters and events in romances such as *Moby-Dick*, according to Chase, have "a kind of abstracted simplicity about them . . . character may be deep but it is narrow and predictable. Events take place within a formalized clarity. And certainly it cannot be argued that society and the social life of man are shown to be complex in these fictions."[81] According to this standard and by now time-worn formulation, the novel has the virtue of realistic representation, whereas the romance, with its use of symbol and allegory (Chase does not distinguish between the various modes of figural discourse), makes human character narrow and abstract and thereby fails to be realistic. The incompatibility of realism and romance simply rehearses Fletcher's opposition between realism and allegory.

The most theoretically sophisticated articulation of this Coleridgean model as it applies to the American Renaissance can be found in the work of Charles Feidelson. He arrives at the same conclusions as Chase but brings a knowledge of linguistic theory to the debate. His disdain for allegory assumes the following form: "Allegory was safe because it preserved the conventional distinction between thought and things. . . . Symbolism leads to an inconclusive luxuriance of meaning, while allegory imposes the pat moral and the simplified character."[82] Although Feidelson, like Chase and Forster, correctly describes allegorical figures as simplified, he incorrectly concludes that this means they are simple. We could begin to challenge this claim by interrogating Feidelson's use of the word character. Are we to assume that Feidelson is referring to the simplicity of the (fictional) character; that is, the way in which the character is drawn? Or might he be referring to the simplicity of the character's character? Clearly, the complexities within the very word character undermine the notion of simplicity. Simplified characters, then, do not by definition have simple functions, especially when those functions are best determined by dialogically reading characters in relation to a variety of complex cultural contexts.

This dialogic reading of allegory has, in fact, already been proposed by Walter Benjamin, whose work has gained increasing influence in the field of literary criticism. His analysis of allegory, which is most fully developed in *The Origin of German Tragic Drama*, significantly differs from the model offered by Coleridge and Fletcher in that Benjamin's interpretation of allegory depends upon history, more specifically the relation between seventeenth-century German culture and German Baroque drama. If the theoretical strength of Benjamin's analysis resides in its rigorous historicizing of seventeenth-century allegory, can one account for Benjamin's applicability to a nineteenth-century study of allegory in America and leave intact that historicization that seemed so compelling in the first place? Yes, says Jonathan Arac. And his explanation makes a great deal of sense. In *Critical Genealogies*, he directly confronts the potential problems of using Benjamin's historicized model of allegory for cultures other than seventeenth-century Germany: "Even if literature and society are interrelated, this does not mean that the 'same' literary features have the 'same' meaning when they appear in different socio-historical circumstances," and as an example of this he cites Benjamin himself, who "did not want simply to repeat in his Baudelaire study the insights into allegory he had achieved in the book on seventeenth-century *Trauerspiel*."[83] At the same time that Benjamin claims for allegory a general relation to history, Arac argues that the meanings generated by this relation are historically specific. History is both the common denominator and the locus of difference.

Let us read the differences between Benjamin and his predecessors. Benjamin challenges the valorization of symbol at the expense of allegory and defends allegory on precisely the ground upon which it had been earlier attacked; that is, the fact that it does not transcend its historical limits. "The decisive category of time . . . permits the incisive, formal definition of the relationship between symbol and allegory. Whereas in the symbol, destruction is idealized and the transfigured face of nature is fleetingly revealed in the light of redemption, in allegory the observer is confronted with the *facies hippocratica* of history as a petrified, primordial landscape."[84] Rather than valorizing allegory by making it more like a symbol, as Fletcher tried to do in *Allegory*, Benjamin highlights their differences. In the symbol, history is revealed as redemptive because nature remains unscathed by the marks of history. Allegory, on the other hand, includes no such idealization or transfiguration. Whereas the symbol attempts to erase the signs of history within nature, allegory is compelled to foreground them.

Benjamin's account of allegory is grounded in a reading of seventeenth-century German culture and, more specifically, the Baroque drama. He connects the presence of ruins in the dramatic landscape and corporeal fragmentation with the Reformation, a cultural movement which, he claims, denied the significance of good works by "making the soul dependent on grace through faith," and created a world in which "human actions were deprived of all value" (138). The ruptured connection between human activity and spiritual fate had grave consequences for the culture's representations of itself. The ruins of the Baroque drama articulated the pain experienced by "those who looked deeper [and] saw the scene of their existence as a rubbish heap of partial, inauthentic actions" (139). The allegory of the German Baroque drama thus spoke to the mournfulness of a culture whose religious foundations depended upon the diminution of human agency.[85]

This disempowerment is figured as a radical change in the body's relation to itself, and it is clear that with this attention to the body, Benjamin distances himself even further from traditional readings of allegory that viewed it as abstract and disembodied. Benjamin uses Dürer's *Melancholia*, where "the utensils of active life are lying around unused on the floor as objects of contemplation" (140), as a representative example of the shift in the experience of one's body. He argues that the body, which up until the Reformation had usefully performed good works, was now consigned to the status of an object of contemplation. He calls this new relation to the body "a symptom of depersonalization" (140), which is a corporealized experience of the loss of agency. This loss, however, becomes the precondition for an even greater gain: "The false appearance of totality is extinguished" in order to behold "the lack of freedom, the imperfection, the collapse of the physical, beautiful, nature" (176). It is only by giving up the illusion of totality, by experiencing one's own lack of freedom, that one can begin to be truly free. It is only by seeing oneself (and all objects) as completely inscribed by history that one can begin, in the words of Terry Eagleton, to be "liberated into polyvalence."[86] This loss of agency, which is figured in the Baroque drama as a depersonalized relation to one's own body, becomes an occasion for a peculiarly postmodern paradigm of liberation.[87] It is necessary to distance ourselves from the misplaced romanticism that underlies both Benjamin and Eagleton's casting of this liberation, because it undermines Benjamin's otherwise compelling historicizing of allegory. The basis of this liberation into polyvalence is, after all, the fact of our complete and utter contextualization.

If allegory is a liberation into polyvalence for Benjamin and Eagleton, it is radically unlike the "vertiginous possibilities of referential aberration" proposed by de Man, whose prominent role requires our attention.[88] Rescuing allegory requires that de Man, like Benjamin before him, rehearse the Coleridgean distinction between symbol and allegory and argue for its incoherence. De Man does this in "Rhetoric and Temporality" by deconstructing the notion of a stable subject who "borrow[ed] from the outside world a temporal stability which it lacked within itself."[89] Thus allegory, in contrast to symbol, acknowledges and foregrounds the temporal disjunction between the subject and nature, a disjunction which allegory is, nevertheless, doomed to repeat because this knowledge does not ultimately matter very much; it does not, indeed it cannot, lead to that temporal stability which de Man has argued is always already a mystification. Benjamin, by contrast, challenges the Coleridgean model by studying the role of allegory in German Baroque drama, where, he discovers, "history merges into the setting. And in the pastoral plays above all, history is scattered like seeds over the ground" (92). Whereas de Man ends up by claiming "the impossibility of our being historical" (211), Benjamin wishes "to make historical content, such as provides the basis of every important work of art, into a philosophical truth" (182). De Man grounds many of his claims about allegory in a reading of Benjamin which sympathizes with the project of releasing allegory from its Coleridgean fate, but his own analysis deletes one of Benjamin's most important claims: "In the last analysis structure and detail are always historically charged" (182). Although de Man makes the relation between allegory and temporality the centerpiece of his discussion, his conception of temporality is shorn of any resemblance to historical context, or, as Frank Lentricchia puts it, "history, at least in its conventional senses, is denied altogether."[90] Temporality, for de Man, means "that the allegorical sign refer[s] to another sign that precedes it. The meaning constituted by the allegorical sign can then consist only in the *repetition* (in the Kierkegaardian sense of the term) of a previous sign with which it can never coincide, since it is of the essence of this previous sign to be pure anteriority" (207). Temporality, in other words, refers not to the possible relations between language and history (which has become as impossible as our being historical) but rather to the intertextual relations within language itself.

Temporality is, indeed, a crucial feature of allegory, but this temporality must be understood in decidedly historical terms, particularly because the antipathy to allegory in American culture was, as I have argued, conceived of in relation to the discursive field of labor. In other words, de Man's ahistorical, or what one critic of deconstruction has called anti-historical, configuration of allegory does not adequately explain allegory in nineteenth-century America.[91] This is not to say, however, that the notion of temporality should simply be dismissed, but rather the repetition that de Man sees as a central feature of allegory needs to be historicized. Benjamin says as much when he claims, "Allegory, like many other old forms of expression, has not simply lost its meaning by 'becoming antiquated.' What takes place here, as so often, is a conflict between the earlier and the later form" (161). The disjunction between the earlier and the later form must be conceptualized not in exclusively linguistic terms but rather in terms of the relation between language and historical context. When "archaic" formations, to use Raymond Williams's terms once again, like allegory are redeployed in different temporal contexts, accretions and transformations of meaning inevitably take place. This requires us to acknowledge and explain the ways in which rhetorical forms, to use de Man's terms, like allegory are mediated, nuanced, and changed by those specific contexts.

Benjamin grounds his account of allegory in the specificity of seventeenth-century Germany, and this is its strength. If some of the same issues raised by Benjamin's analysis resonate in our reading of allegory in nineteenth-century American culture, it is certainly not because Baroque drama anticipated the American novel but rather because the undermining of agency, which Benjamin reads as an effect of the Reformation, has an American counterpart in the dissolution of the work ethic. This historically specific difference, however, opens up a reading of allegory that turns out to be dramatically unlike what Benjamin proposes in *The Origin*, one that reads the antipathy to allegory in the nineteenth century as a consequence of the uncomfortable similarity between allegorical and economic constructions of agency. Hence, we see the development of an "economics of allegory." The work ethic seemed to be a discourse that unified a variety of cultural activities – all professions required an adherence to it. But literary taste urged texts not to foreground the work that went into their construction. The work ethic when applied to literature, then, meant the erasure of literary work. Allegorical texts spurned this advice and often were castigated and marginalized as a consequence. I have up to this point mapped out the ideological motivation behind this advice; now let us look at two tales by Hawthorne and see whether or not he heeds it.

2

Hawthorne and the Economics of Allegory

The question of Hawthorne's relation to allegory has excited and plagued critics of Hawthorne ever since his short stories first appeared in the early 1830s. It even bothered Hawthorne, who in 1854 wrote to his publisher James T. Fields, "Upon my honor, I am not quite sure that I entirely comprehend my own meaning in some of these blasted allegories."[1] Following Hawthorne's own lead, contemporary readers continue to wrestle with the problem of Hawthorne and allegory and have come up with a variety of compelling explanations, many of which assume as their point of departure that Hawthorne was indeed experimenting with traditional allegory to create a new kind of allegory. The agreement ends there, as one cultural critic maintains that Hawthorne "modifi[ed] a sacrosanct Puritan form by mixing it with contemporary themes and styles" in order to "suit modern needs," and another critic, one with a more formalist perspective, argues that Hawthorne "apparently adopts the allegorical mode in order to turn it against allegorical intentions."[2] Although both of these views contribute to a greater understanding of Hawthorne's recasting of traditional allegory, this reading will suggest yet another explanation, in which allegorical characters reveal themselves as dialogically engaged with one of the nineteenth century's most powerful technologies of producing personhood – the developing market economy in antebellum America. If, on the one hand, allegory functions as a reminder of traditional texts (Bunyan would, of course, be the most obvious candidate in the case of Hawthorne) and a repository of traditional values, it becomes, on the other hand, a departure point for radically untraditional configurations of personhood that bear little relation to the religious world of Bunyan. Informed by the logic of the market, personhood is produced and reproduced by acts of exchange and incessant circulation, none more significant perhaps than the exchanges taking place between the texts of Hawthorne and Bunyan in "The Celestial Rail-road" and the circulations taking place between Aylmer and Georgiana in "The Birthmark," two early texts that provide us with especially powerful illustrations of the beginnings of Hawthorne's reconfiguration of allegory. Allegorical characters in these texts function as sites of contestation in which individual agency is suspended or circulating between the poles of possession and dispossession, as was the case with John A. B. C. Smith and Cuticle. Although I will argue that Hawthorne's identification with Georgiana in "The Birth-mark" eventually results in Hawthorne's possession of authorial agency, it is clear that Hawthorne carries the burden of Bunyan's allegory, making it exceedingly difficult for Hawthorne's allegory to signify anything other than his subjection to Bunyan. Hawthorne does, however, get beyond Bunyan, and this is the labor of Hawthorne's allegory in "The Celestial Rail-road" and "The Birth-mark."

Few critics interested in Hawthorne's reconfiguration of allegory have taken seriously the text in which he is most obviously engaged with Bunyan and the meaning of Bunyan's legacy for antebellum American literature – "The Celestial Rail-road."[3] Perhaps with good reason. The comic tone of the tale discourages readers from thinking about it as anything other than an affable, urbane, and humorous recasting of *The Pilgrim's Progress*. Hawthorne's "gently derisive pen," as one critic characterizes it, discourages us from realizing the complexity of the tale.[4] "The Celestial Rail-road" is not only a nostalgic look back at the religious world of Bunyan, which Hawthorne conceives to be no longer available in antebellum America, but also a conceptual look ahead toward a reconfiguration of allegory, an "economics of allegory," which signals Hawthorne's departure from Bunyan and Bunyanesque allegory. Hawthorne's "economics of allegory" registers Fredric Jameson's sense of a "newer allegory [that] is horizontal rather than vertical, [which] if it must still attach its one-on-one conceptual labels to its objects after the fashion of *The Pilgrim's Progress*, it does so in the conviction that those objects (along with their labels) are now profoundly relational, indeed are themselves constructed by their relations to each other."[5] A horizontal model of allegory, in other words, requires that we consider the signifying powers of allegory in relation to a context that is neither stable nor definitive (this would be the vertical model) but has powerfully signifying effects of its own.

"The Celestial Rail-road" must therefore be seen as a central text in any consideration of antebellum allegory, because this marginalized and seemingly simple tale has a great deal to say about the "profoundly relational" relations among Hawthorne, allegory, and antebellum constructions of personhood. This chapter goes on to illustrate the presence of two rival conceptions of allegory in the tale, a traditional one based on Bunyan's *The Pilgrim's Progress* and an economics of allegory constituted in relation to a developing market economy, and then examines how these alternative practices of allegory produce two rather different accounts of the relation between fictional character and identity. The second part of the chapter illustrates how the logic of the market locates itself within and upon the body, in particular the female body. In "The Birth-mark," a story of a woman whose husband sacrifices her life for the sake of erasing a birthmark, which he feels to be the only thing standing between her and perfection, it is possible to read Georgiana's birthmark as making visible and assigning a secure place to what should be, according to the logic of the free market, invisible, fluctuating, and placeless. Aylmer experiences the independent life of the birthmark as a diminution of both his sexual and economic power, which can only be resuscitated by the scientific erasure of "the Crimson Hand."[6] In bringing a halt to the instability and power of the market as it manifests itself on the female body, Aylmer ends up relocating the market, in all of its uncontrollability, potency, and now in its invisibility, within himself. "The Birth-mark" thus continues where "The Celestial Rail-road" leaves off and more fully exemplifies the complex relations among allegory, the market, and the body – the defining nexus of an economics of allegory. My reading of "The Birth-mark" also suggests the ways in which *The Scarlet Letter* might be analyzed in terms of Hawthorne's complex relation to the antebellum aesthetic of invisible labor, which is nowhere more apparent than in Dimmesdale's continued gesture of "holding his hand over his heart."[7] Whereas Hester is forbidden to conceal the sign of her reproductive and productive labors, as represented by Pearl and the scarlet letter, Dimmesdale is/feels compelled to do so. Indeed, Dimmesdale's is the exemplary gesture demanded of authors by the literary marketplace: success is possible only by keeping all evidence of labor invisible. Dimmesdale's gesture and Hawthorne's relation to it is, however, complicated by the fact that the hand that conceals labor is also the hand that metonymically signifies it.

I. EASY RIDER/EASY READER

Of all the tales in *Mosses from an Old Manse*, "The Celestial Rail-road" perhaps has the dubious honor of generating the least amount of critical controversy. There has been little disagreement about this tale, in which a nineteenth-century pilgrim journeys to heaven on board a modern train, ever since one reviewer declared it to be "clothed in forms of equal vividness and simplicity" and another lauded it as one of "the happiest efforts of the author in sketch writing."[8] The tale's simplicity has until now been a sign predominantly of its unambitious design. Appearing in the January 1847 edition of the *New Englander*, however, was a review by Samuel Dutton that managed to raise some of the more fruitful complexities in Hawthorne's story: "The Celestial Rail-road," "which in respect to ease and rapidity, bears a relation to the road of John Bunyan's Pilgrim, like to that which a modern railroad bears to an old fashioned turnpike or county road – a pleasant but keen and truthful satire on modern easy modes of getting to heaven."[9] At first glance, this review simply applauds Hawthorne's story for its clever use of *The Pilgrim's Progress* and interprets "The Celestial Rail-road" as a satire on shortcut approaches to salvation. This is undoubtedly why, according to Bertha Faust in *Hawthorne's Contemporaneous Reputation*, "The Celestial Rail-road" "continued for a long time to be a popular item among the offerings of the American Sunday School Union."[10] Dutton's relatively straightforward response (it "surpasses all his other writings") to Hawthorne's allegedly straightforward tale (his style is "usual[ly] easy and quiet") quickly gets muddled, however, in a series of tortuous analogies that result in the reviewer's (he was, incidentally, a pastor of New Haven's North Church) seeming more like the villainous Mr. Smooth-it-away of "The Celestial Rail-road" than Bunyan's noble pilgrim Christian.

The review begins by asserting "a relation" between "the ease and rapidity" of Hawthorne's tale and "the road of John Bunyan's Pilgrim," which is presumably neither easy nor rapid. The relation between "The Celestial Rail-road" and Bunyan's road is, in turn, "like to that which a modern railroad bears to an old fashioned turnpike or county road." We can see that an analogy is being drawn between two distinct domains – textuality and technology. The realm of textuality is compared, on the one hand, to the world of sophisticated technology in the case of Hawthorne and, on the other, to nature in the case of Bunyan; or to put the point another way, reading "The Celestial Rail-road" is like riding on a modern railroad, and reading Bunyan is like taking an old-fashioned walk in the country. The first is easy, the second is not. Is it better to be fast or slow? and how does religion fit into the comparison? Certainly a relation exists between these two transportation and reading experiences, such as the relation between fast and slow modes of travel or easy and arduous reading experiences, but the relation is ambiguous primarily because of the multivalent significations of ease and rapidity. These terms are obviously positive when understood in terms of railroad technology, negative when applied to religion, and, as I suggested in the first chapter, ambiguous because of the ambiguous status of labor when applied to reading. Dutton's review is therefore complicated by the competing claims of the technological, religious, and aesthetic frameworks that inform his remarks on "The Celestial Rail-road." He seems to be comparing the riding speed of Hawthorne's tale to the speed of the railroad, and the slowness of Bunyan's journey to a county road, but we cannot be sure about which value system, antebellum technology or seventeenth-century religion, is structuring his comparisons. The increasing number of similes, which are meant to clinch the argument, only obfuscate its point even more. His final sentence assures us that the moral of these relations is "a pleasant but keen and truthful satire on modern easy modes of getting to heaven." But the point of *The Pilgrim's Progress* is precisely how difficult getting to heaven actually is. Dutton's Aesop-like ending fails, then, to clarify the ambiguities his text has generated, as he ends up defending the very position that he seemingly wants to critique.

That Dutton takes great pleasure in this story (he goes on to quote nine lengthy passages) because of its "ease," "rapidity," and "truthful satire" is especially evident in his more general description of *The Twice-Told Tales*: "There is nothing strained, and no painfully manifest aim and effort to be brilliant and effective. We have become so wearied with these faults in modern writers, that it is really refreshing to read one who writes unambitiously, and without this apparent labor – one who tells us his thoughts and emotions, without a manifest consciousness of himself."[11] This review conveniently furnishes us with many of the dominant fixtures of nineteenth-century literary taste we have already seen: a lack of strain or effort, an absence of visible labor, and a modest self-consciousness. Hawthorne's "apparent" ease with writing translates into Dutton's effortlessness in reading, which makes for a delightful reading experience. Dutton's aesthetic ideology, which is based on an antipathy to reading (and writing) as labor, gets him into serious spiritual trouble. According to an 1857 address by the Reverend Henry D. Bellows entitled "The Relation of Public Amusements to Public Morality," "life to most men [is] toilful, anxious, serious and sad. And this is what life must be and ought to be. This is what Christianity labors to make it."[12] Clearly, Dutton's text does not uphold the values of work as articulated by Bellows but instead reflects the values of the railroad, as opposed to the old-fashioned turnpike. But if "easy modes of getting to heaven" lack the religious rigor necessary to get to the Celestial City, isn't there something problematic about valorizing the "ease" with which one reads about those "easy modes"? Isn't the journey to the Celestial City *supposed* to be accompanied by strains, labors, and self-consciousness – precisely those qualities Dutton condemns as the faults of modern writers, precisely those qualities exhibited by Christian in *The Pilgrim's Progress*? When characterizing the reading experience as a railroad experience, that is in its technological context, "ease" is good, but "ease" becomes unhinged from this signification when informed by a religious context. Although "the ease and rapidity" of the railroad's progress toward the Celestial City illustrates its wickedness, Dutton would have us believe that the "ease and rapidity" of reading "The Celestial Rail-road" is ideal. Caught between the desire to champion the tortoiselike county road against the harelike railroad when the comparison has to do with religion, the railroad wins out when the comparison has to do with both the technology of riding on the railroad and reading about it. Having mistakenly confused the reading and riding experiences, Dutton's rhetoric maintains that it is possible to be both an easy rider and an easy reader – and get to heaven. This, of course, is precisely what Mr. Smooth-it-away tries to convince the narrator of in Hawthorne's story and presumably not the message we are meant to take away from the story. Dutton's rather contradictory review mirrors the contradictions in Hawthorne's own story. In other words, Dutton's review, which ends up exemplifying the inaccessibility of Bunyan's worldview to nineteenth-century America, has accurately mirrored the contradictions in Hawthorne's story, which at the very moment that it seeks to reestablish Bunyan's importance to Hawthorne's readers ends up displaying his inapplicability. Although Dutton correctly maintains that "The Celestial Rail-road" derives its power from its relation to Bunyan's *Pilgrim's Progress*, it is also clear that Hawthorne's text derives its power from its separation from Bunyan.

Modeling his tale after one of his favorite books, *The Pilgrim's Progress*, Hawthorne scathingly critiques what he sees as the vapid religiosity of antebellum America.[13] In a humorous and pointed rewriting of Bunyan, Hawthorne modernizes Christian's tempestuous journey to the Celestial City. Christian's urgent desire for salvation, for example, finds its nineteenth-century corollary in the narrator's "liberal curiosity" about the Celestial City.[14] In addition, Christian's guide, the Evangelist, has been replaced by Mr. Smooth-it-away, who informs Hawthorne's narrator that Greatheart, who "went off to the Celestial City in a huff, and left us at liberty to choose a more suitable and accommodating man" (811), has also been replaced by "Apollyon, Christian's old enemy, with whom he fought so fierce a battle in the Valley of Humiliation" (811). The repetition of the word "liberty" and its "double-edged" usage, as Matthiessen noted some years ago, clearly indicates Hawthorne's disdain for the "convenient" (809) politics and religious "liberality of the age" (811).[15] In taking such liberties with *The Pilgrim's Progress* – on two occasions he rather disrespectfully refers to Bunyan's book as a "road-book" (812, 814) – the narrator's discourse reveals the wide gulf between nineteenth- and seventeenth-century religious belief and practice. Even so, Bunyan's relevance to the nineteenth century remains intact. If antebellum America fails to live up to the Protestant standards of Bunyan's time, those standards are nevertheless accurate measures of that failure.

The feature that most clearly signals the difference between these two texts is the tonal slipperiness of Hawthorne's text. Whereas *The Pilgrim's Progress* begins with a powerful scene of suffering and confusion brought about by Christian's lack of faith, the opening of "The Celestial Rail-road" hints at no such physical disorientation or spiritual anxiety. A juxtaposition of each text's opening passage makes the point quite clearly. "As I walked through the wilderness of this world, I lighted on a certain place, where was a den; and I laid me down in that place to sleep: and as I slept I dreamed a dream. I dreamed, and behold I saw a man clothed with rags, standing in a certain place, with his face from his own house, a book in his hand, and a great burden upon his back. I looked, and saw him open the book, and read therein; and as he read, he wept and trembled: and not being able longer to contain, he brake out with a lamentable cry; saying, 'What shall I do?'"[6] The pathos of this scene from Bunyan contrasts sharply with the equivocating urbanity of Hawthorne: "Not a great while ago, passing through the gate of dreams, I visited that region of the earth in which lies the famous city of Destruction. It interested me much to learn, that, by the public spirit of some of the inhabitants, a rail-road has recently been established between this populous and flourishing town, and the Celestial City" (808). If Hawthorne had meant "The Celestial Rail-road" to be a homage to Bunyan, the strategy backfired, because the radical difference in tone serves to reinforce the sense of Bunyan's inapplicability to antebellum America. An 1847 review of "The Celestial Rail-road" would appear to make this point: "In 'The Celestial Railroad,' we have a new Pilgrim's Progress performed by *rail*. Instead of the slow, solitary, pensive pilgrimage which John Bunyan describes, we travel in fashionable company, and in the most agreeable manner."[17] Hawthorne so successfully inverted and perverted Bunyan that reviewers such as this one in *Blackwood's Magazine* got the moral of the story all wrong. By "teasing the reader with double explanations and significant omissions," as Frederick Crews has noted, Hawthorne not only registers the ideological gap between his world and Bunyan's but, I would add, makes that gap seem so unbridgeable that Bunyan (and his allegory) are irrecoverable.[18]

"The Celestial Rail-road" presents its readers with a compelling, albeit standard nineteenth-century, explanation for this irrecoverability – technology. Declaring its opposition to the railroad on religious grounds, an Ohio school board called the steam railroad "a device of Satan to lead immortal souls down to Hell," and an 1840 article in *Graham's* magazine entitled "Stage Coaches and Rail Roads" blamed railroad technology for enabling Americans, who "despis[e] every thing but the '*utile*' of life, living only for the sake of making money, and, turning from the finest landscape that the Creator ever wakened into beauty," to continue in their "quick, restless, thrifty" ways.[19] According to these and similar jeremiads against technology, the religious rectitude of Bunyan's time is no longer available to Hawthorne's contemporaries, because technology has made Americans unwilling to endure the hard work necessary to achieve salvation. Unlike the writings of Emerson, for example, which alternately praised the virtues and criticized the vices of technological innovation, Hawthorne's text evinces no such ambiguity but rather demonizes the railroad at every possible turn, and nowhere more clearly than in the following passage:

> The engine now announced the close vicinity of the final Station House, by one last and horrible scream, in which there seemed to be distinguishable every kind of wailing and woe, and bitter fierceness of wrath, all mixed up with the wild laughter of a devil or a madman. Throughout our journey, at every stopping-place, Apollyon had exercised his ingenuity in screwing the most abominable sounds out of the whistle of the steam-engine. (823)

The narrator's vision of a technological hell is surpassed, perhaps, only by Henry Adams, who prophesies in the final chapters of *The Education*: "So long as the rates of progress held good, these bombs would double in force and number every ten years" (494). And like *The Education*, to which I shall return in a later chapter, "The Celestial Rail-road" imagines technology in decidedly corporeal terms. In the passage above, for example, Apollyon "screws out" horrid sounds from the engine, which originate from "the engine's brazen abdomen" (811). In a similar passage, the head engineer violently extracts "a tremendous shriek . . . as if a thousand devils had burst their lungs to utter it" (815). A technological body appears in the narrator's description of the source of the railroad's fuel – that "dismal obscurity of the broad cavern-mouth" where he sees "huge tongues of dusky flame," "strange, half-shaped monsters, and visions of faces horribly grotesque" (815). The engine, as well as the entire apparatus that enables it to function, is represented as a body gone amok.[20] In its possession of a body, the locomotive possesses a crucial aspect of personhood that persons in the story lack. This perverse embodiment of the locomotive is accomplished, as we shall see, at the expense of the individual bodies in "The Celestial Rail-road."

This "mechanical demon" (811), and more specifically its corporeal incarnation, offers a convincing explanation for the moral breach that separates Hawthorne's world from Bunyan's. But technology is, I think, too easy a target. As will become evident, this kind of technological determinism functions strategically for our narrator, who, on the one hand, demonizes the railroad as the root of all evil and, on the other, abdicates responsibility for his own participation in the underlying structures that transform technology into an instrument of, quite literally, the devil. Quick to seize upon the horrors of the railroad engine in all of its technological grotesquerie, the narrator, at other times, possesses what seems to be an almost astonishing capacity for transforming some of the less savory aspects of the market economy, which enables the railroad to go in the first place, into signs of liberal progress. This contradiction

PS 374
.W64
W45
1995

For my mother and my father, whose memory is safe in mine

APR 9 1997

seems unresolvable until we realize that the narrator and the market are one and the same.

II. WHAT'S IN A NAME?

Although *The Pilgrim's Progress* plays an essential role in "The Celestial Rail-road's" social critique, Bunyan's relevance is not limited to the conceptual realm. Hawthorne's formal debt to Bunyan is perhaps nowhere more striking than in the names of characters like Mr. Live-for-the-world, Mr. Hide-sin-in-the-heart, and Mr. Scaly-conscience, whose seventeenth-century family tree undoubtedly includes Bunyan's Timorous, Shame, and Discontent. The names of characters in "The Celestial Rail-road" and *The Pilgrim's Progress* accurately name, describe, and mirror their character. Because no hermeneutic separation exists between a name like Mr. Live-for-the-world and Mr. Live-for-the-world's character, Hawthorne's story effectively does away with the need for interpretation. By making interpretation unnecessary, does Hawthorne leave us with anything at all to say? Although the simplicity of a tale like "The Celestial Rail-road" is disarming, its assumptions about names and the relation between Hawthorne, as namer, and his fictional characters, as named, are, in fact, far from straightforward.

This is most evident in the case of Mr. Smooth-it-away, who conducts the narrator from the city of Destruction to the Celestial City. Although, or because, his name and his character perfectly mirror one another, we most frequently see him trying to drive a wedge between names and what they stand for. Mr. Smooth-it-away's task is to smooth away the hermeneutic gulf between the narrator's experience aboard the Celestial Rail-road and what his experience should be according to *The Pilgrim's Progress*. When they reach the Slough of Despond, for example, Mr. Smooth-it-away testifies "to the solidity of its foundation" (809). And in claiming that he would "be loth to cross it in a crowded omnibus" (809), the narrator initially maintains a rather healthy skepticism toward Mr. Smooth-it-away's "testimony" (809). This skepticism, however, soon gives way to a more liberal-minded affability. When they come upon the Valley of the Shadow of Death, for instance, Mr. Smooth-it-away assures the narrator "that the difficulties of this passage, even in its worst condition, had been vastly exaggerated" (814). Although the narrator has some rather serious doubts about Mr. Smooth-it-away's mollifying explanation and his "heart quake[s]" upon his hearing "a tremendous shriek careering along the Valley as if a thousand devils had burst their lungs to utter it" (815), the narrator soon adopts Mr. Smooth-it-away's perspective by dismissing Bunyan as "a truthful man, but infected with many fantastic notions" (815). Mr. Smooth-it-away's language attempts to tar-

nish the mirror relation between the names of places and fictional characters in *The Pilgrim's Progress*, so that Bunyan's "truthful[ness]" comes to
seem "fantastic" – its very opposite.

The Pilgrim's Progress derives much of its power from its ability to
name people and places correctly. The force of "The Celestial Rail-road"
similarly comes from its concern with naming: Mr. Smooth-it-away's
attempts to misname, the way the narrator, in Delano-like fashion, tries
to convince himself of the truth of these misnomers, and how the narrative critiques this manipulation of names. Fletcher reminds us of the fact
that names play a crucial role in allegory: "To name a person is to fix his
function irrevocably" (50). Although one could certainly interpret this
"fix[ity]" in a negative light, and indeed many readers of allegory did and
still do, one could also experience in this fixity the epistemological satisfaction of knowing that a character's name accurately reflects his character. Mr. Smooth-it-away's name thus cements the relation between his
name and his character at the very moment that his words and actions
attempt to undo the stability between one's name and character.

To name properly a person, a place, or a thing in "The Celestial Rail-
road" means to adhere not only to a semiotic structure in which signs
have stable referents but to an economic one in which, according to
Marx, an individual "directly satisfies his wants with the produce of his
own labour [and] creates, indeed, use-values, but not commodities."[21]
This claim might seem at first unrelated to the story until we see it in
relation to the market economy of "rich commodities" (819) at Vanity
Fair, that "great capital of human business and pleasure" (819). Vanity
Fair, as the name suggests, is a marketplace where the narrator sees self-
absorbed and self-promoting people "making their own market" and
"deeming no price too exorbitant for such commodities as hit their
fancy" (819). Vanity Fair, thus, seems anything but fair as the narrator
observes people making "very foolish bargains" and engaging in "speculations . . . of a questionable character" (819). Such foolishness governs
the exchanges at Vanity Fair, where "if a customer wished to renew his
stock of youth, the dealers offered him a set of false teeth and an auburn
wig; [and] if he demanded peace of mind, they recommended opium or a
brandy-bottle" (820). This principle of "questionable" exchange oversees
all of the activities at Vanity Fair, including its means of communication.
The narrator informs us that "any man may acquire an omnigenous
erudition, without the trouble of even learning to read" from "eminent
divines" and "innumerable lecturers" (818) who spread the word of God.
In this way, the narrator concludes, "literature is etherealized by assuming for its medium the human voice; and knowledge, depositing all its
heavier particles – except, doubtless, its gold – becomes exhaled into a
sound, which forthwith steals into the ever-open ear of the community"

(818). This passage evokes a version of "questionable" exchange where both consumer, in this case the community, and seller, most likely the author, get shafted by a third party, presumably "the capitalists of the city" (817), who have separated out the gold for themselves and dispensed the remainder, or the "sound," to the community. Because of this "etherealiz[ing]" process, sounds and words, as well as the sound of words, have little relation to themselves or to one another in Vanity Fair.[22] Unlike Mr. Smooth-it-away, whose name guarantees his character at the same time that it undermines this relation everywhere else, the "fair" part of Vanity Fair produces on the semantic level the "questionable character(s)" of the Fair. While dedicated to creating the illusion that the Fair is fair, its economy depends for its success upon the fact of its unfairness.

The slippage, or alienation, between name and character in Vanity Fair is clearly a consequence of a market economy that thrives on objects "exchanged at very disadvantageous rates" (820). Language itself, as I have been suggesting, constitutes one of the most significant sites of exchange. When the narrator meets Mr. Stick-to-the-right, for instance, their conversation shows the problematic state of language in Vanity Fair:

> "Sir," inquired he [Mr. Stick-to-the-right], with a sad, yet mild and kindly voice, "do you call yourself a pilgrim?"
> "Yes," I replied. "My right to that appellation is indubitable. I am merely a sojourner here in Vanity Fair, being bound for the Celestial City, by the new rail-road."
> "Alas, friend," rejoined Mr. Stick-to-the-right, "I do assure you, and beseech you to receive the truth of my words . . . you may travel on it all your life-time, were you to live thousands of years, and yet never get beyond the limits of Vanity Fair!" (820–1)

Shortly after this conversation, Mr. Smooth-it-away dismisses "the truth" of Mr. Stick-to-the-right's words by suggesting that he "ought to be indicted for a libel" (821). Mr. Smooth-it-away's invocation of "the law" (821) suggests that language and meaning have become so unhinged at Vanity Fair that a legal apparatus is necessary to arbitrate between competing interpretative claims. Mr. Stick-to-the-right's opening question immediately calls attention to this issue of language in the context of the narrator's identity. Although the narrator calls himself a pilgrim, and indeed asserts his "right" to the "appellation" of "pilgrim," "pilgrim," as Mr. Stick-to-the-right tries to explain, is not exactly the right name.

How then is one to explain the fact that the narrator, the main character of "The Celestial Rail-road," has no "proper" name in a story so invested in the (im)propriety of proper names? There is a curious lopsidedness to the story: on the one hand, a preponderance of names and, on the other, our unnamed narrator. Admittedly, one could (and should) attribute this to Hawthorne's coyness with the reader. He simply and playfully does not give the obvious name, Christian, which no longer fits the revised plot scenario. I would like to suggest, however, a more complicated reading of the narrator's anonymity which connects this anonymity both to the operations of a market economy and to the development of Hawthorne's economics of allegory. This nominative imbalance should first be understood as a disjunction in "The Celestial Rail-road" between a traditional practice of allegory, where the identities of characters are, according to Fletcher, "drawn with extremely sharp-etched outlines," and an economics of allegory, where identities, like the speculations in Vanity Fair, are "of a questionable character" (819).[23] As we have already seen, Mr. Smooth-it-away's name hearkens back to this traditional allegory (à la Bunyan), in which one's name and character are identical, *and* looks forward to an economics of allegory, in which names embody a separation of character from name. As my reading of Mr. Smooth-it-away's name suggests, the principle of an economics of allegory always already existed within the framework of traditional allegory. If, by not having a name, the narrator seems to escape the dilemma posed by Mr. Smooth-it-away (how can there be a disjunction between character and name if there is no name to begin with?), the narrator's lack of a name is precisely the absent origin that most fully speaks to the difference between these two principles of allegory. It is the unnamed narrator who instantiates the market-based personhood produced by an economics of allegory, which fully enacts the logic of the market while imagining itself as transcendent.

The kind of personhood constructed by Hawthorne's nineteenth-century allegory is thus radically different from Bunyan's. Because it is based on imposture, there is, to quote "The Celestial Rail-road," "the same difference as between truth and falsehood" (814). Although Mr. Smooth-it-away's character suggests that the seeds of Hawthorne's allegory exist within Bunyan's, the unnamed narrator is what finally separates the two kinds of allegory. The narrator's first glimpse of Vanity Fair enables us to see how this works:

> It would fill a volume, in an age of pamphlets, were I to record all my observations in this great capital of human business and pleasure. There was an unlimited range of society – the powerful, the wise, the witty, and the famous in every walk of life – princes, presidents, poets, generals, artists, actors, and philanthropists, all making their own market at the Fair, and deeming no price too exorbitant for such commodities as hit their fancy. It was well worth one's while, even if he had no idea of buying or selling, to loiter through the bazaars, and observe the various sorts of traffic that were going forward. (819)

In claiming for himself the objectivity of observation, the narrator positions himself in a protected space that seemingly eludes the traffic of the marketplace. More interesting perhaps is the narrator's representation of himself as a writer, though, of course, one who exists outside the circuit of exchange. In fact, it turns out that everyone at Vanity Fair is a type of writer whose "fancy" determines the price of the Fair's commodities. In her discussion of the "participant observer," Carolyn Porter notes that once one realizes "that observation of the world constitutes a form of participation in its activity, you experience a curious modern version of the Fall, for you become at least theoretically implicated and complicit in events which you presume merely to watch, analyze, and interpret."[24] "The Celestial Rail-road" also railroads the notion that one can transcend one's own complicity in acts of exchange. This is, I take it, the more serious point of the following comic passage, in which the narrator passes the Giant Transcendentalist: "As to his form, his features, his substance, and his nature generally, it is the chief peculiarity of this huge miscreant, that neither he for himself, nor anybody for him, has ever been able to describe them" (817). Porter's observation nicely describes as well our narrator, whose very identity, like the transcendentalist's is constituted by the same traffic that he imagines himself merely to be observing.

The heaviest traffic actually occurs in the imagination itself. The narrator makes this point in his description of "the purchasers" in Vanity Fair, who "made very foolish bargains": "A very pretty girl bartered a heart as clear as crystal, and which seemed her most valuable possession, for another jewel of the same kind, but so worn and defaced as to be utterly worthless" (819). Without imagination, the girl would not trade one jewel for another, nor would others purchase "with almost any sacrifice" the "gilded chains [that] were in great demand" (819). Even more to the point, let us remember that "The Celestial Rail-road" begins with the narrator's "passing through the gate of dreams" (808) and ends with his "thank[ing] Heaven, it was a Dream" (824). Because the narrator's "fancy" becomes the premier site of exchange, his dream plays out the market economy that is his subjectivity. If the narrator's imagination generates images of the market, it is because his subjectivity is not a reflection of the market but an enactment of the market itself.[25]

Constituted by the principles of the market – exchange, accumulation, and transcendence – the narrator imagines himself outside its purview. Although he refuses to exchange any of his wares in Vanity Fair, the narrator's journey to the Celestial City depends upon a series of exchanges, the most significant, of course, being the textual transactions between his version of *The Pilgrim's Progress* and Bunyan's. The tale begins with an exchange of money as our narrator hires a coach, after "paying [his] bill at the hotel" (808), to take him to the Station House. He is accompanied by Mr. Smooth-it-away, "a director of the rail-road corporation and one of its largest stockholders" (808), and their conversation revolves around the benefits of exchange. Even before the narrator sets foot in Vanity Fair and claims for himself the status of nonparticipant observer, his discourse reveals him to have already participated quite fully in an economy based on exchange.

Along with exchange, incorporation stands as one of the defining features within the economy of the market and the narrator's subjectivity. The market's ability to incorporate all activities under the sign of exchange finds its able representative in the figure of the narrator. Incorporation in "The Celestial Rail-road" functions most effectively through accommodation:

> It may be remembered that there was an ancient feud between Prince Beelzebub and the keeper of the Wicket-Gate, and that the adherents of the former distinguished personage were accustomed to shoot deadly arrows at honest pilgrims, while knocking at the door. This dispute, much to the credit as well of the illustrious potentate above-mentioned as of the worthy and enlightened Directors of the rail-road, has been pacifically arranged, on the principle of mutual compromise. The prince's subjects are now pretty numerously employed about the Station House . . . and I can conscientiously affirm, that persons more attentive to their business, more willing to accommodate, or more generally agreeable to the passengers, are not to be found on any railroad. Every good heart must surely exult at so satisfactory an arrangement of an immemorial difficulty. (810)

Given the number of good people who are involved in this conflict, from the "honest pilgrims" to Prince Beelzebub, ironically called "the illustrious potentate," one can scarcely reconstruct the reasons why such "an immemorial difficulty" could not have been solved upon "the principle of mutual compromise" and "accommodat[ion]" years earlier.[26] The principle of incorporation requires that all participants in the "dispute" be "distinguished," "worthy," and "agreeable," including the "benevolent reader [who] will be delighted" to learn about its happy outcome, and that everything be "satisfactory" and "pacifically arranged." Because "all musty prejudices are in a fair way to be obliterated" (811), conflict and difference disappear. The discourse of compromise, improvement, and incorporation successfully turns everyone into a version of everyone else.

Like the market of Vanity Fair, which turns difference into equivalence, the narrator's language generates identities, by which I mean both versions of the same subject and individualized or differentiated subjects. The word identity itself resonates with the kind of doubleness at work in the narrator's subjectivity; that is to say, the construction of "identities" participates in the logic of sameness and difference. The individual subjects at Vanity Fair are, of course, the characters of the narrator's dream. Interestingly, the narrator creates subjects whose identities conform quite closely to their names, for example, "the Rev. Mr. Shallow-deep; the Rev. Mr. Stumble-at-truth; that fine old clerical character, the Rev. Mr. This-to-day, who expects shortly to resign his pulpit to the Rev. Mr. That-to-morrow" (818). Characters with names like this inhabit a severely circumscribed space in which they can only act according to the dictates of their names. If such characters hearken back to a Bunyanesque mode of allegory, they also look forward to, in their utterly repetitive and specialized behavior, the starkest instantiation of an industrialized market economy. While producing these kinds of subjects in his imaginative world, the narrator transcends individual subjectivity by remaining nameless. The specialization of others, or their iterative sameness, serves as the condition of the narrator's individual subjectivity or difference. This difference could not exist, of course, without the very economy the narrator imagines himself to be eluding or, more precisely, transcending. Although he produces allegorical characters typical of seventeenth-century texts, he himself constitutes a new kind of allegorical character based on the unreliability, exchangeability, and disjunction of the nineteenth-century market. Although the names in "The Celestial Rail-road" and *The Pilgrim's Progress* might seem similar, their functions are diametrically opposed. Whereas Bunyan's names are supported by a religious structure that guarantees their reliability, Hawthorne's names are constituted by an economy of unreliability. The narrator's namelessness in "The Celestial Rail-road" means that his identity remains liquid and speculative. The narrator's participation in the market is inseparable from his identity as the market.[27]

In not having a name, the narrator seems to have transcended these competing versions of identity, although, as I have suggested, he fully embodies the transcendent identity of the market. As a paragon of compromise, he is gratified "to learn that there is no longer the want of harmony between the townspeople [of Vanity Fair] and [the] pilgrims" (817), and when he discovers that Christian's old enemy, Apollyon, is the chief engineer of the railroad, he remarks "with irrepressible enthusiasm" upon "the liberality of the age" (811). Like the unnamed narrator in "Bartleby," Hawthorne's narrator speaks the language of gentlemanly benevolence and middle-class liberalism. When he first arrives at the Station House, for example, he approvingly notes that "religion, though indubitably the main thing at heart, was thrown tastefully into the background" (810). As his pilgrimage proceeds, he is surprised by the radiance in the Valley of the Shadow of Death and with Delano-like blindness remarks upon the fearful "changes which it wrought in the visages of my companions," only to dismiss his fears by remarking, "If the reader have ever travelled through the Dark Valley, he will have learned to be thank-ful for any light that he could get" (814).[28] The narrator finds himself in the position of a reader who is interpreting his own experience on the Celestial Rail-road according to *The Pilgrim's Progress*. If he manages to make these texts fit one another, it is through a combination of interpreta-tive gerrymandering and liberal benevolence.[29]

The kinship and the differences between Bunyan's allegory and Haw-thorne's economics of allegory are installed through acts of naming, misnaming, and not naming. I have put a great deal of pressure on this issue of naming both because "The Celestial Rail road" itself demands that we consider what is the narrator's "right appellation" and because naming most clearly exemplifies the exchange that underlies the entire short story, that is the exchange between Hawthorne's and Bunyan's texts. Hawthorne's text cannot transcend the act of exchange, because the text itself is predicated upon exchange – the trace and embodiment of that exchange exists in the figure of the unnamed narrator. As much as Hawthorne himself wishes to align himself with a Bunyanesque kind of allegory, what generates "The Celestial Rail-road," what makes it differ-ent from just another revision of *The Pilgrim's Progress*, is the fact that it, like the railroad itself in the nineteenth century, is fueled by a market economy.

"The Celestial Rail-road" is thus not merely an inversion or perversion of *Pilgrim's Progress*. Simply reversing Hawthorne's terms, in other words, would not give us Bunyan's story. The narrator, in particular, is a figure in Hawthorne's story whose opposite we would be hard put to name.[30] The complexity of this textual relation is suggested early on in the story: "The reader of John Bunyan will be glad to know, that Chris-tian's old friend Evangelist, who was accustomed to supply each pilgrim with a mystic roll, now presides at the ticket-office. Some malicious persons, it is true, deny the identity of this reputable character with the Evangelist of old times, and even pretend to bring competent evidence of an imposture" (809). "The Celestial Rail-road" locates us in a world where identities and impostures cannot be distinguished – and the narra-tor, whose own identity remains unclear, cannot distinguish between them either. His observations about the dilemma above do nothing to help us out: "Without involving myself in the dispute, I shall merely observe, that, so far as my experience goes, the square pieces of paste-board, now delivered to passengers, are much more convenient and use-ful along the road, than the antique roll of parchment. Whether they will be as readily received at the gate of the Celestial City, I decline giving an opinion" (809). The narrator presents himself as a nonparticipant ob-server and, like a good Yankee, invokes the criterion of convenience and usefulness in order to avoid the question of the Evangelist's identity. It is clear that if the hermeneutic stability of Bunyan's text is unavailable to Hawthorne's American pilgrim, Bunyan's "road-book" will not provide a reliable context for Hawthorne's. After all, the narrator's pilgrimage stops at the market of Vanity Fair, never making it to the Celestial City. But the disjunction between these two texts is perhaps nowhere more keenly felt than when the narrator wishes "to visit that old mansion" (812) known as the Interpreter's House and never gets there. The seventeenth-century allegory does not, indeed cannot, explain the historical complexities of nineteenth-century allegory.

III. UNSEPARATING THE SPHERES: DOMESTICITY AND THE LABORATORY

In its reconfiguration of Bunyanesque allegory, "The Celestial Rail-road" invokes an economics of allegory whose defining feature appears to be its rootedness in America's developing market economy. And yet I have been claiming that this economics of allegory can be further characterized by its relation to the body. Bodies in "The Celestial Rail-road," except for the technologized body of the locomotive, remain curiously immaterial; indeed, the "one strange thing that trouble[s]" the narrator is the fact that "amid the occupations or amusements of the Fair, nothing was more common than for a person . . . suddenly to vanish like a soapbubble, and be never more seen of his fellows" (821). It is as if the embodiment of technology effects a disembodiment of persons. We have, of course, seen a version of this anxiety about disembodiment in our analysis of the factory, where the changing relations between workers and their bodies elicited fears about disembodiment and disfiguration. Another version of the lopsidedness of named and unnamed characters in the story thus exists in the imbalance between embodied figures, such as the locomotive, and the actual and potential disembodied persons in Vanity Fair.

The fantasy and fear of disembodiment expressed by the narrator of "The Celestial Rail-road" become the explicit subject matter of "The Birth-mark," where Aylmer's fantasy of disembodiment is Georgiana's fear. Bodies in "The Birth-mark" insist upon their materiality to such an extent that even Hawthorne's body, I shall argue, makes its presence felt.[31] This tale is thus particularly compelling because of the vulnerable status of Hawthorne's own literary labors, which are caught between a literary economy in which the signs of his labor must remain invisible and a market economy which demands that he make visible the fact that he possesses those signs.[32] It is no coincidence that Hawthorne's dilemma revolves around the explicitly allegorical sign of the birthmark, what the narrator calls "this fairy sign-manual" (765), because allegory, as we have seen, insists upon its relation to labor. Like the A. B. C. of John A. B. C. Smith, the birthmark as "sign-manual" signifies the material of writing and announces itself, as all allegories do, according to Maureen Quilligan, as "texts first and last: webs of words woven in such a way as constantly to call attention to themselves as texts."[33] The birthmark is, I shall suggest, a sign of Hawthorne's own literary labors, his mark as maker of "The Birth-mark." The allegorical sign of the birthmark constitutes the site upon which the drama of visible and invisible labor, of non-alienated and alienated labor, of dispossession and possession is staged. At stake in the story, then, is not so much what the birthmark signifies but who gets to claim ownership of it.

We first encounter Aylmer departing from one physical space and entering another; he is leaving his laboratory, quite literally the place of labor, for the charms of a domestic life with Georgiana. In order to accomplish this transition, he has "cleared his fine countenance from the furnace-smoke [and] washed the stain of acids from his fingers" (764). Offering himself as a blank slate to Georgiana, however, does not guarantee that she will respond in kind, and, in fact, he finds upon Georgiana's countenance precisely those stains (in the shape of fingers that go into forming the hand of the birthmark) that he had washed from his own body. He cleanses himself of the marks of his laboratory only to find them re-situated on the body of Georgiana. The boundaries between Aylmer and Georgiana are also compromised by the fact that Aylmer's overzealous devotion to his studies means that "his love for his young wife . . . could only be by intertwining itself with his love of science" (764). From the start, then, Georgiana's and Aylmer's marital future seems a far cry from the separation of spheres in which women had authority over the private home while men dominated the public world that represented the ideal for many white middle-class families of the nineteenth century.[34]

Georgiana's body, and more specifically the birthmark, marks the site where the promises of the laboratory and the home converge. But the laboratory has been none too kind to Aylmer, whose scientific experiments up until this point "were almost invariably failures, if compared with the ideal at which he aimed" (774). The birthmark presents Aylmer with a chance both to right these professional wrongs and, in doing so, to establish Georgiana as the "perfection" of hearth and home "where he would fain have worshipped" (766). In becoming the perfect wife, however, Georgiana must first endure the ordeals that wait for her in the laboratory. The fact that she faints upon being helped over "the threshold of the laboratory" (769) calls attention to the radical nature of her transition from the domestic space to Aylmer's laboratory. Having transgressed the boundaries between the home and laboratory, Georgiana awakens, only to find that this separation has been reproduced once again within the context of the laboratory, only this time Aylmer's magical arts have constructed the domestic space: "Aylmer had converted those smoky, dingy, sombre rooms, where he had spent his brightest years in recondite pursuits, into a series of beautiful apartments, not unfit to be the secluded abode of a lovely woman" (770). Georgiana's new abode represents Aylmer's domestic utopia, a fantasy of invisibility and disembodiment that is manifested (or hidden) in the "rich and ponderous folds" of the curtains that concealed "all angles and straight lines" as well as those "airy figures, absolutely bodiless ideas, and forms of unsubstantial beauty [that] came and danced before her, imprinting their momentary footsteps on beams of light" (770–1). Because Georgiana's seclusion is constituted by the very thing that it pretends to exclude (that is, Aylmer's scientific experiments), it should come as no surprise when the boundaries between her new abode and Aylmer's laboratory fail to remain separate yet again. This next spatial violation occurs when Georgiana, forgetting to inform Aylmer about "a sensation in the fatal birth-mark, not painful, but which induced a restlessness throughout her system," intrudes, "for the first time, into the laboratory" (775).

Georgiana's transgressive entrance into Aylmer's workplace is accompanied by a transference of physical properties between wife and husband as Aylmer "first reddened, then grew paler than ever, on beholding [her]" (776). Georgiana's initial view of Aylmer's laboratory has the same effect on Aylmer's physical system that his "gaze" had on hers, which was to "change the roses of her cheek into a deathlike paleness" (766–7). The geographical restlessness that makes Georgiana unable to remain in her own space reproduces itself in the relation between the bodies of Georgiana and Aylmer. In trying to erase Georgiana's birthmark, Aylmer merely manages to locate its qualities elsewhere, often as not upon his own body. Another example of this corporeal exchange occurs in this same scene when Aylmer violently reacts to what seems to him Georgiana's Pandora-like curiosity about his workspace. When he first discovers her presence, "he rushed towards her, and seized her arm with a gripe that left the print of his fingers upon it" (776). This passage suggests that as Aylmer's desire to erase Georgiana's fingerlike birthmark becomes more and more compulsive, he cannot help inscribing even more fingers upon Georgiana's body and his own, such as when he tells Georgiana that her "Crimson Hand" had "taken a pretty firm hold of [his] fancy" (767). The inescapability of fingers and hands is also made manifest in a dialogue between him and Georgiana where Aylmer solemnly discusses the concoctions in his laboratory, one of which is the Elixir of Life, which "could apportion the lifetime of any mortal at whom you might point your finger," and another is a "powerful cosmetic" which, according to Aylmer, can wash away freckles "as easily as the hands are cleansed"

(773). We have seen, though, from the opening passages of the story, when Aylmer washes the "stain of acids from his fingers" (764), that seemingly erased stains end up manifesting themselves on the body of another. By fetishizing the birthmark, Aylmer turns it into a commodity of sorts. The birthmark is no longer an expression of Georgiana's identity but a thing, to use the language of Marx, "without power of resistance" against which Aylmer can "use force" or which he can "take possession of."[35] Marx's account of the circulation of commodities, and money in particular, proves especially relevant to "The Birth-mark": "When one commodity replaces another, the money-commodity always sticks to the hands of some third person. Circulation sweats money from every pore" (113). The hand of the birthmark bears the sign of the commodity which in circulating through the story leaves that sign upon all that it touches.

Aylmer observes the thematic of circulation in Georgiana's birthmark. This thematic, we might recall, governs the discourse of identity formation in antebellum America. In an 1838 address entitled "Self-Culture," William Ellery Channing observed: "We are able to discern not only what we already are, but what we may become, to see in ourselves germs and promises of a growth to which no bounds can be set, to dart beyond what we have actually gained to the idea of perfection as the end of our being."[36] The boundlessness and never-ending task of self-improvement is recapitulated by Henry Ward Beecher, who claims that "every product of the earth has a susceptibility of improvement."[37] These descriptions suggest that the self is constituted within a perpetual state of circulation, leading, of course, toward the end of self-improvement. In the name of improved selves, Aylmer and Georgiana enact their own version of this circulatory system, only to reveal that one person's immobility becomes the condition for another person's unlimited circulation and capacity for self-improvement. Selves here function according to a model of territoriality in which the construction, transgression, and possession of physical space becomes the way in which characters as well as persons constitute themselves as individual selves. Aylmer's attempts to control the spatial movements in the laboratory, and Georgiana in particular, thus exemplify a self that exists by functioning simultaneously as an object that must defend itself from being possessed by others and as a subject that can only possess itself both in its attempts to possess others and by a continual repossession of itself.[38] This territorial logic informs the spatial movements of "The Birth-mark," where worlds, and in particular Aylmer's, are upset by his entrance into the domestic and Georgiana's (transgressive) intervention in the laboratory. The problematic effect of these incursions is not confined to the spatial realm alone, as I have suggested, but has significant corporeal ramifications as well. It would seem that Aylmer seeks to bring this circulatory system to a conclusion by ridding Georgiana (and himself) of the mark of this economy – the birthmark. The birthmark, after all, instantiates this circulatory economy in all of its changeability, its lack of intentionality, and its horrifying visibility. Aylmer's actions make increasingly clear, however, that it is not the circulatory system as a whole that he wishes to end but rather Georgiana's powerful and problematic participation in it.

There is, though, one character whose lack of participation in this circulatory scenario requires some explanation – Aminadab, the "underworker" (770) in Aylmer's laboratory. Aminadab makes his first appearance in the story when Georgiana enters the magically domesticated space of the laboratory and loses consciousness. Requiring Aminadab's help, Aylmer calls out, and his assistant immediately issues from "an inner apartment" (769). Aminadab's circulations are limited – in fact this is the only time that he leaves the laboratory proper – and controlled by Aylmer. We soon learn that Aylmer relies upon Aminadab's "great mechanical readiness" and his ability to execute properly the "practical details" of an experiment, while at the same time Aminadab, in the final paragraph of the story, is likened to "the gross Fatality of Earth" (780). Aminadab's characterological flexibility is most evident when Aylmer refers to Aminadab as both "thou human machine" and "thou man of clay" (776). The fact that Aminadab can resemble a human machine just as easily as a clod of earth seems less significant than the fact that he is barely a character at all.[39]

The fact that he does not develop, that he is mechanical, that he has done the same thing "during [Aylmer's] whole scientific career" (770) might at first suggest that he is a simple allegorical character whose significance in the text requires little explanation, especially since, as the narrator puts it, "he seemed to represent man's physical nature" (770). But Aminadab is one of those flat, undeveloped, mechanical characters, like John A. B. C. Smith, whose very flatness is allegorical. Through the character of Aminadab, Hawthorne undermines the traditional allegorical framework in which names refer to and explain identities and replaces it with an economics of allegory in which the hermeneutic complexities surrounding Aminadab's name refer to Hawthorne's presence as literary laborer.

The name Aminadab, it turns out, comes from the Bible, appearing most often in genealogical passages such as the following that carry with them little narrative substance: "And these are the names of the men that shall stand with you. Of Reuben: Elizur the son of Shedeur. Of Simeon: Shelumiel the son of Zurishaddai. Of Judah: Nahshon the son of Amminadab" (Numbers 1:5–7).[40] His name, that is, is just one cipher among many that permit the biblical verse to move along. The biblical reference does little to confirm a reading of Aminadab as "man's physical nature," nor does it tell us much of anything else about the character. As was the case with Mr. Smooth-it-away, the traditional way of understanding allegorical characters by appealing to names as stable referents would seem to be obstructed. The name Aminadab asks the reader to view the character allegorically, but the traditional model of allegory does not deliver. Aminadab's unidentifiable identity, however, could easily be rectified by reading his name backwards: bad anima, or bad soul. One might suggest that Aminadab is the visible manifestation of Aylmer's "bad soul." But even this signification, I would maintain, fails to explain Aminadab's character. Although the narrator records Aminadab's "hoarse, chuckling laugh" at the conclusion of the tale and woefully imagines his "invariable triumph over the immortal essence" (780), his allegorical role as bad soul is never convincingly demonstrated, especially given the fact that Aminadab, not Aylmer, is the one who appreciates Georgiana's beauty and voices the danger in Aylmer's attempt at erasing the birthmark. Thus Aminadab's name seems to be allegorical in the sense of referring to some larger, vertical framework, to invoke Jameson, but it turns out to be allegorical in the sense of alluding to the immediate, horizontal framework of Hawthorne's literary labor.[41] The name Aminadab (or bad anima) does not explain the character but cleverly signals Hawthorne's presence as a maker of his character's names. Hawthorne is playing with the reader and tempting her with meaningful wordplay that ultimately clarifies nothing except to foreground his reconfiguration of allegory.

Also making the point about Aminadab's lack of identity is Georgiana's reaction to him, or rather her lack of one. When she enters Aylmer's inner sanctum, where he has been concocting the liquid that will cure her of her birthmark, "the first thing that struck her eye was the furnace, that hot and feverish worker" (775). Indeed, as her gaze turns to Aylmer, she never does recognize Aminadab, the worker, who "was grimed with the vapors of the furnace" (769). Georgiana fails to see Aminadab not only because he is neither human nor machine but because he is invisible. His invisibility, nevertheless, keeps Aylmer's scientific experiments running smoothly (even if they all result in failure). The relation Aylmer has cultivated with Aminadab is a model for the relation Aylmer would like to have with his wife. Aminadab represents an ideal of immobility, stability, and submissiveness. Georgiana's future invisibility will ensure the successful operation of the domestic space that Aylmer has achieved via Aminadab in the workplace. When Aylmer seeks to construct his gender relations along the same lines as those of class, Georgiana proves far more difficult to manage than Aminadab. It is not exactly Georgiana, though, who is resistant to Aylmer's scientific manipulations but rather her birthmark.

The comings and goings of Georgiana's birthmark epitomize the spatial and physical circulations of the story and locate them upon (and within) her female body. The birthmark not only becomes the occasion for the breakdown between the domestic realm and the laboratory but also collapses the private and public domains; that is, the birthmark makes it impossible for Georgiana's private emotions ever to be anything but signs for public (read Aylmer's) consumption. Georgiana is one incessant circulatory system. This fact is made evident by her constant blushing, paling, and crying. The narrator's first description of the birthmark calls attention to this inextricable relation between Georgiana's psychic and physical instability:

> In the usual state of her complexion, – a healthy, though delicate bloom, – the mark wore a tint of deeper crimson, which imperfectly defined its shape amid the surrounding rosiness. When she blushed, it gradually became more indistinct, and finally vanished amid the triumphant rush of blood, that bathed the whole cheek with its brilliant glow. But, if any shifting emotion caused her to turn pale, there was the mark again, a crimson stain upon the snow, in what Aylmer sometimes deemed an almost fearful distinctness. (765)

The birthmark foregrounds the physical and emotional fluctuations that should remain invisible, in particular the nomadic wanderings of her blood supply.[42] And yet it is those very circulations, especially Georgiana's blushing, that make the birthmark invisible. If circulation is the problem (the birthmark marks the circulation of blood in Georgiana's body), it is also the solution. The problem, after all, exists and intensifies when Georgiana's blood is not circulating properly; to take her out of circulation, which is what Aylmer proposes to do by removing the birthmark, will only make things worse – as the conclusion of the story tragically evinces. It seems clear that Aylmer's difficulty with Georgiana's birthmark has less to do with the fact of its presence than with its oscillating presence and absence, which denote the emotional and physical fluctuations that Aylmer would rather not see or, to put it more precisely, that he would prefer to control. Thus, in wishing to erase the sign(s) of Georgiana's circulatory economy, Aylmer does not necessarily want to do away with it – only her participation in it. Aylmer himself makes this point when he confesses to Georgiana, "I have already administered agents powerful enough to do aught except to change your entire physical system" (777). But what he doesn't realize is that the sign and the economy, the birthmark and the circulatory system to which it refers, go hand in hand.

The birthmark seems to act as a transparent conduit between Georgiana's psychic and physical states, and as such it installs a signifying system where private and public, signs and referents, bodies and minds are unmediated. Aylmer, in stark contrast, adheres to an alternative system of signification based on disjunction or representation. This is the point of those lengthy passages detailing Aylmer's many attempts to pacify Georgiana, all of which exemplify the principle of hermeneutic disjunction. In preparing his "smoky, dingy, sombre rooms" for Georgiana's occupancy, for instance, Aylmer creates an atmosphere of "enchantment" and "magic" (770) through a series of optical illusions that make "a picture, an image, or a shadow, so much more attractive than the original" (771). Entertaining her with dioramas, daguerreotypes, and Rappaccini-like floral experiments, all of which are, like his experiments, "mortifying failures" (772), Aylmer celebrates the principles of representational disjunction, and it is this principle that he wishes to inscribe upon Georgiana's body.

But it is already there. Having suggested that Georgiana and Aylmer present us with two versions of signification, the first an unmediated form of circulation and the other a highly mediated one, I now want to argue that this opposition does not in fact adequately account for Aylmer's anxiety about the birthmark, and furthermore that these representational systems locate themselves within a specific economic framework that permits us to understand what is at stake, economically speaking, in Aylmer's desire to remove the birthmark. If we return to the quotation in which the colorations of Georgiana's birthmark are adumbrated, it becomes clear that although the birthmark accurately measures the alterations in her emotions, it does not guarantee whether those emotions will make her turn pale or will cause her to blush. In a related passage, the narrator suggests that Aylmer's revulsion toward the birthmark originates as much in its problematic instability, "now vaguely portrayed, now lost, now stealing forth again, and glimmering to-and-fro with every pulse of emotion that throbbed within her heart," (766) as in the physical presence of "the visible mark of earthly imperfection" (765). Aylmer's hermeneutic response to the birthmark reproduces the instability that, for him, characterizes the very problem posed by the birthmark. In this same passage, for example, he comes up with three different, albeit related, readings of the birthmark. Aylmer first identifies the birthmark as "the fatal flaw of humanity," a description that suffices for a short while until the birthmark more correctly expresses "the ineludible gripe in which mortality clutches the highest and purest of earthly mould," only to become "the symbol of his wife's liability to sin, sorrow, decay, and death" (766). Like the allegorical status of Aminadab, the allegorical birthmark guarantees the presence of meaning for Aylmer, but precisely what that meaning is remains in flux.[43]

Thus, as unmediated as the relation between Georgiana's psychic and physical states may seem at first glance, the changes in the birthmark end up resulting in precisely that kind of hermeneutic disjunction that had seemed most obviously represented by Aylmer's optical illusions. The question of mediation brings us, I think, to the issue of the birthmark's shape. Why a hand? We can begin to answer this question by looking at the passage in which Georgiana reads the records of Aylmer's scientific experiments.

> But, to Georgiana, the most engrossing volume was a large folio from her husband's own *hand*. . . . He *handled* physical details, as if there were nothing beyond them. . . . In his *grasp*, the veriest clod of earth assumed a soul. . . . His brightest diamonds were the merest pebbles, and felt to be so by himself, in comparison with the inestimable gems which lay hidden beyond his *reach*. The volume, rich with achievements that had won renown for its author, was yet as melancholy a record as ever mortal *hand* had *penned*. (774–5; italics mine)

I have edited this lengthy passage in order to highlight the ubiquitous allusions to hands. Furthermore, in this description of Aylmer the scientist, we get our first glimpse of Aylmer the author. In having not only her own two hands but a "mimic hand" (766) as well, Georgiana wears a visible sign that someone, surely not herself, most emphatically not Aylmer, and most likely nature, "our great creative Mother" (769), has authored her first. Thus the "mimic hand" painfully calls attention to the failures of Aylmer's "mortal hand" (775). Mediating all of these hands is, of course, the hand of Hawthorne, which has, I think, often been mistaken for Aylmer's hand.[44] But the case is more complicated than that. Aylmer's desire to erase the "mimic hand" on Georgiana's cheek, which is the product of both "creative Mother" *and* creative father (or Hawthorne, the one engaged in an act of mimesis), seems to be a direct assault on Hawthorne's mediating role as author. Hawthorne imagined just such a scene in an 1835 journal entry: "A person to be writing a tale, and to find that it shapes itself against his intentions; that the characters act otherwise than he thought; that unforeseen events occur; and a catastrophe comes which he strives in vain to avert. It might shadow forth his own fate, – he having made himself one of the personages."[45] This is precisely the situation in which Hawthorne finds himself. The attempt to make invisible Georgiana's hand, in other words, is an attempt to wipe out not only the signs of Georgiana's circulations but the signs of Hawthorne's own labor in the writing of the text. His identity as author is deeply implicated in the visibility of the birthmark. The territorial battle being waged via the birthmark between Aylmer and Georgiana is also being fought between Aylmer and Hawthorne. Aylmer will not do to Hawthorne what he did to Aminadab and Georgiana. For Hawthorne too the birthmark becomes an object to be possessed, and his only chance for possession of it as such exists within the framework of a competitive market economy from which he might rather be exempt. Paradoxically, he can only save the signs of his labor by participating in an economic structure whose primary feature seems to be a desire to erase those signs. At stake here, then, is nothing less than Hawthorne's own agency – an agency that can only be maintained if he subjects himself to an economy that is continually trying to take away his agency. The allegorical birthmark, in other words, is the site upon which the battle for possessing and dispossessing agency, Hawthorne's, Aylmer's, and Georgiana's, is being waged.[46]

"The Birth-mark" is not the only Hawthorne text where this drama of authorial agency is played out. The relations between authorial and characterological agency, between literary and economic labor, are also staged in *The Scarlet Letter*, where Hawthorne yet again finds himself in the productive dilemma of having created fictional characters whose raison d'être seems to be either the concealment or disclosure or both of a mark, a mark with which Hawthorne deeply identifies. For example, before it is disclosed that a scarlet letter covers the bodice of Hester's gown, a young Puritan woman among the crowd of spectators who are there to witness Hester's journey from the prison to the scaffold in the marketplace notes, "Let her cover the mark as she will, the pang of it will be always in her heart" (79). If ever there were a mark that insisted upon its visibility, surely it would be Hester's scarlet letter, "so artistically done, and with so much fertility and gorgeous luxuriance of fancy, that it had all the effect of a last and fitting decoration to the apparel which she wore" (80). And if ever there were a mark that insisted upon its invisibility, indeed its indeterminacy, it would be the companion piece to Hester's letter, or Dimmesdale's scarlet letter. What exactly does Chillingworth see when he "laid his hand upon his bosom, and thrust aside the vestment, that, hitherto, had always covered it even from the professional eye" (159)? Why, for example, after boldly entitling a chapter "The Revelation of the Scarlet Letter" does the narrator reservedly go on to say that "most of the spectators testified to having seen, on the breast of the unhappy minister, a SCARLET LETTER – the very semblance of that worn by Hester Prynne – imprinted in the flesh" (270), only to equivocate even more in the following paragraph by mentioning "that certain persons, who were spectators of the whole scene, and professed never once to have removed their eyes from the Reverend Mr. Dimmesdale, denied that there was any mark whatever on his breast" (271)? Whereas the poles of visibility and invisibility as figured by Hester and Dimmesdale have been understood in the contexts of Puritanism, psychology, or gender, it is also possible to read this dynamic according to the antebellum aesthetic that insists upon the invisibility of authorial labor.[47] In *The Scarlet Letter*, Hawthorne once again concerns himself with the visibility and invisibility of a mark, and as was the case in "The Birthmark," the presence and erasure of that mark are intimately linked to Hawthorne's own authorial position vis-à-vis an aesthetic ideology that demanded the erasure of his marks. Like the earlier short story, *The Scarlet Letter* dramatizes Hawthorne's conflicted relation to this aesthetic by illustrating most compellingly through the figure of Dimmesdale the consequences of invisibility upon the mind and body of the author.

The fact that both Hester and Dimmesdale are artist/author figures has been observed by critics, such as Michael Gilmore, who argue that "the difference in status and behavior of Hawthorne's principal characters dramatizes the conflict in his mind between two radically opposed conceptions of the artist's role and relation to the public."[48] To prove the point, we need only remind ourselves of the chapter "Hester at her Needle," in which Hester's artistry is amply demonstrated in "the finer productions of her handiwork" (106), or "The Minister in a Maze," in which Dimmesdale writes his Election Sermon "with such an impulsive flow of thought and emotion, that he fancied himself inspired" (240). But it is crucial to observe that they are two very different kinds of laborers. Dimmesdale, upon finishing his sermon, finds himself "with the pen still between his fingers, and a vast, immeasurable tract of written space behind him" (240), as if he were the medium rather than the agent of the message; or, to use the image of the text, he "only wondered that Heaven should see fit to transmit the grand and solemn music of its oracles through so foul an organ-pipe as he" (240). Dimmesdale's act of composition reads not unlike Stowe's *Uncle Tom's Cabin* creation myth as the scene of literary labor shares in the logic of invisible authorial labor and the language of sentimentality: "Thus the night fled away, as if it were a winged steed, and he careering on it; morning came, and peeped blushing through the curtains; and at last sunrise threw a golden beam into the study, and laid it right across the minister's bedazzled eyes" (240). Whereas Dimmesdale's compositional labors are done "with earnest haste and ecstasy" (240), Hester's "handiwork" is accomplished "by the faithful labor of her hands" (179), whether it be the "deep ruffs" or the "painfully wrought bands" (106) that she makes for the Puritan magistrates. Furthermore, the laboriousness of Hester's entire existence is continually foregrounded, whether she be "plying her needle at the cottage-window . . . or laboring in her little garden" (106) or bringing up the intractable Pearl.

The visibility of Hester's reproductive labors, in the form of Pearl, signifies her departure from certain moral obligations as defined by her Puritan community. The visibility of her productive labors, in the form of "the letter A"(80), signifies her commitment to an aesthetic ideology that foregrounds individual agency and thereby transgresses the artist's obligations as constructed by the discourse of literary labor. Dimmesdale, on the other hand, is deeply committed to the ideology of invisibility, so much so that "he was often observed, on any slight alarm or other sudden accident, to put his hand over his heart, with first a flush and then a paleness, indicative of pain" (142). The "white-cheeked minister" (157) has inherited Georgiana's birthmark, a mark signifying the visibility of authorial labor, and as such a mark that must be blanched. But he has also inherited Aylmer's desire to erase it.[49] "With his hand upon his heart" (95), Dimmesdale attempts to erase the scarlet letter that now marks his flesh at the same time as the repetitive gesture calls attention to its possible presence. In stark contrast to Hester, who "could scarcely refrain, yet always did refrain, from covering the symbol with her hand" (110), Dimmesdale's "hand – with that gesture so habitual as to have become involuntary – stole over his heart" (225). Dimmesdale's habitual gesture is the corporeal manifestation of the discourse of literary labor that, in the words of Bushnell, demanded that "the writer himself is hidden and can not even suggest his existence."[50] By habitually covering up his own version of the scarlet letter, indeterminate as it might be, Dimmesdale's gesture attempts to conceal his own productive and reproductive acts.

Dimmesdale has written (upon his body) a scarlet letter which turns out to be an allegory of the dilemma of allegory in antebellum America. This dilemma, I have been suggesting, was constituted out of a cultural anxiety about labor, including literary labor, which led to the valorization of the symbol and the mythology of (the author's) invisible hand. The invisible hand of the market had its companion in the invisible hand of authorship which was being promulgated by the literary marketplace. What Dimmesdale both hides and foregrounds through his compulsive gesture is his own allegory of (re)productive labor: the past making of the scarlet letter through his body in the figure of Pearl and the present making of the scarlet letter upon his body.

Hawthorne, of course, articulates his own relation to this dilemma throughout *The Scarlet Letter* and most pointedly in "The Custom-House," where, as with Dimmesdale, the fact of literary paternity competes with the fiction of its invisibility. His elaborate ruse of having discovered a manuscript whose "main facts . . . are authorized and authenticated by the document of Mr. Surveyor Pue" (63), as opposed to having created the manuscript himself, suggests the lengths to which Hawthorne would go to conceal his own agency in the act of literary labor. Even Hawthorne's most (in)famous creation, his theory of the romance, is marked, as Michael Bell has brilliantly explained, by authorial absence: "This well-known passage ["the floor of our familiar room has become a neutral territory, somewhere between the real world and fairy-land, where the Actual and the Imaginary may meet, and each imbue itself with the nature of the other"] doesn't quite make sense – at least as an account of the special art of the romancer. The imaginative quality of this scene comes from the scene itself, from the real combination of familiar objects and ethereal moonlight, and not from Hawthorne's own creative imagination."[51] "The Custom-House" continually minimizes Hawthorne's labor, whether it be through the invention of Surveyor Pue or Hawthorne's diminished labors in his moonlit room, even as that labor is its very subject matter. At the very moment that he seeks "some true relation with his audience" by accounting for the origins of his text through an allegory of his own literary labors, Hawthorne feels compelled to create a myth of his own invisibility. Because allegory must labor to make itself invisible, according to the aesthetic taste of the period, Hawthorne's invisibility at the end of "The Custom-House" only makes sense. Indeed, this self-erasure reaches its logical and comic proportions as Hawthorne aligns himself with the Headless Horseman of Washington Irving and then refers to his work as "the Posthumous Papers of a Decapitated Surveyor," once again suggesting the deleterious effects that this ideology of invisibility might have upon authors.[52] Thus Hawthorne's gestures of concealment, of erasing his own part in the production of *The Scarlet Letter*, function in the same way as Dimmesdale's gesture of putting his hand over his heart: both ultimately call attention to the problematic consequences of authorial invisibility. "The Custom-House," in other words, permits Hawthorne to offer an allegory of his literary labor that would be acceptable to the nineteenth-century literary marketplace at the same time as it allows him to critique that allegory (by revealing its corporeal consequences) on the basis of its concealment of labor and violation of authorial agency.

Given his "inveterate love of allegory," which was anathema to the literary market, Hawthorne could never completely extricate himself from the competing claims of what Mattheissen called his "bias to allegory" and his desire for acclaim.[53] Like the allegorical body of John A. B. C. Smith, the illicit allegories of both Hawthorne and Dimmesdale are concealed beneath seemingly calm exteriors and are prohibited from revealing themselves in public. Dimmesdale's prominence as a public figure, as well as Hawthorne's considerable success upon the publication of *The Scarlet Letter*, is a function of just how completely both character and author managed to conceal their critique of allegory as construed by the literary marketplace. Thus, most readers, except "the good people of Salem, or a portion of them," to quote an 1850 book notice from the *Portland Transcript*, focused less on Hawthorne's somewhat scathing allegory of literary labor as developed in "The Custom-House" and more on what the *Philadelphia Cummings' Evening Telegraphic Bulletin* identified as its "exquisite pen-portraits with passages of rich humor, quiet wit, and genial sentiment, that will warm the heart of every reader."[54]

But the results of this concealment are potentially grave and violent as Dimmesdale's body becomes the site upon which the antebellum aesthetic of invisibility plays itself out. Try as one might to conceal the signs of labor, they will inevitably make themselves visible. In fact, the narrator himself experiences a kind of "imprint[ing] in the flesh" of the scarlet letter: "We have thrown all the light we could acquire upon the portent, and would gladly, now that it has done its office, erase its deep print out of our own brain; where long meditation has fixed it in very undesirable distinctness" (270). The "deep print[ing]" of the scarlet letter ensures its distinctness, desirable or otherwise. Like the birthmark, that sign of literary labor which circulates among Aylmer, Georgiana, and Hawthorne and continues to circulate even after the death of Georgiana, the scarlet letter A, the beginning of language and the medium of Hawthorne's literary labors, will never be fully erased.

IV. THE INVISIBLE HAND MADE VISIBLE: THE BIRTHMARK

"The Custom-House" places us firmly in the world of antebellum America, even as "The Market-Place," Chapter 2 of *The Scarlet Letter*, situates us "not less than two centuries ago" (77). The culture of the nineteenth century unmistakably takes precedence over that of the seventeenth. "The Birth-mark," to the contrary, directs us quite clearly back to "the latter part of the last century" (764). It is thus not beside the point to consider the ways in which economic analyses of the eighteenth century, particularly those relating to the issue of circulation, might pertain to the economic circulations in "The Birth-mark." Another reading of the birthmark that adds to the debate about the "Crimson Hand" (766), the "spectral Hand" (766), the "odious Hand" (767), and the "Bloody Hand" (765) yet one more hand could be construed as this critic's obsessive reproduction of Aylmer's fetishism. To this end, a glance at the invisible hand of Adam Smith, which makes its appearance in perhaps this most famous passage from *The Wealth of Nations*, permits us to view Aylmer's actions from a different and enlightening perspective: "By preferring the support of domestic to that of foreign industry, he intends only his own security; and by directing that industry in such a manner as its produce may be of the greatest value, he intends only his own gain, and he is in this, as in many other cases, led by an invisible hand to promote an end which was no part of his intention."[55] According to Smith, consequences often have little to do with one's intentions, because one's self-interested intention "frequently promotes [the interest] of the society more effectually than when [one] really intends to promote it" (28). This is clearly not the case in "The Birth-mark," where Aylmer's self-interested intentions bring about self-interested results that do everything to preserve "his own security" and nothing to promote "the public good" (28). Have the goals of 1776, the year which saw the publication of *The Wealth of Nations* and the birth pangs of an American nation, been both forsaken by and made unavailable to America in the 1840s? If so, are we to read "The Birth-mark" as a nineteenth-century corrective to the misguided optimism of political economists like Adam Smith and John Locke, who believed that self-interest and the public good were not mutually exclusive in a society that functioned according to a laissez-faire market economy?[56] Tempting as this reading might be, Hawthorne's story seems less an indictment of a laissez-faire economy than of an economy that isn't laissez-faire enough. The tension at the heart of "The Birth-mark" is this: Aylmer's desired end is the invisible hand of Smith's market economy, but the means he deploys in achieving it fly in the face of Smith's economic directives.

What Hawthorne thought of Smith or whether he even read *The Wealth of Nations* has unfortunately not been documented. Sacvan Bercovitch, however, has recently claimed that the brand of irony at work in Hawthorne's representations of the Puritan past is an "historiographical equivalent of laissez-faire," a "counterpart to Adam Smith's concept of the invisible hand."[57] In following Bercovitch's lead, I want to argue that the free-market ideology at work in Smith's ideal of the invisible hand is, in part, what motivates Aylmer to erase the visible hand that is Georgiana's birthmark. But in living up to Smith's principles, Aylmer uses all the wrong strategies: not only is his task deeply intentional, which is antithetical to the unintentionality that governs the marketplace in *The Wealth of Nations*, but Aylmer's active intervention into Georgiana's body is, to say the least, the furthest thing from a policy of laissez-faire. Aylmer's antimarket means, in other words, will make it impossible for him to attain what he desires, the invisible hand and the subsequent power of the market, or something will go awry in the attempt to fulfill his wishes.

My discussion of the circulations in "The Birth-mark" and Georgiana's body, in particular, has thus far focused on the problematics of gender and signification raised by this state of instability. In moving to a discussion of the economic issues suggested by this thematic of circulation, it will be useful to consider another somewhat lengthier passage from *The Wealth of Nations* in which Smith figures the economic circulations of late-eighteenth-century Great Britain in blatantly physiological terms:

> In her present condition, Great Britain resembles one of those unwhole-some bodies in which some of the vital parts are overgrown, and which,

upon that account, are liable to many dangerous disorders scarce incident to those in which all the parts are more properly proportioned. A
small stop in that great blood-vessel, which has been artificially swelled
beyond its natural dimensions, and through which an unnatural proportion of the industry and commerce of the country has been forced to
circulate, is very likely to bring on the most dangerous disorders upon
the whole body politic. . . . The blood, of which the circulation is
stopped in some of the smaller vessels, easily disgorges itself into the
greater, without occasioning any dangerous disorder; but, when it is
stopped in any of the greater vessels, convulsions, apoplexy, or death
are the immediate and unavoidable consequences. (186–7)

According to this description, Georgiana's birthmark could be registering
a deeply disordered market. And this is indeed the case; not, however,
because Georgiana's fluctuating blood supply manifests any disorder (her
paling and blushing would be evidence of a healthy and mobile physiological state) but rather because Aylmer's inability to focus on anything but
Georgiana's birthmark brings about a state not unlike the one described by
Smith, in which "convulsions, apoplexy," *and* death are the "unavoidable
consequences." We are frequently reminded of Aylmer's Ahab-like mono-
mania: "Without intending it – nay, in spite of a purpose to the contrary –
[he] reverted to this one disastrous topic" (766) and a page later, "He had
not been aware of the tyrannizing influence acquired by one idea over his
mind" (767).[58] The problem with the birthmark is not its instability or its
uncontrollability or its mobility but the fact that Georgiana has it and
Aylmer seems to want it. The birthmark registers Georgiana's ineluctable
and successful participation in the market economy. As something Georgiana possesses, the birthmark is also Georgiana, and as such it represents
Georgiana's capacity to possess more, and thus it becomes what Aylmer
must have. Whereas Georgiana both possesses the "charm" (764) of the
birthmark and is possessed by it, Aylmer is clearly possessed by it but
receives none of the benefits of possession. He possesses it at the end of the
story, when, after receiving assurances from Georgiana that she will drink
a potentially fatal elixir, Aylmer has appropriated the power of the market
that had been located in the birthmark: "His spirit was ever on the march –
ever ascending – and each instant required something that was beyond the
scope of the instant before" (777). Capturing the spirit of Beecher and
Channing, Aylmer has recaptured his ever mobile spirit and transcendent
identity by immobilizing and appropriating Georgiana's.

He succeeds in doing this by strategically manipulating the competitive
principles of the market economy that inform the relations among Georgiana, himself, and her/the birthmark. Aylmer's anxieties about the hermeneutic fluctuations of the birthmark are, as has already been sug-

gested, further exacerbated by the fact of its proprietary indeterminacy; in other words, to whom does the birthmark belong? Is it Georgiana? Is Georgiana the birthmark's? These questions underscore the inextricable relation between matters of economy and the self at the same time as they bring us back to the task of defining Hawthorne's economics of allegory. Aylmer's commitment to erasure is also a commitment to ownership, requiring precisely those hermeneutic and proprietary indeterminacies that had seemed most worrisome. Anxiety producing as they may be, these indeterminacies nevertheless enable him to sustain the belief that Georgiana and her property, that is the birthmark, can be disengaged from one another through a process of disembodiment and thus permit Aylmer's territorial raids upon and into Georgiana's body. Aylmer's relation to Georgiana illustrates what Macpherson has called a "possessive market society," where "a man's energy and skill are his own, yet are regarded not as integral parts of his personality, but as possessions."[59] According to this logic, Aylmer assumes that Georgiana cannot both be the birthmark and possess it; therefore, he has an opportunity to own it. Similarly, in order for Georgiana to own the birthmark, she cannot be the birthmark. It is only by not owning the birthmark that she has a chance of owning it. Because her body has been constituted in the name of private property, the issue arises as to whose property she is now and whose she might become; Georgiana's body therefore functions as the site upon which the competitive spirit of the market economy plays itself out. The birthmark is Georgiana's property, and as property its ownership is transferrable or vulnerable, in this case to scientific experimentation. Yet as the ending of the story makes painfully clear, Georgiana *is* her property, or the birthmark. She both is it and owns it. Property that is not alienable is ultimately self-destructive. Because possession and identity are inextricable in the case of the birthmark, Georgiana commits a grave mistake in hoping that they might be separate. Interestingly enough, Aminadab puts his own finger on this logic when he first sees Georgiana lying unconscious in the laboratory: "If she were my wife, I'd never part with that birth-mark" (770). Aminadab might simply be communicating his aesthetic preference for Georgiana with a birthmark as opposed to Georgiana without one, but one can also hear in this sentence the inextricable connection between Georgiana's identity and the birthmark. She thinks, however, that in giving up the birthmark she can still be a person: "Either remove this dreadful Hand, or take my wretched life!" (768). Only when she realizes that her "or" will have to be an "and" will she understand what is at stake in the removal of the birthmark. The problem is not with alienable property but with property that won't be alienable.

Whereas in "The Celestial Rail-road" the disjunction between name and character constituted allegorical subjects who either were controlled by the market or transcended it (and thereby most fully exemplified it), "The Birth-mark" produces allegorical subjects as a consequence of applying the principles of the market economy to the relation between persons and (their) bodies. Georgiana's birthmark marks the surplus of meaning generated by the circulations of her body, which are then transformed by Aylmer into a problem both of allegorical interpretation and economic possessiveness. What does her birthmark signify, and who owns it? That these two questions follow from one another, at least for Aylmer, suggests that allegory and the market economy share the mechanism of generating and containing surplus meaning (or value) in order to make that surplus available for possession. Once Georgiana's proprietary relation to her body unravels as a consequence of Aylmer's successful manipulation of the rules of property, an economics of allegory reveals a configuration in which the omnipotence and transcendence of one character, in this case Aylmer, depend upon the geographical and characterological immobility of others, namely Georgiana and to a lesser extent Aminadab. Like Mr. Smooth-it-away, who in seeming to have escaped the exigencies of the market most clearly represented it, Aylmer controls the instabilities of the market, which were most clearly embodied by Georgiana, but the market cannot exist without precisely those instabilities that continually present the occasions for his acts of transcendence.

In making visible the circulations of the physiological and economic systems that define the late-eighteenth-century world of Aylmer and Georgiana, the birthmark locates upon Georgiana's body a version of the market's circulatory system, whose movements are nicely depicted as Georgiana experiences "a stirring up of her system, – a strange indefinite sensation creeping through her veins, and tingling, half painfully, half pleasurably, at her heart" (773–4). Having destroyed the birthmark as well as his wife, Aylmer has returned the market to its rightful owner – himself. His antipathy to the birthmark was never really the fact of its uncontrollability but rather the fact that Georgiana was both the possessor of and the one possessed by the market's powerful uncontrollability. In the true spirit of Adam Smith, Aylmer has restored the invisibility to the hand that Georgiana had made visible.

3

Melville's Operatives

In late January 1851, Herman Melville toured a paper mill in Dalton, Massachusetts, and four years later fictionalized the visit in "The Paradise of Bachelors and the Tartarus of Maids." The narrator takes a tour of the mill in which he witnesses a frightening scene of production. He describes "a tall girl, feeding the iron animal [the paper machine] with half quires of rose-hued note paper" which "received in the corner the impress of a wreath of roses."[1] The traditional rosy-cheeked young girl is replaced by "pale, blue girl[s]" (327) with "pallid cheek[s]" (328) and "face[s] pale with work" (327). Work, as the debate about the Lowell mill operatives indicated, did not necessarily guarantee spiritual or economic enhancement but increasingly seemed to undermine individual agency and bodily integrity. Instead of developing character in a version of the Romantic symbol, work appeared to flatten it out in an image of Coleridgean allegory. In the tartarus of maids we witness the production of allegorical characters as the paper machine drains the rosiness of the girls' cheeks until the product takes on the quality of natural rosiness, leaving "rows of blank-looking girls, with blank, white folders in their blank hands, all blankly folding blank paper" (328). The machine has replaced Aylmer, the operatives' cheeks have replaced Georgiana's, but rosy cheeks continue to pose a problem; that is, the complex relations among work, writing, and the body remain and continue to be played out upon the bodies of allegorical characters. Whereas Hawthorne imagines his literary labor to be aligned with the visibility of the birthmark, Melville figures his labor, at least in this story, as unavoidably complicitous with and dependent upon the erasure of the girls' rosy cheeks.

Melville's literary labor and the labor of the factory girls are so irrevocably implicated in one another that we are impelled to consider the relations between them. In this story Melville inscribes himself into the industrial process which violently reconstructs the bodies and minds of these girls. On the most obvious level, Melville's profession as a writer requires the paper that has been produced by the exploitation of female bodies. Less obvious, but nevertheless significant, is the way in which Melville makes these characters "march on in unvarying docility to the autocratic cunning of the machine" (333). His construction of fictional character, in other words, seems to recapitulate the machine's relation, its "metallic necessity" and "unbudging fatality," to the "blank-looking girls." Both the paper and the women become "destined to be scribbled on . . . what sort of characters no soul might tell" (333). One might argue that because the factory women in this story object neither to the machine nor to the boss, Melville cannot imagine an alternative to this system of production. And yet like the operatives who "handl[e] such white bits of sheets all the time which makes them so sheety" (331), Melville as a professional writer could become "sheety" through his necessary contact with paper. Melville risks becoming blank at the hands of a literary marketplace that he feels is determined to make him "march on in unvarying docility" to an aesthetic ideology that requires its own version of blankness – the blanking of Melville's presence as literary laborer. To this end, it is crucial to note that the paper is *not* blank. Although the narrator somewhat mystically describes the paper as "destined to be scribbled on," the paper already has a story, which is the story of exploitation. And this is a story, as we saw in the case of Cuticle, Melville is committed to telling. The rose, moreover, signifies the aestheticizing of this clearly unaesthetic story. Melville wants no part of this aesthetic. It is the mark of alienating and disfiguring labor. It is the same story written upon the blank bodies of the women workers. It is the allegory of labor in antebellum America. This chapter claims that Melville's allegorical characters foreground the potentially damaging consequences of industrial labor at the same time as they enable him to devise an alternative narrative of literary labor. Coming up with this alternative is the labor of Melville's allegory.

The economics of Melville's allegory can be mapped out through an analysis of any number of his texts, because Melville was, of all the authors I shall be considering, the most self-conscious about constructing a model of literary labor that differed from the dominant ideology of erasure. That allegory could be a particularly fruitful and ultimately subversive way to go about this construction is evident in the making and receiving of *Mardi*. The inextricable link between allegory and labor in Melville's work cannot be fully comprehended without a close reading of *Mardi* and its array of allegorical characters. These characters powerfully foreground the ways in which an industrialized market economy undermines the founding principles of the work ethic and, by extension, reconstitutes the relations between work and character development as well as between work and leisure. Similarly, allegorical characters in *Moby-Dick*, such as the Carpenter, the Blacksmith, and Ahab, dramatize the corporeal and psychic transformations brought about by new forms of labor. The battle between the organic and the inorganic taking place within Ahab's body serves as an analogy for workers' conflicted relations to changes in labor. In other words, *Moby-Dick* asks the question, who is responsible for what has happened to Ahab's body and Perth's and the many other *Pequod* crew who have lost parts of their bodies and eventually lose their lives? In analyzing the issue of accountability, I offer a reading of several cases decided by Melville's influential father-in-law, Massachusetts Chief Justice Lemuel Shaw, in order to suggest that the legal realm deployed the notion of individual agency as a way of maintaining an unfair distribution of accountability. Quite simply, workers were accountable to themselves and to their employers, and employers were accountable to no one. Although a belief in individual agency was upheld in the legal realm, in the realm of Melville's fiction, individual agency is revealed by Ishmael to be a fiction – and a pernicious one at that. The chapter concludes with an analysis of *Billy Budd*, perhaps the most conventionally allegorical of all of Melville's texts, which situates the unrest aboard the *Bellipotent* and Billy's eventual hanging in the context of the Haymarket riots and the hangings of four Chicago anarchists. By reading Billy's trial alongside the trial of the Haymarket rioters, it is possible to see how Melville's text casts suspicion upon the categories of individual agency, interiority, and naturalness by linking them to Vere's mechanism of discipline and punishment. Melville's refusal to represent Billy as anything other than a flat, mechanical, allegorical character is both a way of not "impressing" Billy into the machinery of Melville's text and "impressing" Billy with the marks of Melville's literary labor.[2]

I. THE CALM BEFORE THE STORM: LABORING THROUGH MARDI

A long calm in the boat, and now, God help us, another in the brigantine. It was airless and profound. In that hot calm, we lay fixed and frozen . . . (*Mardi*)[3]

We had hoped for a pleasant travel ride among the sunny isles of the tropics, instead of which, we were taken bodily, and immersed in the fathomless sea of Allegory, from which we have just emerged gasping for breath. (Review of *Mardi* in *Saroni's Musical Times*)[4]

Melville's *Mardi* committed a number of sins, the most egregious being its contestation of the work ethic, which I have been claiming constituted one of the ideological centerpieces of nineteenth-century American culture. The marginalization of *Mardi* indicates not only the successful dissemination of an aesthetic ideology of invisible labor in the nineteenth century but its continuing power in our own.[5] *Mardi* transgressed the ideology of the work ethic on a number of levels, from the audience's relation to work and leisure time, to the author's relation to the work of writing, to the characters' relation to their work in the fictive economy. By reading the failure of *Mardi* in terms of the dissolution of the work ethic, the narrative of *Mardi*'s reception can no longer be dismissed as an anomalous event in one writer's career but rather must be read as a powerful exemplification of nineteenth-century ideology.[6]

The review from *Saroni's Musical Times* suggests that the allegory of *Mardi* induces an episode of asphyxiation in the reader. The *Athenaeum* also judged *Mardi*'s allegory to be a failure: "If this book be meant as a pleasantry, the mirth has been oddly left out – if as an allegory, the key of the casket is 'buried in ocean deep.'"[7] Surprisingly few reviewers, though, criticized *Mardi* for its overt indictment of such contemporary policies as slavery and imperialism. In fact, William Gilmore Simms was one of the few reviewers who objected to *Mardi*'s representation of nineteenth-century American culture, specifically the "loathsome picture of Mr. Calhoun, in the character of a slave driver which spoils everything to the Southern reader."[8] More often than not, critics attacked *Mardi* for its unnatural and belabored style. Thus, like the review from the *Southern Literary Messenger* with which my first chapter began, an 1849 review complains: "In Mr. Melville's style we notice a too habitual inversion, an overstraining after anti-thesis and Carlyleisms, with the not unfrequent sacrifice of the natural to the quaint."[9] This review provides a classic statement of reading as an activity poised between the categories of leisure and labor: "Parts may be read by the most careless reader, and be enjoyed in the dozes of a summer's afternoon – other parts require a wide-awake application, or, as in *Gulliver's Travels*, one half the aroma will be lost."[10] Most readers, however, felt that *Mardi* had no patience with the "careless reader" and aggressively situated itself on the side of "wide-awake application." The opening chapters of *Mardi* stage the contradictions inherent in a culture that, on the one hand, espoused the virtues of the work ethic and, on the other, demanded that its leisure time, or the time spent reading, be as separate as possible from the world of work and perhaps even undo the physical or psychic damage done by hard or unrewarding work. The first two chapters of *Mardi* not only interrogate the relation between leisure and work time as lived by the narrator of the text but also turn the reading experience into an ordeal of hard labor.

The first chapter of *Mardi* promises to follow the rules set down by literary critics in their discourse on literary labor. The narrator invites us to accompany him on a journey similar to the pleasant and entertaining ones Melville's earlier narrators had conducted. "We are off!" (3), he energetically declares, and we expect to be amused on the trip.[11] There are the anticipation of adventure (the narrator is a sailor on a whaling ship) and the promise of new sights (the setting is the exotic Pacific). We quickly learn that the narrator has decided to jump ship because of what he calls the Captain's "tacit contravention of the agreement between [them]" (6). Having had bad luck in finding and killing sperm whales, the Captain chooses to change the crew's direction in hopes of capturing right whales. Taking advantage of this seemingly unimportant change in plans, the narrator jumps at the opportunity to seek excitement in the islands to the west that are "invested with all the charms of dream-land" (7). Similarly, nineteenth-century readers began *Mardi* with hopes of leaving behind the everyday world of work and entering the exciting and charming world of leisure where they could escape certain people (like the Captain) who might back out of their agreements. Instead *Mardi* itself seems to jump ship, and in the process leaves the reader stranded and, in the words of the *Saroni's* reviewer, "gasping for breath."

Although its opening promises "vistas [which] seemed leading to worlds beyond" (8), *Mardi* quickly retracts this promise and announces its challenge to the reader as early as the second chapter, "A Calm." Meditating on the physical and spiritual experience of being in a calm, the narrator tells us that his entire belief system starts to unravel as "doubts overtake him as to the captain's competency to navigate his ship" (10). The distressed narrator describes his discomfort in terms of reading:

> If a reader of books, Priestley on Necessity occurs to him; and he believes in that old Sir Anthony Absolute to the very last chapter. His faith . . . however, begins to fail; for the geography, which from boyhood he had implicitly confided in, always assured him, that though expatiating all over the globe, the sea was at least margined by land. That over against America, for example, was Asia. But it is a calm, and he grows madly skeptical.
>
> To his alarmed fancy, parallels and meridians become emphatically what they are merely designated as being: imaginary lines drawn round the earth's surface. (9–10)

This passage suggests that when enduring a calm one becomes keenly attentive to the interpretation of books as well as the meaning of the world. A radical change in one's relation to texts occurs, and the authority of eighteenth-century texts, like Priestley and Sheridan's *The Rivals* (one of whose main characters is Sir Anthony Absolute), begins to unravel.[12] This unraveling of authority assumes geographical proportions as the calm problematizes the heretofore seemingly stable relation between places and their global representation. "Parallels and meridians become emphatically what they are merely designated as being"; that is, they no longer appear to have an essential meaning. The language of this final sentence is especially peculiar. The juxtaposition of "emphatically" and "merely" initially leads the reader to believe that the emphasis lies with what the parallels and meridians become. That emphasis, however, is undercut by the word "merely." They reveal themselves as artificial "designat[ions]" and "productions of the imagination." What they are is not what they are but what they have been designated to be. Yet their being and designation are the same. The distinction between the real and the imaginary has collapsed. In a calm, parallels and meridians become emphatically arbitrary in that they become what they have always been – floating signifiers. Furthermore, enduring the calm leads to the questioning of authority: the map is no longer reliable, "the log is a liar" (10), and the Captain is an "ignoramus" (10). For a mid-nineteenth-century American, being in a calm was not only a novelty but an identity-threatening experience.

Departing from the familiar adventure story promised by the first chapter of *Mardi*, the second chapter is completely foreign to all descriptions of American life. Perhaps the most famous one was written by Tocqueville, who incredulously watched as the "American rushes forward to secure his immense booty that fortune offers . . . and urges onward as if time pressed and he was afraid of finding no room for his exertions."[13] In contrast to experiencing the ubiquitous motion described by Tocqueville, the narrator in the calm remains "unable to utilize his glorious liberty of volition" and feels "utter helplessness because his physical organization, obviously intended for locomotion, becomes a fixture" (10). Tocqueville's description points to the continual drive toward progress in antebellum America, one of the main components of the work ethic. Yet the underside of this American preoccupation with "utility" and "locomotion" constantly presented itself as we have already seen it in the texts of nineteenth-century preachers and reformers – this underside was the spectre of idleness, that activity (or lack thereof) that defined itself in direct opposition to the work ethic.

The narrator of *Mardi* is located precisely at the point when he has given up his work aboard the ship and has decided to become the proprietor of his own time. The calm constitutes that interstitial moment in which he will choose either the sweetness of leisure or the path of industry. Unable to "rush forward" or "urge onward" or "find room for his exertions" in typically American fashion, according to Tocqueville, what will the narrator do? According to jeremiads against idleness, the worst thing the narrator could do would be to relax and enjoy the calm. Yet this is precisely what he does when he falls in love with Yillah, a native of Mardi. As his love affair with Yillah unfolds, his initial discomfort with idleness turns into a dangerous enjoyment of it. Under Yillah's influence, he partakes of the intimacies of love: "With Yillah seated at last in [his] arbor, [he] looked round, and wanted for naught" (189). In their first days of romance, he says to Yillah, "Nevermore shall we desire to roam" (161). Although Beecher maintains that "every product of the earth has a susceptibility of improvement," the narrator learns otherwise in his perfect repose with Yillah – until she disappears.

Whereas a delicate balance between Ahab's and Ishmael's narrative impulses is sustained in *Moby-Dick*, the conflict between the narrator's Ishmael-like journey toward knowledge and his Ahab-like pursuit of Yillah overwhelms him and the narrative. The remainder of *Mardi*, or the next 193 chapters, requires us to endure the calm that the narrator experiences in Chapter 2. For the narrator, the experience of a calm forces him to question the meaning of "idleness." Although one might look "idle" while experiencing a calm or while reading, a great deal of work might be going on: "He may sleep if he can, or purposely delude himself into a crazy fancy, that he is merely at leisure . . . but he may not lounge; for to lounge is to be idle; to be idle implies an absence of any thing to do; whereas there is a calm to be endured" (10). Readers who might imagine that reading is a leisurely activity apart from work soon learn, like the narrator, that reading *Mardi* requires a great deal of labor. By forcing the reader to endure the calm that is *Mardi*, the text not only challenges its audience to examine the expectations it brings to a text but transgresses the proper relations between leisure and labor time.

It is crucial to note, however, that *Mardi* is not simply a romantic celebration of the idle life in the tradition of Washington Irving or Walt Whitman. Far from it. Mohi, the historian, tells the story of Donjalolo, who, as ruler of the island of Juam, was not allowed to leave "the little glen of Willamilla" (223). Donjalolo's enforced "idle[ness]" (233) leads to a life of vice and turpitude like the one envisioned by Beecher: Donjalolo "vacillate[s] between virtue and vice; to neither constant, and upbraided by both; his mind, like his person in the glen, was continually passing and repassing between opposite extremes" (224). His inability to move in the direction of virtue leads him to vice, and he becomes intemperate and so sexually promiscuous that "for all his multiplicity of wives, he had never an heir" (244). The chapters about Donjalolo suggest that rather than sentimentalizing the idle life, *Mardi* champions the potential satisfaction that comes from hard work.

And yet hard work is seldom satisfying either. On the island of Juam, for example, Donjalolo requires an army of laborers to enable him to live his idle existence. They function chiefly as "slave[s] to the whims of [Donjalolo's] thirty princesses" (243). The narrator humorously describes the labors of this "band of old men; woe-begone, thin of leg, and puny of frame" (243) as "so laborious . . . that none could discharge them for more than a twelvemonth, at the end of that period giving up the ghost out of pure exhaustion" (243). Characters in *Mardi* are defined by the fact of their relation to labor – either they work or they don't. *Mardi*, in fact, continually calls attention to itself as a world of objects made by workers. Thus we not only read chapters about Media and company drinking wine from gourds, but we learn how those gourds are made:

> They are plucked from the tree; and emptied of their pulp, are scratched over with minute marks, like those of a line engraving. The ground prepared, the various figures are carefully etched. And the outlines filled up with delicate punctures, certain vegetable oils are poured over them, for coloring. Filled with a peculiar species of earth, the gourd is now placed in an oven in the ground. And in due time exhumed, emptied of its contents, and washed in the stream. (180–1)

Everything in the fictional world of *Mardi*, from the gourds used for drinking to the tobacco containers which have been "work[ed] into bowls" (373), is a product of intense labor. Such frequent detailed images of artifice are highly significant, especially once they are understood as versions of Melville's own literary artifice.

Perhaps the most significant artifacts in *Mardi* are the idols that are worshipped, and the material conditions that enable their production are foregrounded in the chapter "Mohi Tells of One Ravoo, and They Land to Visit Hevaneva, a Flourishing Artisan." Step by step, we see how trees are made into idols. First, according to Hevaneva, wood is gotten from "one grove . . . and, on an average, each tree stands us in full fifty idols" (354). Then the wood is made into idols by assembly-line workers. Finally, the idol is made into a commodity. In a remarkable passage, Hevaneva describes this last stage:

> When I cut down the tree[s] for my idols . . . they are nothing but logs; when upon those logs, I chalk out the figures of my images, they yet remain logs; when the chisel is applied, logs they are still; and when all complete, I at last stand them up in my studio, even though then they are logs. Nevertheless when I handle the pay, they are as prime gods. (354)

Hevaneva's appropriation of the journeymen's labor as well as their profits is evident in the use of the first person. More interesting, perhaps, is his description of the magical change that occurs when he handles the pay. Like Marx's description of the transformation that occurs when a product "steps forth as a commodity . . . [and] is changed into something transcendent," here the idol loses its relation to its maker and is changed at the instant of exchange from log to "prime god."[14]

Hevaneva's idol factory illustrates an efficient market economy, and religion is clearly as much an industry on Mardi as anything else. The vast number of demigods enables a sophisticated market economy to produce idols "of every variety of pattern; and of every size; from that of a giant, to the little images worn in the ears of the ultra devout" (353). The idol industry also profits by the perennial squabbling between worshippers of different demigods. At the temple of Oro, for example, Babbalanja notices that "there seems not a single image unmutilated" (345). The competition among demigods ensures a continual supply and demand. In addition, consumers are encouraged to buy new idols, because Hevaneva will take "second-hand images in part pay for new ones" (354). Furthermore, in this picture of the idol factory we learn a great deal more about the product than about the producers, who do their job "with wonderful industry" (353). In fact, the products are far more diverse than the workers. Described solely in terms of function on the assembly line, the body of the worker disappears and the body of the product is foregrounded: "The journeymen were plying their tools; – some chiseling noses; some trenching for mouths; and others, with heated flints, boring for ears" (353). Instead of describing the eyes and ears of the journeymen, Hevaneva explains how the workers repair damaged idols by "touching up the eyes and ears [and] resetting their noses" (354). It as though the specialization or narrowness of the journeymen serves as the precondition for the variety of the commodity.

Mardi, however, issues a challenge to the kind of market economy represented by Hevaneva's factory, which features specialized laborers doing unoriginal work. Their idols are the products of their mechanical work, which for Melville is a kind of idleness. Just as idleness and work were turned inside out in the first two chapters of *Mardi*, this chapter undermines work (the particular kind of work illustrated by the factory) by suggesting its kinship with idleness/idolness. Although the journeymen work hard, they too are stuck in a kind of calm in which they, like our narrator, can neither "rush forward" nor "urge onward" nor "find room for their exertions" in the manner characterized by Tocqueville and promised by the work ethic. If idleness subverts the work ethic, the work exemplified by Hevaneva's idol factory does as well. Whereas idleness in the opening chapters unravels so as to become a kind of work, here work unravels so as to become a kind of idleness. By unraveling this dichotomy which aligns literature with idleness, Melville's text works toward a redefinition of literature as work and, more specifically, literature as meaningful and rewarding work.

Moreover, the version of work at Hevaneva's factory profoundly reorganizes the relation between work and individual agency. The effect of factory work on the journeymen is not a development of characterological identity but rather its flattening out. This labor produces allegorical characters who can do only one thing. We shall see that the effect of idleness on characters in *Mardi* is, paradoxically, the same. Characters become allegorical as a consequence of either laboring too much or not laboring at all. As was evident in the case of Cuticle, the agency of allegorical characters is severely limited by the antebellum work ethic – precisely the ethic that seeks to instill a sense of unlimited agency through hard work. Because the work ethic, at least as presented here by Melville, constitutes behavior as either idleness or work, allegorical characters in *Mardi* signify their complete adherence to or disregard of either one of the terms in this opposition. But the fact that idleness and work *both* produce allegorical characters indicates that the opposition between idleness and work is itself destabilized. The flatness of allegorical characters, in other words, alludes to a market economy that produces persons who are either mechanical laborers or idlers. We need only look at the characters of Oh-Oh, the antiquarian, and Jiji, the collector of teeth (the specie of Mardi), to see that they, like Hevaneva's workers, are allegorical characters in their two-dimensionality. One of the first things we learn about Oh-Oh, the antiquarian, is that Oh-Oh is not his name. Although his real name remains a mystery, the narrator tells us that Oh-Oh "went by the exclamatory cognomen 'Oh-Oh'; a name bestowed upon him, by reason of the delighted interjections, with which he welcomed all accessions to his museum" (378). Rather than making a name for himself in the tradition of the self-made man and through dedication to the work ethic, his purchases name or make him. The narrator then describes this "old man [who] was a sight to see" (378). He possessed a Rabelaisian nose; "the rest of his person was crooked, and dwarfed, and surmounted by a hump, that sat on his back like a burden . . . thus old, and antiquated, and gable-ended, was the tabernacle of Oh-Oh's soul" (379). Like Oh-Oh's ancient and curious manuscripts, which he "preserve[s] in a vault" (382), the strange body of the antiquarian remains "housed in as curious a structure" (379). The rest of the chapter lists the many pamphlets and books in his museumlike house. Significantly, Oh-Oh omits the authors' names when discussing his collection. No sign of the labor (or laborer) that went into the production of these texts appears. Only when Babbalanja finds "a few crumbling, illegible, black-letter sheets of his favorite old essayist, brave Bardianna" (385) is an author's name even mentioned. When Babbalanja asks Oh-Oh for "one shred of those most precious pages" (385), Oh-Oh responds, "Philosopher, ask me for my limbs, my life, my heart, but ask me not for these" (385). Willing to give up his body parts rather than his possessions, Oh-Oh will never part from them even in death.

Oh-Oh's mirror image, Jiji, lives on the other side of the island. Whereas the antiquarian collects manuscripts, Jiji collects teeth, the currency of Mardi. Jiji's body is equally grotesque: "[His] great head shook with a tremulous motion, as one by one, to a clicking sound from the old man's mouth, the strings of teeth were slowly drawn forth, and let fall, again and again, with a rattle" (391). Jiji is paradoxically both a rich man and a pauper, because even though he has a great deal of money (or teeth, as is the case in Mardi), upon "opening his mouth, he aver[s] he ha[s] none" (391). The biological function of his teeth (chewing food) has been exchanged for their economic use. Jiji mutilates himself because he is drawn to teeth, his as well as others', in their inorganic, abstracted state.

It seems obvious that these characters do not conform to the normative standards of antebellum reviewers. First, they are radically "unnatural." Jiji and Oh-Oh become increasingly artificialized as their manuscript and specie collections take on lives of their own. Second, as their names suggest, their characters do not develop. They simply repeat themselves by collecting more of the same thing. Rather than evincing "the progressive development of character,"[15] they seem to develop, in their utter repetitiveness, toward what Forster identified as "flatness."[16]

At the same time that *Mardi* presents and critiques a number of unacceptable versions of production (and nonproduction), Melville is attempting to come up with a satisfying version of labor, specifically authorial labor, of which these repetitions are, I think, a part. Allegory plays a crucial role in the model of literary labor that Melville offers.[17] Rather than effacing the traces of his own work, Melville calls attention to *Mardi* as a product of hard labor by including an allegory about his own making of *Mardi*. Richard Brodhead characterizes the kind of work Melville had done in writing *Mardi*: "He comes to see that its true action is not his characters' adventures but his own creative process: that its real voyage is the imaginative one he has undertaken in conceiving *Mardi*, that the real object of its quest is nothing his characters seek but the mental world he himself discloses through the act of creating his book."[18] This mental labor is nowhere more evident than in a chapter about Lombardo's Koztanza, a text much like *Mardi* by an author much like Melville, in which Melville draws our attention to his efforts. Babbalanja quotes the following words of Lombardo's: "Who will read me? Say one thousand pages – twenty-five lines each – every line ten words – every word ten letters. That's two million five hundred thousand a's, and i's, and o's to read" (601). If the reader had any doubt that she should read this discussion about the Koztanza in terms of Melville's *Mardi*, the reference to the a's, i's, and o's makes the connection perfectly clear, since one of *Mardi*'s chapters is entitled "A, I and O." More significant, though, is the way in which textuality is reduced to its most fundamental terms – the letters of the alphabet. We might usefully compare this passage from *Mardi* with Beecher's essay "Reading": "The ready reader never thinks of *letters*. It is only the *word* that he sees. And even the word seems to lose individuality, and is but a member of something else, – a sentence. But even the sentence seems not to be seen, but to be seen through."[19] When we read, according to Beecher, a gradual distancing from the materiality of the text should herald our entrance into "a train of pure thought, or the flow of sentiment" and lead us away from "the symbol by which [the thought] is set forth" (188). Beecher here rehearses Coleridge's distinction between the symbol, which creates an experience of coherence by transcending individual parts, and allegory, which creates an experience of fragmentation by breaking things down into their individual parts (in Melville's case, the letters of the alphabet). *Mardi*'s materiality is, of course, precisely what Melville insists upon throughout the text. Melville allows no such distancing. He refuses to let his text become a part of an economy that requires the erasure of his labor. Whereas Wai-chee Dimock interprets this refusal as "a radical aggrandizement of the self," I think that it is better understood as Melville's attempt to reconceptualize a textual economy that incorporates the signs of authorial labor into the finished artifact.[20]

Allegory is at once a manifestation of the problems with the work ethic and a way for Melville to reconfigure the work ethic according to his own ideology and ideal of literary labor. Melville's allegory in *Mardi* thus functions to liberate Melville from the constraints of the work ethic, at least as it applies to authorial labor. Let us remind ourselves of the dominant literary version of the work ethic by turning to an 1842 review of John Pendleton Kennedy's oeuvre: "It is very plain that Mr. Kennedy has had scant time to study, frame, and perfect the novels, which during this busy life, he has given to the public; and consequently, *Swallow Barn*, which required no labor of this sort, which was but a collection of sketches without a plot . . . is, as a whole, the best of his productions."[21] The critique of allegory and the elevation of texts "which required no labor" are, as we have seen, elements of the antebellum aesthetic ideology that sought to erase any evidence of literary labor that would make visible the fact of authorial agency. Melville's ideal of literary labor radically differs from this articulation of aesthetic taste, and nowhere more dramatically than in his use of allegory, whose primary attraction (or detraction) is the self-referentiality and laboriousness that this reviewer (and the literary marketplace which he represents) finds aesthetically inferior.

Mardi appropriately ends with the travelers reaching the island of Serenia and discovering upon it the possibility of fulfilling labor where "men strive to live together in gentle bonds of peace and charity" (623). Although our travelers initially dismiss this experimental utopia as being "based upon the idlest of theories" (623), they come to see the wisdom of its religious and economic ways. In contrast to what obtains on Hevaneva's island of Uma, the religion of Serenia requires neither temples nor idols, because "this isle is all one temple to his praise [and] every leaf is consecrated his" (628). Its religion is based on a true understanding of Christian principles, which significantly include the fair distribution of labor: Let "no man toil too hard, that thou may'st idle be" (637). Although the Serenians resemble Donjalolo and our becalmed narrator in that they "rove no more" (637), unlike them, these islanders desire "no calmer strand [and] no sweeter land" (623). What first looks like idleness is, in fact, the calm that one attains through fair and rewarding labor.

II. WAILING AND WHALING

Although reviewers greeted *Moby-Dick* with much more enthusiasm than *Mardi*, they were, for the most part, harsh. The *Morning Post* was an exception in that, while recognizing certain "occasional extravagancies," it acknowledged the fact that *Moby-Dick* "is a book of extraordinary merit, and one which will do great things for the literary reputation of its author."[22] The majority of reviewers, though, felt that Melville deserved to be accused of "eccentricity and oddity," "wilfulness," and "purposeless extravagance," because once again the renowned author of *Typee* and *Omoo* had failed to give the public what it wanted.[23] In one of the most vituperative critiques of *Moby-Dick*, the *London Atlas* not only castigated Melville for "a certain besetting sin of extravagance" but also wrote, "This unbridled extravagance in writing, this listless and profitless dreaming, and maundering with the pen in the hand, is as it were supported and backed by the wildness of conception and semi-supernatural tone of the whole story."[24] As with *Mardi*, the literati were attempting to pressure Melville into returning to the amusing narrative voice of his earlier texts. More important, the economic language of this review reveals the inextricability of Melville's crimes as a writer – his "extravagance, listless[ness], and profitless[ness]" – and as an inefficient American worker in the antebellum market economy. His product is, for example, "supported and backed" by wildness as opposed to steady progress. Moreover, this reviewer even imagines the scene of literary labor as Melville, pen in hand, fails to live up to a set of aesthetic standards that are here defined in relation to an economy of writing.

This economy of writing (or lack thereof) is concisely delineated in an 1850 *Harper's* article, "The Literary Profession – Authors and Publishers," which states that "there is something altogether fitful, irregular, spasmodic in their [professional writers'] way of life": "It may be assumed, as we have already hinted, that no small proportion of those who adopt literature as a profession have enlisted in the army of authors because they have lacked the necessary amount of patience and perseverance – the systematic orderly habits – the industry and the self-denial by which alone it is possible to attain success in other paths of professional life. "[25] This article suggests that the lack of a work ethic among literary professionals, their "irregular distribution of time, and with it irregular social and moral habits" (550), should be corrected so as to avoid a situation in which they are "weary of the work before [they] ha[ve] traced out the first parallel" (550) or they are "compelled to live a life of fever, between excitement and exhaustion of the mind" (551). Like workers of the period, for whom leisure was becoming an increasingly popular antidote to the damage done by labor, literary professionals were advised to partake of "rest and recreation, fresh air and bodily exercise [which] are essential to an author" (551). Although the *Harper's* piece acknowledges the fact that literary laborers are different from other kinds of laborers in their "occasional paroxysms of industry" (550) as opposed to the "orderly methodical habits" (550) of industry, authors nevertheless receive the same advice as workers who suffer from the potentially damaging effects of too much order. Although they neither adhere to the demands of the work ethic nor engage in factorylike labor, the discourse of the work ethic and anxieties about the factory provide the discursive materials out of which an experience of literary labor is represented and a restructuring of literary labor is advised. *Moby-Dick* is about the painful restructuring of laborers: both the workers who kill whales and the worker who writes about killing whales. Melville's text is preoccupied both with articulating and accounting for the pain and mournfulness that are involved in this transformation of labor and the maintenance of individual agency, and Melville is committed to reconfiguring his own status as literary laborer so as to avoid such pain.[26] This reconfiguration is accomplished by sabotaging the notion of individual agency and revealing it as a myth, which makes laborers accountable for an individual self that simply does not exist.

These acerbic reviews of *Moby-Dick* are typical of the negative attention the book received. Evert Duyckinck's more positive 1851 review in the *Literary World* examines, though rather ironically, a mournfulness about *Moby-Dick* that had eluded other reviewers. In describing the characters aboard the *Pequod*, Duyckinck notes:

> They are striking characters withal, of the romantic spiritual cast of the German drama; realities of some kinds at bottom, but veiled in all sorts of poetical incidents and expressions. As a bit of German melodrama, with Captain Ahab for the Faust of the quarter-deck, and Queequeg with the crew, for Walpurgis night revellers in the forecastle, it has its strong points, though here the limits as to space and treatment of the stage would improve it. Moby Dick in this view becomes a sort of fishy moralist, a leviathan metaphysician, a folio Doctor Dubitantium, in fact, in the fresh water illustration of Mrs. Malaprop "an allegory on the banks of the Nile." After pursuing him in this melancholic company

over a few hundred squares of latitude and longitude, we begin to have
some faint idea of the association of whaling and lamentation, and why
blubber is popularly synonymous with tears.[27]

Duyckinck is drawn to the allegorical characters of the text, whom he
depicts as melancholic. Although he does not explain the source of their
melancholy, he nonetheless realizes its thematic importance in *Moby-
Dick.* By punning on "wailing" and "whaling," and on "blubber" as it
refers both to whale's blubber and blubber as tears, Duyckinck once
more refers to the theme of melancholy, but the humor of his wordplay
functions to deflect one's attention away from the significance of his
observations: who, for example, is wailing? is it just the melancholic
company of the *Pequod,* or is it also the reader of Melville's text? and what
is the relation between the blubber of a whale and the blubber of a
discontented reader?

Clearly, Duyckinck is covertly alluding to his own tears while reading
Moby-Dick; tears that do not signify sympathy for the *Pequod*'s melancholic company but rather impatience with their adventures over "a few
hundred squares of latitude and longitude." In *Moby-Dick* Melville's ex-
pansiveness organizes itself around the killing of whales and the process-
ing of whale blubber into oil to be sold in the marketplace. But unlike the
blubber of whales, the blubber of a reader almost always translates into
poor market sales. In other words, the blubber of whales is produced as a
desirable commodity, whereas Melville's representation of the blubber of
whales is, according to Duyckinck's half hinted-at aesthetic criterion,
produced as an undesirable commodity. In contrast to whale blubber,
which is exchanged for money in the market, the representation of mar-
ketable whale blubber is unprofitably "exchanged" for the profitless blubber of readers. This review, then, is of particular interest because the
terms that describe the commercial activity in *Moby-Dick,* whaling and
blubber, are also the terms that characterize the reader's experience of the
text, wailing and blubber; terms that are then brought to bear upon each
other and ultimately used against Melville.

In his journal entry of November 27, 1849, Melville records "a shocking
accident [which] occurred to one of the hands of the boat. His foot was
ruined in the machinery."[28] Although Melville does not make much of
this incident, we know that this injured sailor would have received no
compensation from his employer because of the decision handed down
by Chief Justice Lemuel Shaw in the 1842 case *Farwell* v. *Boston and
Worcester Railroad.* In this landmark case, Shaw argued that the railroad
could not be held responsible for Farwell's injury, since Farwell had taken
the job with "full knowledge of the risks that were as likely to be foreseen

and guarded against by employees as by their employer."[29] Shaw used this same reasoning eight years later in *Albro* v. *Agawam Canal Company* to reject a textile spinner's grievance against her employers for gross negligence: She "can have no legal right to complain of his carelessness or unfaithfulness; for he had made himself, by no act or contract, accountable to her." In the name of free agency, American individualism, and worker mobility, Shaw contended that employers could not be held responsible – "accountable," to use his word – for accidents incurred on the job. Thus, Farwell, Albro, and the seaman aboard the *Emerald* received no compensation or "indemnity in case of loss."[30]

Advocates, like Shaw, of an American industrialized market economy strategically denied workers power by arguing that technology would, in fact, make them more powerful. Beecher's meditations on technology, which can be found in an 1862 collection of essays, *Eyes and Ears*, illustrate a similar attitude. While musing upon the economic and moral value of mowing machines and steam ploughs, he anticipates the day when "the farmer shall no longer be a drudge; and work shall not exact much, and give but little." The most significant payoff will take the shape of books that will be "no longer the product of cities, but [will] come fresh and glowing from Nature, from unlopped men, whose side branches, having had room to grow, [will] give the full and noble proportions of manhood from top to bottom."[31] By eliminating much of the drudgery intrinsic to the farmer's life (drudgery that had once been idealized, most notably by Crèvecoeur and Jefferson in the myth of the noble farmer), these inventions will certainly benefit the farmer. No benefit, however, will be more welcomed than the opportunity to write books. But Beecher's comparison implies that the farmer's gains are the urban dweller's losses: the unlopped men who create literature from Nature will replace the lopped men who have written books in the city. Not only is the laborer who writes books in the city erased from the picture, but workers who make the mowing machines and steam ploughs mysteriously disappear as well. Precisely when Beecher attempts to show the value of these mechanical contrivances, he ends up "lop[ping]" workers from the picture. This description offers a glimpse of the potentially troubled relationship between machinery and workers.

Even as factory conditions and new machinery altered the relationship between employer and employee, opinions like those of Shaw and Beecher reflected a stubborn denial of these changes. Because no one could be held accountable for injuries done to workers' bodies, Shaw's decisions effectively allowed those losses to continue. Although the *Farwell* decision, according to Leonard Levy, had "harsh consequences, [it] was in keeping with the strict individualism which pervaded [Shaw's] whole opinion, as well as the common law and American philosophy."[32]

In other words, having workers maintain responsibility for physical injuries on the job meant that they remained independent entities, even though their bodies had become instrumentalized for greater profits. The law insisted upon viewing them as free agents. In contrast to Shaw's legal response to industrialized labor, Melville's *Moby-Dick* describes the exploitation of workers' bodies and explodes the myth of the workers' free and individual agency in the factory aboard the *Pequod*.

In *Mardi*, Melville had attempted to "give the full and noble proportions of [his] manhood" and ended up feeling lopped. He experienced this feeling once more with the composition of *Redburn* and *White-Jacket*. Identifying himself as a laborer in a famous letter to Shaw, Melville writes of these two books: "They are two *jobs*, which I have done for money – being forced to it, as other men are to sawing wood." This revealing letter begins with assurances to his father-in-law that though Melville must go to England with his manuscripts, his "travels will have to be bounded by [his] purse & by prudential considerations." A seemingly financially responsible Melville claims, "Economy . . . is my motto," only to conclude with the following: "So far as I am individually concerned, & independent of my pocket, it is my earnest desire to write those sort of books which are said to 'fail.'"[33] Melville is not a happy worker. To make money, he must undertake labor that does not satisfy him, and when he does work that satisfies him, he does not make much money.

And he finds himself in a position not unlike Farwell and Albro. Like them, Melville is accountable to employers (readers and reviewers) who in turn are not accountable to him. Because he has entered into a contract with them having "full knowledge of the risks," Melville can, de jure, hold no one but himself responsible, though he vacillates between blaming himself and reviewers. This is also the situation in which Ahab finds himself. If what Ahab seeks is a figure of accountability, whom else except himself (and the whale) can he hold responsible for his dismemberment? Surely not Captain Peleg or Captain Bildad, who describe themselves as "part owners and agents" of the *Pequod*; their accountability as agents is protected by their status as part owners.[34] Rather than seeing Melville and Ahab engaged in what Dimock calls a "battle for sovereignty," I read them as both pursuing a solution to the problem of accountability. If Ahab's pursuit ends in death, it is not because Melville wishes "to command absolutely" but because he finds in Ishmael a less self-destructive means of existing in a world where accountability is the burden of individual agents (like Farwell or Ahab, Albro or Ishmael) who, de facto, function neither as individuals nor as agents.[35] Indeed, the logic of Shaw's legal strategy comes back with a vengeance, for whom else but himself can Ahab hold responsible? The principle of individual agency had won the day, but the individuals themselves began to bear little resemblance to the ideal of individual empowerment Shaw had imagined, and looked more like allegorical agents whose bodies transgressed the boundary between organic and mechanical and whose relation to individual agency was, as we have seen, deeply problematic.

From this perspective, two of the most important figures in *Moby-Dick* are the Carpenter and the Blacksmith, because, as allegorical characters, they register the extent to which new forms of labor produce new forms of personhood. Although critics have addressed the issue of labor in *Moby-Dick*, most have ignored the significance of these characters because of their seeming simplicity. The legacy of antebellum aesthetic ideology is powerfully exemplified in R. P. Blackmur's new critical critique of the Carpenter and the Blacksmith, who lack the necessary qualities of any respectable fictional character: "[They] are only pulled out at intervals and are usually given stock jobs to do, [and] set speeches to make. . . . To be successful and maintain interest they must be given enough to do to seem everywhere natural, and never obviously used, as here only to make the wheels go round."[36] Blackmur's language reveals his allegiance to a model of "round," or symbolic, as opposed to "flat," or allegorical, characters, as well as to an ideal of nonmechanical and "non-obvious" labor. Characters should be neither "stock" nor "set." They should be "natural" and never "obviously used." If a character is being "used," that use should be hidden so that the character can appear natural. The work in the fiction that the character does should, in other words, be made not to look like work.

Presumably Blackmur strenuously objects to allegorical characters such as the Carpenter, whose "brain, if he had ever had one, must have early oozed along into the muscles of his fingers. He was like one of those unreasoning but still highly useful, *multum in parvo*, Sheffield contrivances, assuming the exterior – though a little swelled – of a common pocket knife" (468). One might argue that the Carpenter is a model craftsman removed from the exigencies of an industrialized workplace. But clearly the Carpenter's "unreasoning but still highly useful" identity registers many of the anxieties that surrounded factory labor, including the reconfiguration of the body and the numbing of the mind. Designated according to the work that he performs on the *Pequod*, the Carpenter's identity and his work are inseparable. The Carpenter's lack of an individual name is particularly important in this respect; even a Sheffield contrivance possesses a degree of individuality missing in the Carpenter. Having completely adapted to the demands of the workplace, Melville's Carpenter is the perfect worker, unlike Ishmael, who contemplates "Descartian vortices" (159) while allegedly looking for whales. Not only has his brain "oozed along into the muscles of his fingers," but his body has rearranged itself so that "it so shaded off into the surrounding infinite of things that it seemed one with the general stolidity discernible in the whole visible world" (467). The Carpenter's body and the "visible world" are not in conflict; in fact, his body has thoroughly merged with that world. He and his tools have become indistinguishable, so that now he is the perfect instrument, a model of usefulness and "pure manipulat[ion]" (468). Although the narrator notices a "half-horrible stolidity in him, involving, too, as it appeared, an all-ramifying heartlessness" (467), the Carpenter, like Cuticle, whose "heartlessness must have been of a purely scientific origin" (*White-Jacket,* 251), seems to be one of the few men at peace with his position aboard the *Pequod.* Blackmur's negative evaluation, and the antebellum aesthetic from which it derives, of characters who are used "only to make the wheels go round" misses the cultural significance of such figures in Melville.[37] The Carpenter exemplifies the ideal mechanical worker in a market economy.

Unlike the Carpenter, who "was prepared at all points, and alike indifferent and without respect in all" (467), many characters in *Moby-Dick,* including Perth, the Blacksmith, have not adapted themselves so smoothly to the demands of America's industrial society.[38] The chapter "The Blacksmith" records Perth's difficult passage from Perth to Perth the Blacksmith, from a character with an individual name to an allegorical character whose name and occupation are now inextricable. Although Perth's body, like the Carpenter's, eventually "rearrange[s] itself," the narrator calls attention to the violence that has accompanied Perth's reconstruction. Before becoming the Blacksmith on the *Pequod,* Perth had been "an artisan of famed excellence" (485). After battling to keep his artisanal workshop, one night he suffered "the loss of the extremities of both feet" (485). One casualty of the new economic order, among the many aboard the *Pequod,* is Perth, who has "toiled away, as if toil were life itself, and the heavy beating of his hammer the heavy beating of his heart" (484). The fabric of the work ethic is severely mangled when a complete adherence to the work ethic evidenced by Perth leads not to spiritual and economic reward but to psychic and corporeal damage. Perth's wounded body becomes the topic of conversation as Ahab observes the seabirds that follow the *Pequod* and remarks to Perth, "Thou liv'st among them without a scorch" (487). Perth responds: "I am scorched all over, Captain Ahab . . . I am past scorching; not easily can'st thou scorch a scar" (487). Like the forge at which he works, the Blacksmith's body must become scorched all over in order to accomplish its necessary tasks. Only when he is "past scorching" can he be the perfect worker who toils "as if toil were life itself" (484). No longer different from the machine that he operates, "this old man's was a patient hammer wielded by a patient arm" (484): the success of the market can be seen in the transference of agency from Perth's body to Perth's tools. The attributes of his body parts, whether they be his heavy heart or his patient arm, are now an effect not of Perth's agency but of the agency of his hammer.

Both Perth and Ahab have suffered the loss of part of their bodies because of their inability to "shade off into the surrounding infinity of things." Although Ahab describes Perth's acceptance of his own loss and subsequent limitations as "sanely woful" (487), Ahab can accept neither the instrumentalization of his own body nor the fact that he can hold no one accountable. Unlike Perth, Ahab does not learn the necessity of adaptation. Like the Carpenter, Perth's body has become purely instrumental – "No murmur, no impatience, no petulance did come from [Perth]" (484) – because the loss that once seemed to be a part of himself (his feet) has been translated into a loss outside himself. The economic system that creates the loss also provides the system with which to mourn that loss; that is, Perth's bodily wound only matters if he conceives of his body as an agent. Once his body becomes an instrument, the loss loses its personalized relation (and thus its agency/ urgency), and he can take his place as an efficient worker in the industrial workshop. On the other hand, Ahab, "impatient of all misery in others that is not mad" (487), protests against this depersonalization while at the same time he insists on instrumentalizing and depersonalizing every man on the *Pequod*. Although Ahab allegedly despises the technological apparatuses of the market economy, he nevertheless desires the power they can confer. Appropriating their power, he recapitulates the very structures of exploitation and experiences of loss he wishes to destroy – as does Melville.[39] Allegorical figures in *Moby-Dick*, like the operatives in the tartarus of maids, reveal the consequences of an industrializing market economy that Melville himself cannot help reproducing in his authorial relation to those characters. But it is only through these allegorical characters that Melville's text can begin to challenge the politics of an aesthetic ideology that wants nothing to do with such characters precisely because their mental and physical disfigurations allude to economic changes that are accompanied by great pain.

The corporeal losses experienced by Perth and Ahab are just two of the many examples of bodily mutilation in *Moby-Dick*. In fact, these characters suggest that the changing expectations for work and workers in mid-nineteenth-century America produced melancholy on a vast scale.[40] Ahab's mourning is, however, paradoxical because, while mourning his own loss, he inflicts versions of that loss upon the members of his ship. Even though he rages against his own fragmented body, he nevertheless makes the crew of the *Pequod* his own utensils and becomes, according to Michael Rogin, "the [negative] image of American hopes that technology would empower free men" (138). Like the nineteenth-century manager, Ahab first disassembles the individual bodies aboard the *Pequod* and then reconstructs them in "the *Pequod*'s organic, communal, social body" (128). Yet his own body undergoes this same process of reconstruction – and this he finds unbearable.

III. AHAB: THE MACHINE AND THE MECHANIC

In his discussion of Dürer's *Melancholia*, Benjamin notes that "the utensils of active life are lying around unused on the floor, as objects of contemplation" (140). Once active, now unused. A powerful and devastating picture of melancholy appears in the chapter "Of Whales in Paint" as Ishmael describes "a crippled beggar . . . holding a painted board before him, representing the tragic scene in which he lost his leg . . . with downcast eyes, [he] stands ruefully contemplating his own amputation" (269). In *Moby-Dick*, these "utensils of active life" are body parts; fragments of the body that were once active, but now are "objects of contemplation." Killing whales in *Moby-Dick* enacts a similar fragmentation, only this time of the cetacean body. "The utensils of [the whale's] active life" not only become the basis for "monstrous pictures of whales" (260) and oil for the lamplight, but also objects for the crew's contemplation. By mutilating the whale, the members of the *Pequod* brutally turn an agent into useful material. The dismemberment of the whale accounts for many chapters of *Moby-Dick*, and the reader is continually forced to face the bloody transformation of the whale's wholeness and omnipotence into fragmentariness and commodification.

One of the most powerful of these confrontations occurs in the chapter "Stowing Down and Clearing Up." After the whale has been cut up, sapped of its sperm oil, and enclosed in casks,

> the unmanufactured sperm oil possesses a singularly cleansing virtue. This is the reason why the decks never look so white as just after what they call an affair of oil. Besides, from the ashes of the burned scraps of the whale, a potent ley is made; and whenever any adhesiveness from the back of the whale remains clinging to the side, that ley quickly exterminates it. (428)

Here is an example, par excellence, of a living thing turned into a useful instrument offering no resistance to its own commodification: the whale has been disassembled and remade so that it offers no bodily obstacle to the whalemen. The whale even tidies up its own mess. By cleaning up after itself, the whale is made to participate in mystifying the process of its own disembodiment and eventual commodification. All evidence of labor seems to be completely erased by the whale himself/itself, except for the fact that he does not "consume his own smoke" (422). Those fumes are, of course, the final signs of the whale's life and the labor that went into destroying that life. Invisible though those fumes may be, they are all the more powerful precisely because of that invisibility. It is possible to close one's eyes, but it is impossible to stop oneself from smelling that "unspeakable, wild, Hindoo odor" (422).

Yet the whale is not the only agent turned into an instrument aboard the ship. The crew themselves, the agents of the whale's mutilation, become instruments in the factory system aboard the *Pequod*; that is, as the crew participates in the mutilation of the whale's body, their bodies also become disfigured. In *Moby-Dick*, bodies are constantly being torn apart, unmade, and remade: from Stubb, who "would almost as soon have turn[ed] out of his bunk without his nose as without his pipe" (119), to Flask, who "as a carpenter's nails . . . [was] made to clinch tight and last long" (119), to Ahab, whose "whole high, broad form, seemed made of solid bronze, and shaped in an unalterable mould, like Cellini's cast Perseus" (123). Describing the state of the crew, the narrator claims, "Alike, joy and sorrow, hope and fear, seemed ground to finest dust, and powdered, for the time, in the clamped mortar of Ahab's iron soul. Like machines, they dumbly moved about the deck, ever conscious that the old man's despot eye was on them" (536). This machinelike quality of the crew recapitulates the mechanical qualities of the more powerful Ahab.[41]

Indeed, Ahab's power is likened to the power of the machine. By "closely calculating . . . every minute atmospheric influence which it was possible for his crew to be subjected to" (213), Ahab makes sure that the workers' bodies will pose no obstacle to "the mechanical humming of the wheels of his vitality" (162). The efficiency of the whale-killing machine depends upon Ahab's control of the crew, a control that is achieved through the destruction of individual character: "All of the individualities of the crew, this man's valor, that man's fear; guilt and guiltiness, all varieties were welded into oneness, and were all directed to that fatal goal which Ahab their one lord and keel did point to" (557). In this sentence, both the crew and Ahab are instrumentalized. The words "Ahab their one lord and keel" hint at Ahab's own mechanization – one he both detests and passionately desires. This hint is fully developed in his man order to the Carpenter, in which Ahab says, "Imprimis, fifty feet high in his socks; then, chest modelled after the Thames tunnel; then, legs with roots to 'em, to stay in one place; then arms, three feet through the wrist; no heart at all, brass forehead, and about a quarter of an acre of fine brains" (470). Although Ahab hates the fact that technology (in the form of his prosthetic leg) has become necessary to his body, the man order reveals Ahab's avid desire for a complete mechanization of that body that would empower him. Ahab does not hate technology as much as he desires the power that resides in it; a power he wishes to appropriate for his wounded body.

Ahab instantiates the melancholic temper in the contemplation of his own corporeal fragmentation; that is, he sees his body becoming "the utensil of [his] active life." In his mournfulness, Ahab, who was "before [a] living agent, [but] now . . . [a] living instrument" (185), becomes a slave to the meaning that he imagines resides in Moby Dick, and, in fact, to the meaning he sees in "all visible objects" (164). Like the melancholic of Benjamin's Baroque drama, Ahab responds to his instrumentalization by resignifying the world in the form of a mask.[42] Thus Ahab, the melancholic, whose "only pleasure . . . is allegory" (185), forces worldly objects (which are essentially empty of meaning) to produce meaning. By making all objects signify, Ahab becomes the maker of meaning and can thus claim to be an agent. His dependence upon those objects to signify, however, ultimately signifies his own instrumentality. By trying to locate the place where all meaning emanates, Ahab hopes to discover and destroy what has instrumentalized him. However, the belief that Moby Dick constitutes this point of origin enslaves him from the start.

Ahab's mournfulness is, moreover, the emotional ground that makes possible the simultaneous possession and dispossession of agency that is one of the defining features of allegorical characters. Ahab's inorganic leg destabilizes his identity as a whole, organic agent. Replacing his human leg with an artificial limb destroys the categories of the human and the nonhuman, the organic and the machine, by which he had understood the world (and himself) and thus opens up all experience to a potentially endless reconfiguration of meaning. Ahab's melancholic response to this loss turns the world into a mask, and his allegory transforms the world into a machine which unceasingly makes meaning. In his famous speech on the quarterdeck, Ahab proclaims: "All visible objects, man, are but as pasteboard masks. But in each event – in the living act, the undoubted deed – there some unknown but still unreasoning thing puts forth the mouldings of its features from behind the unreasoning mask" (220). Like a machine that will not stop producing, Ahab's allegory (like Aylmer's) forces everything in the world to signify, from Moby Dick to the "veriest trifles [which] capriciously carry meanings" (237). Like workers who feel controlled and oppressed by the machines they operate, so too Ahab feels operated by the machine of his creation, whose meaning he cannot control.

Clearly Ahab wants to be the producer of meaning. Throughout much of *Moby-Dick*, he imposes his understanding of the whale and other objects in the world upon the crew. When Ahab gets himself fitted for a new leg, he finds the Carpenter and Perth at work. Noticing the white fire of Perth's forge, Ahab comments: "I do deem it now a most meaning thing, that that old Greek, Prometheus, who made men, they say, should have been a blacksmith, and animated them with fire; for what's made in fire must properly belong to fire; and so hell's probable" (470). Here Ahab's imperial language, "I do deem it now," underscores his complete control over both the occasion when something is meaningful and what that meaning is. But the final meaning produced by Ahab, "hell's proba- ble," has no clear connection to his initial point about Prometheus's being a blacksmith or to his claim that "what's made in fire must properly belong to fire," a claim that requires further elucidation to make sense. True, the conjunctions "for" and "and" suggest a logical progression of thought, but the sense of Ahab's language depends upon the control he exerts over language and the meaning he deems it to signify. This control is nowhere more vividly illustrated than when Ahab stands before the doubloon and thunderously declares, "The firm tower, that is Ahab; the volcano, that is Ahab; the courageous, the undaunted, and victorious fowl, that, too, is Ahab; all are Ahab" (431).[43]

Yet Ahab also wants meaning to produce itself; in this respect he wishes to be an instrument which receives meaning. In the chapter enti- tled "The Sphynx," Ahab pleads with the decapitated head of the whale, "Speak, thou vast and venerable head . . . speak, mighty head, and tell us the secret thing that is in thee" (311). Unlike the example of the dou- bloon, in which Ahab seeks to control meaning, here he wishes to be a receptacle for the "secret thing" within the whale's "venerable head." Ahab, as the captain of the ship, wants to destroy the resistance of his crew. Ahab, as the worker whose self-imposed task is to make meaning at what I would call the "meaning machine," wishes to be "past scorch- ing" (487); he desires the destruction of his own resistance. In the one case, he wants to be the machine that annihilates the identities of his crew, and in the other, he wants his own agency to be destroyed by the machine of meaning.

Ahab's desire to produce meaning is thus as great as his desire to take himself out of the circuit of producing meaning. He wildly vacillates between a commitment to the visibility of his own imperial labors of signification and a commitment to the logic of commodity fetishism, in which, Marx claims, "the productions of the human brain appear as independent beings endowed with life" (72). Even in the following pas- sage from "The Quarter-Deck," which one might argue can be used to illustrate Ahab's fetishizing of the whale, he acknowledges that the ma- levolence of Moby Dick is an arbitrary and interpreted, not an essential, quality: "He tasks me; he heaps me; *I see in him* outrageous strength, with an inscrutable malice sinewing it" (164; italics mine). Ahab's language acknowledges, as it were, the fact that the meaning of *Moby-Dick* is a product of his signifying labor. Ahab cannot completely surrender to the lure of commodity fetishism, because to do so would be to erase himself as lead actor, or, more precisely, only actor, in the act of making meaning. Ahab, like Hawthorne and Melville, is thus contesting a model of labor that demands an act of self-erasure. In refusing this model, Ahab adopts another that ensures the presence of his own acts of individual labor by virtue of erasing all others.[44] Clearly, he is no better off with this alternative model, because it eventuates in a literal act of self-erasure.

Ahab's body constitutes the site upon which this allegorical drama of self-erasure and the erasure of others, of reconstruction from agent to instrument, takes place. Ahab fights this reconstruction as ardently as he desires it. His resistance to the machine of meaning impels him to hold onto a conception of an organic, whole human nature which his very body denies. Once he has created this machine, he can either be the agent of its signifying potential as well as its instrument, or he can die protesting against the machine he himself has constructed.[45] The position of allegorist allows Ahab the possibility of doing both: he can exercise his power over the object while in turn conceding the power of the object over him. As allegorist, he approaches the state of the Blacksmith: he is both the agent and the instrument of meaning in a world void of meaning. He might achieve the kind of indifference displayed by the Carpenter when asked to construct Queequeg's coffin: "No sooner was the carpenter apprised of the order, than taking his rule, he forthwith with all the indifferent promptitude of his character, proceeded into the forecastle and took Queequeg's measure with great accuracy" (478). The machine and the person are not in conflict. They do not resist each other. Ahab could both operate the machine that produces the allegory and be the machine upon which allegory produces itself. In either case, the machine is and must be incorporated into his reconfiguration of agency. Although allegory provides Ahab with a way out of his dilemma, he ultimately refuses it. Ishmael, in contrast, succumbs to allegory's power and dramatizes Benjamin's description of the allegorist who "fall[s] from emblem to emblem down into the dizziness of its bottomless depths" (232). Unlike Ahab, Ishmael recognizes his instrumental relationship to the machine of meaning and attempts to exploit that relationship.

Ahab and Ishmael each have a distinctly different position vis-à-vis the machine of meaning.[46] This difference is powerfully elucidated in the relation each character has to his name. "To be called Ahab," Dimock convincingly argues, "is to inhabit a narrative tautology, in which the ending is already immanent in the beginning, and in which all temporal development merely reenacts what is in place from the very first."[47] In contrast to Ahab, who Captain Peleg reminds us "did not name himself" (79), the narrator of *Moby-Dick* begins his narrative with an act of self-naming. It is significant that he does not choose just any name but one from the Bible. As he appears in Genesis, Ishmael is fated not only to be an outcast but a violent man as well: "His hand will be against every man, and every man's hand against him" (Genesis 16:12). True, the nineteenth-century American Ishmael becomes an outcast like the Ishmael of the Bible, but Ishmael's friendship with Queequeg and the intimacy Ishmael shares with his mates in the famous chapter "A Squeeze of the Hand" suggest that the Ishmael of *Moby-Dick* produces a narrative different from the one we might have expected from a character named Ishmael. More-over, this act of self-naming radically departs from the tradition of the self-made man who names himself, because the name Ishmael, like the name Ahab, carries with it an entire history of religious significance and textual authority. In deciding upon this name, then, the narrator of *Moby-Dick* is immediately a receptacle of the meanings invoked by "Ishmael." He at once possesses agency by naming himself and is dispossessed of individual agency by bearing the signifying weight of the name of Ishmael.

Through the character of Ishmael, Melville reconfigures literary labor as at once an individual and collective, a centered and disseminated, enter-prise. To the extent that Ishmael takes upon himself the literary burden of authoring a "systematization of cetology" (136), it makes sense to read his way of going about such a project as an allegory of Melville's own literary labors in constructing *Moby-Dick*. In contrast to Oh-Oh, the book collec-tor of *Mardi* who fails to mention the authors whose books fill his antiquar-ian library, the "Extracts" section of *Moby-Dick* is a moving homage to authorial labor. Quotation after quotation, all having to do with whale sightings or whale lore, records not only the continued interest in whales through the ages but also the vast number of literary laborers who devoted their energies to compiling and constructing such records. In the tradition of the Homeric catalogue of ships, here we have a catalogue of authors' names. The extracts suggest that Melville's authority as author depends upon this community of writers even as that authority is simultaneously undermined through parody. The presence of this community is continu-ally foregrounded throughout the text and most visibly in "Cetology," where Ishmael acknowledges that his own cetological taxonomy will have "to be filled in all its departments by subsequent laborers" (136) and later confesses, "This whole book is but a draught – nay, but the draught of a draught" (145), presumably to be completed by future writers.

In making visible Ishmael's labor, Melville foregrounds his own indi-vidual labor. As readers of *Moby-Dick* have noted, Ishmael ceaselessly calls attention to himself as a writer, particularly in "The Affidavit," where he acknowledges, "I care not to perform this part of my task methodically" (203) or "I do not know where I can find a better place than just here, to make mention of one or two other things, which to me seem important" (205).[48] This self-consciousness reaches its pinnacle in Ishmael's remarks about the uses to which a certain layer of dead whale skin can be put: "I have several such dried bits, which I use for marks in my whale-books. It is transparent, as I said before; and being laid upon the printed page, I have sometimes pleased myself with fancying it exerted a magnifying influence. At any rate, it is pleasant to read about whales through their own spectacles, as you may say. But what I am driving at here is this" (305–6). This passage seems especially interesting in that, like reviews of Melville (and like the article from the *New York Review*), which featured a scene of literary labor, here Melville includes a scene of the labor of reading and, more particularly, a tableau of reading a whale book not unlike *Moby-Dick*. The scene of reading is here imagined not in terms of the words on the page but rather in terms of the object (or former subject) used, in this case whale skin, to magnify the words on the page. Ishmael is not being a good reader in the conventional sense, because he gets caught up in a reading of the whale skin – the mechanism that is supposed to make the task of reading easier. Although the whale skin is transparent, its transparency (like the blankness of the operatives in the tartarus of maids) tells a very powerful story if readers are willing to read it. Ishmael's reading leads to a confrontation with an entire economy that has turned the whale into a magnifying glass. This story of the whale's disembodiment, moreover, is hard, even painful to read – as is *Moby-Dick*, as is the very passage describing the scene of reading: "That same infinitely thin, isinglass substance, which, I admit, invests the entire body of the whale, is not so much to be regarded as the skin of the creature, as the skin of the skin, so to speak; for it were simply ridiculous to say, that the proper skin of the tremendous whale is thinner and more tender than the skin of a new-born child. But no more of this" (306). Perhaps the magnifying glass will make the reader's labor less onerous. More important, however, is the difficulty of the passage itself. The work the reader must do in making her way through the self-referentiality, the repetitive diction, and the halting prose suggests both the laborer who writes such prose and the laborer who reads it. Ishmael's writing makes visible not only the economy that has turned the whale into a transparent magnifying glass but also the economy that tries to turn Melville into a transparent, invisible author. The visible labors of Melville's allegory, in other words, make visible the allegory of labor (literary and nonliterary) in antebellum America.

Ahab is one possible outcome of Shaw's *Farwell* and *Albro* decisions and the market economy logic that informed them. Ishmael is another. Shaw upheld individual accountability, to the detriment of individuals and the benefit of companies that were, like Bildad's and Peleg's, "part owners and agents." Whereas Ahab illustrates the results of this decision taken to its most extreme position, Ishmael avoids Ahab's demise not by simply reascribing accountability to the market economy but rather by challeng-

ing the very foundation upon which accountability rested – individual
agency. Without an individual, Shaw's notion of accountability is invalid.
Ishmael's notion of labor, which constitutes individual labor as always
already genealogical, radically differs from Ahab's. Whereas Ahab's dedication to the visibility of his own labor means the erasure of others' labors
and the assumption of individual accountability, Ishmael's adherence to
the principle of visible labor means the foregrounding of *all* labor and
laborers and the (utopian) dissemination of individual accountability. And
this, I take it, is the function of Ishmael's frequent invocation of historical
communities, whether it be the genealogy of texts in "The Extracts" out of
which *Moby-Dick* is produced or the community of whales in "The Grand
Armada," from which the community of workers on the *Pequod* gets its
oil. Accountability is thus no longer the burden of individual agents, who
in Ishmael's configuration of labor exist only in relation to a community of
laborers, but the burden of everyone. If accountability is disseminated,
even the Boston and Worcester Railroad and the Agawam Canal Company
will have to accept some responsibility.

IV. BILLY BUDD *AND "BENITO CERENO": INSIDE* NARRATIVES FROM THE OUTSIDE

With the exception of *Mardi*, *Billy Budd* is Melville's most
overtly allegorical text. A list of characters' names suffices to make the
point: Billy Budd is designated the "Handsome Sailor," Captain Vere is
called "Starry Vere," Claggart is referred to as "Jemmy Legs," and then
there are the Dansker and Red Whiskers. Such names would seem to
imply that unreal people or allegorical types populate the fictional world
of *Billy Budd*, disconnecting Melville's final text from anything remotely
historical.[49] I want to argue precisely the opposite; that is, the mechanicalness, flatness, and what we might call "surfaceness" of allegorical characters register Melville's attempt to separate himself from those disciplinary
structures that deploy individual agency and, more specifically, interiority as the foundation for social order. A belief in Melville's interiority,
after all, was the basis upon which literary critics constructed an image of
Melville as an "aimless" and "listless" literary laborer. Take away this
foundation and maybe one could be safe from such intrusions. As was the
case in *Moby-Dick*, the legal system is seen to be an especially powerful
locus wherein the category of interiority is strategically deployed and
persons are subsequently disciplined. In illustrating the ways in which
Billy Budd relies on and challenges constructions of interiority that are
historically specific to late-nineteenth-century American legal discourse,
this section juxtaposes Billy's trial with the Haymarket trial of 1886, in
which the discourse of interiority was used to convict the Haymarket

rioters of anarchy. The legal manipulations in *Billy Budd*, like those in the Haymarket trial, aimed at disciplining unruly bodies, whether they be anarchists' bodies, and the uncontrolled body politic they represented, or Billy's body. A reading of Haymarket, moreover, permits us to see the extent to which *Billy Budd* is imbricated in not only legal discourse but the discourses of labor and scientific management as well. The allegorical characters of *Billy Budd* are set, like "The Birth-mark" to which it alludes, in the eighteenth century and thus not only look ahead to a modern world of systemic management but simultaneously refer back to an archaic world, "the time before steamships."[50] The archaic layering calls attention to the profound differences between Melville's economics of allegory and allegory in its earlier incarnation. Thus, when seen in relation to Melville's own history with readers and the history of late-nineteenth-century constructions of personhood, the allegorical characters of *Billy Budd*, in their very absence of interiority, signal Melville's desire to avoid experiencing and inflicting the psychic and bodily pains that, for Melville, characterize the ideological space of interiority.

From the very start of *Billy Budd, Sailor (An Inside Narrative)*, whose subtitle, "an inside narrative," is itself inside parentheses, the knowledge of Billy's insides is invoked and deferred. This issue of insides is powerfully foregrounded by the Purser and the Surgeon in their discussion of the unusual absence of motion that follows Billy's hanging. In short, they try to explain why Billy didn't ejaculate.[51] This scene, to which I shall return later, merely stages yet again what has been a recurring feature in the text – the attempt to get at Billy's insides. The earliest example of this occurs while Billy is packing his belongings and preparing to join the crew of the *Bellipotent*. The captain of the *Rights of Man* shares with Lieutenant Ratcliffe, the officer of the *Bellipotent* responsible for Billy's impressment, some stories about Billy: "In the second dogwatch one day, the Red Whiskers in presence of the others, under pretense of showing Billy just whence a sirloin steak was cut – for the fellow had once been a butcher – insultingly gave him a dig under the ribs" (47). Billy responds to this violation of corporeal boundaries with a violation of his own as he "let[s] fly his arm" (47), although this blow, unlike the one that proves fatal to Claggart, does not seriously injure Red Whiskers.

We have, of course, witnessed before this digging under the ribs in *Moby-Dick*, with whale meat for the sirloin steak, whalemen for butchers, and the cetacean body for Billy's body. And just as the anthropological digging in *Moby-Dick* required a whale corpse and produced very little knowledge from it, such digging has similar results in *Billy Budd*. Furthermore, the importance of digging, corporeal violation, and lost knowledge is confirmed by the fact that of all of the Hawthorne stories to which Melville might have alluded in *Billy Budd* (one thinks of "Rappaccini's

Daughter" and "My Kinsman, Major Molineux"), he cites "The Birth-mark." Just as the circulating economy of Georgiana's body expresses itself through the oscillations of the birthmark, Billy's "dimples . . . mys-teriously form in the cheek, silently coming and going there . . . a serene happy light born of some wandering reminiscence or dream [that] would diffuse itself over his face, and then wane away only anew to return" (119–20). And just as Aylmer wishes to gaze upon and discipline these oscillations by limiting Georgiana's physical movements to a chamber of his own devising, the comings and goings of Billy's facial colorations are the only signs of circulation that exist once his body has been placed "lying prone in irons in one of the bays formed by the regular spacing of the guns comprising the batteries on either side" (118).

The attention to surfaces is apparent, for example, as the narrator contentedly comments upon Billy's complexion, in which, "thanks to his sea-going, the lily was quite suppressed and the rose had some ado visi-bly to flush through the tan" (50) or says that "he was soon at home in the service, not at all disliked for his unpretentious good looks and a sort of genial happy-go-lucky air" (49). Unlike Aylmer, the narrator of *Billy Budd* never tires of simply remarking upon "the rose-tan in [Billy's] cheek" (77). At other times, the narrator invokes the language of interior-ity while refusing to enter into Billy's consciousness: "The moral nature was seldom out of keeping with the physical make. Indeed, except as toned by the former, the comeliness and power, always attractive in masculine conjunction, hardly could have drawn the sort of honest hom-age the Handsome Sailor in some examples received from his less gifted associates" (44). How the interior workings of Billy's body are repre-sented, whether from the inside or the outside, is a crucial narrative problem in *Billy Budd*.[52] Getting inside Billy seems to yoke an act of negative homoeroticism with the construction of interiority. The narra-tor avoids this dangerous conjunction by exteriorizing Billy and situating his own depiction of Billy at the specular borders of homoeroticism. Throughout the text he insists upon remaining at the surfaces of Billy's body even though he claims that his story is "restricted . . . to the inner life of one particular ship and the career of an individual sailor" (54). Because interiority functions as the strategic category that ultimately dooms Billy, the narrator prefers to remain on the outside. Melville prefers not to "impress" Billy. He prefers not to imprint or mark the surfaces of Billy's body in the way the paper manufactured by the tar-tarus of maids was imprinted with a rose, nor does he wish to force Billy into narrative (or naval, as is the case with Vere) service.

Claggart, on the other hand, is committed both to the military strategy of impressment and the notion of characterological depth. We might even think of him as a literary critic who deploys a fiction of depth, knowing full well what he will find when the depths are plumbed. In flagrant contrast to the narrator, Claggart warns Vere that Billy conceals "a man-trap . . . under the ruddy-tipped daisies [of his cheeks]" or that he is "a deep one" (94). Claggart's words suggest that Billy *must* have an inside potentially at odds with the surfaces of his body. The idea of depth, which posits an interiority at odds with Billy's "youth and good looks" (94), fuels the legal machinery that is used to discipline the surfaces of Billy's body and to convict him of mutiny if necessary. Presumably, by countering depth with superficiality, interiority with exteriority, Billy could effectively challenge Claggart's position. But by making Billy and his world completely mechanical and narrating that world from the exterior, Melville's text reveals that Claggart's appeal to Billy's interiority is merely a fiction that provides him the necessary excuse to get the disciplinary machine going, a machine that Vere himself is only too happy to keep running. It is not the case that the narrator denies Billy interiority; he just won't try to represent it, for to represent it would be to reproduce the kind of violations committed by Claggart and Vere.[53]

The problematics of inside and outside, of intention and act, also determined the fate of the self-proclaimed anarchists at Haymarket. What it came down to was not who actually threw the bomb that killed a number of policemen (to this day we still do not know) but rather who had the intent to do so. Interiority became the vehicle for prosecuting and hanging the anarchists. What became the Haymarket affair started out as a protest against a police force that had killed striking workers at the McCormick Harvester factory on May 4, 1886. The next day, a group of 3,000 people committed to the eight-hour day were gathered to hear their leaders speak on behalf of workers' rights, and Captain John Bonfield of the Chicago police force ordered the crowd to disperse. A bomb was then hurled toward the police, killing several members of the police force, which responded by opening fire on the restive crowd, killing and wounding at least 200.[54] The riot resulted in the arrest of several self-proclaimed anarchists, the suicide of one, and the hanging of four of them.

The history of the Haymarket trial includes one appalling breach of protocol after another. In his history of the riots, the trial, and its aftermath, Paul Avrich notes, "The state exhibited bombs, fulminating caps, shells, melting-ladles, and other paraphernalia of the dynamiter's craft, although they had not been traced to any of the defendants."[55] Years later, Captain Frederick Ebersold, Chicago chief of police, conceded that Captain Schaack, chief investigator of the Haymarket affair, "deliberately set about organizing anarchist societies and planted bombs and ammunition at these organizations."[56] Historian Henry David confirms this in the following account: "Newspapers published details of impossible plots and conspiracies which Schaack, the master-detective, had uncovered. Most of the bombs were either non-existent or had been planted by the police."[57] When all of the evidence had been heard, the plaintiffs were unable to prove the identity of the bomb thrower, thus making it "impossible to determine his motives or to show that he had known the defendants or read any of their writings or heard any of their speeches."[58] Nevertheless, Judge Gary advised the jury that the identity of the bomb thrower was irrelevant. All they needed to consider was whether or not the defendants "by print or speech advised, or encouraged the commission of murder, without designating time, place or occasion at which it should be done, and in pursuance of, and induced by such advice and encouragement, murder was committed, then all of such conspirators are guilty of such murder, whether the person who perpetrated such murder can be identified or not."[59] The fact that the anarchists often referred to themselves as heirs to John Brown, another infamous anarchist in nineteenth-century American culture, did not help matters.[60] Doing away with the complicated matter of the bomb thrower's identity radically altered the trial. Gary advised the jurors to consider only the consequences of the occurrences at Haymarket and whether or not the individuals had ever expressed intentions whose effects were realized at Haymarket. In his final address to the jury, defendant Samuel Fielden claimed, "If I had known that I was being tried for Anarchy I could have answered that charge. I could have justified it under the constitution. . . . I was told that I was to be hung for being an Anarchist, after I got through defending myself on the charge of murder."[61]

Seven years later, after all but one of the defendants had been hung, Illinois governor John Altgeld pardoned the Haymarket rioters and maintained that "the evidence utterly fails to show that the man who did throw [the bomb] ever heard or read a word coming from the defendants."[62] It was obvious that the accused men never received a fair trial. Not only had Judge Gary ensured a guilty verdict through his final instructions to the jury, he also allowed prejudiced jurors to serve on the case. Juryman Theodore Denker had announced before the trial, "The whole damn crowd ought to be hanged." Special bailiff Henry Ryce had confided to one of the prospective jurors, "I am managing this case, and know what I am about. These fellows are going to be hanged as certain as death."[63] That the method of choosing a jury was illegal can be further deduced from Judge Gary's Vere-like confession in 1893, "If I had a little *strained the law* . . . I was to be commended for so doing."[64]

Melville had, of course, been interested in such legal strainings well before he wrote *Billy Budd*. In *Moby-Dick*, he had parodically undermined legal authority in "The Affidavit." In "Bartleby the Scrivener," he had savagely exposed the legal profession as a paternalistic institution that required its workers to engage in labor that was a waste of time. But it is the critique of law in "Benito Cereno," as well as the narrator's representation (or lack thereof) of interiority, that speaks most directly to my reading of *Billy Budd*. This story of slave mutiny, we recall, is perhaps best characterized by an excruciating degree of hermeneutic uncertainty (which takes place in a *Mardi*-like calm) both for Captain Amasa Delano and Melville's readers. A particularly compelling example of interpretative difficulty occurs when Delano first sees Babo and Benito and notes how, "like a shepherd's dog, he mutely turned [his face] up into the Spaniard's [so that] sorrow and affection were equally blended."[65] Delano assumes that since Babo looks subservient, he is. Although Delano can imagine Benito "playing a part" (64), he will not permit himself to imagine that Babo himself might be a "wicked imposture" (64). But Babo and Benito are not the only ones who may or may not be playing a part in this early scene. The narrator's simile "like a shepherd's dog" suggests that the reader must beware of the narrator, whose "craft . . . [might] at present, be of a piratical character" (68). Is the narrator using this simile to convey Delano's attitude toward blacks, or might the narrator himself harbor this unflattering opinion of blacks (and if so, how might this affect the accuracy with which he reports Delano's thoughts?), or might he be trapping the reader into admitting her own ideological and racist complicity in the events aboard the *San Dominick*?[66]

The language of the text continually posits Delano's desire to equate exteriority with interiority and then challenges that desire by introducing the possibility of their disjunction. Although he acknowledges this disjunction in the case of Captain Cereno, Delano believes that he doesn't have to worry about the interiority of slaves, not because they don't have any but because he knows out of what it is constituted – "pure tenderness and love" (73), possessing "a certain easy cheerfulness, harmonious in every glance and gesture" (83). But the theatricality of "Benito Cereno" relentlessly foregrounds the potential divide between interiority and exteriority. In an early scene, for example, Delano waits for his boat to deliver supplies to the decrepit Spanish ship. As his boat moves farther and farther away, disappearing into the "leaden ocean [that] seemed laid out and leaded up, its course finished, soul gone, defunct" (78), Delano grows impatient, and his eyes begin to wander "as from a stage-box into the pit, upon the strange crowd before and below him" (78). The theatrical simile allows the narrator to intimate ironically that Delano is, in fact, watching a play and that his role on the *San Dominick* is that of audience or reader. If Delano is indeed witnessing a play, Babo must be some kind of impostor, wicked or otherwise.

The similes and metaphors are the most effective means used to install a chasm between interiority and exteriority. The overwhelmingly figurative language of the text foregrounds the fact of representation and potential disjunction. In the following scene, for example, Babo comments upon Benito's punishment of Atufal: " 'How like a mute Atufal moves,' murmured the servant. The black mounted the steps of the poop, and, like a brave prisoner, brought up to receive sentence, stood in unquailing muteness before Don Benito. . . . This is some mulish mutineer, thought Captain Delano" (61–2). In this scene, Delano believes that Benito has authority over Atufal. Because he believes what he sees, Delano assumes that Atufal is being punished for wrongdoings and even asks Benito to "remit him his penalty" (63).[67]

Melville's refusal to give us an interior view of the slaves aboard the *San Dominick* creates a cast of allegorical characters, all of whom, according to Rogin, "perform static, ritualized motions which, unlike genuine rituals, shut out meaning instead of embodying it."[68] These static rituals do not so much exclude meaning in "Benito Cereno" as embody the possibility of meanings at one and the same time. Because we never get inside the consciousness of the characters performing the rituals, we can never be sure about their status as genuine or not. Allegorical characters, as I have been claiming, instantiate the most exterior kind of characterization imaginable even as they allude to a knowledge of interiority. Thus, in remaining outside the slave consciousness, "Benito Cereno" focuses attention on exteriority and, in particular, the black body.

Whereas *Billy Budd* attends to the multiple significations of workers' bodies, this text "places special privilege on the bodies of the blacks."[69] Black bodies, like workers' bodies, were sites of ideological struggle as northern industrialists, southern slave owners, and slaves themselves battled to control the meanings of their bodies. Citing the United States Census as evidence for his proslavery position, John C. Calhoun argued, "In all instances in which the States have changed the former relation between the two races [from slaveholding to nonslaveholding] . . . [Africans] have been invariably sunk into vice and pauperism . . . deafness, blindness, insanity and idiocy."[70] Using the same language for their antislavery position, health reformers feared that the rampant sexuality of the South would lead to "idiocy, insanity, disfigurement of body, and imbecility of mind."[71] The most interesting image of the black body appears in an 1850 issue of the *Southern Quarterly Review* in which the language used to characterize the problem with the black body is the language of allegory. The "problem" with the black body, it would seem, is its allegorical quality: "The muscles and the limbs still move, without their natural nerves and sinews, by the artificial and spasmodic agency of an extrinsic influence."[72] An exterior and artificial agency, what Fletcher would call the allegorical "daimon," operates to control the black body. By getting into the inside, one could presumably make "natural" (or white) the "artificial" (or black) agent. Melville does not so much deny interiority to the slaves as he refuses to depict it, because to do so would be to take away the power that resides on surfaces. The interiority of allegorical characters in "Benito Cereno" is everywhere suggested and nowhere confirmed. This absence of represented interiority is, I think, the source of Babo's power, the narrator's power, and Melville's as well – a power that Melville will deploy, once again, in *Billy Budd*.

Furthermore, these examples illustrate that the language of "Benito Cereno" produces such excesses of meaning that the din of competing significations makes it impossible to determine which meaning is the true one. Of course, no one true meaning exists, even though the legal language of the depositions suggests otherwise. These legal documents, which are meant to correct "*the fictitious story dictated to the deponent by Babo, and through the deponent imposed upon Captain Delano*" (110), fail to explore why there was a mutiny in the first place. Sundquist writes about the deposition, "The language of the court and the coldblooded documents of history cannot fully *contain*" what has occurred aboard the *San Dominick*, and his argument is supported by the fact that the legal depositions do not conclude Melville's text.[73] Even though the court hearings occur last in the history of the events, "Benito Cereno" ends with a conversation between Delano and Benito and, more precisely, with the twinned images of Babo's head and "the recovered bones of Aranda" (117). Although Babo is silenced at the end of the story by death, his silence relentlessly produces meaning through the voice of the narrator. Far from containing the significance and significations of the mutiny, the legal depositions only produce more. The attempt to exclude history, specifically the history of the African slave trade, is itself the clearest marker of history.

It would seem to be the case that Vere's manipulation of the law, like the legal depositions in "Benito Cereno," is an attempt to interpret history, and in particular the history of the Great Mutiny, so as to contain the potentially ambiguous significations of Billy's actions vis-à-vis Claggart. Even the narrator of *Billy Budd* raises the twinned issues of history and law when commenting upon certain "views of policy" (55) that had been taken during the crisis of the Great Mutiny and had been "shade[d] . . . off into the historical background" (55). "Such events," he acknowledges, "cannot be ignored, but there is a considerate way of historically treating them" which means refraining from "blazoning aught amiss or calamitous" (55). Clearly, *Billy Budd* does not blazon anything (its use of negatives and passive-voice constructions often makes for painfully obscure sentences), but it does exemplify the cultural logic and legal gerrymanderings that sanction the hangings not only of Billy Budd but of the Haymarket rioters as well.[74]

Indeed, recent critics of *Billy Budd* have carefully detailed Vere's blatant manipulation of the law.[75] Vere "deviat[es] from general custom" (104) in a number of particulars. For example, instead of "postpon[ing] further action in so extraordinary a case to such time as they should rejoin the squadron" (101), he immediately calls for a drumhead court. Convincing himself that he "would not be at variance with usage" if he "elect[ed] the individuals composing [the drumhead court]" (104), Vere selects an officer of marines, a sea lieutenant, and a sailing master. *A Collection of the Statutes Relating to the Admiralty, Navy, Shipping, and Navigation* reveals that not only had the British navy made no provisions for a drumhead court in such unusual circumstances but that "regular naval court-martials consisted of commanders and captains."[76] Like the prosecutor of the Haymarket case who argued, "Gentlemen of the jury; convict these men, make examples of them, hang them and you save our institutions, our society,"[77] Vere reminds the drumhead court that "to the people the foretopman's deed, however it be worded in the announcement, will be plain homicide committed in a flagrant act of mutiny. What penalty for that should follow, they know" (112). Of course this statement is untrue. Billy's actions will be perceived as "a flagrant act of mutiny" only if Vere presents them as such. Vere's rhetoric throughout the trial reveals precisely the opposite of what he says here; that is, "the words in the announcement" will construct Billy's innocence or guilt, not vice versa. Echoing Gary's advice to the jury, Vere's final injunction to the drumhead court, "Budd's intent or non-intent is nothing to the purpose" (112), ensures a guilty verdict. In an inversion of Judge Gary's instructions, which stresses the anarchic "intent or non-intent" of the Chicago eight, as opposed to their actions, Vere insists that the drumhead consider only Budd's actions, his "intent or non-intent" being irrelevant to their decision. Although Gary stressed intent and Vere action, both men did away with the complications of the case, complications effected by either not considering intent or considering intent, and manipulated the jurors to get the desired verdict.

V. CONTEXTUALIZED BODIES

Billy's final words, "God bless Captain Vere" (123), both affirm and ironically subvert Vere's official code. Billy, the worker, who "made no demur" (45) when impressed into naval service, blesses his executioner. More interesting, perhaps, is the issue of Billy's body, which remains just the least bit untamed, even though it has been domesticated through the legalistic, humanistic, and scientific discourses of Vere, the Purser, and the Surgeon. The "absence of spasmodic movement" (125), as the narrator calls it, ends up producing an excess of meaning. His body remains untamed enough to evoke a "murmur" (126) among the crew which makes Vere realize "the necessity for unusual action" (128). What calls for such unusual action on Vere's part is the unusual inaction of Billy's body; that is, the fact that he doesn't ejaculate. What is inside never gets outside, and what is "natural" remains invisible. Billy's body remains consistently impenetrable, or, more precisely, unpenetrated by the narrator.

Billy's body, however, like Babo's head in "Benito Cereno," "cast[s] such a shadow" (116) over *Billy Budd*, complicating the text in a way that Gary's instructions attempted to uncomplicate the hangings of the Chicago anarchists. The clearest example of the body's conflicting significa- tion occurs in the discussion that follows Billy's hanging. The Purser and the Surgeon analyze why "no motion was apparent" (124) when Billy was hanged. When the Purser suggests that the lack of movement is a "testi- mony to the force lodged in will power" (124), the Surgeon responds:

> Your pardon, Mr. Purser. In a hanging scientifically conducted – and under special orders I myself directed how Budd's was to be effected – any movement following the completed suspension and originating in the body suspended, such movement indicates mechanical spasm in the muscular system. Hence the absence of that is no more attributable to will power, as you call it, than to horsepower – begging your pardon. (124–5)

Like Vere, for whom "measured forms are everything" (128), the scien- tist accepts only measurable information. Data about personality, such as Billy's willpower, is labeled "imaginative and metaphysical" (125) and dismissed. Just as we see Vere pare down the potential complexities of Billy's actions in order to act within the parameters of martial law, the scientist similarly reconstructs Billy's body through the language of "me- chanical spasm" and "horsepower" in order to discipline, according to scientific law, the complexities of the hanging. Although the Purser and the Surgeon differently "read" the unusual absence of motion in Billy's body at the moment of the hanging, both men participate in what Fou- cault has called "a 'mechanics of power' . . . [which] defined how one may have a hold over others' bodies."[78] On the one hand, the Purser argues that the "absence of spasmodic movement" (125) denotes will- power, while on the other hand, the Surgeon does not "pretend to ac- count for it at all" (125). The Purser's perspective relies on the existence of Billy's interiority, which was Claggart's strategy in formulating the theory of Billy's mutinous intentions. The Surgeon's rhetoric, although claiming not to give an account of "an appearance the cause of which is not immediately to be assigned" (125), nevertheless culminates in the scientific domination of Billy's body which "produces subjected and practised bodies, 'docile' bodies."[79]

Melville gives us a very good idea of what these persons and their bodies might look like. The characters in *Billy Budd* are distinctively allegorical, peculiarly inorganic. Even Billy, who has been described as "one of Nature's innocents" or "the vital urge incarnate," seems as much a product of art as of nature.[80] The completely anatural world of the *Bellipotent* functions to reveal how "nature" gets used to control its crew. The story takes place in a world of mechanically produced people:

> Every sailor, too, is accustomed to obey orders without debating them; his life afloat is externally ruled for him; he is not brought into that promiscuous commerce with mankind where unobstructed free agency on equal terms – equal superficially, at least – soon teaches one that unless upon occasion he exercise a distrust keen in proportion to the fairness of the appearance, some foul turn may be served him. A ruled undemonstrative distrustfulness is so habitual, not with businessmen so much as with men who know their kind in less shallow relations than business, namely, certain men of the world, that they come at last to employ it all but unconsciously; and some of them would very likely feel real surprise at being charged with it as one of their general characteristics. (87)

In this description everyone is constructed by a code, whether it be the martial law which dictates the identity of the sailors aboard the *Bellipotent* or the code of "undemonstrative distrustfulness" which constitutes the identity of even those men who participate in "less shallow relations than business." Such codes are essential, because without them people might naively assume that "unobstructed free agency" is something good and true, something about which one does not have to be profoundly distrustful. This quotation also reveals the constructed codes through which people organize their lives and which are fundamental to one's self-representation. Because they remain invisible to "men of the world," who "come at last to employ [them] all but unconsciously," they "very likely feel real surprise" when confronted with the artificiality of (what had seemed to be) their nature. The narrator depicts Billy as "cast in a mold . . . which the Greek sculptor in some instances gave to his heroic strong man, Hercules" (51). The laborers aboard the *Bellipotent* mechanically obey their masters. After Billy's hanging, a temporary glitch in the routine, the sailors respond with an "impulse whose operation at the official word of command much resembles in its promptitude the effect of an instinct" (127). As a unit, they function so efficiently aboard the *Bellipotent* that the narrator finds it "not necessary here to particularize" (63) any other crew members besides Claggart. Even though the workers aboard the *Bellipotent*, a military machine "fed with the oil supplied by war contractors" (119), appear perfectly obedient, the narrative of the text is nevertheless based on the supposed mutinous intention of the sailors.

The categories of interiority and nature, as we have seen in the Haymarket trial and *Billy Budd*, permit workers' bodies to be read as resistant and therefore fuel the cultural machinery which then disciplines those bodies. This strategy, though, is a phenomenon specific to late-nineteenth-century American culture, and it is especially enlightening to analyze Melville's construction of fictional character in the context of late-nineteenth-century debates about workers' bodies. In stark contrast to labor reformers and management spokespersons, who were united in their commitment to the categories of interiority and the "natural," *Billy Budd* is committed to a notion of allegorical character because these are precisely the categories that are deployed to discipline bodies. Only when read in the context of this debate about workers' bodies can one see how radical the complete lack of interiority and distinct unnaturalness of Melville's characters actually was.

Labor reformer Henry George, for example, advocated an oppositional stance toward industrialization based on the belief that machinery prohibits workers from gaining the potential rewards of the work ethic as well as developing into anything other than mindless addenda to their machines: its "tendency . . . [is] not merely to place [everything] out of the power of the workman to become his own employer, but to reduce him to the position of a mere attendant or feeder."[81] George positions the worker's "natural" body against the machine's "artificial" constitution. Similarly, Henry D. Lloyd argues that "through the body only can [workers] approach the higher realms of truth; they therefore believe the body to be as sacred as the soul, and that if one is to be holy the other must be whole."[82] Lloyd's religious language alerts us to the nostalgic element inherent in certain labor reformers' appeals to workers' rights. It is significant that we are, once again, in the realm of the Coleridgean symbol as both George and Lloyd critique industrialization on the ground that it prohibits transcendence to "the higher realms of truth" and prevents workers from being "whole." This antagonism to industrialization is, of course, voiced in the same language that Coleridge, as well as nineteenth-century literary critics, had used to critique allegory.

Labor commissioner Carroll Wright advocates the use of machinery precisely on the ground that it leads to an increased opportunity for character development. Thus, unlike those who worried about the anesthetizing effects of machinery on workers, he claimed that "machinery [was] constantly lifting men out of low into high grades of employment [and] constantly surrounding them with an intellectual atmosphere."[83] Wright further argues that "factories are . . . the legitimate outgrowth of the universal tendency to association which is inherent in our nature, and by the development of which every advance in human improvement and human happiness has been gained" (93). Wright's organicist rhetoric also appears in the work of Washington Gladden, religious spokesperson for the necessity of integrating morality and economic progress, who claimed that "improvement of implements and machinery [was] one powerful means not only of ameliorating the physical condition of laboring man, but also of cultivating his intellect."[84] Far from hampering the development of individual character according to the paradigm of the work ethic, machinery brings out the best in the workers' natures. After all, machines "are the handiwork of God . . . [like] the flowers and the grains that grow on the face of the earth" (14–15). His argument is based on maintaining the naturalness of the worker's nature under factory conditions and on naturalizing machinery itself. Moreover, Gladden's discourse aestheticizes, sanctifies, and naturalizes machinery in the same way that Lloyd and George were attempting to aestheticize, sanctify, and naturalize workers' bodies. Of course George and Lloyd would have seen themselves in opposition to the opinions of Wright and Gladden. Both sides, however, share one important rhetorical technique: the use of "nature" as a strategy for bolstering their positions.[85]

By dispensing with any pretense of the workers' naturalness, Melville's text undercuts arguments like these that rely on the immutability of the worker's nature in their attempts to reconstruct that nature through mechanization. Characterization in *Billy Budd* is contingent upon a fundamental "unnaturalness" that exposes the category of nature as a straw man with which Vere permits himself the opportunity to execute his power. By destabilizing the categories of the natural and the artificial, Melville exposes the basis upon which those in power excuse themselves for disempowering others. The term nature is used so often in *Billy Budd* that its meaning is quickly seen to be wholly arbitrary. This is precisely Melville's point. Vere's orchestration of the trial effectively deploys the category of nature as he reminds the members of the drumhead court that they have "ceased to be natural free agents" because "martial law [is] operating through" (110) them. The categories of nature and interiority here converge as Vere presents a model of interiority that can be manipulated, depending upon whether or not a particular situation requires an "allegiance . . . to Nature" or "to the King" (110). The notion that this allegiance to nature is somehow more valid, more "natural" than the allegiance to the king is shown to be a fiction, because the term nature itself undergoes so many permutations. When, for example, Vere speaks to the illegally formed jury that will decide Billy's fate, he assures them that "did he know our hearts, I take him to be of that generous nature that he would feel even for us on whom in this military necessity so heavy a compulsion is laid" (113). The deployment of Billy's "generous nature" is tactical and effective. It comes precisely at the moment when Vere is about to leave the jurors so that they can make their decision. Vere gets the desired verdict. The best example of the arbitrary meaning of "nature" appears in the narrator's account of Claggart: "In a list of definitions included in the authentic translation of Plato, a list attributed to him, occurs this: 'Natural Depravity: a depravity according to nature'" (75). The fear that the worker's "nature" will arise and protest its mechanized condition allows those in power to anticipate the mutiny which then permits the exercise of authority. Both men fear "what sailors are" (112); that is, what their nature is. But their nature is, of course, constructed by these "Benthamites of War" (57) who have erected a Panopticon-like structure on the *Bellipotent* and will not "tolerat[e] an infraction of discipline" (60). Even though Vere has no reason to believe Claggart's accusation against Billy and claims that he will not "permit himself to be unduly disturbed by the general tenor of his subordinate's report" (93), once the charge is articulated, the martial machinery begins to move – all because of "what sailors are." Whether or not Billy committed the crime makes no difference. A "real" mutiny and a "fictional" mutiny become the same thing. Vere makes this point while admonishing the judges: "Your clement sentence they would account pusillanimous. They would think that we flinch, that we are afraid of them – afraid of practicing a lawful rigor singularly demanded at this juncture, lest it should provoke new troubles. What shame to us such a conjecture on their part, and how deadly to discipline" (113). Those in power must respond to an alleged mutiny the same way they would react to an actual one. And the historical fact of an actual one, in this case the Nore Mutiny, adds one more bit of evidence proving that a sailor's nature is mutinous. By relying on Billy's supposed instinctual or natural anger about his impressment (after all, he is a deep one), Claggart easily raises the spectre of mutiny, which then permits Vere to exercise his beloved "forms" (128).

The insides of Billy's body do not circulate, but externalized representations of that body do in the several conclusions of the text. After the execution, for example, an article in a naval chronicle, like the depositions in "Benito Cereno," reports that "the criminal paid the penalty of his crime. The promptitude of the punishment has proved salutary. Nothing amiss is now apprehended aboard H.M.S. *Bellipotent*" (131). But like Babo's decapitated head, Billy's body continues to "cast a shadow" over the text. According to Brook Thomas, "the ragged edges of *Billy Budd* subvert more than attempts at formal closure. Generated by the subversive negativity of Melville's vision, they turn us to a historical world beyond a closed textual universe in which all possibility for transformation has vanished and keep open a space in which an alternative to our present condition can be imagined."[86] That space is, I think, the space occupied by

Billy's body and how that body will be read and represented. The ragged edges of the text, like the ragged edges of Billy's body, figure texts and bodies as surfaces that the narrator will not smooth away by positing a clear cut meaning on either language or persons. Melville's narrator, although he cannot protect Billy from the likes of Vere, can protect Billy from himself (that is, the narrator). It is as if the narrator of *Billy Budd* has learned well the lesson of "The Birth-mark." He thus metamorphoses the desire for invisibility that destroyed Georgiana into an invisibility that provides a space of relative freedom. These ragged edges appear throughout *Billy Budd*, whether as the "sanctioned irregularities" of governments that for obvious reasons "would hardly think to parade at the time" (66) or "that harassed frame of mind" (113) which "actuated the commander of the U.S. brig-of-war *Somers* to resolve, under the so-called Articles of War, . . . upon the execution at sea of a midshipman and two sailors" (113). Exteriorizing Billy, as we have seen, allows the narrator to remain outside the cultural logic that destroys him by imputing interiority to him. Similarly, at the conclusion of *Billy Budd* the narrator, in quoting "history . . . without comment" (114) as well as in citing newspaper articles (also without comment) that depict Claggart as "vindictively stabbed to the heart by the suddenly drawn sheath knife of Budd" (130), imputes no interiority or agency to the logic that informs this version of the story and thereby undermines it completely.

Billy's body enters history, along with the bodies of John Brown, the men killed on the U.S.S. *Somers*, and the Haymarket anarchists – bodies which then perform the task that, according to Benjamin, cultural "treasures" do. Billy, who is referred to as a "jewel" (46) in the text, is like one of these Benjaminian treasures in that his body records the fact that "there is no document of civilization which is not at the same time a document of barbarism."[87] The power of Billy's allegorical body resides not in a transcendence of cultural context but in the fact of its utter saturation.

4

Twain in the Man-factory

Like Melville, Twain imagined the scene of writing to be inextricably connected to the scene of industrial production. And like Melville, Twain imagined that the act of inventing fictional characters for a literary economy was analogous to the act of producing laborers for a market economy. The relation between these scenes of production was even more vexed for Twain than for Melville. Twain in his capacity as entrepreneur continually shuttled back and forth between the two scenes, inventing characters to populate his fictions and constructing laborers to operate the machines in which he had invested. The encounter between these two scenes of production is itself written into Twain's texts. After all, what is the Man-factory of *A Connecticut Yankee in King Arthur's Court* if not a site both of the manufacturing of persons for Hank's market economy and for Twain's literary economy?

It is the powerful and productive encounter between these two scenes of producing persons that this chapter analyzes in order to map out Twain's own relation to the work ethic as it applied to literary labor and to delineate the economics of Twain's allegory. Whereas Melville's texts destabilized conventional oppositions between work and leisure in order to install a new notion of literary labor, Twain's texts interrogate traditional relations between efficiency and inefficiency in order to suggest that literary labor, particularly humorous literary labor, is subject to different notions of efficiency. In the case of Twain, these relations are particularly complex. His activities in the world of manufacturing, for example, demonstrate his deep commitment to efficiency techniques that workers felt to be damaging not only the ideals of the work ethic but their minds and bodies as well. The efficiency strategies which Twain praises throughout his letters and journals produced a kind of flattened character in the workplace that had little place, as we have seen, in a fictional text. And a kind of character with which Twain himself was uncomfortable. When Twain's commitment to efficiency is translated

129

into literary practice, in other words, an aesthetic problem arises. His fictional characters begin to resemble the flattened, mechanical persons he believes to be ideal workers. His fictional characters become allegorical characters – ideal perhaps in a factory or in a market economy but problematic in a fiction or in a literary economy.

Admittedly, critics have not had much to say about allegory and Twain.[1] There is a sense, perhaps, in which the Civil War utterly eradicated the legacy of antebellum writers like Hawthorne and Melville, making it impossible for someone like Twain to write allegory. There is a sense, perhaps, in which Twain's iconic status as realist might be diminished if he were considered to be an allegorist. But the divide between allegory and realism is not nearly as great as theorists and readers have thought, and so to think about Twain in relation to allegory is not necessarily to challenge his qualifications (and merits) as a realist. To the contrary, the presence of allegorical characters is itself an indication of realism. Allegory in Twain, like allegory in Hawthorne and Melville, is powerfully related to the concerns of realism to the degree that the visibility of Twain's own labors and the visible effects of labor on his characters are thought to constitute the real.[2]

The allegory of labor in Twain is best understood through examining Twain's vexed allegiances to the construction of persons as constituted in the market and literary economies. Indeed, it becomes increasingly clear that Twain has an enormous amount of difficulty with the construction and what we might call the survivability of his fictional characters. Just as the engineers in *Life on the Mississippi* have the power to make and unmake persons, Twain's position as author confers upon him the power to produce fictional persons as well as to destroy them. The texts that will be taken up in this chapter offer especially powerful representations of the problem of fictional persons in Twain, whether it be the endlessly proliferating characters who more often than not end up dead in the case of *Life on the Mississippi*, or the ideal characters in Hank's Man-factory of *A Connecticut Yankee* whose military expertise leads to the Battle of the Sand-Belt, or the "original" and "duplicate" characters whose subversive indistinguishability culminates in the procession of the dead with which *The Mysterious Stranger, #44* concludes. A pattern emerges whereby Twain appears to expend as much energy in figuring out ways to destroy his characters as he does in producing them. One arrives at the conclusion that only by erasing the products of his imaginative labor does Twain complete the labor process itself.[3] Moreover, Twain's career permits us to witness the drama of the author as engineer who must now find the solution to the problem of inventing too many characters – or, more precisely, too many characters of the "wrong" or allegorical type. These texts thus labor to undo the characterological labor that they have done.

Twain's own version of literary labor is constituted out of an aesthetic ideology that not only required the erasure of his literary labors but also demanded that his literary labors adhere to a principle of strict efficiency as defined by the newly developing disciplines of engineering and scientific management.[4] Because efficiency requires the complete erasure of the signs of one's labor, Twain's texts often contain seemingly random episodes of violence and conclude with violent scenes of erasure. Twain's literary work ethic takes the aesthetic ideology of invisible labor to new heights, since now texts should not only erase the signs of the labor that go into their making but must also figure the erasure of themselves. In a last-ditch effort at efficiency, Twain erases narratives that are best characterized by their inefficiencies, such as the seemingly irrelevant compilation of detail in the second part of *Life on the Mississippi*; the accretion of episodic adventures that seem unrelated to the main narrative, as in *A Connecticut Yankee*; and the often unmanageable plot complications, as in *The Mysterious Stranger, #44*. These inefficiencies are, I think, the signs of Twain's construction of an alternative version of literary labor that, far from demanding an ideal of efficiency, celebrates an ideal of inefficient (or is it now efficient?) narrative that is digressive and, more important, humorous. This chapter claims that Twain's narratives are torn between adhering to a conventional notion of literary labor and inventing an alternative. This invention is the labor of Twain's allegory.

I. ENGINEERING THE MISSISSIPPI

Life on the Mississippi plays a crucial role in delineating Twain's economics of allegory, because it overtly stages Twain's conflicted allegiances to the activity of literary labor, including the construction of fictional character, as it would be understood by the engineering profession and a practice of literary labor as defined by the profession of authorship. My reading thus begins by analyzing the complex relations between Twain's status as author of *Life on the Mississippi* and the engineer's position as reconstructor of the Mississippi and the pilot's role as navigator of the Mississippi – relations that Twain himself foregrounds throughout the text. The narrative can usefully be thought of as vacillating between documentary and digressive storytelling. Furthermore, the tension between documentary efficiency and digressive inefficiency also exists on the level of characterization, where an allegorical or flattened configuration of personhood competes with a symbolic or rounded one. Twain's flat characters are allegorical in the sense that they signify the fact that personhood is constituted in relation to a market economy. These flat characters exist on the borders of the Mississippi and on the margins of *Life on the Mississippi*. They are present in the statistical populations that become an increasingly significant feature of the second half of the text. It is necessary to pay particular attention to the allegorical populations in this text, because they become an increasingly recognizable presence in Twain's later works, which feature similar populations in Hank's Man-factory and the "duplicate" population in the Bible factory of *The Mysterious Stranger, #44.*

When the narrator of *Life on the Mississippi* first learns to pilot the river, much of his excitement comes from surprises in the river's geography, such as changes in the shape of the shoreline and rocks in the river bottom, which threaten to wreak havoc upon the steamboat at any moment. In an often quoted passage, the narrator describes his experience of a Mississippi sunset before he "had mastered the language of this water and had come to know every trifling feature that bordered the great river":

> A broad expanse of the river was turned to blood; in the middle distance the red hue brightened into gold, through which a solitary log came floating, black and conspicuous; in one place a long, slanting mark lay sparkling upon the water; in another the surface was broken by boiling, tumbling rings, that were as many-tinted as an opal; where the ruddy flush was faintest, was a smooth spot that was covered with graceful circles and radiating lines, ever so delicately traced; the shore on our left was densely wooded, and the sombre shadow that fell from this forest was broken in one place by a long, ruffled trail that shone like silver.[5]

Leo Marx argues that the conventional language of this passage illustrates Twain's inability to "affirm the landscape's beauty *in its actuality.*"[6] Similarly, Henry Nash Smith claims that Twain's highly artificial discourse "implies that the rhetoric is false, the prosaic reality true."[7] As both critics point out, the "language of this water" is anything but "natural." The artificiality of this passage is especially important to note because, precisely when the narrator attempts to describe the "natural" river, his language becomes conventionalized through simile ("rings, that were as many-tinted as an opal") and metaphor ("the river was turned to blood"). The presence of such obviously literary language suggests that the romantic view of the river is no less contrived and no more natural than the technological perspective of the West Point engineers offered later on in the text.

But even as the narrator offers us this highly wrought description with the humility of one who has not yet "mastered the language of this water" (95), it is apparent that at least two languages of the water exist – the pilot's and the author's – and the narrator has certainly mastered the latter. This mastery of authorial artifice is further evident as the passage resonates with the literary authority of Hawthorne's "Birth-mark."[8] One can find many thematic parallels between these two texts: "the face of the water" is "a wonderful book" (94) the way Georgiana's birthmark is "a fairy-sign manual"; the river's "new marvels of coloring" evoke Georgiana's continually changing birthmark; and, most significant of all, when the narrator can no longer see "the romance and the beauty" (96) of the river, he asks, "What does the lovely flush in a beauty's cheek mean to a doctor but a 'break' that ripples above some deadly disease?" (96). But the similarities between the two texts are less interesting than the way in which Twain's narrator deploys the notion of textuality itself. The passage begins by celebrating his newly acquired ability to read the river and uses the language of textuality to do so as we learn that the river contains "*italicized*" passages, "a legend of the largest capitals," and "a string of shouting exclamation points" (94). The narrator then acknowledges the loss of a presumably less mediated reading experience of the river when he laments, "All the grace, the beauty, the poetry had gone out of the majestic river!" (95) and then concludes by comparing a pilot's experience of reading the river with a doctor's approach to his patient. What seems so interesting about this passage is that at the very moment the narrator wants to make an antitextual argument, that is to say an argument on behalf of an unmediated, purely experiential relation to the river, his language invokes the authority of poetry. (One might argue that conceiving of the river as poetry is itself the more appropriate subject of lamentation.) The literary discourse here undermines the narrator's attempt to characterize romantically the river in a pretextual form. To interpret the signs of the river within a language of textuality is to lose what the narrator imagines as a pretextual relationship to the river. There can be, in other words, no position outside the place of textuality.

Not only do the professions of piloting and literature deploy their own discourses in order to read the river, but the engineering profession also has its hermeneutic techniques. The engineers in Twain's text advocate a principle of efficient and disciplined circulation not unlike Aylmer's notion of the invisible hand in "The Birth-mark." Although the engineers spend most of their time devising ways to control the dangerous circulations of the Mississippi River, they also turn their attention to the circulations occurring beneath the cities it borders. They need look no further than the New Orleans drainage system to discover the diseases lurking and breeding beneath the beauty's cheek: "The water in the gutters used to be stagnant and slimy, and a potent disease-breeder; but the gutters are flushed now, two or three times a day, by powerful machinery; in many of the gutters the water never stands still, but has a steady current" (302). Here the stagnant water does not exemplify the workings of nature but rather the need for technological improvement. The beauty of New Orleans, like the beauty of the Mississippi, conceals an "unwholesome condition" (96) which can only be treated by "progressive men – thinking, sagacious, long-headed men" (302), men like Aylmer and like Twain in his more "progressive" moments. In fact, like Georgiana, the entire South is a haven for disease which "might suffocate one in his sleep" (285). And the South, like the river, is female. The narrator obviously sees the female body reflected in the river when he compares the "ruddy flush" (96) of the river to the "lovely flush in a beauty's cheek" (96). The female qualities of the South stand out as the narrator derides "the 'Female Institute' of Columbia, Tennessee" (286) and the "Kentucky 'Female College'" (286) because they stand "as a symbol and breeder and sustainer of maudlin Middle-Age romanticism" (286). These institutions, so clearly demarcated by their femaleness, are "necessarily a hurtful thing and a mistake" (286). Like the irregularities in the female river, the mistakes of the South need to be cured.[9]

The engineering community thus conceives of the river as a set of problems in need of a solution. Their desire to make the river "as safe and simple as driving stage" (204) induces the United States River Commission to make a new river:

> The military engineers of the Commission have taken upon their shoulders the job of making the Mississippi over again, – a job transcended in size only by the original job of creating it. They are building wing-dams here and there to deflect the current; and dikes to confine it in narrower bounds; and other dikes to make it stay there; and for unnumbered miles along the Mississippi, they are felling the timber-front for fifty yards back, with the purpose of shaving the bank down to low-water mark with the slant of a house-roof, and ballasting it with stones; and in many places they have protected the wasting shores with rows of piles. (205)

The untamed body of the Mississippi confronts the engineers with a host of other so-called problems. The darkness of the river, for example, poses the greatest threat to pilots and entrepreneurs, whose goods might be endangered by "that lawless stream" (205). In response to this apparent danger, "the national government has turned the Mississippi river into a sort of two-thousand-mile torch-light procession . . . the government has set up a clear-burning lamp. You are never entirely in the dark, now; there is always a beacon in sight, either before you, or behind you, or abreast. . . . Lamps in such places are of course not wasted. . . . The government's snag-boats go patrolling up and down" (203–4). The presence of the government is now inescapable. Like the Panopticon, which was meant to be a more tolerant form of punishment in nineteenth-century England, the government has created an all-seeing mechanism whereby one is always surrounded by a beacon of light "either before

you, or behind you, or abreast" (203). Along with the engineers who
have brought about such increased efficiency, an entire ideological apparatus, which alludes to the constant supervision of the penitentiary and
includes, more specifically, the patrolling boats, comes with them.[10] Another example of this governmental supervision includes the "signal for
meeting boats," which has been "rendered obligatory by act of Congress" (350). The pilot, whom Twain had earlier celebrated as "the only
unfettered and entirely independent human being that lived in the earth"
(122), has been remade in the shape of engineering laws and Congressional Acts.

A similar zest for efficiency pervades Twain's own construction of the
text; that is, the "lawless stream" (205) of the Mississippi has an analogue
in the lawlessness of *Life on the Mississippi*, which Twain feels he must
discipline. Twain, like the U.S. Commission, would like to transform the
disordered body of his text about the Mississippi with its "snags" (204)
and other "perils and anxieties" (204) into a "confine[d]" and "narrower"
body. Twain's desire is evident in an 1882 letter to Howells detailing his
problems with the book: "I am going to write all day and two thirds of
the night, until the thing is done, or break down at it."[11] A month later,
Twain again wrote to Howells complaining that "I never had such a fight
over a book in my life before" and that "large areas of it are condemned
here and there and yonder, and I have the burden of these unfilled gaps
harassing me and the thought of the broken continuity of the work,
while I am at the same time trying to build. . . . I have got everything at
a dead stand-still, and that is where it ought to be, and that is where it
must remain."[12] The reconstruction of the Mississippi is, of course, designed to prevent precisely the kind of "dead stand-still" about which
Twain complains. Similarly, "the unfilled gaps" and "the broken continuity of the work" allude as much to the task of the U.S. Commission as to
Twain's task of composition. In other words, the efficiency brought to
the Mississippi by the West Point engineers is a model for Twain of the
efficiency he would like to bring to his text about the Mississippi.

But the model of efficient engineering turns out to be a vexed one for
Twain. The engineer of Twain's imagination would seem to challenge
Cecilia Tichi's conclusion that this newly developing professional "signified stability in a changing world" and thus reassured Americans that
"the world of gears and girders combined rationality with humanity."[13]
In fact, at precisely the moment when Twain's engineers take steps to
provide this kind of reassurance, whether it be remodeling the Mississippi River in order to make it more navigable or bringing technology to
the world of Camelot in order to make it more efficient, Twain's narratives become increasingly unstable as the very nexus of rationality and
humanity starts to unravel. Thus the engineer ultimately functions for

Twain as an ambiguous figure who, though an expert problem solver, is bent upon creating the very problems to be solved – a position not unlike the one in which Twain the author finds himself as he tries to devise solutions to some of the most infamous plot complications in American literature, which he himself created.[14]

Throughout *Life on the Mississippi*, the narrator articulates an ideology of efficiency which he both deplores and celebrates as the herald of progress. While recognizing the greater efficiency that electric lamps bring to the navigation of the Mississippi, he complains that "this thing has knocked the romance out of piloting" (204) and "has taken away its state and dignity" (205). In his discussion of New Orleans, however, he boasts, "It was the best lighted city in the Union, electrically speaking. The New Orleans electric lights were more numerous than those of New York, and very much better. One had this modified noonday not only in Canal and some neighboring chief streets, but all along a stretch of five miles of river frontage" (303). Similarly, we have seen that he does not ignore the benefits of the reconstructed Mississippi. There is a new ease in navigating the river that both pleases and disconcerts him. Frequently he discusses this irritation in the language of a disappointed and displaced romantic; other times he speaks the language of the engineer. In the chapter "The Metropolis of the South," the narrator explains the need for a reconstructed river: "In high-river stage, in the New Orleans region, the water is up to the top of the enclosing levee-rim, the flat country behind it lies low . . . and as the boat swims along, high on the flood, one looks down upon the houses and into the upper windows. There is nothing but that frail breastwork of earth between the people and destruction" (301). This description illustrates in the language of the engineer why the Mississippi should be reconstructed. On the other hand, when the river is changed the narrator laments, "The Government has taken away the romance of our calling" (205) or "The noble science of piloting" was a thing "of the dead and pathetic past" (137). Certainly this allegiance to the romantic tradition of steamboat piloting compromises the narrator's dogged hatred of Sir Walter Scott. According to the narrator, Scott's romances have brought to the South an "admiration of his fantastic heroes and their grotesque 'chivalry' doings and romantic juvenilities" (285). The South can only recover from this influence with "the wholesome and practical nineteenth-century smell of cotton-factories and locomotives" (285) – the same instruments of technology that have destroyed the steamboat profession about which he fondly reminisces.

Thus, while lambasting the romantic tradition of Sir Walter Scott, the narrator indulges in his own form of nostalgia through his idealization of the river. The contradictions in the narrator's perspective are also evident

in his discussion of the engineering strategies of the West Pointers, because at the same time as he critiques the engineers' reformation of the
river, the narrator himself uses some of these same reforming techniques
on the narrative of his companion pilot, Mr. Brown. The narrator describes Mr. Brown's amazing memory, which makes him incapable of
"distinguish[ing] an interesting circumstance from an uninteresting one"
(118). Using diction similar to that of the engineer's description of the
Mississippi, the narrator writes of Brown: "As a talker, he is bound to
clog his narrative with tiresome details and make himself an insufferable
bore. Moreover, he cannot stick to his subject. He picks up every little
grain of memory he discerns in his way, and so is led aside" (118). Like
the river that contains "drifting dead logs, broken boughs, and great trees
that had caved in and been washed away" (100) and requires careful
navigation, Brown's memory "picks up every little grain . . . and is led
aside." Unable to operate efficiently, Brown's narrative suffers from improper and directionless circulations. We would expect the narrator to
experience the same "exquisite misery of uncertainty" (106) while listen-
ing to Brown's rambling narratives that he felt while navigating the river.
This is not the case, however, and eventually the narrator finds himself
"reform[ing] his [Brown's] ferocious speeches for him, and put[ting]
them into good English, calling his attention to the advantage of pure
English over the bastard dialect of the Pennsylvania collieries whence he
was extracted" (158). As the engineers discipline the river, the narrator
civilizes the "ferocious speeches" and "bastard dialect" in order to discipline, and therefore exert his power over, Brown's disorderly language.

Using this example of Brown, we might convincingly argue that, like
the military engineers who "try to bully the Mississippi into right and
reasonable conduct" (205), the narrator attempts to correct the conduct of
Brown's undisciplined memory. We might even claim that the narrator
recapitulates on the level of narrative the very ideology he wishes to condemn. The case becomes more complicated, however, when we look at
the chapter entitled "Uncle Mumford Unloads." This chapter explores the
role of the United States River Commission in the reconstruction of the
river and also includes, in a subsection, Uncle Mumford's "Impressions of
the River." Before presenting these impressions, the narrator explains,

> I consulted Uncle Mumford concerning this and cognate matters. . . . I
> have here and there left out remarks which were addressed to the men,
> such as "*where* in blazes are you going with that barrel now?" and which
> seemed to me to break the flow of the written statement, without
> compensation by adding to its information or its clearness. Not that I
> have ventured to strike out all such interjections; I have removed only
> those which were obviously irrelevant. (206)[15]

The narrator's emphasis on "information" and "clearness" suggests that he is as efficiency oriented with respect to the narrative as the engineers are with respect to the river. The so-called edited version, however, brilliantly parodies the technique of literary reform in the very act of imitation. Here is Uncle Mumford on the transformation of the river:

> Away down yonder, they have driven two rows of piles straight through the middle of a dry bar half a mile long, which is forty foot out of the water when the river is low. What do you reckon that is for? If I know, I wish I may land in – HUMP *yourself, you son of an undertaker! – out with that coal-oil, now lively,* LIVELY! And just look at what they are trying to do down there at Milliken's Bend. There's been a cut off in that section, and Vicksburg is left out in the cold. (207)

The subject matter as well as the style of this passage work together to challenge the engineer's notion of efficiency. To begin with, Uncle Mumford describes the engineer's reconstruction of this small segment of the Mississippi in the name of greater efficiency which ends up condemning Vicksburg to a less than promising future. Second, and here we should remember that the narrator has edited this version of Uncle Mumford's story in the name of greater clarity, the narrator shows that these qualities may be far from universally understood by including Uncle Mumford's hilarious interjection. Does this interjection give us any information? Does it help to clarify anything about the engineer's activities? Not really. In fact, it seems at first to be utterly irrelevant, especially if one's definition of information relies upon Uncle Mumford's presentation of the facts about the river. If, however, one wishes to know about Uncle Mumford's style of language, then his narrative interruptions assume much greater importance. Thus, what appears to be relevant to the engineer is only relevant in a sphere limited to the beliefs in efficiency and discipline as understood according to the logic of the engineering profession. The logic of another profession, say that of authorship, might view efficiency in terms of the text's ability to communicate facts about individual character or to provide the reader with an individual's linguistic style. The dictates of efficiency as understood in the context of authorship would surely demand that the narrator include "HUMP *yourself, you son of an undertaker!*" whereas efficiency when understood in the framework of engineering would require its exclusion. Humor, it seems, is not efficient.

Twain's narrative dramatically vacillates between an allegiance to two diametrically opposed principles of efficiency, the first as understood by engineers and the second, by storytellers like Uncle Mumford. A self-consciousness about efficiency (or lack thereof) pervades the text, especially in the chapter "The River Rises," where the narrator charts the movements of both the river and the narrative of the river. While informing us that a tree has gotten in the way of his boat's smooth passage down the river, the narrator pauses to say, "This will serve to show how narrow some of the chutes were," as if he feels the need to explain its inclusion in the narrative, as if the tree not only blocks the movement of the boats but, by analogy, blocks the even flow of the narrative. He wants to assure us that what might seem at first glance to be inefficient narrative meandering is, in fact, coherent narrative development. This already heightened self-consciousness escalates even further when he concludes his description of the "exquisite misery of uncertainty" (106) that accompanied him while he performed his piloting duties with the following: "I thought I had finished this chapter, but I wish to add a curious thing, while it is in my mind. It is only relevant in that it is connected with piloting" (106). Given that the entire chapter and, for that matter, the whole book are about piloting, why should the narrator have to point out the relevance of this story, which, after all, is about piloting? The narrator's difficulty stems from the fact that the subsequent story deals with the issue of piloting (a certain pilot X manages to navigate a very difficult section of the Mississippi while asleep, and X's fellow pilot thinks that X is wide awake), yet he uses the topic in order to tell a funny story. It makes sense, then, for the narrator to emphasize the story's connection to piloting and yet to feel some anxiety about its actual relevance. The anxiety comes from the fact that humor, in this case, requires digression and a certain degree of narrative inefficiency.

This kind of dis-ease about what does and does not belong in the narrative comprises a defining feature of the story itself and appears quite often. Similarly, the chapter "A Pilot's Needs" begins with the admission "I am wandering from what I was intending to do, that is, make plainer than perhaps appears in the previous chapters, some of the peculiar requirements of the science of piloting" (115). This narrative nomadism sounds suspiciously like the wandering of the young pilot caught in the impossible-to-navigate Mississippi: "You find yourself away out in the midst of a vague dim sea that is shoreless, that fades out and loses itself in the murky distances" (105–6). And finally, unlike the "placidly effortless" (116) memory of the pilot and more like Mr. Brown, who "picks up every little grain of memory he discerns in his way, and so is led aside" (118), our narrator pauses to tell us a story which he introduces in the following way: "Here is a story which I picked up on board the boat that night. I insert it in this place merely because it is a good story, not because it belongs here – for it does n't" (267).[16]

The narrative of *Life on the Mississippi*, like the Mississippi itself, encounters its own versions of dangerously projecting reefs or water that is too shoal in the textual form of seductive, because humorous, stories that interfere with the smooth and efficient operation of the story. The text both calls attention to these narrative reefs and attempts to navigate them by stressing their relation to its shape: "My reference, a moment ago, to the fact that a pilot's peculiar official position placed him out of the reach of criticism or command, brings Stephen W—— naturally to my mind" (125). Or, in the following passages, the narrator gives up all attempts at transition and simply reports, "Anecdote illustrative of influence of reputation in the changing of opinion" (226) or "Piece of history illustrative of the violent style of some of the people down along here" (227). For *Life on the Mississippi* to avoid the textual reefs that take away from the efficiency of the story, the narrator resorts to the documentary style that upholds the principles of efficiency by directly communicating the significance of the passage but whose very presence undermines the kind of efficiency (as defined by the profession of authorship) represented by Uncle Mumford's style of storytelling. The price of this documentary narrative style was high indeed. It cost *Life on the Mississippi*, particularly the second half, which relies more and more on this technique, its reputation.[17]

II. POPULATION EXPLOSIONS

Thus far, we have contrasted the engineer's efficient remaking of the Mississippi River with the narrator's contradictory allegiances to efficiency as signified by the engineer and efficiency as practiced by the principles of the storyteller. Significantly, the tension between a documentary style and a more conventional mode of storytelling reappears on the level of character, where a demographic paradigm of constructing and accounting for personhood vies with what we might call a more traditional model of making characters. This alternative mode asserts itself most powerfully in the narrative passages that list the population statistics of towns bordering the Mississippi. The presence of these statistics has attracted little critical attention other than the kind offered by the hero of Sherwood Anderson's 1925 novel *Dark Laughter*, who remarks, "He filled the book mostly with statistics [and] wrote stale jokes."[18] But what might it mean for a fictional text, whose primary task one might argue is the invention of persons, to acknowledge and to incorporate this alternative method of producing people? Demography functions as a crucial paradigm in *Life on the Mississippi* because of the text's ambivalent relation to the efficient construction, accounting of, and disposal of persons.[19] Furthermore, the unnamed and undescribed persons who make up the demographic statistics in passages such as "Muscatine, ten thousand; Winona, ten thousand; Moline, ten thousand; Rock Island, twelve thousand" (397) – and the list continues – represent the beginnings of allegorical personhood in Twain's texts, which will be succeeded by Hank in his Man-factory and #44 in the book factory.

The field of demography was, in fact, becoming an increasingly important area of the social sciences, as is made evident by the work of Edward
Atkinson (who is mentioned in another context in the appendix to *Life on
the Mississippi*) and Francis A. Walker, whose analysis of the operations of
the United States Census Bureau enables us to situate Twain's statistical
populations in their cultural context. Although censuses had been taken
before the Civil War, the devastation of the war left many wondering
exactly what (and who) of the nation remained. Thus in an 1890 article
that appeared in *Publications of the American Statistical Association*, Walker
laments the haphazard fashion in which the census of 1865 was done:
"Had Congress, in an enlightened view of the immense importance of
ascertaining precisely where that great struggle left us, provided for the
taking of a census in 1865, with improved modern machinery of enumera-
tion, we should have obtained results of almost priceless value."[20] In an
earlier article, "American Industry in the Census," Walker complains
about the "vast disproportion between objects and results" in the 1860
census: "The volume on Manufactures (including, besides manufactures
proper, all mechanical and mining operations) professes to give, among
others, the products of four of the more common trades, – coopering,
blacksmithing, carpentering, and painting. Yet a comparison of these
tables with the 'Occupations of the People,' in the volume on Population,
exhibits the startling fact that, of 43,624 coopers working at their trade,
the production of only 13,750 is accounted for among the 'products of
industry'; of 112,357 blacksmiths enumerated, only 15,720, including
one heroic woman, contribute to the reported production of their craft;
of 242,958 carpenters, only 9,006; and of 51,695 painters, only 913, find a
place in the tables of industry."[21] Walker is continually startled to discover
that bodies and numbers do not match up. But whereas he seeks to
correct these disjunctions by more accurately counting the bodies that go
along with the numbers, Twain's text, while invoking the statistical logic
of demography, takes great pleasure in unraveling the logic by explicitly
foregrounding the ability of fiction to create such disjunctions. One
might argue that fiction is itself the construction of persons without
bodies, populations that don't add up.

An incalculable difference would seem to exist between the characters
created by the narrator of *Life on the Mississippi* and those anonymous (or,
more precisely, ones named by numbers rather than names) persons who
populate the 1860 census as described by Walker or the towns along the
river, such as Greenville, which has "three thousand inhabitants, it is said,
and doing a gross trade of $2,500,000 annually" (249). In contrast to this
highly efficient statistical description of Greenville's population, most of
the characters in *Life on the Mississippi* exist not so much to be counted but
rather to account for themselves, and, like the tales told by the passengers

in Melville's *The Confidence-Man*, their self-accountings function more as obfuscations than illustrations of personal identity. Examples abound, but to prove the point we need only look at the chapter "Episodes in Pilot Life," which lives up to its title by narrating a series of pilots' stories, all qualifying for inclusion in this rather schematic chapter by virtue of its rather broad topic sentence, "Some of the pilots whom I had known had had adventures" (345). A list of adventures follows, some with named heroes, some with unnamed ones. The names, however, hardly matter at all. There is little difference, for example, between the stories of Dick Kennet, who died in the war, and George Ritchie, "who had been blown up near Memphis" (347), and "a young fellow who perished at the wheel a great many years ago" (346) or "one of the pilots" known to the narrator who died when "his boat caught fire" (345). The personal quality of these stories becomes less and less apparent as it becomes increasingly clear that their stories are, for the most part, the same. They work on the Mississippi, and they die on (or near) the Mississippi. Named or not, the characters thus join the ranks of the anonymous. The chapter concludes, appropriately enough, with an account of persons who, though named, do not exist. Also appropriately enough, the narrator introduces the story with the fact that the protagonist, in this case a steamboat clerk, is dead. The story concerns a young man and woman who, though unmarried, have assured the woman's father that they are, in fact, betrothed. The young woman's parents eventually die and bequeath a large inheritance to their daughter, using the daughter's married name in the will. Because no such person exists, the couple cannot collect the money. The nonexistence of named persons, however, occurs on more than one level of the story. Although the narrator tells us that the name of the young man is George Johnson, he eventually confesses that the name of the young man "was not George Johnson, but who shall be called George Johnson for the purposes of this narrative" (347). Here is a story about a nonexistent person (Mrs. George Johnson) based on the existence of another nonexistent person (Mr. George Johnson).[22]

Names, as this story so clearly demonstrates, do not necessarily register the fact of personhood. Although these names seem to offer the promise of personal identity and assume, of course, the bodily presence of the person, the stories function to undermine both the correlation between name and identity and the one between name and personal presence. This is, of course, what fiction does: nonexistent persons act in a community of other nonexistent persons as if they were real. These nonexistent persons, furthermore, usually have names that signify their participation in a world that more often than not bears some relation to the reader's. Giving a name to someone usually implies a someone to whom one gives the name. Names, however, in *Life on the Mississippi* guarantee neither personal identity nor corporeal presence. In the case of demography, bodies increase without the names to identify them, whereas in the examples we have analyzed, names proliferate without the bodies to fill them. When accounting for persons in the traditional sense of telling their stories leads to the kind of circularity and identic confusion we see in the case of the Johnsons and in the example of "The Undying Head" in the appendix to *Life on the Mississippi*, counting persons seems to offer an alternative way of describing and marking personal identity. Counting provides just as coherent (or incoherent) a barometer for identity and corporeality as accounting. In other words, the populations which are identified not by names but by numbers (and here we can see the beginnings of the boys in the Man-factory and the mysterious stranger, #44) at the borders of the Mississippi have as great a reality as, if not a greater reality than, the individual stories in the text.[23] One of the final chapters, "An Archangel," begins with the observation, "From St. Louis northward there are all the enlivening signs of the presence of active, energetic, intelligent, prosperous, practical nineteenth-century populations" (392). Populations rather than persons constitute the cities bordering the Mississippi, and the cities themselves don the discursive garb of individual personhood: Marion City, which has "gone backwards in a most unaccountable way" (392), or "Quincy is a notable example, – a brisk, handsome, well-ordered city; and now, as formerly, interested in art, letters, and other high things" (392), or Burlington, "a fine and flourishing city, with a population of twenty-five thousand, and belted with busy factories of nearly every imaginable description" (395).

This oscillation between a statistical and nonstatistical model of personhood presents yet another version of the efficiency problem, only this time applied to the issue of personal identity. And as quickly as the names and bodies increase, they either die or are killed off. This erasure of persons partakes of the logic of efficiency in that the unaccountable and uncountable persons in the texts form a fictional population that can only be kept track of and therefore controlled by the fact of its destruction. Thus the text spends an inordinate amount of time introducing a character who, a mere few paragraphs later, dies. When the narrator returns to Hannibal, for example, he regrets not being able to visit a mausoleum housing the body of a fourteen-year-old girl which was "put into a copper cylinder filled with alcohol, and this was suspended in one of the dismal avenues of the cave" (386). People in this text die at breakneck speed. The stories of their demise are sometimes funny, sometimes serious. The chapter "Episodes in Pilot Life," for example, illustrates the ubiquity of death: "Several others whom I had known had fallen in the war – one or two of them shot down at the wheel. . . . Ben Thornburgh was dead long ago; also his wild 'cub' whom I used to quarrel with" (346). Because similar passages occur throughout – for example, in "My Boyhood's Home" the narrator asks about a number of people from his past, only to discover that they have died in the war or in an insane asylum (374) or in Mexico (373) – it should come as no surprise when Memphis is described as "a mighty graveyard" (217) or the Mississippi becomes a kind of cemetery where the remains of the woodyard man and other less savory characters are buried. (212)

The desire to attend to the population growing on the borders of the river as well as the fictional population within the text generates a related desire to keep track of the people who die. And, as was the case with the construction of personhood, there are more and less efficient ways of taking the body count. Undertakers frequently appear in *Life on the Mississippi* because, having (re)created the Mississippi, the engineers must now take care of the remaining debris, which is all too often human. Although the engineers give birth to a new Mississippi, they also bring death in their wake. For example, when the narrator returns to the river "after twenty-one years' absence" (167), he remarks: "The towboat and the railroad had done their work, and done it well and completely. The mighty bridge, stretching along over our heads, had done its share in the slaughter and spoliation. Remains of former steamboatmen told me, with wan satisfaction, that the bridge does n't pay. Still, it can be no sufficient compensation to a corpse, to know that the dynamite that laid him out was not of as good quality as it had been supposed to be" (173). Sometimes the narrator is saddened by these "remains," whereas other times he feels that these remains are better off dead, as is evident when he happily reports the destruction of the southern way of life: "We mourn, of course as filial duty requires – yet it was good rotten material for burial" (295).

Inhumation provides the narrator with both humorous subject matter and a point of departure for critiquing the engineer's activities. In "The Art of Inhumation," for example, the narrator discusses the economic benefits of "the dead-surest business in Christendom" (310) – undertaking. J.B.——, Undertaker, tells him that an epidemic "don't pay in proportion to the regular thing" (311). In an epidemic, an undertaker has no time to tempt the mourning person with expensive varieties of funereal preparation, such as fancy techniques for embalming and special coffins with "silver door-plate and bronze handles" (310). Certainly the narrator is making fun of the business person who will do anything for a buck, especially someone who will take advantage of a grief-stricken person.

A competing and more serious representation of death, however, suggests that this commodification of death is a consequence of the engineering reform of the Mississippi. The narrator frequently mourns the loss of

those who no longer populate the river. The narrator observes "the absence of the river man" (169) and concludes that "he was absent because
he is no more. His occupation is gone, his power has passed away" (172).
Similarly, the industrial complex created by the military engineers and
the government has left many endangered (and extinct) species. The
narrator asks, "And where now is the whittler? Does he still vex the
foreign tourist with his universality and his never-tranquil jack-knife, or
is he gone down into the shades forever, with the vanished woodyard-
man of the Mississippi? He does seem to have passed utterly away and
left no heir" (300). The ubiquity of death, either because of "the lesson
taught by a desolating visitation of the yellow-fever" (217) or because of
the Civil War, which created streets of "*iron* litter" (260), is frequently
paired with the engineers' technology which wipes out various people
who then are "absorbed into the common herd" (172).

Being absorbed into the common herd is not unlike being inhumed
and is rather like being out of circulation. Paradoxically, the very people
in charge of making the river circulate more efficiently are responsible for
the inability of those like the woodyard man to circulate. The military
engineers both bring about the deaths of the steamboatman and the
woodyard man and create the sanitary means of dispensing with them.
Their tactics of efficiency, furthermore, manage to organize the suffering
of those who are mourning and to aestheticize their experience.[24] Inhumation allows the mourner to feel better through purchasing state-of-the-art
funeral adornments, and thus death gets engineered and sentimentalized à
la Mount Auburn in such a way that the mourner, rather than confront-
ing the loss of the person, thinks about the virtues of the expensive oak
casket as opposed to the more inexpensive pine.

In contrast to the engineers who count the living and the dead, the
narrator accounts for the stories of these people and their deaths in nonstatistical ways. Nonstatistical but not quite individual either. That is to
say, the deaths of the woodyard man and the whittler are obviously not
the deaths of Mr. So-and-So, the woodyard man, or Mr. So-and-So, the
whittler, with identifiable names and bodies. We would seem to be in the
realm of statistical persons where bodies exist without names. But with a
difference. Even though the accounts of the deaths of the woodyard man
and the whittler are not individual accounts, neither are they statistical
accounts. Like the Carpenter in *Moby-Dick*, these characters possess neither names nor numbers. They have become what we should recognize
as allegorical: they simultaneously hearken back to a premarket world
that the engineers, according to the argument of the book, have recreated
and look ahead to a market economy that incorporates or expels persons
according to the value of their labor. It is true that the allegorical nomina-

tion of these characters partakes of the engineer's way of understanding persons, but the narrator crucially and critically maintains the difference between counting and accounting by offering accounts of why the wood-yard man and the whittler have disappeared – clearly a story (not an individual one but an allegorical one) left untold by demographic statistics. Their stories surely remain hidden by statistics such as those that repute to represent St. Paul and Minneapolis, "the former seventy-one thousand, and the latter seventy-eight thousand" (398), or Helena, with "$1,000,000 invested in manufacturing industries" (231). Computed by the engineer, these demographic and monetary statistics define the success or failure of a town. But these numbers also hide the individual persons and the collective stories, inefficient as they have become in the culture of the Mississippi and within the narrative of *Life on the Mississippi*, of the steamboatman or the woodyard man that the narrator attempts to unveil. Allegorical characters, it would seem, can go both ways. They can embody the demographic model of personhood while simultaneously demonstrating its partiality and fictionality. The remainder of the chapter will in fact argue that the Man-factory of *A Connecticut Yankee* produces allegorical characters in the demographic mode which then resurface in the Bible factory of *The Mysterious Stranger, #44* with surprisingly subversive results.

III. TYPING AT THE TYPESETTER

When Hank Morgan enters King Arthur's Court, a labor of Herculean proportion awaits him; or rather, uninvited, he sets himself the task of transforming medieval England into nineteenth-century America. In order to accomplish this, he first promotes himself from "head superintendent" (8) of the Colt Arms Factory to head engineer of the world, whose job qualifications include the efficient management of newspaper offices, a patent office, and a hygiene franchise as well as the production and destruction of men. The West Point engineers of *Life on the Mississippi* become fully realized in the figure of Hank Morgan, and Twain's ambivalent attitude toward engineering and efficiency takes on even greater intensity as the Rock Island of *Life on the Mississippi*, with its "national armory and arsenal" (399), effects the apocalyptic Battle of the Sand-Belt in *A Connecticut Yankee*. The engineer has now turned from his work on the river to the reform of human beings – and not just their reform, but also their construction in a Man-factory. That Twain imagined a scene of literary production like the one in the Man-factory is no coincidence, given his long-term entanglement with James Paige and the infamous Paige typesetter, which to Twain's great displeasure never made it to the scene of factory production. Twain's literary pursuits, engineering interests, and profit motives were inextricably related during the composition of *A Connecticut Yankee*. By making reproducible boys in a Man-factory, Hank accomplishes what Twain (and Paige) could not. Furthermore, the allegorical populations that bordered the Mississippi have been relocated to the Man-factory, the center of Hank's civilization and of Twain's text. At this center one finds the scenes of Hank's labors and Twain's literary labors, whose erasure is required, according to the logic of Twain's literary work ethic, and hence accomplished in the Battle of the Sand-Belt.

The notebooks Mark Twain composed during the years 1884–90 read more like the memos of an entrepreneur and budding engineer than of a writer of literature. Statistical charts measuring the efficiency of the Paige typesetter against its rivals, mathematical equations describing the relation among labor, cost, and output necessary for maintaining the machine, and intricate notes detailing patent negotiations illustrate Twain's immersion in the world of invention, money, and management, as well as his intense interest in labor: "The P.S. [Paige typesetter] does the work of 5 men; a slow operator does the work of 5 slow men; a fast one the work of 5 fast men: therefore the new wages should be 1/5 of the old. . . . At <5,000>4,500 an hour he would make $2.70 a day (he gets full *10 hours'* work) as against $2.40 & $2.50 now. Whoso pays us 10 cents & his man 9, saves <24C>27C on a M paper."[25] By looking at Twain's involvement with the typesetter, we can deduce the situation of American businesses during the late nineteenth century. Not all commercial enterprises, of course, followed this exact development, but the story of the Paige typesetter typifies much in American industry in the late nineteenth century, especially with respect to the patenting of new inventions and the conceptualizing of the human laborer in increasingly economic terms.

Like many other documents of American progress in the post–Civil War years, *The Great Industries of the United States,* by Horace Greeley and others, published in 1873, promised "an insight into the various arts which distinguish the present period of scientific industry in the United States of America." Greeley's paean to technology intended "to convey an adequate impression of the magnitude of the manufactures treated upon, their mechanical subtleties, and everything connected therewith." The section on typesetting machines, more specifically, discusses proofs and distributing machines while also giving the reader a brief account of Isaac Adams, who "patented, in 1830 and 1836, a press," and of "the Napier press [which] was introduced into the United States in 1830."[26] That "the introduction of the Napier and Adams presses threw nine tenths of these men out of employment" is omitted.[27] Not only were the negative effects of invention on the laboring classes left out of this celebration of American progress, but "everything connected therewith" also excluded the system by which inventions were "introduced into the United States" and the process by which inventors (or more frequently companies) got patents. Inventions were not merely "introduced" to Americans, especially by the time Twain was investing in the Paige typesetter; rather, inventors and their financial backers had to contend with a bureaucratically organized Patent Office, ubiquitous competition for patent claims, and corporations which often had the power to influence decisions in the Patent Office.

The bureaucracy of the Patent Office, combined with Paige's irresponsibility, turned Twain's dreams of success into a twelve-year nightmare. The growing antagonism between Twain and Paige primarily revolved around the patent issue. A eulogy to the Paige typesetter, "The Last Chapter in the History of the Paige Typesetting Machine. Bankrupted Mark Twain. A Good Many Hartford People Helped Carry the Load," noted, "Paige's great feat consisted in not taking out his patents, but holding them back, so that when one set of investors got through he was in good shape to go on with another crowd."[28] After the initial month of examination in 1887, the patent application was pending for eight years. The Paige typesetter became infamous, especially when Paige filed his "204 sheets of drawings, with over a thousand separate views" and officials from the Patent Office spent a month examining the machine.[29] According to historian Richard Huss, "The Patent Office had on its hands the most voluminous and time-consuming siege on one invention in its entire history." The lengthy amount of time required by the Patent Office to issue three patents in 1895 which "contained 275 sheets of drawings, 123 sheets of specifications and 613 claims" caused Twain great financial and mental anxiety.[30]

In one of his more optimistic moments, Twain projected the following future for his business: "He was absolutely certain that he could sell 350 machines in New York City alone right away, and that this sale would breed a minimum sale of two thousand a year for the life of the patent and earn for the company an annual profit of at least twenty million dollars, with other millions pouring in each year from Europe."[31] Yet Paige was not nearly as interested in sharing the profits with his benefactor as in creating and recreating a perfect machine. Perfecting the machine meant abandoning the original project, spending another ten years working on a machine that would include a mechanical justifier, and, according to Justin Kaplan, "extend[ing] the patent life of the machine for an additional seventeen."[32] As long as Twain sent Paige his monthly income of $3,000, he was content to toy with the machine, and happily did so for fifteen years, backed by over $190,000 provided by Twain and an esti-

mated $2,000,000 overall.[33] Paige continually seduced Twain into provid-
ing more money. On August 20, 1885, Paige wrote, "I shall continue to
push matters as fast as possible, and hope to be able to complete the
machine within a few weeks." Three months later, Paige informed Twain
that he could "expect the machines out in a week or so," and two years
later, Paige assured Twain, "Our machine will be ready in the early fall,
with automatic justifyer attached."[34] Not surprisingly, Twain felt be-
trayed by Paige's inventive approach to patents and profits. Twain's anger with Paige culminated in a letter written to his brother Orion, "I've
shook the machine and never wish to see it or hear it mentioned
again. . . . It is worth billions; and when the pig-headed lunatic, its
inventor, dies, it will instantly be capitalized and make the Clemens
children rich."[35]

Needless to say, the Paige typesetter never made anyone rich.[36] The
Mergenthaler Linotype Company purchased the Paige typesetter, and the
machine was never mass-produced. Huss contends that the typesetter
was never manufactured because of Paige's refusal to engage himself with
the capitalists necessary to underwrite such a venture and not because of
"any mechanical failure or defect in the machine."[37] Most historians of
American invention disagree with Huss's evaluation and argue that the
machine's complexity and delicacy made it impossible to manufacture.[38]
In his *History of Composing Machines*, for example, John Thompson explains that the mechanical sophistication of the typesetter was "such as to
demand the attendance of experts, and the impossibility of training mechanics to the degree of skill required made it a commercial impossibility.
There were about eighteen thousand separate parts, eight hundred shaft
bearings, and cams and springs innumerable."[39] The inordinate number
of parts and their complicated relation to one another meant that laborers
could not be trained to use such machines, nor mechanics to repair them.
Paige had created a perfect machine which resisted its own reproduction.
In *A Connecticut Yankee*, Twain creates both a mirror image and an inversion of the typesetter. His invention is the constructed boy of the Man-
factory, who, unlike the typesetter, can be reproduced and yet, like the
typesetter, brings with it its own demise.

IV. "A MAN IS A MAN, AT BOTTOM," OR IS HE?[40]

One of the Yankee's first confessions is "I am a Yankee of the
Yankees – and practical; yes, and nearly barren of sentiment, I suppose –
or poetry, in other words" (8). This is not true. Hank is full of sentiment.
When Clarence appears for the first time, Hank remarks, "He was pretty
enough to frame" (15). Moments before Hank blows up Merlin's tower,
he picturesquely describes the scene from the palace: "These people, and

the old turrets, being partly in deep shadow and partly in the red glow from the great torch-baskets overhead, made a good deal of a picture" (39). Last, when Hank and the king journey through Camelot disguised as peasants, they come across several knights to whom they must bow. Reluctant to comply with such a menial request, the king forces Hank to come up with an alternative plan. "When they [the knights] were within fifteen yards, I sent that bomb with a sure aim, and it struck the ground just under the horses' noses. . . . Yes, it was a neat thing, very neat and pretty to see. It resembled a steamboat explosion on the Mississippi; and during the next fifteen minutes we stood under a steady drizzle of microscopic fragments of knights and hardware and horse flesh" (158).

This combination of machinery and body parts, of the mechanical and the organic, appears early on in the text when Hank destroys Merlin's tower: "[There were] a thousand acres of human beings groveling on the ground in a general collapse of consternation. Well, it rained mortar and masonry the rest of the week" (39). The best and most famous example of this occurs when Hank, wandering through Camelot, discovers a man "bowing his body ceaselessly and rapidly almost to his feet" (120). Although "it was his way of praying" (120), Hank seizes such an investment opportunity. In a foreshadowing of Frederick Winslow Taylor's scientific management, Hank "timed him with a stop-watch and he made 1244 revolutions in 24 minutes and 46 seconds. It seemed a pity to have all this power going to waste. It was one of the most useful motions in mechanics. . . . So I made a note in my memorandum book, purposing some day to apply a system of elastic cords to him and run a sewing-machine with it. . . . He was going, Sundays, the same as week-days, and it was no use to waste the power" (120).[41] Certainly this scene is meant to be humorous in its iconoclastic stance toward prayer and ever-watchful Yankee ingenuity. If Hank's claim that he wants to liberate the people of Camelot from their "dumb uncomplaining acceptance of whatever might befal them in this life" (101) is true, then hooking up this man to a machine would seriously damage that claim.

Efficiency, though, is not necessarily the final result when people behave according to the logic of the machine. In the example of the praying man getting hooked up to a machine, efficiency is unarguably achieved. The case of Sandy is, however, more complicated. Like Uncle Mumford, who "is bound to clog his narrative with tiresome details" (118), Sandy "would be thirty days getting down to those facts" (72). Although Hank characterizes Sandy's flow of talk as being "as steady as a mill" (62) and Sir Kay as "fir[ing] up on his history-mill" (25), these discursive mills possess a kind of efficiency that makes for inefficient storytelling. Sandy's "clack was going all day, and you would think something would surely happen to her works, by and by; but no, they never got out of order; and she never had to slack up for words. She could grind and pump, and churn and buzz by the week, and never stop to oil or blow out" (62). The result of such discursive efficiency is "monotony" (72) and narratives which "run too much to level Saharas of fact" (75). Her narratives are inefficient in the sense that persons are indistinguishable from one another and all events seem alike because they are narrated in the exact same way. Here is just one example of this Sahara-like style of narration: "And so they rode and came into a deep valley full of stones, and thereby they saw a fair stream of water; above thereby was the head of the stream, a fair fountain, and three damsels sitting thereby. In this country, said Sir Marhaus, came never knight since it was christened, but he found strange adventures" (76). Such leveling induces a state of stupor in Hank such that he "lost the thread there, and dozed off to slumber" (76), only to discover upon awaking that he "had lost another chapter" (76). Sandy's (in)efficient monotony, however, becomes a wellspring of humor as Hank interrupts Sandy's "conversational mill" (70) to instruct her in the techniques of realism: "Sir Marhaus, the king's son of Ireland talks like all the rest; you ought to give him a brogue, or at least a characteristic expletive. . . . You should make him say, 'In this country, be jabers, came never knight since it was christened, but he found strange adventures, be jabers'" (76). Hank frequently reminds us of his reactions to Sandy's narrative: "I could not follow Alisande's further explanation of who our captured knights were, now – I mean in case she should ever get to explaining who they were" (77). The humor of passages like this comes not from the content or style of Alisande's narratives but rather from Hank's response to and characterization of them. Through the continued linkage of machinery and narrative – "I had set her works agoing . . . a person would die if he let her monotony drip on him right along all day" (72) and "Her steam soared steadily up again" (75) – Twain humorously (and hilariously) reveals the necessary divide between machinery and narrative. Twain's humor comes from the presence of *both* Sandy's efficient (and inefficient) style of narration and Hank's response to it. If Sandy's narrative style were altered so as to appeal to Hank's aesthetic taste, the humor in passages like this would be lost. This is precisely what happens as the book progresses. Sandy's voice (she hardly speaks in the last half of the book) and the voice of the knights disappear as Hank takes charge. As a consequence, the humor of the book also seems to disappear, or, at the very least, it becomes increasingly difficult to figure out the jokes. Moreover, Hank ends up installing in the Man-factory an ideology of efficiency that produces persons who "are all alike" (75); persons who share precisely the qualities of Sandy's Sahara-like narratives, with their lack of "picturesque detail," their "certain air of the monotonous" (75), that Hank had critiqued. As was the case with Poe and John A. B. C. Smith and Hawthorne and Aylmer, Hank threatens to erase Twain's literary labor (of humor). Hank's ideology of efficiency begins to take over the narrative, leaving Twain no choice but to invent a Battle of the Sand-Belt so as to destroy the character who threatens to destroy him and his literary labors.

Twain, however, had great sympathy with Hank's efficient production of persons in the Man-factory, being quite familiar himself with strategies for increasing production among laborers. For example, his publisher, Fred Hall, suggested to the author the following inducements "to keep a [General Agent] spurred up to his work" by taking "$500 and divid[ing] it into prizes to be given to agents who sell the greatest number of books in one year after its publication, for instance, the agent who sold the greatest number should receive $200.00 the second should receive $100.00 the third $75.00 the fourth $60.00 the fifth $50.00 and the sixth $40.00, this would make $525.00 in prizes."[42] Unsurprisingly, Twain's interest in various management techniques also applied to the Paige typesetter and its operatives. The matter of accurate timing, for example, was crucial in Twain's experiments with workers. He constructs the following scene, employing the time-study man and the stopwatch (two of the most controversial techniques in scientific management), in order to determine "how long it takes to *cast*": "Put the man at his utmost speed for one entire hour, noting in a book every hitch or delay or interruption of any sort. . . . Set down the errs he does in the hour – and during the hour see that nobody touches the bars he is making, upon any pretext. . . . Time him from the instant he touches the handle that sends the line of matrices away from before his face till that bunch of matrices has been elevated to the top of the machine preparatory to being distributed."[43]

Twain's statistical accounts of the typesetter and its workforce exhibit promanagement attitudes that were being vigorously challenged by increasing labor activities during the 1880s and 1890s. Explaining the reasons for labor strikes, Robert Layton, Grand Secretary of the Knights of Labor, observed the degradation of workers: "When the men entered [the workplace] in the morning they were numbered by checks. A man lost his identity as a man and took a number like a prisoner in a penitentiary."[44] Confirming Layton's description was Samuel Gompers, who, in testimony before the Senate Committee on Education and Labor, quoted a Massachusetts manufacturer as saying, "I regard my employés the same as I would an old machine, which, when it becomes rusty, I thrust into the street."[45] Such statements illustrated the need for organized labor and created some of the most violent union uprisings in American history, most notably the railroad strikes of 1877. Let us recall that *A Connecticut Yankee* was written during this time of enormous transformation in both labor and management and was published in

1889, just two years before Melville completed *Billy Budd* and only three years after the Haymarket riots.

Twain's position while writing the book unsurprisingly straddled the views of management and labor. On the one hand, we have seen how easily his work on the typesetter places him in the managerial position of power. In fact, in his journals of April through August 1885, Twain lists the following strong points of the typesetter machine as opposed to human operatives: "This type-setter does not get drunk. He does not join the Printers' Union. He does not distribute a dirty case, he does not set a dirty proof."[46] This reference to the printers' union suggests that Twain's position was antiunion. Similarly, in a letter to Fred Hall about the type-setting of *A Connecticut Yankee*, Twain reiterates his instructions to a proofreader: "*I told him plainly, that he must have no opinion whatever regarding the punctuation, that he was simply to make himself into a machine and follow the copy.*"[47] The ideal efficient worker is the mechanical one.

But Twain also occupies the position of the disempowered laborer in his relationship to Paige. He continually finds himself in the predicament of giving money to an inventor who cares more about his machine than about Twain's situation. In a speech to the Monday Evening Club of Hartford, "The New Dynasty," Twain's empathy for the laborer is evident. "Who are the oppressors? the few: the King, the capitalist, & a handful of other overseers & superintendents. Who are the oppressed? . . . The nations of the earth; the valuable personages; the workers; they that *make* the bread that the soft-handed & the idle eat."[48] Twain clearly identifies himself with "the valuable personages; the workers." Furthermore, his contention that he must finish *A Connecticut Yankee* on the same day that the typesetter was supposed to be completed suggests that Twain, like the workers we have discussed, identified with the machine. Twain's own relation to the typeset-ter recapitulates the problems experienced by machine operators in the workplace: as they felt increasingly mechanized by the growing manage-ment system and the sophistication of the machines, the machines seem to take on qualities of the organic, and the persons become mechanical. When the Paige typesetter failed the *Chicago Herald* test (a sixty-day competition which pitted the Paige typesetter against rival machines), Twain told Henry Huttleston Rogers, "I must be there and see it die. That is, if it must die; and maybe if I were there we might hatch up some next-to-impossible way to make it take up its bed and take a walk."[49] The Paige typesetter embroils Twain in the problems of nineteenth-century business and fi-nance. Desiring profit, he fetishizes the machine and mechanizes the labor force. The one becomes anthropomorphized, the other dehumanized.

Like Twain, Hank Morgan becomes interested in exactly how organic or mechanical a person is, since his self-appointed task is "to turn groping and grubbing automata into *men*" (89). Like the engineers of the Mississippi who want the river to be efficient, productive, and profitable, Hank wishes to re-form or "train a crowd of ignorant folk into experts – experts in every sort of handiwork and scientific calling" (50). Hank, however, gets caught in a dilemma. On the one hand, he argues:

> Training is everything; training is all there is *to* a person. We speak of nature; it is folly; there is no such thing as nature; what we call by that misleading name is merely heredity and training. We have no thoughts of our own, no opinions of our own; they are transmitted to us, trained into us. All that is original in us, and therefore fairly creditable or discreditable to us, can be covered up and hidden by the point of a cambric needle, all the rest being atoms contributed by, and inherited from, a procession of ancestors. (90)

For all of his talk about the omnipotence of training and the illusion of nature, Hank insists upon that part "hidden by the point of a cambric needle" or that "one microscopic atom in me that is truly *me*" (90). Hank's denial of nature is contradicted by his assertion that "a man *is* a man, at bottom. Whole ages of abuse and oppression cannot crush the manhood clear out of him" (173). Even with continual training in "abuse and oppression," that "one microscopic atom" (90) that is a man cannot be trained out of him.

At the very moment that he insists that people, like machines, can be trained to do whatever he wishes, Hank tries to maintain the difference between the organic person and the mechanically created "person." His ability to deploy the mechanical depends upon the existence of the organic. Yet his whole project is an attempt to wipe out whatever the people of Camelot imagine is organic or natural in their lives. By believing that a man remains a man even if trained by abuse and oppression to be an automaton in the workplace, Hank exculpates himself from any anxiety about treating people like machines. Unsurprisingly, these categories get confused in Hank's mind. While watching the king's reaction to his subjects' being brutally beaten, Hank notes, "It was merely the fault of his training, his natural and unalterable sympathies" (136). This sentence concisely reveals Hank's confusion about training. Throughout the text, Hank opposes training to what is natural and unalterable. Here training and the natural have merged. The categories of the mechanical and the organic have unraveled as training becomes a form of nature – a second nature. The category of original or first nature no longer has any meaning, because the distinction between first and second nature cannot be made.

Just as it was necessary to read Vere's use of the category of nature in the context of the conflict between labor and capital, so too Hank's interest in the nature of human beings must be analyzed within this larger cultural debate. Interestingly, those who most successfully manipulate human nature through mechanization are the same people who stubbornly articulate the supremacy of human nature over technology. In *Natural Law in the Business World*, for example, Henry Wood argued that conflict is not between laborers and "employers or capitalists, but with the law of supply and demand. They [labor] are, apparently, not aware that their contest is with nature, and that it is impossible to overcome or repeal a Natural Law."[50] This position assumes that if something is natural, such as the law of supply and demand, then nothing, including legislation to assure workers of fair pay, can be done. Only nature can challenge nature. Only the nature of workers, their desire to work as best they can, will allow them to take advantage of "Natural Law."

In *Social Problems*, Henry George pointed out the popularity and unfairness of this laissez-faire theory of natural law: "The comfortable theory that it is in the nature of things that some should be poor and some should be rich, and that the gross and constantly increasing inequalities in the distribution of wealth imply no fault in our institutions, pervades our literature, and is taught in the press, in the church, in school and in college."[51] Critics of George's prolabor position countered with the indictment that strikers who found "fault in our institutions" were unwilling to battle with their own lazy and immoral nature. For example, Jay Gould claimed, "The poorest part of your labor generally are at the bottom of a strike. Your best men do not care how many hours they work, or anything of that kind; they are looking to get higher up."[52] Gould's position is repeated time and again by conservatives, who use the "nature argument" to avoid the consequences of their laissez-faire economics. In testimony before the Senate Committee on Education and Labor, Edward A. Atkinson says, "If men are poor to-day in this land it is either because they are incapable of doing the work which is waiting to be done, or are unwilling to accept the conditions of the work."[53] Successful businessmen like Wood, Gould, and Atkinson insisted that the nature of workers determined their position in the system. Even though this nature was being radically reconstructed by new forms of labor, the power of the organic self remained intact.

The battle to define the worker's nature in *A Connecticut Yankee* can best be illustrated by Hank's attempts to make the king "look as little like a king" (161) as possible. When he and the king set out to tour the countryside of Camelot, Hank attempts to teach the king how to look like a member of the "working class." Frustrated by the kingliness of the king, Hank exclaims about the king's transformation into a lower-class subject, "It's all *amateur* – mechanical details all right, almost to a hair; everything about the delusion perfect, except that it don't delude" (159). The king learns almost all of the mechanical motions necessary to achieve a "sort of deceptive naturalness" (161), but the king "don't delude." Hank tells us, "[The king] is just a cheap and hollow artificiality when you don't know he is a king. . . . A king is a mere artificiality, and so a king's feelings, like the impulses of an automatic doll, are mere artificialities" (201). Nevertheless, he also maintains that "as a man, he is reality, and his feelings, as a man, are real, not phantoms" (201). According to Hank, the king's nature has been constructed; however, his nature "as a man" is "real," is "essential," is organic. What complicates Hank's distinction between the king, who is an artificial construct, and "man," who is an organic essence, is Hank's own construction of persons, his own indomitable belief in training. Although Hank wants to insist upon the difference between first and second nature, between training and the organic, the distinction falls apart. Even the distinction between medieval England and nineteenth-century America cannot be maintained, because Hank responds to all of these dichotomies in the same way: he destroys one of the terms (whether it be the organic, first nature, medieval England), all the while insisting upon the integrity of those oppositions. The presence of the Man-factory most clearly expresses why these oppositions cannot be maintained.

The Man-factory, though, has been consistently ignored even among critics who agree that technology is a significant theme in the book. Henry Nash Smith dismisses the Man-factory because, of the "fifty-two shadowy boy technicians in the cave at the end, none of them [is] given an identity or even a name, and none [is] represented as performing any concrete action."[54] To dismiss the shadowy boys in the Man-factory is to repeat the antipathy toward allegorical characters who are flat and mechanical in favor of characters who are round and organic. Benjamin offers a persuasive account of allegorical figures that helps to explain the reasoning behind these dismissals: "There is not the faintest glimmer of any spiritualization of the physical. The whole of nature is personalized, not so as to be made more inward, but, on the contrary – so as to be deprived of soul. That awkward heavy-handedness, which has been attributed either to lack of talent on the part of the artist or lack of insight on the part of the patron, is essential to allegory."[55] Just because allegorical figures are despiritualized and deprived of soul, they do not signify the author's lack of ability. Instead, the lack of soul in Twain's allegorical characters reveals Hank's desire to mechanize everything and everyone. The transcendent existence of the soul is precisely what Hank depended upon in order to dominate the daily lives of the people in Camelot. The creation of these allegorical characters thus reveals Hank's commitment to the thinglike rather than the lifelike quality of persons. Furthermore, the boys in the Man-factory allude not only to Hank's view of the people and civilization of medieval England but also to Hank's attitude toward nineteenth-century America: both populations are opportunities for Hank to construct human beings according to the ideology of efficiency.

These unidentified, shadowy, unreal figures are quite significant in that they point to Hank's vision of an ideal world in which he both controls the production of human personhood and need not apologize for the desire to construct people upon the model of the machine. In the Man-factory, the notion that people are organic is completely dispensed with. No longer worried about maintaining the distinction between the organic and the mechanical, Hank gets to do what he wants most – to destroy the organic and replace it with the purely mechanical. The boys are like the newspapers, in which Hank takes enormous delight: "A thousand of these sheets have been made, all exactly like this, in every minute detail – they can't be told apart" (151–2). Like the sheets, these boys have no identities and no names, because each one is exactly the same. One could even compare them to the narrations that come out of Sandy's "conversational mill," since the boys "suffer in the matter of variety; they run too much to level Saharas of fact" (75). Their "shadowiness" perfectly embodies their lack of individuation, their "abstractness" comes from their complete mechanicalness, their unreality comes from their shocking reproducibility.

This reproducibility is shocking because it is ultimately homoerotic. Hank's production of boys in the Man-factory for his market economy and Twain's production of boys in the Man-factory for his literary economy are both based on a kind of homoerotic economy that substitutes mechanical reproduction for biological reproduction. "The intimacy between technological and biological ways of making persons" that Seltzer has identified as a crucial component in Twain's text is here given an explicitly gendered twist as Hank and Clarence stand in for the technological way of making persons, and Hank and Sandy conform to the biological way. *A Connecticut Yankee* presents us, in other words, with two competing representations of making persons. On the one hand, Hank has a traditional family with his wife, Sandy, and their daughter, Hello-Central, and, on the other hand, Hank is part of a less conventional family with Clarence as his mate and the boys of the Man-factory as his children. Hank's attitudes toward the two families are quite different. In contrast to his rancorous relationship with Sandy, Hank's affection for Clarence remains constant. When Hank telephones Camelot and Clarence picks up the phone, Hank reports, "It was good to hear my boy's voice again. It was like being home" (131). Their "affectionate interchanges" contrast sharply with Hank's reaction to Sandy's "jaw, jaw, jaw, talk, talk, talk, jabber, jabber, jabber" (62). Another comparison between Clarence and Sandy suggests that Clarence knows Hank more intimately than Sandy. After the Church has returned Camelot to its state of "darkness" (235), Hank disguises himself in order to find out what has hap-

pened while he has been tending to the ailing Hello-Central. Upon entering Clarence's quarters, Hank remarks, "[Clarence] knew me as easily as
if I hadn't been disguised at all" (237). A parallel scene occurs when the
slave driver captures Hank and takes him to London. Unlike Clarence,
who immediately recognized the disguised Hank, "Sandy passed within
ten yards" (207) and failed to recognize him with his "rags and dirt and
raw welts and bruises" (207). Unfazed by Sandy's lack of recognition,
Hank lets his attention quickly be captured by "the sight of a newsboy"
(208). Hank happily concludes, "Here was proof that Clarence was still
alive and banging away. I meant to be with him before long; the thought
was full of cheer" (208). Rather than looking forward to the time when
he and Sandy will be together, Hank anticipates his reunion, his "banging
away," with Clarence.

The Battle of the Sand-Belt is the apotheosis of and punishment for
such homoerotic desire. What makes "a man a man at bottom" is a man
and a woman, and Hank's mechanical reproductions threaten to erase the
female body. In Hank's technological utopia, the female is alive only as a
simile and a simulation. As Hank attempts to stir his troops to action, he
remarks, "They were a darling fifty-two! As pretty as girls, too" (248).
Sandy and Hello-Central do not return to Camelot with Hank, but he has
their picture. In one of his letters to Sandy (which he cannot send because
he cannot leave Merlin's Cave), he writes, "Sandy, if you and Hello-
Central were here in the cave, instead of only your photographs, what
good times we could have!" (246). An all-male family has replaced the
conventional heterosexual family, and the female remains only in a figure
of speech and a photograph.

Hank's attempts to maintain sexual difference, like his attempts to
separate the mechanical and the organic, fail because in the same way that
he wished to make all things mechanical, he desires to make all things
male. By separating the spheres of homoerotic activity in the Man-
factory from the heterosexual reproduction of Hello-Central, Hank tries
to preserve the "naturalness" of male–female reproduction, while at the
same time setting up a competing system of reproduction that attempts
to destroy the very category of the natural. Although Sandy and Hello-
Central are protected from the ravages of the Battle of the Sand-Belt, the
domestic space occupied by mother and child ironically embodies the
very technology it sought to oppose; that is, Hello-Central, an artifact of
Hank's nineteenth-century industrialized world, represents the melding
of the natural and the technological.

The site where persons are made must be destroyed in *A Connecticut
Yankee* not only because it is the scene of a threatening homoerotic economy but also because Twain's notion of literary labor requires it. The
allegorical population in the Man-factory, while signifying Hank's effi-

cient making of persons in a market economy, registers a breakdown in Twain's literary economy. Twain's worries about the vulnerability of his own literary labor are evident in Hank's acknowledgment that "do what one may, there is no getting an air of variety into a court circular" (150). He continues, "There is a profound monotonousness about its facts that baffles and defeats one's sincerest efforts to make them sparkle and enthuse. The best way to manage – in fact, the only sensible way – is to disguise repetitiousness of fact under variety of form: skin your fact each time and lay on a new cuticle of words. It deceives the eye; you think it is a new fact" (150–1). Unlike Hank, who is relatively confident about his production of new facts, Twain is not. "A new cuticle of words" might fool the eye of most readers, but it doesn't fool Twain's. And thus the new cuticle must be torn away at the very moment that it is laid on. The signs of Twain's labor must not only remain "fenced away from the public view" (51) in the same way as Hank's "future civilization . . . went smoothly and privately along undisturbed in [its] country retreats" (50) but must be erased as well.

The signs of Hank's efficient labor, that is the boys in the Man-factory, are also the signs of Twain's inefficient labor vis-à-vis the construction of conventional fictional characters, making it impossible for Twain to do anything but destroy the primary scene of production, the Man-factory. The boys in the Man-factory are like those allegorical populations bordering the Mississippi – numbers without stories. If Hank is allowed to continue making boys in the factory, they will end up being precisely like the knights, who have been "reduced to a monotonous dead level of patience, resignation, dumb uncomplaining acceptance of whatever might befal them in this life" (101). Hank's impatience with all things monotonous is belied by his zest for newspaper sheets that "can't be told apart." Although Hank's sheets do not have to be distinguished one from the other, Twain's do. Hank's desire for all things the same reveals his commitment to efficiency as defined by a market economy, which for a literary economy spells disaster. Hank's manufacturing of an allegorical population in the Man-factory thus threatens Twain's construction of characters in *A Connecticut Yankee*, which is a macrocosm of the Man-factory. The construction of the Man-factory portends "the rising hell" that will be directed at the civilization of Camelot and at *A Connecticut Yankee* itself. To the extent that the production of boys in Hank's Man-factory is an allegory of Twain's literary labors, it must be destroyed. The Man-factory is both the site of personhood and the source of its extinction.

It is no coincidence that Hank chooses Clarence to be his partner in the operations of his technological family. When they first meet, Clarence "informed me that he was a page" (15). The boundaries between Twain's writing of *A Connecticut Yankee* and his involvement with the Paige typesetter are, as I have been suggesting, exceedingly permeable. Whereas the Paige typesetter could not be mass-produced because of its complexity, Twain creates a character who mechanically reproduces people. Twain succeeds in the literary realm where he failed in the business world. Both the typesetter and the shadowy boys, however, end up being destroyed. Cox argues that Twain was able to finish *A Connecticut Yankee* only by destroying "the vicious identification between it and the machine. . . . In bringing Morgan to death Twain was symbolically killing the machine madness which possessed him."[56] Although Cox's reading is highly suggestive, the destruction of Hank's world at the end of the novel signifies not the killing of the machine but rather the killing of those allegorical characters Twain finds so threatening to his view of the world in which people are people and machines are machines. His experience with the Paige typesetter begins to question the stability of these categories. As I have argued, he pushes the limits of these categories even further in his fictional work. Allegorical characters do not permit the kind of mystification that Hank relies on throughout the text and that Twain himself was experiencing with the Paige typesetter. The end of the book signifies a victory for the writer, but it does not lead to the death of the machine; in fact, Twain was investing in an electric cash register machine. Instead, it represents the birth and hesitant incorporation of an economics of allegory that gets fully articulated in *The Mysterious Stranger, #44*, in which Twain completely immerses himself in the production of allegorical persons. In fact, it signifies Twain's hesitant acceptance of himself and his text as permutations of the machine. Allegorical characters are no longer a threat to Twain's production of fictional character and conception of literary labor but are rather their very instantiation.

V. THE MYSTERIOUS STRANGER, *#44 AND BENJAMIN'S WORK IN THE AGE OF MECHANICAL REPRODUCTION*

In Twain's *The Mysterious Stranger, #44*, the laborers of a Bible factory in medieval Austria protest the rapid advancement of nonunion laborer #44. When they go on strike, little do they know that #44's technological wizardry enables him to produce "duplicate" workers, thus making ineffectual the "original" workers' strike (they are called "duplicates" and "originals" in the text). The creation of these "duplicates" is a dream come true for any boss, and for a scientific manager in particular: "You would see a sponge get up and dip itself in a basin of water; see it sail along through the air, see it halt an inch above a galley of dead matter and squeeze itself and drench the galley, then toss itself aside . . . in another minute or two there would be a mountain of wet type in every box and the job [would be] finished."[57] This tableau and others like it, which we shall explore in greater detail, represent the successful culmination of scientific management: human laborers, and any obstacles they might present, are eliminated by this new and efficient machinery of production. We have returned not only to the temporal world of *A Connecticut Yankee* but to the issues raised in it. The Man-factory is, however, no longer hidden in the text, "giving no sign of the rising hell in its bowels" (*A Connecticut Yankee*, 51). It is the explicit subject of *The Mysterious Stranger, #44*.

Like *Life on the Mississippi* and *A Connecticut Yankee*, *The Mysterious Stranger, #44* poses the question of Twain's efficient or inefficient, productive or unproductive, construction of fictional character. A reading of this often marginalized text is required for an understanding of Twain's economics of allegory because of its explicit focus on the relation between constructing laborers for a market economy and producing fictional characters for a textual economy. Just as the allegorical characters in *Billy Budd* became the means by which Melville interrogated the categories of interiority and nature, allegorical characters in *The Mysterious Stranger, #44* function to subvert the logic of efficiency and, more specifically, scientific management. They are not simply the instantiation of economic efficiency but become the site of inefficiency – and humor. Whereas Twain needed to destroy the allegorical population of the Man-factory produced by Hank because of its threat to his own literary labors, here Twain's literary labors are explicitly linked to the construction of an allegorical population which, far from registering an efficient production of personhood, brings about the disintegration of efficiency. As an allegory of Twain's literary labor, *The Mysterious Stranger, #44* demonstrates Twain's breathtaking and potentially never-ending production of characters. But true to the logic of Twain's notion of literary labor, the erasure of that production is figured in #44's final words to August, "I am but a dream . . . you will banish me from your visions and I shall dissolve into the nothingness out of which you made me" (186).

The text begins with the story of a worker who got a raw deal. If our sympathies immediately go to the wronged worker, they are perhaps only slightly modified by the fact that the worker is the Devil. The town of Eseldorf needs a bridge and asks the Devil to build it. He agrees and contracts with the town to receive the first Christian to cross the bridge as payment for his labor. The Church finds a terminally ill monk, who "tottered across, and just had strength to get over; then he fell dead just as the Devil was reaching for him, and as his soul escaped the angels swooped down and caught it and flew up to heaven with it, laughing and jeering" (8). This story of a broken contract, which introduces labor–management conflict to the text, suggests that workers may indeed have good reason to strike.

Not all of the workers in the print-shop factory, however, are as diligent as the Devil. When we first see the print-shop workers at their tasks, Twain presents a *tableau vivant*:

> In the corner old Binks was bowed over a proof-slip; Katzenyammer was bending over the imposing-stone making up a form; Ernest, with ink-ball and coarse brush, was proving a galley; I was overrunning a page of Haas's to correct an out; Fischer, with paste-pot and brown linen, was new-covering the tympan; Moses was setting type, pulling down his guide for every line, weaving right and left, bobbing over his case with every type he picked up, fetching the box-partition a wipe with it as he brought it away, making two false motions before he put it in the stick and a third one with a click on his rule, justifying like a rail fence, spacing like an old witch's teeth – hair-spaces and m-quads turn about – just a living allegory of falseness and pretence from his green silk eye-shade down to his lifting and sinking heels, making show and bustle enough for 3,000 an hour, yet never good for 600 on a fat take and double-leaded at that. (37)

In this representation of the workers, everyone, save Moses, conscientiously does his job. The task identifies the operative, not vice versa, and the character of the worker is not individualized so much as the work is. Moses stands out because he merely pretends to be efficiently doing his work; instead, he is "soldiering," or spending his time "studying just how slowly he can work and still convince his employer that he is going at a good pace."[58] The perfect worker will not stand out. Scientific management should reconstruct him and make him an efficient, honest worker. Because of his soldiering, Moses is "a living allegory of falseness and pretence." All of the workers in this tableau are living allegories of some variety, whether a living allegory of proper proofreading, of form making, or of correcting. The point is that to be a living allegory is acceptable, in fact desirable, but one should not be a living allegory of pretense and inefficiency.

Moses distinguishes himself in yet another way, or, more precisely, the description of Moses sets itself apart from the others. One need only note the similes "justifying like a rail fence" and "spacing like an old witch's teeth," the humorous tone of the description (comparing his spacing to the witch's teeth), and the rather unusual appearance of the word allegory to realize that Moses has a strikingly literary persona when compared to the other workers in the scene. In other words, the tricks of Twain's trade, the tools of his literary profession, become a part of the narrative and call attention to themselves. One might even venture to guess that

Moses' very soldiering, the very act of not doing his work, somehow invites the narrator (and Twain) to deploy his literary techniques. As was the case with Twain's humor in *A Connecticut Yankee,* which played off Sandy's inefficiency and Hank's response to it, here Twain's literary labor requires Moses' inefficiency. Moses needs to look efficient so that the boss doesn't complain, but this is quite different from being efficient, and the mock efficiency represented by him could potentially lead to a disintegration of efficiency itself – which is exactly what happens in *The Mysterious Stranger, #44.*

Moses' soldiering and the insurgent attitude that accompanies this practice spread throughout the print shop once #44 enters the scene. The owner of the shop, to the chagrin of the union workers, allows the stranger to participate in high-level tasks previously reserved for union members. The presence of #44 elicits hostility among the other workers, and eventually they strike. Presumably the strike will call a halt to the mechanical reproduction of "two hundred Bibles" (51) – "a formidable piece of work for the University of Prague" (47). Not only does the strike fail to frustrate the owner's wishes; the work gets done for free through the creation of duplicate workers.[59] If the workers fail to reproduce mechanically the texts, then the workers themselves will be mechanically reproduced. The reproduction of workers who "did not need to eat or drink or sleep, so long as the Originals did those things" (89) promises to solve the labor problem. Like #44, the duplicates are machines in their ability to work efficiently, uncomplainingly, and free.

The technical expertise of #44 lies in his ability to reproduce laborers in the print shop so that the employer will succeed in honoring his business contracts. His full name, "Number 44, New Series 864,962" (20), registers his birth on the assembly line and his membership in an allegorical population not unlike the statistical ones bordering the Mississippi. As a consequence of his mechanical birth, #44 possesses an intimate knowledge of technology. After one of his many visits into the future, he returns to August, the main character, with a tape recorder, "a camera and some photographs" (146). It is no coincidence that #44, who can unceasingly duplicate himself and others, introduces even more mechanisms of mechanical reproduction into the text. As a master of duplication, #44 explains to August, "We don't need those people, you know. No one needs them, so far as I can see. There's plenty of them around, you can get as many as you want . . . in a couple of hours I can fetch a whole swarm" (139). Like Hank's Man-factory, #44's feats of duplication lead to the creation of perfect workers and the subsequent disposal of inefficient ones.

Scientific management attempts this very reconstruction of bad workers, such as Moses, into ideal laborers, such as the duplicates.[60] In 1911, a year after Twain's death, Frederick Winslow Taylor, the father of scientific management, boldly declared: "What we are looking for . . . is the ready-made, competent man . . . in the past the man has been first, in the future the system must be first." According to Taylor, managers should "talk to and deal with only one man at a time, since each workman has his own special abilities and limitations, and since we are not dealing with men in masses, but are trying to develop each individual man to his highest state of efficiency and prosperity."[61] Taylor's system continually makes such appeals to the individual, when the very basis of that system is the denial of the individual and the construction of the generic worker. Haber characterizes Taylor's program as one in which "methods were primary, not particular men."[62] The particularities of individuals disappear even though Taylor denies "dealing with men in masses."

But the labor movement read Taylor's program as a direct threat to their own understanding of the labor process and the dignity of their work. Seen as an attempt to silence the voices and discipline the bodies of laborers, labor leaders and reformers vigorously protested the institutionalization of scientific management in the workplace. "Damning Taylor's system as reducing men to 'mere machines,'" the American Labor Movement, first under the direction of Terence Powderly and then Samuel Gompers, challenged the unchecked accumulators of wealth as well as the cult of efficiency.[63] George argued that a worker "becomes a slave, a machine, a commodity – a thing," and Lloyd lashed out, "The worthlessness of the body and the advantages of poverty are the favorite doctrines of those who fare sumptuously every day."[64] Claims like these were supported by Josephine Goldmark's *Fatigue and Efficiency*, a fascinating study of the effects of mechanical labor on workers which illustrated the competitive relationship between the rhythms of the machines and those of the human body: "It is apparent that the rhythm of any power-driven machinery is fixed and mechanical, depending upon its construction and its rate of speed. Now it is true also that human beings tend to work rhythmically, and when the individual's natural swing or rhythmic tendency must be wholly subordinated to the machine's more rapid mechanical rhythm, fatigue is likely to ensue."[65] Goldmark's description pits the natural body of the worker, with its "natural swing or rhythmic tendency," against the "more rapid mechanical rhythm" of the machine's unnatural body.

As my historicized reading of *Billy Budd* indicated, the battle between scientific management and the labor movement centered on the laborer's body. Management maintained that the disciplining of the body through monotonous labor offered not only the means of controlling "the pleasures, amusements, and temptations" of a potentially threatening class of people but, on the more positive side, "relieved the strain of mind and body which varied hard labor entails, and [even] left the workman not too tired at night to go to his club or his union and hear discussions as to rights and wrongs of labor."[66] Although workers claimed that "[they] cannot leave that particular branch and go to any other; [they have] got no chance whatever to learn anything else because [they are] kept steadily and constantly at that particular thing," management asserted that workers who were well matched to their machines would "provide everything needed for [an] easy and wasteless performance." The worker's body must be treated like a machine, and it should be "realized that high wages paid to a man may be as truly an investment as a high price paid for a machine."[67]

The Mysterious Stranger, #44 stages the conflict between labor and management in late-nineteenth-century America in the Bible factory of medieval Austria, and, as one might predict, the narrator (and Twain) straddles the positions. Amidst all of the complexity of the narrative voice, one can say that Taylor's ideal workplace finds, to a certain extent, a fictional equivalent in Twain's text. One can also say, however, that the efficiency of Taylor's utopia quickly disintegrates as the basic distinctions that permit that efficiency – the distinctions between shadow and substance, between original and duplicate, between persons and machines – begin to break down. Twain pits the natural body of the original against the mechanical body of the duplicate, not so as to champion one or the other but to "damn Taylor's system" altogether (as well as all others) by making it impossible to tell them apart. As was the case in *Billy Budd, The Mysterious Stranger, #44* centers on the legibility and controllability of the worker's body. Whereas Melville refuses to participate in the ideology of interiority and nature through which that body is read and disciplined, Twain completely undermines the ideology of nature, which is based on the difference between the natural and the mechanical, by making it impossible to distinguish the one from the other. If efficiency is one of the desired outcomes of this distinction, Twain's construction of flat, allegorical characters makes efficiency impossible. His efficient duplicate workers unravel the distinctions not only between original and duplicate but between efficiency and inefficiency. They can, as I shall suggest, be neither read nor disciplined. Indeed, one might even say that they instantiate the very principle of inefficiency.

The mechanical duplicates induce a state of shock when they are first detected by the striking workers in the print factory. The narrator, August Feldner, says: "We were paralyzed; we couldn't even cross ourselves, we were so nerveless. And we couldn't look away, the spectacle of those familiar objects drifting about in the air unsupported, and doing their complex and beautiful work without visible help, was so terrifyingly fascinating that we had to look and keep on looking, we couldn't help it" (65). Upon seeing the duplicates, the originals recognize "the spectacle of those familiar objects" (65). Later on, when August comments upon the duplicates, he says, "It is a new and strange and fearful idea: a person who is a person and yet *not a human being*" (100).

The duplicates simultaneously possess the qualities of familiarity and strangeness. They are like the originals and yet different. Dumbfounded by the duplicates, the originals experience the power of the uncanny, which Freud explains in his essay "The Uncanny": "The 'double' was originally an insurance against the destruction of the ego, 'an energetic denial of the power of death,' as Rank says; and probably the 'immortal' soul was the first 'double' of the body. . . . The 'double' [however] reverses its aspect. From having been an assurance of immortality, it becomes the uncanny harbinger of death."[68] There is a temporality in this account of the uncanny that pertains to the temporality of allegory. The uncanny signifies both an earlier moment in which the double functions to stave off death and a later moment in which the double alludes to the coming of death. The temporal layering of the allegorical character similarly registers its link to the archaic as well as to the modern. The duplicates of *The Mysterious Stranger, #44,* like so many of the allegorical characters we have analyzed, refer back to their origins in medieval Austria at the same time as they allude to their mechanical reproduction in the twentieth-century imagination of Twain.

Through the duplicates, the originals witness the temporal and thematic reversal of a double's aspect. The "strange and uncanny" (93) duplicates, to use Twain's words, embody the qualities of the uncanny, the most important feature being "the fact that the subject identifies himself with someone else, so that he is in doubt as to which his self is."[69] These duplicates, who "stuck industriously to their work [and] did not speak except when spoken to" (93), are in fact "the uncanny harbinger[s] of [the originals'] death." Because the duplicates are perfect workers requiring no food, no sleep, and no pay, they challenge the function of the originals, who are no longer necessary. In fact, the duplicates are the uncanny harbingers of the procession of the dead which concludes the text. The uncanniness of the duplicates resides in their simultaneous familiarity and unfamiliarity – they are persons but not persons. They are new and yet familiar. How can this be? What makes a person a human being? They are allegorical, but their meaning is suspended. As with John A. B. C. Smith, their bodies resonate with significance, but the content of that significance is indeterminate. The gap between personhood and humanness is an important one in this text, but it is a gap that cannot be bridged. Let us recall that the duplicates are not completely independent beings. Although "the Duplicates did not need to eat or drink or sleep" (89), they require the nutrition and sleep of their originals. The duplicates being dependent upon the originals for food and rest, the duplicate–original relation is not unlike the relation between the fetus and the maternal body. The duplicates are thus familiar in that they have a maternal/corporeal relation to their originals, and unfamiliar in that #44 has produced them.

The familiarity of the maternal model is itself made unfamiliar, since the direction of *The Mysterious Stranger, #44* is undoubtedly toward mechanization and duplication. The best example of this duplicating frenzy can be found in the many versions of Twain's own text, which includes "The Mysterious Stranger," "The Chronicle of Young Satan," "Schoolhouse Hill," and *The Mysterious Stranger, #44*.[70] In addition, #44 brings inventions related to the duplication of images or voices back to medieval Austria; original workers are replaced by duplicate ones, and, as if that weren't enough, another duplication, or rather triplication, is introduced when #44 explains that "each human being contains not merely two independent entities, but three – the Waking-Self, the Dream-Self, and the Soul" (124). The original–duplicate relation is itself duplicated. This obsessive insistence on unfamiliar models of reproduction makes it seem particularly odd that the relation between originals and duplicates is predicated on a maternal body. And yet the narrative insists on this model. When August, for example, first meets his duplicate, named Emil Schwarz, August says, "Although we had been born together, at the same moment and of the same womb, there was no spiritual kinship between us; spiritually we were a couple of distinctly independent and unrelated individuals, with equal rights in a common fleshly property" (125). And later when Emil Schwarz asks August's permission to return to his (that is Emil's) unfleshed state, Emil says, "Say you will be my friend, as well as brother! for brothers indeed we are; the same womb was mother to us both, I live by you, I perish when you die" (151).

The interconnectedness between duplicate and original should call to mind the rhetoric of promanagement spokespersons like Henry Wood and Washington Gladden, both of whom invoked the symbiotic relation between capital and labor as they argued for the dependency of labor and capital in a vision of economic domesticity or domestic economy. In the preface to *The Political Economy of Natural Law*, for example, Wood claims, "The fault is not with the 'social system,' but with abuses which are the fruitage of moral delinquency in personal character. Labor and capital, when deeply defined, melt into each other."[71] Echoing Wood's sentiment is Gladden, who explains, "If the capitalist would measure his profits, and the working-man his wages, by the Golden Rule, there would be instant peace."[72] The opposing sides in *The Mysterious Stranger, #44* neither "melt into each other" nor achieve "instant peace." In fact, the workers in the text have good reason to go on strike.

The anecdote about the Devil with which the book begins illustrates the incompatible interests of labor and management. Employers want to get the most out of laborers (the ultimate coup would be to get the labor without paying for it), and workers want to get the best possible pay for their labor. No matter how many times writers concerned with the "labor problem" spoke of the mutual interests of the worker and the employer, workers understood that their rights were not the concern of the employer and that these rights needed to be fought for, usually through striking. The strike in the text, however, is more complex than this opposition between worker and employer might initially suggest. Who is being victimized – the laborers whose union is being challenged by the presence of #44 and his rapid ascent into the print-shop profession? or the boss whom "the men had in their power" (47)? The narrator first suggests that the labor dispute might be solved simply if "the Duplicates do the work and the Originals take the pay" and then realizes that "the plan wouldn't answer; it would not be lawful for unions and scabs to have dealings together" (89).

The fact is that the labor–management conflict can easily be taken care of in this text. But something is getting in the way of this resolution. Not only does mechanical reproduction make the difference between the original and duplicate indiscernible (who would be the union man and who the scab?), but the very fact of mechanical reproduction seems to undo the labor–management dichotomy itself. Management, like labor, will inevitably undergo a similar process of duplication. In this respect, workers and managers are equally threatened by the unending spectacle of the mechanically reproduced. Although the strike is a significant element in the plot of the text, the relationship between labor and mechanical reproduction becomes the central issue; that is, as long as there is mechanical reproduction, the strike will go on forever. The text becomes less about the actual strike than about the role of mechanical reproduction in the workplace.

In contrast to the representation of domestic economy or the maternal womb, #44 is often described as the sole creator of the duplicates, such as when he chastises August for not being able to "conceive of something being made out of nothing" (114). Unlike August, #44 and his race "need no contributed materials [because] we *create* them – out of thought" (115). Sometimes the text invokes a maternal presence to explain the existence of the duplicates, and other times it insists on #44's autogenetic creation of the duplicates. As we saw in *A Connecticut Yankee*, a familial discourse thus competes with an unfamily-based or technological discourse. The maternal or domestic discourse in Twain's text, as well as in the texts of Wright, Wood, and others, seems to function as a way of naturalizing and familiarizing the technological model of reproduction. Perhaps locating the maternal body would put an end to this unraveling of identic categories. But this body is nowhere to be found.

VI. SCIENTIFIC MANAGEMENT MADE UNMANAGEABLE

Although the work of producing Bibles has been accomplished by the duplicates, the work they have done in, or rather done to the text *The Mysterious Stranger, #44*, has been inefficient and confusing. Very few characters and even fewer readers have been able to distinguish between originals and duplicates. Katzenyammer's duplicate is introduced in the following way: "A heavy step was heard, all glanced up nervously, and yonder in the door appeared *a duplicate Katzenyammer!* . . . then the house sat paralyzed and gazing. This creature was in shop-costume, and had a 'take' in its hand. It was the exact reproduction of the other Katzenyammer to the last shade and detail, a mirror couldn't have told them apart" (87). Similarly, another character notes, "One of them's the Duplicate, the other's the Original, but I can't tell t'other from which, and I don't suppose *they* can" (154). This frenzy of duplication creates what Susan Gillman has recently described as a "narrative [that] aims to decenter the reader" and the very characters in the text.[73] Paradoxically, the construction of efficient duplicates leads to massive hermeneutic problems in the text. Part of the reader's difficulty is that the duplicates and the originals usually have the same name, with August as a notable exception, making it difficult to know exactly whether the duplicate or the original is speaking. The narrator, for example, quotes his friend Fischer but then adds, "Of course it could have been his Duplicate that said it, there's never any telling, in this bewitched place, whether you are talking to a person himself, or only to his heathen image" (155). August refers to this nominal chaos as "the enigma of those names" (124) or "the secret of this mystery, the how of it, the why of it, the explanation of it" (122). August, as well as the reader, must "unpuzzle the puzzle" (125) and "unriddle the riddle" (128) of these names that paradoxically do not name. As #44 says to Emil Schwarz, "I try to make you out, I try to understand you, but it's all fog, fog, fog – you're just a riddle, nobody *can* understand you" (150–1). Duplicates cannot be distinguished from originals, and even dream selves (which it turns out is another term for duplicates) get confused. Thus #44 playfully suggests that they "turn the maid into a cat, and make some *more* Schwarzes, then Marget would not be able to tell t'other from which, and couldn't choose the right one" (140).

Having the same name and not having the same name prove to be equally confusing. Marget, one of the characters in the text, falls in love with August's duplicate, Emil Schwarz. Marget's dream self, however, named Elisabet Von Arnheim, insists she is in love with Martin Von Giesbach, who, we are told, is the dream self of Emil Schwarz, himself a dream self of August. The only thing clear about the proliferation of names is that they do nothing to clarify the identities of persons. Like names in *Life on the Mississippi,* which are not necessarily reliable indices of persons, names in *The Mysterious Stranger, #44* allude to an allegorical population that may or may not be made up of embodied persons. This quagmire is further confused by the end of the text, in which it is revealed that #44 is August's allegedly true dream self.

The unreadability or, in the language of scientific management, the inefficiency of characters (are they originals, duplicates, dream selves?) is in the text itself – characters no longer know their own voices, and words, or the typographical characters on the page, are no longer recognizable. For example, after one of his transhistorical, cross-continental voyages, #44 asks August to "talk into the thing which he brought" – a tape recorder. "#44 then reversed the machine and allowed me to listen to my voice as other people were used to hearing it" (146). August feels alienated from his disembodied voice and reports, "I recognized that it had so little resemblance to the voice *I* was accustomed to hearing that I should have said it was not my voice at all if the proof had not been present that it was" (146). Like the names in the text that cannot designate their rightful owner (because there are always at least two owners to a name), voices are also disowned. Like the duplicates, August's duplicated voice is both familiar and unfamiliar. A similar disorientation and reversal occur at the end of the text when #44 decides to "turn time backward for a day or two" (177). About two pages of the text are then played backward. Not only are the events of the text's last twenty-four hours retold, but the dialogue itself reads backward. Thus, when #44 says, "I've taken a lot of pains with that reputation; I've taken more interest in it than anything I've planned out in centuries" (178–9), two pages later the words now sound and look like gibberish: "Centuries; in out planned I've anything than it in interest more taken I've reputation; that with pains of lot a taken I've" (180). Although the narrative has revealed itself as simply one more piece of machinery that can either be fast forwarded or rewound, it has also become illegible.

Like the original workers who protest the mechanical reproduction of themselves, the mechanical reproduction of the narrative voice is inscribed in the text in the form of the tape recorder and is then undermined. The culmination of scientific management is thus achieved in the text in the construction of efficient workers and the making of a machinelike text, and yet that very culmination proves to be its own undoing. Scientific management, though creating efficient workers in an industrial economy, wreaks havoc upon a literary one. A paradigm of characterological reproduction based on technology ends up resulting in a deconstructed world of proliferating characters whose identity is unattached to any coherent signifying structure. Thus #44 tells August, "We have no character, no *one* character, we have all characters" (152), and later he reminds August that there is "*nothing* permanent about a dream-sprite's character, constitution, beliefs, opinions, intentions, likes, dislikes, or anything else" (160).[74] Such characters lack any trace of interiority, and they are often described as "leather-headed" (139, 140) or "wooden" (69, 79). They are "honest in one dream, dishonest in the next" (152), or sometimes "duplicates know languages – everything, – sometimes, and then again they don't know anything at all" (155). They are profoundly arbitrary, mechanical, and allegorical. But their mechanicalness, far from alluding to a kind of mechanical efficiency, signifies a complete absence of interiority that cannot be disciplined. Thus August's frustration with #44's "vacant" (148) expressions and unmotivated actions: "You are as indifferent about this as you are about everything else. You show no feeling whatever, you don't even show interest" (150). The solution to one labor problem, that is the originals' strike and the creation of duplicates, generates another version of another labor problem, that is the technological reproduction of allegorical, unidentifiable persons. Although the text seems to hold out the possibility that a maternal body might put an end to this deconstruction, the appearance of that body, of that "original," is forever deferred.

The only thing that does put an end to this drama of mechanical reproduction is its status as a dream. The dream ending of *The Mysterious Stranger, #44* has been the subject of much critical debate, with Edwin Fussell arguing that the final chapter "outlines a general theory of solipsism" and Bruce Michelson claiming that the dream is the logical conclusion to a text that has all along induced "a kind of vertigo, with every structural and thematic rug pulled out from under us."[75] It is also possible to read the conclusion of this text in the context of Twain's attitude toward the efficiencies and inefficiencies of his literary labors. As in the case of *Life on the Mississippi* and *A Connecticut Yankee*, Twain imagines his literary labor to be complete only when the signs of that labor are erased, which is accomplished either by killing off characters, blowing up the Man-factory in the Battle of the Sand-Belt or, in this case, erasing the Bible factory (and everything/everyone else) through the dream ending. Thus #44 says to August, "In a moment you will have realized, this [I am but a dream], then you will banish me from your visions and I shall dissolve into the nothingness out of which you made me" (186). As the characters in the text disappear into a kind of "Dream-mush" (129), so too does Twain's labor disappear. But with a difference. It seems particularly important that #44 also tells August, "I your poor servant have revealed you to yourself and set you free" (186). Like #44, Twain's labor is free from the restraints of efficiency that had vexed him in his earlier texts. He is free to create all kinds of characters, whether they be duplicates, dream selves, or originals. His repertoire of characters can even include people who were once dead, as is evident in the Assembly of the Dead. This assembly, it turns out, can also include characters from Twain's earlier texts, such as "King Arthur [who] came along, by and by, with all his knights" (184). The digressiveness of these final scenes is astounding indeed. Not only does Twain return to characters from previous texts, he plays back the events of *The Mysterious Stranger, #44* itself, and he even goes back to the world of the dead.

The dream ending, while erasing the allegorical population of the text, nevertheless aligns it with the logic of (humorous) inefficiency. What gets erased are not so much the signs of Twain's labor (as in the case of *A Connecticut Yankee,* where the Man-factory is completely destroyed) as the signs of a certain kind of managed labor from which Twain is able to disentangle himself in this final text. Having "no *one* character" (in the sense of an individual, consistent identity) permits Twain to "have *all* characters" (152). When #44 explains to August, "The Duplicates are not real, they are fictions" (97), it is powerfully clear that fiction operates under the sign of inefficiency. They have become invulnerable to discipline. The labor of Twain's allegory and the allegory of labor in this text have succeeded in wreaking havoc both on a literary economy that requires fictional characters to possess qualities such as interiority and originality and on a market economy that, above all, demands that its laborers be efficient. This humorous havoc, this unmanageable freedom, comes from unraveling the very basis of efficiency by applying it to a literary text. Inefficiency is the result of completely surrendering to the logic of efficiency. Taylor's system is, in the end, "damned altogether" not by being challenged by its opposite but simply by letting it destroy itself. In *The Mysterious Stranger, #44* Twain has staged an encounter between the fictive and market economies that manages to unmanage them both. "The best way to manage" is not to "skin your fact each time and lay on a new cuticle of words" (151), as Hank would have it, but to let management unmanage itself.

The Manikin, the Machine, and the Virgin Mary

The burden of individualized, interiorized characters is abandoned in *The Mysterious Stranger, #44* as Twain discovers a kind of liberation from the constraints of efficiency in the construction of duplicated characters. To be sure, the manikin in the preface to *The Education of Henry Adams* looks extremely familiar after our discussion of duplicates and #44. Such characters participate in a strikingly different narrative of American identity, a narrative of allegorical personhood as opposed to the customary symbolic one. They have an unconventional, to say the least, relation to nature, interiority, and individuality, and their mere presence issues a perilous warning to all traditional notions of coherent and organic identity. Nevertheless, how each of them comes to subvert conventional configurations of personhood is slightly different. For example, the unraveling of identity brought about by the indistinguishability of duplicates and originals in *The Mysterious Stranger, #44* does not exist in *The Education,* because there are no originals with which/whom duplicates can be confused in Adams's world. There are only manikins. The confusion of a manikin, furthermore, has less to do with its relation to an original identity, as was the case with Twain, and more to do with its relation to the proliferating number of fictional identities it may inhabit. Will it wear the clothes of a banker or a mechanic? Will it occupy the shop window of Macy's or a less expensive imitation? And how successful will it be at selling the products it dons? But for all of the differences between Twain's duplicates and Adams's manikin – and we shall get to them – these unlikely fictional characters, these allegorical characters, primarily exist in relation to the discourse of work. To put it even more forcefully and precisely, their being is directly necessitated by changes in the nature of work; the duplicates because of the factory strike and the manikin because of the consumer society's need to create as efficient as possible a labor force that will produce and continue to stimulate consumption.

This chapter begins, then, by focusing upon the manikin as a literal object that exists at the border between the worlds of work and leisure – in the shop window dividing those who work from those who buy and translating one into the other. The elegant transparency of the window, and the manikin that both passively and actively waits within/behind it, belies the complicated performance of that manikin to bring about a syn-chronicity of production and consumption, labor and leisure. The bound-aries between these two terms, as we have seen, function to organize and normalize any number of activities, including the writing of literature. The oppositionality of these terms has greater and lesser degrees of stabil-ity, and it is clear that the manikin, in powerfully innovative ways, trans-gresses this boundary yet again. To read *The Education* in the context of this continuing and by now familiar debate about work and leisure, and the place of literature in that opposition, is to understand Adams's work as one of our culture's most powerful meditations upon, enactments of, and sustained critiques of the work ethic. Like Twain, Adams mounts this critique by challenging the categories of labor and leisure, efficiency and inefficiency, as defined by scientific management. Even someone like Ad-ams, a member of an American dynasty, a representative of upper-class gentility, could not conceive of his own story outside the discursive frame-work of the work ethic. When it seems that Adams cannot be more anti-thetical to all that his culture represents, for example when he espouses his allegiance to the ideals of his eighteenth-century forebears or when he stands worshipping the Virgin at Chartres in *Mont-Saint-Michel and Chartres*, Adams, it turns out, cannot be more implicated in his nineteenth-century historical context. Like Melville, Adams found the work ethic to be a problematic means of constructing identity in that it promised a coherent and satisfying identity that it could not deliver. Both fulfilling labor and the individual identity that was to be its reward seemed fictional. If the allegory of labor in *The Education* makes this point, Adams's labor of allegory delineates an alternative work ethic that abandons the burden of individual identity.

I. TAILORS, PATRONS, AND MANIKINS

The manikin, with its absence of interiority, its mechanical body, and its function in the network of production and consumption, inaugu-rates Adams's allegory of labor. Approaching the manikin as first and foremost a material object opens up new ways of understanding the place of the manikin in the preface and in *The Education* as a whole. First, the presence of the manikin situates Adams in the department store, that shrine of consumerism which was as representative of the cultural ideol-ogy of nineteenth-century America as the Chicago World's Fair. Second, the presence of the manikin grounds Adams's text in the discourse of scientific management and efficiency. The manikin, who has the paradoxical status of worker and consumer, functions for Adams as an ideal for both his labors (textual, political, and otherwise) and his inability to labor. Third, the manikin exemplifies an ideal of bodily efficiency that liberates Adams to imagine the possibility of a coherent identity but imprisons him in that very search for coherence. Like the manikin's ability to project simultaneously an experience of absence and completion, Adams's configuration of bodies projects his own sense of fragmentation onto them and imagines them as potentially complete persons. Throughout *The Education*, Adams puts forth education, and later the cult of the Virgin, as possible "cures" for his manikinlike position vis-à-vis the world. But whether or not Adams wants to be cured, whether or not he is willing to trade in his frustratingly incoherent identity for an identity based on his culture's errant work ethic, is the unresolved issue that generates Adams's entire text. And last, the manikin firmly situates Adams in the debate that has been the subject of this book – the relation between literature and labor, between representations of work in texts that specifically designate themselves as literary and texts that do not. Whereas the manikin seamlessly encapsulates the principles of production and consumption, Adams ultimately seeks to occupy an alternative position outside the paradigms of production–consumption and labor–leisure.

In the preface to *The Education*, the narrator introduces a tailor, a patron, and a manikin. The patron wishes to purchase a particular garment which the tailor then makes which the manikin then models. As any reader of the text knows, Henry Adams, surely one of the best-educated Americans of his time, uses this sartorial scenario to suggest that finding an education that will prepare him for the complexities of life in twentieth-century America is an arduous task indeed, one made especially difficult by the fact that the clothes of the fathers no longer fit the sons. In other words, what Adams half-regretfully (and always half-ironically) realizes is that the younger generation must begin, in the words of Stephen Greenblatt, the process of "self-fashioning."[1] The manikin thus provides Adams with a figure upon which to drape "the toilet of education . . . in order to show the fit or misfit of the clothes."[2]

To complicate matters even further, the manikin is just one of several identities adopted by Adams in the preface: "The tailor adapts the manikin as well as the clothes to his patron's wants. The tailor's object, in this volume, is to fit young men, in universities or elsewhere, to be men of the world, equipped for any emergency; and the garment offered to them is meant to show the faults of the patchwork fitted on their fathers" (xxx). Although Adams initially figures himself as a manikin, with "the same value as any other geometrical figure of three or more dimensions" (xxx), it turns out that he is also the tailor, whose object is "to fit young men, in universities or elsewhere, to be men of the world" (xxx). Throughout *The Education*, Adams the tailor will make a variety of garments for Adams the manikin to sample. Adams, however, occupies not only these two positions, but also a third, the patron, and his relation to the patron is particularly vexed. In control of the situation, the patron communicates his/her wants to the tailor, who then materializes those desires into the manikin's garment. Much of this chapter will be devoted to studying those garments and the problems generated when the patron's desires conflict – and they frequently do – with the garments adopted by Adams.[3] The sole representative of authority in this triangle, the patron, is continually undermined by Adams, whose text works to subvert the authority not just of the patron of the preface but of all the patrons in *The Education*.

With this preface, Adams invokes a tailor–patron relationship that was becoming increasingly rare in stores like Macy's, which had already opened workshops "for the manufacture of men's shirts" in 1879 and by 1885 was manufacturing everything from children's underwear to linen collars. Although the tailor certainly had a place in the manufacture of clothes, he or she had become less of an independent craftsperson and more of an adjunct to the department store, often in the position of seamstress.[4] The manikin played a crucial role in the developing culture of department stores because it enabled shoppers, individually and en masse, to visualize a fantasy of what they might look like in a new set of clothes. The manikin in the shop window was one of the most powerful signifiers of the fact that for the first time American consumers could purchase mass quantities of mass-made garments in large department stores. The increasing use of manikins, ornate window displays, and stately architectural schemes made department stores, such as Macy's and Marshall Field's, more than just places to buy necessities. The window displays of Arthur Fraser, designer of the Marshall Field's windows, became famous throughout the world because of his lavish displays using "mannequins in Parisian gowns" and sometimes even "headless mannequins."[5] According to one historian, Chicago department stores, such as Field's and Selfridge's, turned the Loop into "a vast promenade of huge glass windows in which mannequins stood as mistresses of taste to teach people how to embody their secret longings for status in things of great price."[6] Like the secret-bearing sphynx, the silent manikins imparted all manner of valuable advice from the latest fashions to hints for the upwardly mobile.

As the arbiters (or the vehicles for the arbiters) of taste, manikins played a crucial role in the dissemination of cultural value. They encouraged the purchase of specific products that bore the marks of American ideology. But the manikin was itself a cultural product as well. It not only displayed what colors and fashions were in or out of season, but it also helped construct and maintain a model body that simultaneously worked and consumed at an ideal level of efficiency. The manikin possesses a purely inorganic, disembodied, and disemboweled body that permits it to be at once purely productive and purely consumptive, or productive of consumption – purely productive in that it produces the desire to consume and purely consumptive in its ability to generate that desire ad infinitum. The construction of this ideal body, whose scientific efficiency is guaranteed by an interiority that does not exist but relentlessly demands fulfillment, became essential to the development of a consumer-oriented economy during the 1890s.

Whereas Taylorism offered a guide for the construction of an efficient worker's body, Thorstein Veblen's theory of "conspicuous consumption" analyzed the culture's strategies for the invention of the perfect consumer body. The efficiency of, for lack of a better term, "salesman[ikin]ship" derives from what Stuart Culver has described as the dual signification of the manikin's body: the manikin, he suggests, must "project the image of a complete body while simultaneously dramatizing a present lack."[7] That is, the manikin has to represent the consumer's body as fragmented in order to sell the commodities required to restore his/her "intactness" at the same time that it must create a competing representation of its "intact body" in order for consumers to imagine the fulfillment of their desires. But the manikin did not only embody an image of the consumer. It also provided workers with an ideal image of themselves. The manikin's lack of a circulating and circulatory body, after all, made it an ideal worker. Without having to be cared for (other than getting an occasional dusting), without requiring any respite for food, rest, or hygiene, a manikin's work is never done, or rather it is always done. In fact, it cannot do anything else but work. Furthermore, because the manikin has no body upon which those signs can be seen, the signs of labor remain invisible. The logic of the work ethic is fulfilled by the manikin's bodiless body. The manikin thus represented the ideal consumer whose body could be made to fit any garment and the ideal laborer whose services required no attendance and whose pockets, like Twain's duplicates, needed no wages. Representing both consumer and worker in the space of the shop window, the visual space that has the power to transform workers into consumers and rewrites consumption as labor, in particular the labor of middle-class women, the manikin became one of the ultimate strategies of worker and consumer efficiency in the department store.[8]

Worker efficiency had become the watchword in these new department stores as sophisticated technologies enabled management to maximize the space of the store and to train the laborers in it. The manikin participated in these changes, for, after all, it was the body constructed in the factory for the purpose of selling commodities in the department store – a retailing space which, as Susan Porter Benson reminds us, imitated the very structure of the factory. Department stores used the factory as a model for discipline and profit. Time and motion studies, like those in Taylor's workshops, were conducted because management suspected that customers "with the apparent intention of buying . . . went away without being served."[9] Clarence Bertrand Thompson, advocate of Taylor's system, claimed that along with "a science of production . . . there is a science of selling, too, and many people are trying to find out what it is, thus recognizing the application of this manufacturing principle to marketing." Speaking like a good scientific manager, Thompson recommended that department stores "eliminate wastes of equipment, materials, and later of effort."[10] Labor that looks effortless, that seems erased, is of course one of the hallmarks of the work ethic. Not only did architects and managers rearrange the space of the store and departmentalize the tasks of salespersons in order to make shopping more enjoyable, profitable, and effortless, but the use of manikins dovetailed with this "science of selling" and elimination of wastefulness. Producing neither physical nor temporal waste, the manikin did not even have to undergo the training in scientific management required by wasteful (read "human") workers.

II. A MASTER OF DISGUISE: LABORER OR LOAFER?

Throughout *The Education*, Adams the manikin tries on the garments of the medieval historian and the Washington socialite, the clothing of a drifter (367) and a beggar (337), and the worn-out garb of the unemployed laborer (322). Most criticism of this text, however, has focused on only one of Adams's multiple self-fashionings: Adams the displaced patrician, doomed to unhappiness because of his inability to adapt to the demands of an industrialized America. We recognize this portrait as the Henry Adams presented to us in many of the most famous passages of *The Education*, but as I have already begun to suggest, the less famous passages might give us a considerably different view of Adams, the suffering elitist alienated from all aspects of nineteenth-century culture. Along these lines, we would do well to keep in mind that when Adams journeyed to the Chicago World's Fair in 1893, he not only "sat down helpless before a mechanical sequence" (342), he also "haunt[ed] the lowest fakes of the Midway day and night."[11] Like the other 27.5 million travelers who visited the World's Columbian Exposition to witness the "rapid advancement, the gravitating attractiveness, and the grandeur of American civilization,"

Adams derived great pleasure from observing some of its more frolicsome exhibitions, such as the snake charmers, the gladitorial contests, and "the most popular citizen of the village . . . Mr. Claas, the big orang-outang from Sumatra."[12]

Although Adams thoroughly enjoyed the "sweet repose" of the Midway Plaisance, he omits such frivolous activities from *The Education* and emphasizes his chronic suffering and "helplessness" (341). Historians have been drawn to this elite Adams who spent a lifetime grappling with the effects of Darwin's theory of natural selection upon society or the impact of the laws of thermodynamics upon historiography, while literary critics have concentrated on Adams's use of language to argue either for a formal unity or a linguistic instability in the text.[13] By departing from these more traditional views of Adams, which "connect him with Harvard dandies and Wildean poseurs," it is possible to place him in a more immediate relationship with the pressing issues facing turn-of-the-century American society, the most significant being, for the purposes of this analysis, Adams's relation to Taylor's scientific management and its doppelganger, the labor movement of the early twentieth century.[14] Adams was not only "harnessed to the family go-cart" (265), as Jackson Lears has argued, but also to an entire cultural apparatus that required continual demonstrations of loyalty and was met with continued protest. Adams's hitherto neglected postures in *The Education* will situate this Boston Brahmin in some highly unusual and strikingly original (for an Adams, that is) contexts.

Connecting Henry Adams, great-grandson of President John Adams and grandson of President John Quincy Adams, to the issue of labor in the late nineteenth century might seem odd indeed. But preceding his metaphysical talk about unity, multiplicity, and his struggle to synthesize them, Adams is primarily concerned with the fact that "he reached his twenty-sixth birthday without the power of earning five dollars in any occupation" (194). Even though Adams holds a variety of positions throughout *The Education*, whether as private secretary to his father, professor of medieval history at Harvard University, or editor of the influential magazine the *North American Review*, he continually returns to the problem of a métier and obsesses about the ambiguous value of his labor.

Adams finds himself in this quandary, one which will last throughout the book, as early as its opening chapter, "Quincy." The paradox of Adams's labor is actually a paradox of education; namely, that education does not occur when one is trying to get educated but rather when one is not looking. Contrasting the discipline of the Boston schoolhouse to the freedom of summer life, Adams writes of his happiest and most productive moments: Education "passed in summer lying on a musty heap of

Congressional Documents in the old farmhouse at Quincy, reading 'Quentin Durward,' 'Ivanhoe,' and 'The Talisman,' and raiding the garden at intervals for peaches and pears. On the whole he learned most then" (39). Adams's sensual education – reading fiction, eating fruit, and simply wasting time – during the summer months in Quincy proves more valuable than institutionalized education, which "he always reckoned . . . as time thrown away" (38). Against a self-conscious search for enlightenment, Adams posits this more spontaneous, haphazard approach to learning as more worthwhile and more conducive to true education.

Such an inversion of the conventional ways in which education has been perceived might be dismissed as just another instance of Adams's perverseness and/or pomposity or as evidence of Adams's allegiance to an upper-class, genteel approach to labor. Throughout *The Education*, however, Adams delights in exposing the ignorance of his teachers in order to reveal his superior intellect. For example, when Samuel Langley guides Adams through "the great hall of dynamos" (380), Adams piercingly writes, "A historian who asked only to learn enough to be as futile as Langley or Kelvin, made rapid progress under this teaching" (381). Adams reserves his most scornful words for teachers, perhaps because he himself was one. But even if the educative thrill he derives from eating peaches or reading by himself is a part of his attack on authority figures in general and teachers in particular, these scenes also exemplify Adams's earliest attempts to challenge conventional definitions of leisure and labor. In fact, Adams's disdain for authority and his transgressions against the work ethic are inextricable. By championing the educative value of leisure time rather than traditional labor or school time, *The Education* launches its critique of the work ethic.

Adams's position as private secretary to his father, Charles Francis Adams, during the Civil War years best exemplifies the vague borders of Adams's labor and leisure time. He acknowledges that though his post as private secretary "was irregular . . . yet it lent itself to a sort of irregular education that seemed to be the only sort of education the young man was ever to get" (145). The irregularity of Adams's position takes on greater significance as the vagaries of his career become associated with his lack of a coherent identity. "The young man knew no longer what character he bore. Private secretary in the morning, son in the afternoon, young man about town in the evening, the only character he never bore was that of diplomatist, except when he wanted a card to some great function" (194), the meaning of which "he never knew" (197). Adams's description of his daily round suggests a similar lack of direction: "He had only to reckon so many breakfasts; so many dinners; so many receptions . . . all counting for nothing in sum, because, even if it had been his official duty – which it was not – it was mere routine, a single, continuous, unbroken act" (212). If these various engagements do not make up his official duty, which is what Adams claims here amidst an impressive proliferation of negatives, it is difficult to know exactly what would. One of Adams's most pressing problems is, therefore, his inability to distinguish between leisure and labor time. If only he could tell the difference, he could figure out his character; or that at least is the implicit assumption of the passage. His labor turns into leisure and vice versa, leaving Adams with an overwhelming sense of his own wastefulness and unproductivity.

Relating to his father like a servant to his master, Adams finds himself enacting some version of labor that is not quite labor and something that is not quite leisure either. The problematic categories of leisure and labor also occupied one of Adams's most famous contemporaries, Thorstein Veblen, who describes the experience of household servants in the employ of the leisure class, a situation not unlike the one faced by Adams in his own relation to his father. Veblen states the case quite emphatically:

> By virtue of their serving as evidence of ability to pay, the office of such domestics regularly tends to include continually fewer duties, and their service tends in the end to become nominal only. This is especially true of those servants who are in most immediate and obvious attendance upon their master. So that the utility of these comes to consist, in great part, in their conspicuous exemption from productive labour and in the evidence which this exemption affords of their master's wealth and power.[15]

This is clearly Adams's relation to his own work at the American delegation, "which led to nothing and nowhere except Portland Place and the grave" (212). This lack of clearly productive (or unproductive) labor as well as an absence of clearly productive (or unproductive) leisure haunts Adams throughout *The Education*: "For Henry Adams – not private secretary – all the time taken up by such duties was wasted" (205).

"The law of conspicuously wasteful expenditure of time and substance" (82), as understood by Veblen, is the law Adams both obeys and wishes to undermine. But to rebel against the obligation to waste time as freely as possible would be an odd rebellion indeed, and one with which Adams will have nothing to do. Presumably such a rebellion would establish a new and more rewarding relation between Adams and his work, something akin to Veblen's "instinct of workmanship," which "disposes men to look with favour upon productive efficiency and on whatever is of human use. It disposes them to deprecate waste of substance or effort" (93). But this deprecation of waste is certainly not forthcoming in *The Education*, where Adams observes about himself (in the third person, as always), "The student's only clear gain – his single step to a higher life – came from time wasted" (80). Adams's text turns Veblen's relatively stable categories of conspicuous consumption and the instinct of workmanship inside out as the student finds himself in a situation where time wasted and time not wasted are equally questionable. Although Veblen powerfully problematizes the role of inefficient productivity (or, to use the more general and popular term, conspicuous consumption), his allegiance to the instinct of workmanship remains unshaken and unquestioned because of his ultimate belief in the ideology of the work ethic. In contrast to Veblen, then, the radically unstable position in which Adams finds himself, with respect to both the value of his labor and the nature of his identity, is a function of his fundamental lack of faith in the dominant ideology of the culture that constructs and organizes personal identity – the work ethic.

Adams spends most of *The Education* mounting a critique of the definitions of efficiency and inefficiency as provided by the work ethic, but in order to launch a truly devastating attack he must first be prepared to give up the most prized benefit bestowed upon those who agree to live according to the principles of the work ethic, individual identity. Even though the work ethic has miserably failed Adams, and neither his work nor his leisure time provides him with anything other than a sense of "the sheer chaos of human nature" (153), and especially his own, the cause-and-effect relation between work and identity still exerts a powerful influence upon the text. This relation promises Adams that if he can only find work that will be meaningful, he will find (the meaning of) himself. Thus, while Adams enjoys the chameleonlike position that enables him to inhabit various identities and offers him the illusion of freedom, he finds that position ultimately lacking in that it prevents him from becoming individuated. Like a manikin, he simply adopts one persona after another, never finding the garment that truly fits. Even if "it now became possible to have a size," as Walter Benn Michaels suggests in his brilliant analysis of standardization in late-nineteenth-century America, Adams can't figure his out.[16] If having a size suited to one's individual needs involves one's membership in a larger class of similar-sized individuals, Adams's inability to find the right size suggests an ambivalence about both his individuality as an Adams and his class identity as an Adams. We might think of Adams as an emperor with no clothes going from one shopping emporium to another, only to discover that not only does no one carry his size, but they can't figure out what that size is because it is always changing.

Although we shall return to this portrait of Adams the ideal consumer whose needs can never be completely fulfilled, it is important to keep in mind that his narrative includes an important psychological component as well. In a father–son version of object relations, Adams's lack of individuation is a direct consequence of his undefined relationship to his father. In the chapter "Diplomacy," Adams describes his problematic status as private secretary to his father. On the one hand, "he was [a] most fortunate person . . . having for master only his father who never fretted, never dictated, [and] never disciplined" (112). On the other hand, however, "most secretaries detested their chiefs, and wished to be anything but useful" (117). Adams is both grateful to his father for being a kind master and angry at the minister for being his master in the first place. His sense of uselessness is thus predicated upon an attachment to his father which not only circumscribes but precludes all attempts to become something other than son or secretary. Rather than considering Adams as a man without any profession whatsoever, we might begin to think about him as so completely professionalized, as so inextricably defined by the work that he does, that his continual search for a career is also an attempt to eschew the careers that seem to find him (and here we might remember that Harvard sought Adams for the position of medieval historian and editor of the *North American Review*). This identification of father and son finds its fullest expression in "Political Morality" as Adams recalls the circumstances which made him private secretary: "It was the first – and last – office ever offered him, if indeed he could claim what was offered in fact to his father. . . . Any young man could make some sort of Assistant Secretary; only one, just at that moment, could make an Assistant Son" (145). Adams's career as assistant secretary becomes indistinguishable from his role as son; hence, his identity as an assistant son. His professional identity becomes hopelessly obscured by his filial obligations, as in this passage, where the language of filial dependence is inseparable from Adams's account of his professional duties: "By courtesy [he was] allowed to go to Court as Attaché, though he was never attached. . . . In society, when official, he was attached to the Minister; when unofficial, he was a young man without any position at all" (145). Adams's attachment to his father paradoxically functions to make him feel personally adrift and professionally useless.

Adams's "helpless sense of being" (111, 384) is a consequence of (his experience of) failed labor and, as such, needs to be understood in the discursive context of the early-twentieth-century debates about labor that enabled us to historicize the late works of Melville and Twain. Characterizing himself as a "drift[er]" (426), "a vagrant as well as a pauper" (93), and "a beggar" (337), Adams keeps company with some of the foremost writers of American literature, like Washington Irving and Walt Whitman, as well as a new breed of potentially dangerous vagrants.[17] According to Michael Denning, this rather innocuous image of the tramp began to change in response to the 1873 depression and the 1877 railroad strikes.

The category of the tramp, he argues, was an "ideological naming of the new phenomenon of unemployment."[18] Once magazines, legal institutions, and charity organizations began to problematize this mental and physical nomadology, tramping gradually lost its romantic mystique and came to be known as vagrancy, a category of idleness invented and controlled by the law, which defined vagrants as "idle persons . . . having [no] visible means of support [and] liv[ing] without lawful employment."[19] In an article entitled "The American Tramp," the writer quotes Jack the Hobo, a magazine version of Huck Finn: "I seen places where you wouldn't never want to do nothin' all day, but just lay there, smellin' them flowers and listenin' to them birds." Beneath this "dream of the Golden Age of Vagrancy," however, are grave sanitary and ethical problems for American society.[20] Vagrants, warned this author, could no longer be left to their own devices, because they threatened the physical and moral health of America. Tramps did not work presumably because they wished not to, but what about vagrants? Were they just modernized versions of tramps, or were vagrants unemployed because they could not find work?

Leaving aside the possibility that vagrants might signify deep fissures in America's social fabric, Washington Gladden in 1876 urged his readers to "shovel dirt, saw wood, do any kind of reputable work, rather than abide in idleness."[21] The simple act of doing work, even work that did not pay, would begin to solve the vagrancy problem. The mere invocation of the work ethic would apparently release its restorative powers and heal the economic depressions and class conflicts that marked nineteenth-century America. Yet, as American laborers became increasingly vulnerable to the fluctuations of a market economy, even those who preferred not to "abide in idleness" found themselves unemployed.[22] As the words of Gladden illustrate, the appearance of vagrants and tramps evoked calls for reform in the workplace as well as jeremiads against what Henry Ward Beecher had years before called "the sins of idleness."[23]

Although Americans had always disapproved of idleness, the sophisticated cultural mechanisms with which to stamp out this unproductive behavior had not yet been constructed. As efficiency became the anthem of politicians, preachers, and management, a reciprocal taxonomy of inefficiency was established in order to distinguish among the various levels of unproductivity.[24] The transformation of the relatively innocuous tramp of the antebellum years into the turn-of-the-century dangerous vagrant is just one element of this elaborate taxonomy. By far the greatest danger was posed by idlers who did not work while they were at work. These were called soldierers. Scientific management became the technology through which the unacceptable behavior of soldiering, or "deliberately working slowly so as to avoid doing a full day's work," could be made visible and disciplined.[25] Unlike tramps, idlers could not be clearly distinguished from workers; the problem for Taylor, then, was that persons could simultaneously be both workers and idlers. The task of scientific management included rooting out the idling behavior in workers and turning them into efficient laborers.

In *The Principles of Scientific Management*, Taylor sings the praises of "the ready-made, competent Man" created by his system. In an allusion to his time-and-motion studies, Taylor explains how one of his followers, Frank B. Gilbreth, "reduced [a bricklayer's] movements from eighteen motions per brick to five, and even in one case to as low as two motions per brick." Gilbreth accomplished this feat by determining "the best height for the mortar box and brick pile, and then designed a scaffold, with a table on it, upon which all the materials are placed, so as to keep the bricks, the mortar, the man, and the wall in their proper relative positions. . . . The bricklayer avoids either having to turn the block over or end for end to examine it before laying it, and he saves, also, the time taken in deciding which is the best edge and end to place on the outside of the wall."[26] The importance of this description lies not only in the "man" walled in between the mortar and the wall (certainly reminiscent of Bartleby) but also in the simultaneous restricted motion and increased speed of the bricklayer's body. Successful Taylorism required the elimination of any physical movement or personality trait that interfered with efficiency. This excision of extraneous movement combined with continual, efficient speed characterized the manikinlike "ready-made man" of scientific management.

What Taylor attempted to achieve in the domain of labor efficiency, Adams tried to do in the sphere of personal identity. Twain's dual commitments to efficiency and inefficiency are repeated in Adams's contradictory allegiances to scientific management and wastefulness. Indeed, according to the logic of scientific management, Adams is a wasteful, inefficient worker. If the manikin constitutes the ideal Taylorized worker, then Adams must become a manikin. He therefore applies the laws of thermodynamics to the human personality and studies himself, in Taylor-like fashion, as a potential worker in order to formulate the most efficient and productive management scheme for his labor. The principles of scientific management promise to discipline Adams, who is caught in drift – a state of locomotion which might best be defined as movement minus teleology. For example, in the midst of office seekers surrounding President Grant's administration, Adams feels himself to be "drift[ing] among them, unnoticed, glad to learn his work under cover of the confusion" (255). Similarly, the discussion of the 1893 Chicago World's Fair finds Adams observing that "the American people probably knew no more than he did; but that they might still be driving or drifting unconsciously to some point in thought, as their solar system was said to be drifting towards some point in space" (343). From the broad perspective of the work ethic (the departure point for both the advocacy of scientific management and the resistance of organized labor against it), drift possesses no educative value. As we have seen, though, Adams is uncomfortable with both the work ethic and the conventional understanding of education which the work ethic promulgates. Although Adams eventually celebrates drift as a third term outside the binary opposition between labor and leisure, he first adopts the discursive garments made by Taylor and his opponents to see if, perhaps, they might give him the coherent identity he seeks.

The discourse of efficiency thus appears as frequently as the language of drift in *The Education*. Adams's analysis of President McKinley's administrative style makes the point: "Mr. McKinley brought to the problem of American government a solution which lay very far outside of Henry Adams's education, but which seemed to be at least practical and American. He undertook to pool interests in a general trust into which every interest should be taken, more or less at its own valuation, and whose mass should, under his management, create efficiency" (373). Adams's praise of McKinley's scientifically managed administration comes to an ironically grinding halt. "He achieved very remarkable results. How much they cost was another matter; if the public is ever driven to its last resources and the usual remedies of chaos, the result will probably cost more" (373–4). McKinley, though "a marvellous manager of men" (374), is thoroughly undermined by Adams's rejection of the conventional formula "efficient means good." The discourse of scientific management appears yet again when Adams characterizes German state education as "a sort of dynamo machine for polarizing the popular mind; for turning and holding its lines of force in the direction supposed to be most effective for State purposes" (78). He concludes this seemingly objective account with damning praise: "The German machine was terribly efficient. Its effect on the children was pathetic" (78). Although Adams uses the language of scientific management to measure the success or failure of his employment, he simultaneously critiques the very process that tabulates "work" according to a scientific procedure. Adams undermines scientific management, like all discourses in the text, as soon as he presents it as authoritative.

To focus exclusively upon the fact that the discourse of scientific management almost always works against itself throughout *The Education* is to overlook the more complicated ways in which Adams's appropriation of this discourse allows him to narrativize his dilemma as that of the abused and misunderstood laborer in late-nineteenth-century America.

Like many contemporary workers, Adams presents himself and other characters in *The Education* as attempting to deal with new industrial techniques that had begun to dominate factories and had spread to the spheres of politics, art, and literature. For example, in the chapter "President Grant," Adams speaks the language of a dissatisfied laborer: "In such an atmosphere, one made no great pretence of hard work. If the world wants hard work, the world must pay for it; and, if it will not pay, it has no fault to find with the worker" (257). Similarly, like workers who felt themselves becoming more like the machines they operated, Adams could say that his mind also "felt itself helpless . . . as though he were a Branley coherer" (384). Or he might claim that "every man . . . if only as a machine, has had to account to himself for himself somehow" (472).

The capacity to account for oneself, however, becomes increasingly problematic as men become machines. How does a machine account for itself? This is precisely the dilemma in which characters in *The Education* find themselves as Taylor's construction of the ideal worker and Adams's scientific management of himself lead to the mechanization and "manikinization" of bodies in the workplace and in the text. "The Abyss of Ignorance" begins with Adams's account of how his "mind stepped into the mechanical theory of the universe before knowing it" (427): "Adams never knew why, knowing nothing of Faraday, he began to mimic Faraday's trick of seeing lines of force all about him, where he had always seen lines of will" (426). This passage not only describes but also enacts the disappearance of "lines of will." "Faraday's trick of seeing lines" magnetizes and attracts Adams, so that without ever understanding Faraday's theory, Adams enters the realm of mechanical theory. Adams responds to Faraday not as a person but as a force; an understanding of Faraday the individual is irrelevant. By representing his mind as mechanized, Adams once again appropriates laborers' fears that new industrial methods were threatening their place in the factory.

Perhaps the clearest example of the effects of scientific management on the human personality, or the substitution of "lines of force" for "lines of will," occurs in Adams's description of his onetime close friend Charles Sumner:

> Sumner's mind had reached the calm of water which receives and reflects images without absorbing them; it contained nothing but itself. The images from without, the objects mechanically perceived by the senses, existed by courtesy until the mental surface was ruffled, but never became part of the thought. Henry Adams roused no emotion; if he had roused a disagreeable one, he would have ceased to exist. The mind would have mechanically rejected, as it had mechanically admitted him. (252)

Adams does not want us to miss the point that Sumner's mind has become mechanized. He uses the word "mechanically" three times in three sentences. Sumner, like the Carpenter of *Moby-Dick*, "reject[s]" and "admit[s]" people as if they were computer data. He is pure surface, lacking any interiority that could integrate "images from without." In his discussion of scientific management, Samuel Haber explains that Taylor's "concept of mechanical efficiency developed out of the application of the laws of thermodynamics to the technology of the steam engine" and then condemns it as an attack on "the cult of personality."[27] In Sumner, Taylor's program as described by Haber has been realized. In addition, the mechanization of Sumner prefigures what Adams will later describe as an entire "mechanical consolidation of force" (345) as well as a new kind of humanity which is a "product of so much mechanical power" that bears "no distinctive marks but that of its pressure" (466). By abandoning human nature and embracing force, Adams imagines himself as participating in a fantastic vision of pantomime with himself as "an acrobat, with a dwarf on his back, crossing a chasm on a slack-rope, and commonly breaking his neck" (434).

Adams's almost melodramatic helplessness is, of course, always mitigated by the fact that, unlike the laborers with whom he compares himself, he has enough money so as not to have to work. He makes this point while describing his nonpaying position as assistant secretary to his father: "No one had made a suggestion of pay for any work that Adams had done or could do; if he worked at all, it was for social consideration, and social pleasure was his pay" (257). As this passage makes clear, even if Adams uses the language of discontented laborers, his comparative monetary ease permits him to get paid a nonmonetary salary and therefore distinguishes him quite emphatically from workers whose livelihoods depended upon their adjustment to new techniques in the workplace. Furthermore, an equally important distinction between the two obtains by comparing what we have seen as laborers' relatively solid commitment to and Adams's basic lack of faith in the work ethic, which is most evident in his developing sense of drift.

Adams ultimately finds himself a stranger to the positions espoused by both scientific management and labor. We witness Adams's search for a position outside the traditional opposition between worker and vagrant, and yet his training in the Protestant work ethic affords him no terms outside that opposition, except for drift. The experience of drift eventually enables him to locate a third term outside this dichotomy, outside their reliance upon the work ethic. But drift does not initially possess this liberating quality. At first, it conveys nothing more than Adams's fundamental lack of direction and vexed relation to the work ethic. On the one hand, for instance, he claims that "his single step to a higher life . . . came

from time wasted; studies neglected; vices indulged; education reversed"
(80), and yet he apologizes for "drift[ing] into the mental indolence of
history" (36). Throughout *The Education*, Adams presents himself as pow-
erless to do anything about the permanent drift in which he seems to be
caught. He writes of "flounder[ing] between worlds passed and worlds
coming" (83) and confesses to "consciously pursu[ing] nothing, but drift-
[ing] as attraction offered itself" (366–7). But as we have seen in our
discussion of *Mardi*, drift can be a powerful way of challenging the traditional boundaries between leisure and labor, and this is precisely its function in *The Education*. By forcing the reader to endure a literary version of
drift, *Mardi* contested the opposition between reading and labor and
thereby challenged the assumptions of the work ethic. In the process, we
recall, the unraveling of this dichotomy undermined the patriarchal authority of the captain. Like *Mardi*, the presence of drift in *The Education*
destabilizes a constellation of authoritative discourses and authority figures, from the work ethic and the field of science to the power of teachers,
patrons, and fathers.

Adams's vexed relationship to labor, however, leads not to a denial of
social issues but to a direct confrontation. Adams adopts no single, unifying strategy (how could he when as a conservative Christian anarchist, he
is committed to the belief that "unity was chaos"[406]?) in his attempts to
dismantle this ideology of work that so powerfully and successfully unifies American culture. His celebration of drift, that term outside the work
ethic, suggests one way to undermine the nexus of identity and work,
and his appropriation and subversion of the work ethic offers still another. Adams's challenge to the Protestant work ethic in no way signals a
retreat from American life but rather forces Adams to analyze the very
foundations of American culture and identity out of which his subversive
identity as manikin, as conservative Christian anarchist, as destroyer of
all patrons, is constituted. In other words, Adams's challenge to a traditional configuration of identity based on the work ethic illustrates all the
more powerfully how Adams's identity is, in part, constituted by the
very paradigm of identity he wishes to undermine.[28]

III. LIKE MANIKINS: THE ADAMS FAMILY

Recall for a moment the process whereby Ahab's strangely organic and inorganic body produces the fragmentation of bodies aboard
the *Pequod*. The categories by which Ahab had understood the world
quickly unravel as Ahab's body undergoes its reconstruction. Simultaneously desiring to control and hasten the destabilization of his own body,
Ahab empowers himself by inflicting this corporeal mortification upon
his crew. Adams's use of the manikin body completes Ahab's dismember-

ment, but instead of waiting for some whale to come along, Adams dismembers himself. And like Ahab, Adams ends up turning himself into an allegorical character as well as everyone else. Then he rages about this state of affairs and places the blame upon technology. Paradoxically, he assumes the task of dismantling the very system of technology which he had created to help explain his own experience of bodily and psychic "manikinization." Adams's experience of corporeal "manikinization" is, as this section explains, painfully related to the fact that the Adamses could not have children. The images of sterility and fertility that pervade *Mont-Saint-Michel and Chartres* and *The Education* thus need to be understood in both their intensely personal and cultural contexts.

Any discussion of Adams's representation of bodies must attempt to deal with the little information available to us about Henry and Marian Adams's inability to have children. Unfortunately, Mrs. Adams's letters give no information about her response to their childlessness, and Adams's prolific correspondence omits any direct reference to the subject.[29] Yet scattered allusions to Adams's desire for children are not hard to find. Mrs. Alexander Whiteside, Mrs. Adams's lifelong friend, wrote that although Mrs. Adams wanted children, "not having any was a greater grief to Mr. Adams than to her."[30] And in response to the news of Mr. and Mrs. Charles Milnes Gaskell's first child, Adams offers his congratulations "on getting happily over this first great condition of marriage." This letter ends with a bittersweet acknowledgment that "one consequence of having no children is that husband and wife become very dependent on each other and live very much together."[31] Although Adams acknowledges a vital closeness with his wife, the letter clearly indicates that the degree of their mutual dependence is the price they pay for having no children.

The Adamses' acquaintance with S. Weir Mitchell, doctor to such well-known women as Jane Addams, Edith Wharton, and Charlotte Perkins Gilman, also suggests that they sought the advice of medical experts. Unfortunately, it is impossible to determine precisely how influential Mitchell's ideas about "the increase of nervous diseases . . . and the dying out of the maternal instinct" were upon the Adamses.[32] In addition to the occasional remarks about their childlessness and their relationship to Mitchell, Adams had apparently acquired the famous tract on female sterility by James Marion Sims, *Clinical Notes on Uterine Surgery – With Special Reference to the Management of Sterile Conditions.*[33] The word "management" in the subtitle of the book clues us in to Sims's view of female sexuality and the male's managerial responsibility toward maximizing the efficiency of his wife's reproductive labors. Thus his description of a gynecological examination sounds remarkably like Twain's experiments with workers at the typesetter and Taylor's attempts to reconstruct workers' bodies. "The knees are to be separated eight or ten inches; the thighs are to be at about right angles with the table; thus the plane of the table, the axis of the thighs, and that of the body, would form a right-angled triangle, of which the thighs and table would make the right angle and the body the hypotenuse."[34] Medical and managerial discourse converge upon the female body, the only difference being that Sims's "efficiency studies" occur with women on an examining table and Taylor's are performed upon the bodies of factory workers. Like Taylor, who insisted upon the uniqueness of each worker, Sims claimed that "the object of having two blades or specula to one shaft is merely to have them of different sizes so as to suit different vaginas; for there are no two vaginas exactly alike, any more than there are two faces precisely alike."[35] This concern for individuality served the larger project of scientific (and reproductive) management, which, according to Taylor, was the "*enforced* standardization of methods, *enforced* adoption of the best implements and working conditions, and *enforced* cooperation."[36] Sims's mechanical view of female sexuality, like Taylor's scientific approach to factory labor, gave birth to an entire technology of reproduction.[37] According to Seale Harris's biography of Sims, the doctor had a unique talent for "inventing new instruments to fit every occasion."[38] Even though the influence of Sims's opinions on Adams's view of his wife cannot be definitely determined, a discourse of biological sterility and mechanized reproduction can be found throughout *The Education*.

This anxiety about technological fecundity and female sterility, very much like the one in Melville's "The Paradise of Bachelors and the Tartarus of Maids," becomes Adams's topic in "Vis Inertiae." Whereas Melville's story suggests that the maids are being victimized by an unfair economic order, Adams holds women responsible for the situation in which they find themselves:

> So far as she succeeded, she must become sexless like the bees, and must leave the old energy of inertia to carry on the race . . . but the American woman had no illusions or ambitions or new resources, and nothing to rebel against, except her own maternity; yet the rebels increased by millions from year to year till they blocked the path of rebellion. Even her field of good works was narrower. . . . Socialism, communism, collectivism, philosophical anarchism, which promised paradise on earth for every male, cut off the few avenues of escape which capitalism had opened to the woman, and she saw before her only the future reserved for machine-made, collectivist females. (446)

Here the American woman rebels against maternity by becoming sexless, but her challenge to motherhood ends up producing another version of reproduction. Ironically, her very rebellion reproduces itself by "millions from year to year" until "the rebels blocked the path of rebellion." The image of the blocked path, the narrowed field, and the closed avenues of escape figure the body of this new woman as reproductively disabled, only capable of giving birth to "machine-made collectivist females." But reproduce she must.

Adams's text participates in a popular discourse of the late nineteenth and the early twentieth century that voiced a great deal of anxiety about the changing body of the "New Woman." As early as 1869, Horace Bushnell had spoken about the physiological consequences brought about by female reforms, such as suffrage: "[Women] will become taller and more brawny, and get bigger hands and feet, and a heavier weight of brain . . . [and] at the same time thinner, sharp-featured, lank and dry."[39] George Beard's medical research on neurasthenia, which was published in 1881, describes the increasing difficulty American women had during childbirth: owing to the pressures of "modern civilization . . . the simple act of giving birth to a child opens the door to unnumbered woes; beginning with lacerations and relaxations, extending to displacements and ovarian imprisonments, and ending by setting the whole system on fire with neuralgias, tremors, etc., and compelling a life-long slavery to sleeplessness, hysteria, or insanity."[40] These jeremiads about the New Woman constituted the female body as the ideological space most susceptible to the contaminations of modern life and most in need of its technological in(ter)ventions.

To understand the trajectory of Adams's thought from the barrenness of the female body to the reproductive capacity of the machine, one does not need to look any further than Adams's own home. We know that one of Mrs. Adams's greatest pleasures was photography, the mechanical reproduction of images. The body that could not reproduce a child turned to the reproduction of photographs. Once Adams's avocation, photography had soon become one of Mrs. Adams's favorite activities; she photographed historian George Bancroft and architect H. H. Richardson. That Adams introduced his wife to the pleasures of photography and that she eventually committed suicide by ingesting the chemicals used to develop pictures was an irony from which he never recovered.[41]

Although photography does not explicitly appear in *The Education*, the paradigm of female infertility and mechanical reproduction in Adams's text seems analogous to the Adamses' own experience of childlessness and artistic accomplishment and failure.[42] Photography does, however, make a crucial appearance in the preface to *Mont-Saint-Michel and Chartres*, in the form of the Kodak camera: "One niece is much more likely than two to carry a kodak and take interest in it, since she has nothing else, except her uncle, to interest her. . . . One cannot assume, even in a niece, too emotional a nature, but one may assume a kodak."[43] Although the Kodak appears only once in *Mont-Saint-Michel and Chartres*, it continually asserts itself as a rival scheme to Adams's own way of understanding Gothic art. Not only does the Kodak threaten Adams's description of medieval culture, it "jeopardize[s] by reproduction" Adams's belief in what he calls in *The Education* "the old occult or fetish-power" (479).[44] The language used by Walter Benjamin in his essay "The Work of Art in the Age of Mechanical Reproduction" and by Adams to describe the phenomenon of art's losing its "fetish-power" or "cult value" is remarkably similar. But whereas Benjamin, perhaps nostalgically, sees a form of liberation and democratization in these new techniques, Adams finds only cause for lamentation. Adams's task, as he imagines it, is to collapse the distance between himself and this earlier medieval culture, but the Kodak seems to embody and reinforce his separation. Although at moments Adams believes that he has captured the unity of the medieval world, particularly in his ecstatic union with the Virgin Mary, he represents history and technology as dooming his enterprise to failure. Unable to accept the potentially liberating elements of technological reproduction, Adams continues to mourn the loss of an allegedly unified world.

The irony of *Mont-Saint-Michel and Chartres* is that while complaining about this crisis of unity and blaming it on technology, Adams creates a separation himself by abandoning any relation to his nieces. Like the camera which disappears from the text, so too does the audience. Not only does Adams turn away from technology, he also alienates himself from the only available living community in his book – his nieces. Adams blames the Kodak for his alienation instead of the inattentiveness of his nieces or the character of their uncle. Obviously, he needs technology to explain the lack of relationship between himself and his community. This strategy of using technology in order to account for a more personal loss of community that Adams himself has helped to bring about also operates in *The Education* and can be seen most clearly in "The Dynamo and the Virgin," Adams's famous disquisition on the 1900 Paris Exposition.[45]

Following Adams's lead, critics of *The Education* have traditionally focused on his failures and have often pointed to this chapter as an illustration of the artistic problems in the book as a whole. Ralph Maud, for example, condemns the symbolism of the Virgin and the dynamo as "muddy and lethargic" and adds that "as a symbol [the Virgin] has been frittered away in the talk about forces."[46] In a more sophisticated reading, Melvin Lyon identifies two kinds of symbolism in *The Education*: "complex" and "rhetorical" symbolism. Without using the language of symbol and allegory, Lyon's interpretation of the dynamo and the Virgin nevertheless invokes the Coleridgean model and, unsurprisingly, ends up valorizing the "complex" symbol as opposed to "rhetorical" allegory: "Adams uses images in this narrowly rhetorical way . . . the imagery is still further devitalized [in *The Tendency of History*]. . . . The result is expression almost wholly lacking in that imaginative quality which more poetic images give most of his poetic work."[47] Lyon's evaluation fails to take into account that *The Education* exposes the fact that life in nineteenth- and early-twentieth-century America has fundamentally altered the notion of aesthetic images and has problematized the Coleridgean model which he upholds. This "lack in imaginative quality" is, in fact, constitutive of Adams's literary labor, which has dispensed with the possibility of transcendence and unity and has embraced a signifying logic of arbitrariness.[48] Adams himself alludes to this paradigmatic shift when he wryly notes in the chapter "Harvard College," "He did not lack the wish to be transcendental" (63).

The wish to be transcendental is, of course, different from the fact of being transcendental, and this distinction is duly noted in Adams's famous commentary in "The Dynamo and the Virgin" upon the role of symbols in culture: "The symbol was force, as a compass-needle or a triangle was force. . . . Symbol or energy, the Virgin had acted as the greatest force the Western world ever felt" (388). Adams seeks to discover whether or not the power of the symbol, as embodied by the Virgin, exists in American culture. Adams provides us with the answer at the conclusion of the chapter when he describes the process of artistic creation. "The pen works for itself, and acts like a hand, modelling the plastic material over and over again to the form that suits it best. The form is never arbitrary, but is a sort of growth like crystallization, as any artist knows too well; for often the pencil or pen runs into side-paths and shapelessness, loses its relations, stops or is bogged" (389). Like a good Coleridgean, Adams speaks of his writing in terms of the symbol, with its disdain of "arbitrar[iness]" and its valorizing language of "crystallization." The results of this organic procedure are, however, anything but symbolic in the Coleridgean sense of the word as "Adams covered more thousands of pages with figures as formal as though they were algebra, laboriously striking out, altering, burning, [and] experimenting" (390). Instead of achieving symbolic transcendence, Adams has written formal algebraic equations or "translation[s] of abstract notions into a picture-language," or what Coleridge had defined as allegory.[49]

At the same time as this passage yokes Adams's literary activity to the Coleridgean symbol, the results of his writing betray the presence of allegory. Adams's discourse certainly alludes to the romantic ideology of the mid nineteenth century, but the products of that romanticism are inveterately modern. In fact, Adams's attempt at a transcendental account of his own literary labors results in a rather untranscendental account of the act of literary labor as we witness Adams "laboriously striking out, altering, burning [and] experimenting" (390). This passage is unique in that throughout *The Education* Adams denies the fact of his labor. He barely mentions the voluminous *History of the United States During the Administrations of Jefferson and Madison*, which he wrote during the years covered in *The Education*, and when he discusses his dual role as Harvard professor and editor of the *North American Review* he remarks, "He had become a small spring in a large mechanism, and his work counted only in the sum" (309). It is significant that Adams's explicit acknowledgment of his labors occurs in a passage about literary labor and, more important, a passage that conceives of that labor according to the logic of allegory rather than symbol. This passage explains, in the language of literary labor, why Adams's labors never translate into the transcendental, coherent identity promised by the work ethic. It is because the work that goes into Adams's labors (literary and otherwise) can be neither transcended nor ultimately erased. Although Adams claims that "the result of a year's work depends more on what is struck out than on what is left in" (389), Adams, at least in this passage, leaves everything in. Like a manikin's, Adams's work is never done, but unlike a manikin's, his labors are both visible and wasteful. If Adams had deleted all of the labors he considers to be wasteful, and those labors that would be deemed wasteful according to the logic of scientific management, one might safely assume that *The Education of Henry Adams* would not exist. Although Adams claims not to be able to tell the difference between his labor and leisure time, between efficiency and inefficiency, between wastefulness and productivity, the effect of this indistinguishability is an undermining of a work ethic that defines and bifurcates these categories in the first place.

It is a sign of the enduring power of romantic ideology that this scene of visible labor is the one critics have found particularly displeasing. The presence of allegedly "devitalized," allegorical images in *The Education* suggests the power of the inorganic and the abstract, whereas symbolism depends upon a belief in transcendence and organicity. Cecilia Tichi, then, misses the point of allegory in *The Education* when she claims that "instead of liberating his symbols, Adams restricts them despite prodigious efforts to the contrary. In bondage to each other, the dynamo and the Virgin become the Siamese twins of literary symbols, attached, mutually restrictive, and ultimately grotesque."[50] It is interesting to note that the language of twentieth-century Adams criticism replicates nineteenth-century anxieties about the female body. Like the narrowed body of the New Woman that led to difficult pregnancies and horrific labors, Adams's restricted symbols give birth to the grotesquerie of Siamese twins. Adams's allegory replicates a perverted version of the female work ethic. Allegory, in other words, is messy labor.

Instead of debating the aesthetic value of these images, however, it will be more instructive to think about them, and particularly the Virgin, in the context of our analysis of Adams and the work ethic. When the work ethic is gendered, when the issues of efficiency, productivity, and consumption are applied to female labor and to reproductive labor in particular, new questions about identity based not on the relation between production and identity but between reproduction and identity take on a heightened degree of urgency. There is a sense in which the female work ethic as represented by the Virgin will provide Adams with an authenticated and stable identity. But this is something that not even the Virgin can do.

The Virgin is, to say the least, a key figure for Adams. In *Mont-Saint-Michel and Chartres* she inspires those who worship her to heights of religious ecstasy and sexual passion, to excellent architecture and exquisite taste. Indeed, she is the legitimate representative of the cult of true womanhood who, in her thirteenth-century manifestation, combines beauty, grace, and power. "She never calls for sympathy by hysterical appeals to our feelings; she does not even altogether command, but rather accepts the voluntary, unquestioning, unhesitating, instinctive faith, love, and devotion of mankind" (148). But to understand the Virgin as Adams's nostalgic backward glance at women in the good old medieval days is to miss the ways in which the Virgin ineluctably locates Adams in the rich discursive context of early-twentieth-century American culture. The figure of the Virgin, like the manikin before her, generates a strikingly similar constellation of issues, such as production, consumption, and labor, only now the male triangle of patron–tailor–manikin is complicated by the presence of a woman. In addition, like so many of the allegorical characters already discussed, whose temporality is at once archaic and modern, the Virgin looks back to a medieval religious tradition and looks ahead to a culture of conspicuous consumption.

Like the manikin, the Virgin illustrates the inextricability of consumption and production. Although Adams would like to imagine the Virgin in her purely religious incarnation, his account of her cathedral suggests that it is, among other things, a tribute to wealth and shopping. Adams's descriptions of her in *Mont-Saint-Michel and Chartres* attest to a surprising similarity between nineteenth-century women and this extraordinary thirteenth-century woman "who loved grace, beauty, ornament [and cared for her] toilette, robes, [and] jewels; – who considered the arrangements of her palace with attention, and liked both light and colour" (90). Like the woman in Veblen's leisure class whose defining activity was to ensure "the good name of the household to which she belongs" by putting "in evidence her household's ability to pay" (180), the Virgin of Chartres "was never cheap" (108) and required for her extravagant home "all the resources of art" (108). Adams admiringly notes how the Virgin's "feminine taste" (162) dominates all aspects of Chartres, whether it be the "space, light, [and] convenience" or the "colour decoration" that would "unite and harmonize the whole" (100). Because her desire is insatiable, she illustrates the ideal consumer who looks at the manikin through the window and imagines herself as always incomplete.[51]

As a female version of the manikin, the Virgin speaks to the culture's developing consumer ethos and provides a suitable object with which Adams can fill up his conspicuous leisure time. In her analysis of consumerism, Benson cogently explains the ideology of late-nineteenth-century department stores and their managers: "[They] urged a new therapeutic ethic upon their customers. . . . Shopping offered a cure for neurasthenia, an activity exciting enough to engage even the most jaded."[52] Adams constructs the Virgin as the solution to his neurasthenia, which he claimed "was really very good fun when you got used to it."[53] The Virgin, who "did not shut her costly Exposition on Sunday" (468), was, in fact, a consumer's dream. In "Vis Nova," Adams describes himself traveling through the twelfth, thirteenth, and fourteenth centuries as the "Virgin's glass opened rich preserves" (470). Always available, always "so winning" (472), she functions as an antidote to Adams's neurasthenia as she offers herself, in contrast to the "monthly-magazine-made American female" (384) of his time, to Adams as a perfect commodity. By turning the Virgin into a commodity, however, he becomes forever separated from her; or he comes to possess her in the only way he can – as a commodity. Just as he had disengaged himself from his nieces in *Mont-Saint-Michel and Chartres* and blamed technology for his loneliness, Adams once again finds himself alienated from the Virgin in his commodification of her and desperately trying to account for it.

But like the manikin, the Virgin does not only conspicuously consume. She illustrates an ideal of work or, more precisely, two ideals of work which turn out to be antithetical. On the one hand, the labor performed in the service of the Virgin is of a kind that freely and proudly calls attention to itself as labor, and, on the other, her body exemplifies that perfection of labor which erases the signs of labor at the very moment that it produces them. Adams keenly felt what Veblen had called the instinct of workmanship in the windows of Chartres: "We see, and the artists meant that we should see, only the great lines, the colour, and the Virgin" (195). In contrast to Adams's own mode of production, with its "labyrinths" and "gutters" (389) and its loss of relation, the artists at Chartres work collectively and, more specifically, within guilds; that is, the windows were donated and made by a variety of guilds ranging from stoneworkers to shoemakers. The window made by the merchant tailors, for example, features their signature at the bottom as well as an illustration of a thirteenth-century tailor's shop in Chartres where a "shop-boy takes cloth from chests for his master to show to customers, and to measure off by his ell" (166). Similarly, the signature of the furriers decorates their window, "where a merchant shows a fur-lined cloak to his customer" (168). The signatures in the windows, which include both a handwritten and pictorial representation of the appropriate guild, foreground the fact of labor. One's proper name has utterly given way to one's professional identity, which is doubly inscribed by the signature of the guild and the artistically rendered performance of the work done by the guild. Adams himself points to this erasure, or what amounts to it, of individual identity when he notes that even though an individual name does occasionally appear on a window, "the name tells nothing, even if the identity could be proved. Clement the glassmaker may have worked on his own account, or for others" (172). Far from lamenting this loss of identity and accountability, Adams finds the communal labor at Chartres liberating, because it evokes the foundational principles of the work ethic, where work signified one's relation to a higher power, in this case the divinity of the Virgin Mary.[54] Although one might argue that an individual's labor is similarly diminished in guilds and factories, guild workers benefit from such diminishment by gaining entree into the Virgin's spiritual kingdom, whereas factory workers get nothing.

What Adams witnesses in the cathedral at Chartres is an alternative to the American work ethic as organized by scientific management and deployed in factories – where identity and work are inextricable, without the existential asphyxiation produced by the work ethic of Adams's own culture, and where one works not for the sake of work itself but for a higher, indeed, a religious power. For Adams, Chartres restores the transcendental potential of work, in the tradition of Emerson, Channing, and others, that had been gutted by divisions in labor and the advent of the factory. Adams's vision of Chartres is not unlike Channing's ideal of labor with which my Introduction began; work allows us to become "one of God's nobility" (42). This is clearly not the work ethic of Washington Gladden's telling people to shovel dirt because idleness is inherently bad, but something radically different:

> The architect at Chartres was required by the Virgin to provide more space for her worshippers within the church, without destroying the old portal and flèche which she loved. That this order came directly from the Virgin, may be taken for granted . . . one sees her give orders, and architects obey them; but very rarely a hesitation as though the architect were deciding for himself. In his western front, the architect has obeyed

orders so literally that he has not even taken the trouble to apologize for leaving unfinished the details which, if he had been responsible for them, would have been his anxious care . . . the work shows blind obedience, as though he were doing his best to please the Virgin without trying to please himself. (112)

This image of work offers a powerful alternative to the "thickets of ignorance" (389) in which Adams finds himself as he tries to complete his education/*Education*. Adams also calls attention to the fact that the signs of the architect's labor remain visible to all, and enviously observes the artistic relief that this visibility permits. The work ethic of medieval culture guarantees that one's identity, whether inscribed by a personal name, a guild name, or a picture, is authenticated by the Virgin, who gives meaning to her worshippers. Adams's signature clearly has no such authorization. That *The Education* is an autobiography makes this fact all the more remarkable. It is as if Adams's signature, which appears on practically every page of *The Education*, title page included, cannot authorize itself. It is as if the signature alludes to a series of proliferating identities and disjunctions: it stands for the unbridgeable gap between the signature as that which inscribes the writer of the work into his own work and that which transforms the writer of the work into a character in that work, as well as the gap that exists between Adams's corporeal absence as writer of text and his presence as fictional character. Because these signatures are ultimately inextricable, Adams's "work" ends up producing multiple identities, or what Gregory Jay calls "an inevitable doubling," at the very moment when he is engaged in a quest to find his single, singular identity.[55] This doubling is, of course, most evident in the use of the third person. His signature, which should be the most visible sign of his literary labors and his individual identity, paradoxically registers the untenability of that (first-person) identity. Adams's signature bears a burden that the signatures in the windows of Chartres do not. Whereas the Virgin authorizes the signatures of the laborers of Chartres and values their labors as well (the evidence of their labor does not need to be erased), Adams is forced to authorize his own signature and his own labor. He cannot do this because his labors, literary and otherwise, do not give him the individual identity that is registered by the signature. Furthermore, the aesthetic ideology that calls for an erasure of labor (the signature being the most visible sign of that labor) undermines the signature itself. Thus the work ethic, as conceived of by Adams, simultaneously holds out the possibility of individual identity through rewarding labor and proves to be the greatest obstruction both to rewarding labor and to individual identity.

The greatest difference, then, between the work ethics of Chartres and

The Education would have to be the difference between the medieval principle of community labor and communal identity and the American version, with its nexus of labor and individualism. Adams concludes "The Dynamo and the Virgin" with a commentary on his own labor:

> Only with the instinct of despair could one force one's self into this old thicket of ignorance after having been repulsed at a score of entrances more promising and more popular. . . . The secret of education still hid itself somewhere behind ignorance, and one fumbled over it as feebly as ever. In such labyrinths, the staff is a force almost more necessary than the legs; the pen becomes a sort of blind-man's dog, to keep him from falling into the gutters. (389)

The educated, and therefore authentic, identity promised by this version of labor simply cannot deliver. Like a carrot on a stick – or, to be truer to the imagery of the passage, like a woman who promises what she will not deliver – the identity Adams seeks exists only by virtue of its unattainability. The closer one gets, the farther away it recedes. This disjunctive relation between work and identity is borne out in Adams's remarks about the relation between Langley, inventor of the bolometer and Adams's guide through the Paris Exposition, and his scientific discoveries: "He was not responsible for the new rays, that were little short of parricidal in their wicked spirit towards science. . . . The rays that Langley disowned, as well as those which he fathered, were occult, supersensual, irrational" (381–3). The language of the family and of ownership are here enlisted only to illustrate the radical disassociation, radical to the point of murderous, between Langley and his labor. Indeed, this version of labor can only result in disappointment when one discovers that work can, at most, prevent one from falling into gutters. It cannot confer individual identity.

V. THE PROMISE OF ANARCHY/THE END OF WORK

It is precisely that Ishmaelian liberation from individuality which nevertheless allows for the possibility of identity, only an identity as conceived through one's membership in a guild, that Adams longs for in *Mont-Saint-Michel and Chartres*. He celebrates the fact that "at Chartres no one – no suggestion of a human agency – was allowed to appear" (136), an absence of agency that proponents of the work ethic would certainly condemn as dangerously un-American and assuredly identity-threatening. But instead of a nightmare of mechanical, agentless workers whose lack of agency signifies their lack of identity, Adams discovers that this absence of individual agency could potentially lead to greater freedom and, oddly enough, to great art. Adams is thus surprised to discover that even though the cathedral has been made without a thought to individual desire and without the individual hand of an artist, "some controlling hand has given more or less identical taste to all" (172). He had expected that the various guilds with their different tastes would create an object of questionable aesthetic merit.[56] The hand of the Virgin, however, has the power not only to inspire great works of art but to make the act of labor itself an experience of transcendence. Her divine hand, unlike the invisible hand of the market, does not make individual identity impossible by turning people into "hands" but rather takes their individual hands and combines them to form a collective and satisfying identity. The religious transcendence made possible by this notion of labor is, therefore, accomplished by the individual's absorption into a communal religious identity. In stark contrast to a divine hand that directs and unifies the labors of the medieval guilds in a utopia of labor, Adams's human and individual pen, which "acts like a hand" (389), gets caught in "side-paths and shapelessness" (389). As much as Adams wishes to be directed and absorbed by the divine hand, he is too well versed and too committed to the logic of the work ethic of his time. Thus, as appealing as the notion of collective labor might be, Adams is unwilling, indeed unable, to abandon completely the promise of individual identity through labor as espoused by the work ethic.

The Virgin is an especially complex figure in Adams because at the same time as she encourages a kind of labor radically at odds with the work ethic as understood by most Americans in Adams's time, she also embodies that work ethic in its most pristine and ideal form. Only now the principles of the work ethic have shifted from the house of prayer to the bedroom, and the logic of the work ethic is brought to bear on labor, as in reproductive labor. In a comparison between American women, for whom "sex was sin" (384), and the Virgin, who had inspired "the highest energy ever known to man" (385), Adams writes in *The Education* that the Virgin was a "goddess because of her force; she was the animated dynamo; she was reproduction – the greatest and most mysterious of all energies; all she needed was to be fecund" (384). What seems particularly interesting about the role Adams has assigned to the Virgin is that not only does she constitute force but also fecundity and "the power of sex" (385). Although Adams celebrates the power of the maternal Virgin and the sexuality that is a part of her identity as a mother, he has chosen an extremely unusual "woman" as the representative of female sexuality. Not only does the Virgin immaculately conceive her child, but the birth is painless. Adams's knowledge of Saint Thomas Aquinas, as evidenced by his lengthy discussion of Aquinas in *Mont-Saint-Michel and Chartres*, would have meant his familiarity with Aquinas's views about the Virgin Mother in *Summa Theologiae*: "The pangs of childbirth are caused by the baby opening the passage from the womb. Now we have said that Christ came from his mother's closed womb without forcing a way. Consequently there was no pain in the birth and no injury done,"[57] Her fecundity thus has nothing to do with her biological body. As in a manikin, the signs of her (reproductive) labor remain invisible. Her labor is, in other words, labor-free.

It is ironic that even as Adams laments the fact that American "society regarded this victory over sex as its greatest triumph" (385), he presents as ideal a version of sexuality which would seem to be one of the greatest victories over sex and of female labor one could imagine. The woman's body in Adams's representation of perfect sexuality is actually the closest thing possible to the dynamo. Like the dynamo, which creates force without sexuality, so too the Virgin produces children and forces which require little if any help from the body. Adams's representation of the female body, then, would appear to suggest two antithetical positions: either "women were dead" (383) because American society had become "as far as possible sexless" (385), or women, in the image of the Virgin, could be "potent, not merely as a sentiment, but as a force" (384). Both of these identities, however, ultimately lead to an anesthetized, deadened female body. Moreover, Adams celebrates female reproductive power inasmuch as he imagines the impossibility of its return. Passages such as "his mind was ready to feel the force of all, though the rays were unborn and the women were dead" (383) or "in America neither Venus nor Virgin ever had value as force" (383) or "an American Virgin would never dare command; an American Venus would never dare exist" (385) suggest the relatively safe position from which Adams launches his attack on American sexlessness. Because an American Virgin would not dare to exist, Adams can plead with her to appear. And once she does appear in her incarnation as the dynamo, Adams no longer finds comfort in her: Adams, "the baby lying close against [the dynamo's] frame" (380), finds himself "lying in the Gallery of Machines at the Great Exposition of 1900, with his historical neck broken by the sudden irruption of forces totally new" (382), unable to turn to the Virgin because she and the dynamo have become one and the same. In a twentieth-century reenactment of the end of *Hamlet*, the dead body of the Virgin, the dead bodies of women, the lethal rays of Langley, and the body of Adams, victim of infanticide and death (by forces), conclude Adams's appeal to the Virgin.

The deadness of bodies in "The Dynamo and the Virgin" is intimately related not only to the Adamses' unreproductive bodies but also to a cultural concern with the technologizing of the female body and the formation of the New Woman. Yet the figures of the dynamo and the Virgin function less as antithetical images of sterility and productivity than as kindred images through which Adams's "mournfulness finds satisfaction."[58] If Adams's melancholy derives from a feeling of corporeal emptiness, or what we might call "manikinization," the cure resides in the power of that body to reinvigorate itself. This is precisely what takes place in a letter Adams wrote to Elizabeth Cameron about his infatuation with babies. He records a dream in which he had one: "One of my minds was rather surprised, and asked, in a puzzled way, whether men had babies as a rule; and my other mind at once replied with my usual positiveness and passion for generalisation, that men always had babies."[59] Like Hank Morgan's appropriation of maternity, in this dream Adams's body becomes female and gives birth to children. The dynamo, the Virgin, and the feminization of Adams's body rely on immaculate conceptions – a possibility denied to the Adamses.

This reading of *The Education* has thus far suggested that the discourse of the worker's and the woman's mechanized body permits Adams the historian to speak about his helplessness while concealing the rather ahistorical conviction that "we have always been the victims, never the causes. Disease, Insanity, Vice, Stupidity, have ruined our lives through those on whom we depended; we have been bankrupted by our partners, and commonly our partners have suffered first and worst."[60] Technology, though certainly bringing about enormous changes during Adams's lifetime, for instance "the great mechanical energies [of] coal, iron, [and] steam" (238), ultimately serves as a scapegoat for his experience of feeling like "a flotsam or jetsam of wreckage" (238). Adams's neurasthenia is the analogue to Ahab's melancholy. Unable to find a cure for his own mournfulness, Adams, like Ahab, reproduces his melancholy in the allegorical bodies of his text. Adams thus creates this elaborate representation of technology in *The Education* and then blames it for his own as well as his culture's problems. But Adams does not stop there. He also unmakes the system of his own making, and the concluding chapters of the text are the clearest evidence of this decreation. Although many critics of the final chapters of *The Education* point out the lack of narrative movement or the scientific quackery of his schemes, it is possible to read Adams's use of these scientific theories as an attempt to bring about "a universe of motions . . . of vertiginous violence" (495), a blitz of motion radically unlike the disciplined motions advocated by Taylor. This "universe of motions," which depends upon scientific theory for its representability, will bring about the destruction of the scientific world – the final and most powerful patron in *The Education*.

Writing to Elizabeth Cameron about *A Letter to American Teachers of History*, Adams observes: "I'm amusing myself by printing a little volume to make fun of my fellow historians. The fun of it is that not one of them will understand the fun. The *pince-sans-rire* is not an American form of humor."[61] This letter suggests that, at least with respect to his *Letter to*

Teachers, Adams sees his appropriation of historical discourse as something of a joke on his fellow historians. In *The Education*, his use of scientific language similarly functions as a joke on scientists. By using the theories of acceleration and thermodynamics, Adams turns the vision of science against itself. He confirms this ironic use of science when writing to Harvard English professor Barrett Wendell that his *Letter to Teachers* is a "scientific demonstration that Socialism, Collectivism, Humanitarianism, Universalism, Philanthropism, and every other ism has come . . . there is nothing possibly beyond, and they can all go play, and, on the whole, base-ball is best."[62] What critics have assumed to be Adams's definitive view of science, then, might be just one of his many challenges to authority, in this case to teachers.[63] Similarly, "A Dynamic Theory of History" and "A Law of Acceleration" do not necessarily constitute Adams's last effort to "arrange sequences" (382). Rather, in the late chapters of *The Education*, Adams wishes to undercut the very scientific theories he presumably attempts to authenticate.

These final chapters recapitulate the ironic lesson evident in an earlier chapter, "Dilettantism." Adams the dilettante of European art wishes to know if he has purchased a valuable painting. After he receives a series of contradictory opinions about a particular Rembrandt from the allegedly great British art authorities, he feels "as though the world had not been enough upset in his time [and] he was eager to see it upset more" (225). So too in his seemingly sincere attempt to find authority and sequence in the most sophisticated scientific laws of his day. Let us recall that in the earlier chapters Adams ironically portrays himself as a victim of people or institutions: "The young man was not very quick, and he had almost religious respect for his guides and advisers" (75). This respect for authority is quickly compromised when, only a few sentences later, Adams claims that he and the other students in his law class "could have learned from books or discussion in a day more than they could learn from [the professor] in a month" (75). Adams's "respect for his guides" thus rapidly develops into a critique of his "guides and advisers." A similar pattern can be observed in Adams's discussion of Darwin: "Every curate in England dabbled in geology and hunted for vestiges of Creation. Darwin hunted only for vestiges of Natural Selection, and Adams followed him, although he cared nothing about Selection, unless perhaps for the indirect amusement of upsetting curates" (225). Given Adams's penchant for "upsetting curates," it comes as no surprise when we read that "he could detect no more evolution in life since the *Ptersaspis* than he could detect it in architecture since the Abbey" (230). Adams's "respect for his guides and advisers" once again seems like empty rhetoric as he successfully challenges the authority not only of Darwin but also of another famous evolutionist, Sir Charles Lyell, whose work he allegedly respects.

So too in these later chapters, Adams's attitude toward such authorities as the chemist Wolcott Gibbs and the mathematician Karl Pearson is critical. In "The Grammar of Science," Adams characterizes himself, using the language of "Helmholz, Ernst Mach, and Arthur Balfour," as "a conscious ball of vibrating motions, traversed in every direction by infinite lines of rotation or vibration" (460). Given Adams's manikin persona, this "conscious ball of vibrating motions" can and should be seen as one among a series of garments he tries on throughout *The Education*. And yet because Adams wears this garment of science longest, readers have assumed correctly that he is most threatened by its power but deduced incorrectly that he has fallen a victim to it. Hence, critics have judged the garment authentic: Adams, the victimized Brahmin, "rolling at the feet of the Virgin at Chartres or of M. Poincaré in an attic at Paris, a centre of supersensual chaos" (460). By adopting the scientific theories of these men, however, Adams can use science against itself, just as he used the art expertise of the British curators to destroy their authority. If Adams's goal is to destroy the cultural authority that has inflicted immeasurable loss upon him, what better strategy than to infiltrate the scientific mind and attack it from within?

Although few critics of *The Education* have considered Adams's anarchist pose as anything other than the dilettantism of a Boston Brahmin, it is possible to see a genuine element of anarchy in Adams's understanding and deployment of mechanical forces. In "Vis Inertiae," for instance, Adams describes the typical American man with his "hand on a lever and his eye on a curve in his road [whose] living depended on keeping up an average speed of forty miles an hour, tending always to become sixty, eighty, or a hundred" (445). Earlier in *The Education*, Adams confesses that he has a certain inclination toward accelerating speeds when he writes: "What he valued most was Motion, and what attracted his mind was Change" (231). Although one might imagine that Adams's medieval sensibility was deeply offended by these new rates of speed, we find him learning how to ride a bicycle and traveling in an automobile while touring Gothic cathedrals in the French countryside.

And indeed, Adams now celebrates the power of speed. In *The Education*, the virtue of speed assumes a subversive quality, similar to the anarchy produced by drift, the difference being that speed is fast drift without a telos: "As anarchist, conservative and Christian, he had no motive or duty but to attain the end; and to hasten it, he was bound to accelerate progress; to concentrate energy; to accumulate power; to multiply and intensify forces; to reduce friction, increase velocity and magnify momentum" (406). Here Adams's language calls up a model worker who wishes "to accelerate progress"; however, his Luddite vision suggests the opposite – it is an attempt to push the scientific machine to its utmost limits in the hopes of destroying its power. Adams accomplishes this "multipl[ication] and intensif[ication] of forces" by assuming the bodily identity of the scientifically managed laborer. "Reduc[ing] friction, increas[ing] velocity and magnify[ing] momentum" are precisely what Taylor's system attempted. By pushing the scientific machine from "forty miles an hour . . . to sixty, eighty, or a hundred," Adams can, in effect, create a theater of motion which will ultimately self-destruct. And this is precisely what Adams does in the final chapters of the book. At the rate of at least one major scientific theory per chapter, these "lines of force" (as opposed to the more human "lines of will") take over the narrative, only to become "motion in a universe of motions, with an acceleration, in their own case, of vertiginous violence" (495). In Adams's appropriation of scientific management, this accelerated body, constructed in the name of technological progress, in the image of scientific management and the work ethic, effects the end of progress, the end of work.

Afterword

When President Theodore Roosevelt addressed an audience of journalists at the Gridiron Club in Washington, D.C., in 1906, little did he know that his speech would bequeath a name to a group of newspaper writers who brought to the public's attention the corruption of politics, business, and labor unions that would define their journalistic efforts as an historical movement of the early twentieth century. These were, of course, the muckrakers, a coterie of writers dedicated to exposing the worst in American society, whether they found it in the Standard Oil Company, as did Ida Tarbell, or in Chicago's meatpacking industry, as did Upton Sinclair. The muckrakers considered everything and everyone fair game. Indeed, when *Cosmopolitan* featured an article by David Graham Phillips about Chauncey Depew, the United States senator from New York, Roosevelt felt that he could no longer refrain from speaking out against the methods and intent of this new journalism. "With the muckrake," Roosevelt claims, this kind of writer "speedily becomes, not a help to society, not an incitement to good, but one of the most potent forces of evil."[1] In choosing the figure of the muckraker, Roosevelt firmly situated himself in the tradition of American allegory initiated in Hawthorne's texts – the radical tradition of an economics of allegory whose contours have been the subject of this book. That Roosevelt used the figure of the muckraker, who, after all, made his first appearance in *The Pilgrim's Progress*, to describe the activities of these journalists speaks to the enduring cultural power of Bunyan's text and, more important, makes fully explicit the critique of American individualism and the work ethic that had always inhered within allegory but had remained relatively implicit. Furthermore, the relation between individual agency and the muckraker's enterprise circulates within the highly charged context of Roosevelt's own campaign against the agency of corporations. By the early twentieth century, Hawthorne's Celestial Rail-road traveled exclusively on rails owned and operated by the Standard Oil Company.[2]

207

The muckrakers, many of whom wrote for *McClure's Magazine* at the turn of the century, deployed an array of authorial weaponry in an attempt to write stories that appealed to their audience's twin desires for realistic and emotional reportage. Their investigative pieces often included transcripts from legal trials and personal interviews and official documents from corporate headquarters, as in William Hard's 1907 exposé of the South Chicago plant of the United States Steel Corporation. A typical muckraking article combined the techniques of what would later characterize the documentary film with a fictional style condemned by Roosevelt as "sensational, lurid and untruthful" (60). "Lurid" accurately describes many of the articles, including Hard's, which details the horrible conditions endured by laborers at U.S. Steel and concludes with an image of the company undertakers who vulturelike wait at the gates of the plant to transfer its daily casualties: "You see them coming closer and closer. You see them settling down and waiting. And then you see the dead bodies coming out from the plant and being carried into the back rooms and being lawfully viewed and having true presentment made as to how and in what manner and by whom or what they came to be what they are now."[3] Almost any muckraking article attests to the effectiveness of this style to call forth sympathy, to evoke anger, and often to do both at once. Muckrakers successfully tapped into public outrage about economic, political, and social conditions either by melodramatically telling the story of an individual's desperate and ultimately thwarted attempt at Bunyanesque progress or by narrating, in a hard-boiled detective style, the story of individual corruption. Lincoln Steffens's piece on Doc Ames, "The Shame of Minneapolis," illustrates this second approach most pronouncedly in its opening paragraph: "Whenever anything extraordinary is done in American municipal politics, whether for good or for evil, you can trace it almost invariably to one man. . . . St. Louis is a conspicuous example of this form. Minneapolis is another. Colonel Ed Butler is the unscrupulous opportunist who handled the nonpartisan minority which turned St. Louis into a 'boodle town.' In Minneapolis 'Doc' Ames was the man."[4] The short sentences, simple and to the point, exemplify a no-nonsense style that delivers the unadorned facts to the reader, who can then respond to them with the appropriate outrage and, hopefully, with an ignited social conscience.

The style of the muckrakers displays a desire to reach their audience by any means possible as well as an ideological commitment to individual agency. One need only glance at the titles of many of their articles to realize that the motivation for such journalism stemmed, in part, from a belief that persons and their individual desires were ultimately accountable for social ills whose origins seemed at first so impossible to locate that they would appear to bear little relation to individual agency. One needed to rake the muck in order to expose the individuals who created the muck in the first place. For example, *Cosmopolitan* in 1906 included an article by David Graham Phillips, "The Treason of the Senate: Aldrich, the Head of it All," whose first paragraph concluded with an emphatic statement of blame: "For the organizer of this treason we must look at Nelson W. Aldrich, senior senator from Rhode Island."[5] Similarly, John L. Mathews, writer for *Hampton's Magazine*, locates the source of all corruption relating to the government's management of property claims in the person of the Secretary of the Interior, Richard Ballinger. Mathews's article, entitled "Mr. Ballinger and the National Grab Bag," starts out with a description of the riches contained in Oregon's Des Chutes River and then turns to the issue of individual culpability: "Mr. Ballinger has unloosed the drawstrings of the grab bag just enough to allow the whole Des Chutes River to be pulled out by two of the most earnest grabbers of the Northwest – James J. Hill and the late Edward H. Harriman."[6] It is certainly possible to conclude that this exposure of individual responsibility reflects a desire to sell magazines through sensationalizing and simplifying conduct that if seen in a broader context of institutional contingencies and social forces would, perhaps, lead one to denounce corporations rather than individuals. Roosevelt asks us to consider just this possibility in his 1906 speech.

Whereas the muckrakers saw their exposure of individual corruption as the best way to maintain individual agency, Roosevelt thought they failed miserably. Rather than personalizing corruption, they accomplished, he claimed, precisely the opposite: "There are beautiful things above and round about them; and if they gradually grow to feel that the whole world is nothing but muck their power of usefulness is gone. If the whole picture is painted black there remains no hue whereby to single out the rascals for distinction from their fellows. Such painting finally induces a kind of moral color blindness" (60). The aesthetic sensibility that informs this critique of muckraking is, unsurprisingly, antipathy toward allegory. Roosevelt perceives the muckrakers' attack on individuals as what he calls at one point an "indiscriminate assault upon character" (59), at another "the destruction of character" (59), and once more, the "gross and reckless assaults on character" (59–60). In the muckrakers' zeal to expose the corruption of individual agents, they end up destroying individual agency by producing allegorical characters who are invented out of "hysterical exaggeration" (59) and "sweeping generalizations" (60). Roosevelt subjects himself, of course, to the charge of hysterically exaggerating the position of the muckrakers (or is it the corporations?) when he transforms their individual identities into the individual identity of the muckraker – and an allegorical identity at that. Roosevelt here uses an allegorical figure from an allegorical text to critique what he sees as the muckrakers' predilection for turning individuals into allegorical figures and thus tautologically reinscribes the very dilemma from which he was trying to escape.

It should also be noted that the dangers of the muckrakers' character assassination assume an economic form typical of the economics of allegory we have seen throughout our analysis. "At this moment we are passing through a period of great unrest – social, political and industrial unrest. It is of the utmost importance for our future that this should prove to be not the unrest of mere rebelliousness against life, of mere dissatisfaction with the inevitable inequality of conditions, but the unrest of a resolute and eager ambition to secure the betterment of the individual and the nation" (62). Although Roosevelt has formulated the critique in a slightly different context, we see once more that the attack on allegory is based on its affinity with an economic state of affairs specifically having to do with class consciousness and deeply at odds with America's faith in liberal individualism. Moreover, the unrest and ambition required for the betterment of individuals and nations should also call to mind the discourse of the work ethic. If the muckrakers' exposure of the work ethic gone awry could not be redeployed to (re)secure the ideology of the work ethic and American individualism, their efforts offered no payoff. Their exposures only revealed the sediments of a dissolving work ethic and an American identity. They proposed no solutions.[7] Roosevelt's critique issues from precisely the fear that the muckrakers in their very attempt to uphold individual agency were undermining it.

Whereas the muckrakers exposed individual corruption in the name of individual agency, Roosevelt, at the conclusion of his address and throughout his political career, attacked corporations in the name of individual agency. The corporations of Roosevelt's speech, it turns out, have many of the same problems as the muckrakers. Both require "regulation and control" (64); both threaten the health of the body politic, the muckrakers with their "spasm of reform" (62) and corporations with their "swollen[ness] beyond all healthy limits" (63); and both are prone to "violent excesses" (64). It makes sense to find these similarities between muckrakers and corporations in Roosevelt's speech, because he sees them as fundamentally connected by their attack on individual agency. But Roosevelt himself could be charged with what he would see as a similar criminal offense. In his attempt to maintain individual agency by holding trusts responsible for their actions (rather than individuals), his position can be interpreted as an attack far more damaging to individual agency than anything proposed by the muckrakers. In a particularly enlightening passage, Roosevelt champions the muckrakers "so far as this movement of agitation throughout the country takes the form of a fierce discontent with evil, of a determination to punish the authors of evil, whether in

industry, or politics" (62). Roosevelt had earlier worried about the potential of the muckrakers to become "one of the most potent forces of evil"
(59). Exactly who are the authors of evil? Roosevelt's language clearly
collapses the differences between the corporations who author the evil
and the muckrakers who author the evil by exposing it. According to
Roosevelt, authors who expose evil can do as much damage as, if not
more than, those who authorize the evil in the first place. If this is the
case, the figure of the muckraker takes on new meaning. The muck is not
only authored by corporations but by the muckrakers themselves – the
muckrakers' rake figures as the pen that produces the muck, which
would seem to be a kind of excrescent ink. Roosevelt's critique of the
allegorical figure of the muckraker thus becomes an attack on authorial
labor – a conjunction that we have seen throughout our analysis of allegory. His critique of the muckrakers in the name of individual agency
collapses in upon itself as he undermines the authorial agency of the
muckrakers.

According to Roosevelt, "the high individual character of the average
citizen" (65) must be preserved at all costs, by exposing either individual
or corporate corruption, and this individuality of character is precisely
what allegorical characters would deny and what Roosevelt himself denies to the muckrakers when he classifies them in terms of an allegorical
figure. At the very moment that Roosevelt claims his allegiance to "individuality," he deploys the deindividualizing of allegorical characterization. Roosevelt's speech would seem to suggest that the most powerful
expressions of American identity depend upon an invocation and deployment of an opposite configuration of that identity – an economics of
allegory that challenges the ideological foundations of the work ethic and
the individual identity that was to be its reward.

Notes

INTRODUCTION

1. Edgar Allan Poe, "The Man That Was Used Up," in *The Complete Tales and Poems of Edgar Allan Poe* (New York: Random House, 1975), 406. All further quotations from Poe will be from this edition and will be noted in the text.
2. From *The Works of William Ellery Channing* (1882; rpt. New York: Burt Franklin, 1970), 39.
3. Samuel Taylor Coleridge, "Lay Sermons" (1816), in *The Collected Works of Samuel Taylor Coleridge*, ed. R. J. White (London: Routledge & Kegan Paul, 1972), 30. All further quotations from "Lay Sermons" will be from this edition and will be noted in the text.
4. See Jonathan Auerbach, "Poe's Other Double: The Reader in the Fiction," *Criticism*, 24 (1982), 341–361. Auerbach's assessment of Smith as a repudiation of the self-made man seems exactly right, although I think this repudiation needs to be extended to the level of Poe's relation to fictional character; that is, Poe's critique of the self-made man is also a critique of a particular kind of character readers had come to expect and even demand from authors. Also see Michael J. S. Williams, *A World of Words: Language and Displacement in the Fiction of Edgar Allan Poe* (Durham: Duke Univ. Press, 1988), 17–24.
5. Angus Fletcher, *Allegory: The Theory of a Symbolic Mode* (Ithaca: Cornell Univ. Press, 1964), 55. Fletcher's explanation of allegorical character can be found in the chapters "The Daemonic Agent," which includes a section, "Daemonic Mechanism and Allegorical 'Machines,'" that develops the connection between allegorical characters and machines (55–9), and "The Cosmic Image" (70–146). Charles Feidelson, *Symbolism and American Literature* (Chicago: Univ. of Chicago Press, 1953), 13. Feidelson is here discussing *The Marble Faun* and Hawthorne's predilection for allegory, which Feidelson describes as "the brake that Hawthorne applied to his sensibility" (14–15).
6. Walter Benjamin's *The Origin of German Tragic Drama*, trans. John Osborne (London: New Left Books, 1977), marks allegory's first entrance into the field of cultural studies, and my work has been profoundly inspired by his. Other

texts that have been influenced by Benjamin and have begun to explore the relation between allegory and cultural production include Wai-chee Dimock, *Empire for Liberty: Melville and the Poetics of Individualism* (Princeton: Princeton Univ. Press, 1989), Jonathan Arac, *Critical Genealogies: Historical Situations for Postmodern Literary Studies* (New York: Columbia Univ. Press, 1987), Donald Pease, *Visionary Compacts: American Renaissance Writings in Cultural Context* (Madison: Univ. of Wisconsin Press, 1987), Russell Reising, *The Unusable Past: Theory and Study of American Literature* (New York: Methuen, 1986), and Jane Tompkins, *Sensational Designs: The Cultural Work of American Fiction, 1790–1860* (New York: Oxford Univ. Press, 1985).

7. E. M. Forster, *Aspects of the Novel* (New York: Harcourt Brace & World, 1927), 78.

8. For a reading of flatness in a postmodern context, see Fredric Jameson, *Postmodernism, or, The Cultural Logic of Late Capitalism* (Durham: Duke Univ. Press, 1992).

9. Smith's body is exposed as a product of labor in the home. Thus, Poe's text undermines the myth of *hauteur* by positing authorship as labor *and* collapses the boundary between the domestic space of leisure and the marketplace of work. Gillian Brown's *Domestic Individualism: Imagining Self in Nineteenth-Century America* (Berkeley and Los Angeles: Univ. of California Press, 1990) offers a powerful analysis of domesticity and work. Also see Nicholas K. Bromell's *By the Sweat of the Brow: Literature and Labor in Antebellum America* (Chicago: Univ. of Chicago Press, 1993), which looks at how the distinction between manual and mental labor operated in antebellum culture. Although the problematic of literary labor is our shared subject, our analyses diverge in that Bromell does not consider its relation to allegory or to postbellum culture.

10. *Harper's*, 4 (1852), 709, quoted in *The Portable Hawthorne*, ed. Malcolm Cowley (New York: Penguin, 1977), 284.

11. *Graham's*, 18 (1841), 201. Equally (in)famous is his review of Hawthorne's *Mosses from an Old Manse*, in which he writes, "In defense of allegory, (however, or for whatever object, employed,) there is scarcely one respectable word to be said" (quoted in *The Recognition of Nathaniel Hawthorne*, ed. B. Bernard Cohen [Ann Arbor: Univ. of Michigan Press, 1969], 24).

12. Karl Marx, *Capital: A Critique of Political Economy,* ed. Frederick Engels (New York: International Publishers, 1967), vol. 1, 72.

13. Lloyd Spencer makes a related point in "Allegory in the World of the Commodity: The Importance of *Central Park*": allegory "register[s] the *dissolution* of the stable, hierarchised and meaningful existence which most allegory seems to imply. . . . Allegories, even those which proclaim the stability and fullness of meaning in the (hierarchised) universe can thus be seen as deconstructing themselves, as revealing the opposite of that which they seek to imply" (*New German Critique*, 34 [1985], 63). Similarly, Jean Christophe-Agnew in his reading of Melville's *The Confidence-Man* claims, "Thus Janus-like, *The Confidence-Man* points in two directions at once: backward toward an ancient tradition of corrective criticism, and at the same time forward, toward the modernist's stance of indeterminacy" (*Worlds Apart: The Market*

and the Theater in Anglo-American Thought, 1550–1750 (Cambridge: Cambridge Univ. Press, 1986), 201.

14. In contrast to Ahab, who rages against this state of affairs, Smith is relatively comfortable with it. See Michael Rogin, *Fathers and Children: Andrew Jackson and the Subjugation of the American Indian* (New York: Random House, 1976), and Richard Slotkin, *The Fatal Environment: The Myth of the Frontier in the Age of Industrialization, 1800–1890* (New York: Atheneum, 1985).

15. I see this as Poe's attempt to overcome what Marx describes as the alienation between worker and object in a market economy: "In the finished product the labour by means of which it has acquired its useful qualities is not palpable, has apparently vanished" (*Capital,* vol. 1, 183).

16. Whereas Christopher Wilson argues in *The Labor of Words: Literary Professionalism in the Progressive Era* (Athens: Univ. of Georgia Press, 1985) that the gentleman ideal of authorship was most strenuously contested in the latter decades of the nineteenth century, especially in the writings of the muckrakers, I want to argue that this construction of the author as divorced from "the driving impetus of bourgeois society – the ideal of productivity" (9) was, in fact, being challenged in the antebellum period.

17. Auerbach, "Poe's Other Double," 341. Another reading of Poe's relation to labor can be found in Terence Whalen, "Edgar Allan Poe and the Horrid Laws of Political Economy," *American Quarterly,* 44 (1992), 381–417. For a brilliant deconstructive reading of Poe, see Louis A. Renza, "Poe's Secret Autobiography," in *The Other American Renaissance,* ed. Walter Michaels and Donald Pease (Baltimore: Johns Hopkins Univ. Press, 1985), 58–89.

18. This project is indebted to Daniel Rodgers, *The Work Ethic in Industrial America, 1850–1920* (Chicago: Univ. of Chicago Press, 1974).

19. Darko Suvin, "Can People Be (Re)Presented in Fiction? Toward a Theory of Narrative Agents and a Materialist Critique Beyond Technocracy or Reductionism," in *Marxism and the Interpretation of Cultures,* ed. Cary Nelson and Lawrence Grossberg (Urbana: Univ. of Illinois Press, 1988), 667–8.

20. Michel Foucault, "Nietzsche, Genealogy, History," in *Language, Counter-Memory, Practice,* ed. Donald F. Bouchard (Ithaca: Cornell Univ. Press, 1977), 148.

21. Carolyn Porter, "After the New Historicism," *New Literary History,* 21 (1990), 269.

22. Raymond Williams, *Marxism and Literature* (Oxford: Oxford Univ. Press, 1977), 122.

23. Benjamin, *The Origin,* 177. Although he uses slightly different terms, Benjamin makes the same point as Williams: "Allegory, like many other old forms of expression, has not simply lost its meaning by 'becoming antiquated.' What takes place here, as so often, is a conflict between the earlier and the later form" (161).

CHAPTER 1. THE PROBLEM WITH LABOR AND THE PROMISE OF LEISURE

1. Quoted in Jay Leyda, *The Melville Log: A Documentary Life of Herman Melville, 1819–1891,* vol. 1 (New York: Gordian, 1969), 305.

2. *Harper's*, 1 (1850), 140.

3. The gentlemanly ideal is, perhaps, nowhere more evident than in Washington Irving's preface to *The Sketch Book of Geoffrey Crayon, Gent.* (New York: New American Library, 1961), in which he confesses, "My whole course of life . . . has been desultory, and I am unfitted for any periodically recurring task, or any stipulated labor of body or mind. I have no command of my talents. Practice and training may bring me more into rule; but at Present I am as useless for regular service as one of my own country Indians or a Don Cossack" (x).

4. In *Bodies and Machines,* Mark Seltzer makes a similar point: "Naturalist writing instances a fundamentally different understanding of the work process and of the relation of writing and representing to the work process. What this involves in part is the incorporation of the representation of the work process into the work process itself. But, beyond that, it involves the incorporation of the representation of the work process *as* the work process itself" (New York: Routledge, 1992), 14. The "fundamentally different understanding of the work process" requires us to ask, different from what? What Seltzer identifies as a "turn of the century" (11) phenomenon in America can and should be seen as a defining feature of antebellum culture and, more important, a feature of an aesthetic ideology developed within the discursive context of and specific to antebellum America: a disintegrating work ethic.

5. Ralph Waldo Emerson, *Essays: First and Second Series* (New York: Library of America, 1983), 37.

6. *The Works of William Ellery Channing* (1882; rpt. New York: Burt Franklin, 1970), 39.

7. Augustus Woodbury, *Plain Words to Young Men* (Concord, N.H.: Edson C. Eastman, 1858), 104–5.

8. Horace Greeley, *Hints Toward Reform* (New York: Harper Bros., 1850), 86–7.

9. Henry Ward Beecher, *Lectures to Young Men on Various Important Subjects* (1844; rpt. Boston: Jewett, 1853), 33.

10. *Voice of Industry*, 1, no. 15 (September 4, 1845), 4.

11. Ibid., 1, no. 35 (February 13, 1846), 3.

12. Ibid., 1, no. 13 (August 21, 1845), 2.

13. Ibid., 1, no. 22 (November 14, 1845), 2.

14. Ibid., 1, no. 13 (August 21, 1845), 2.

15. Thomas Skidmore, *The Rights of Man to Property* (1829; rpt. New York: Burt Franklin, 1967), 231.

16. William Heighton, *Address to Members of Trade Societies and the Working Classes* (Philadelphia: William Heighton, 1827), 4.

17. Unlike Leo Marx, who argues that "the pastoral ideal remained of service long after the machine's appearance in the landscape" and "enabled the nation to continue defining its purpose as the pursuit of rural happiness while devoting itself to productivity" (*The Machine in the Garden: Technology and the Pastoral Ideal in America* [Oxford: Oxford Univ. Press, 1964], 228), I argue that the pastoral ideal was always complicated by the fact that it could not be invoked outside the context of mechanization.

18. Daniel Rodgers, *The Work Ethic in Industrial America, 1850–1920* (Chicago: Univ. of Chicago Press, 1974), 67.

19. See Merritt Roe Smith, *Harper's Ferry Armory and the New Technology: Challenge of Change* (Ithaca: Cornell Univ. Press, 1977), 80.

20. David Montgomery, *Workers' Control in America* (Cambridge: Cambridge Univ. Press, 1979), 13.

21. Quoted in Philip S. Foner, *The Factory Girls* (Urbana: Univ. of Illinois Press, 1977), 135.

22. See John Kasson, *Civilizing the Machine: Technology and Republican Values in America, 1776–1900* (New York: Penguin, 1976). Also see Thomas Dublin, *Farm to Factory: Women's Letters, 1830–1860* (New York: Columbia Univ. Press, 1981), Thomas Dublin, "Women and Outwork in a Nineteenth-Century New England Town: Fitzwilliam, New Hampshire," in *The Countryside in the Age of Capitalist Transformation*, ed. Steven Hahn and Jonathan Prude (Chapel Hill: Univ. of North Carolina Press, 1985), Jonathan Prude, "The Social System of Early New England Textile Mills: A Case Study, 1812–40," in *The New England Working Class and the New Labor History*, ed. Herbert G. Gutman and Donald H. Bell (Urbana: Univ. of Illinois Press, 1987).

23. Quoted in Foner, *The Factory Girls*, 134.

24. *Voice of Industry*, 1, no. 14 (August 28, 1845), 3. For a further discussion of this conjunction, see Ronald Walters, *The Anti-Slavery Appeal: Abolitionism After 1830* (Baltimore: Johns Hopkins Univ. Press, 1976). In "Bodily Bonds: The Intersecting Rhetorics of Feminism and Abolition" (*Representations*, 24 [1988], 28–59), Karen Sanchez-Eppler focuses more particularly on the discursive relation between women and slaves.

25. *Lowell Offering*, ser. II, vol. 3 (1842–3; rpt. Westport, Conn.: Greenwood, 1970), 191.

26. Elisha Bartlett, *A Vindication of the Character and Condition of the Females Employed in the Lowell Mills* (1839; rpt. New York: Arno, 1974), 13.

27. *Corporations and Operatives: Being an Exposition of the Condition [of] Factory Operatives, and a Review of the "Vindication," by Elisha Bartlett, M.D.* (1841; rpt. Lowell: Samuel J. Varney, 1843), 16.

28. William Scoresby, *American Factories and Their Female Operatives; with an Appeal on Behalf of the British Factory Population and Suggestions for the Improvement of Their Condition* (Boston: Ticknor, 1845), 64.

29. In her reading of Andrew Jackson Downing's American Gothic, Gillian Brown argues, "Downing's house plans obscured every sign of work" (*Domestic Individualism: Imagining Self in Nineteenth-Century America* [Berkeley and Los Angeles: Univ. of California Press], 77). Whereas Brown understands "the corporeality of women's work" (64) as the special target of erasure, I would argue that these erasures are not limited to female labor but apply to labor in general and that these erasures omit not only "woman's agency from her own labor" (64) but men's agency as well.

30. Woodbury, *Plain Words*, 137, 80.

31. Daniel Eddy, *The Young Man's Friend: Containing Admonitions for the Erring; Counsel for the Tempted; Encouragement for the Desponding; Hope for the Fallen* (Lowell: Nathaniel L. Dayton, 1851), 84.

32. Edward Bruce, *The Century: Its Fruits and Its Festival. Being a History and*

Description of the Centennial Exhibition, with a Preliminary Outline of Modern Progress (Philadelphia: Lippincott, 1877), 42.

33. Theodore D. Woolsey, David Wells, E. P. Whipple, et al., *The First Century of the Republic: A Review of American Progress* (New York: Harper Bros., 1876), 209.

34. Edward Everett Hale, *Public Amusement for Poor and Rich* (Boston: Phillips, Sampson, 1857), 4.

35. Catharine Beecher, *Letters to the People on Health and Happiness* (New York: Harper Bros., 1855), 88.

36. Catharine Beecher, *Temple of Health* (New York: Harper Bros., 1854), 169.

37. Throughout this discussion of leisure I heed Gareth Stedman Jones, who issues the following warning: "It would be a fundamental mistake to develop [research into nonwork time] into a subject in its own right," because "leisure time is clearly constricted by type and hours of work" (*Languages of Class: Studies in English Working Class History, 1832–1982* [Cambridge: Cambridge Univ. Press, 1983], 87).

38. Quoted in Herbert Gutman, *Work, Culture and Society in Industrializing America* (New York: Random House, 1977), 15.

39. Ann Douglas, *The Feminization of American Culture* (New York: Avon, 1977), 252; see, in particular, her chapter "The Domestication of Death: The Posthumous Congregation" (240–72). Like Douglas, I am interested in how Mount Auburn, by exemplifying an ideal of invisible labor, provides an ideal text for antebellum Americans.

40. Jacob Bigelow, *History of the Mount Auburn Cemetery* (Boston: James Munroe, 1860), 13. See Neil Harris, *The Artist in American Society: The Formative Years, 1790-1860* (Chicago: Univ. of Chicago Press, 1982), for an analysis of the cemetery movement.

41. Jacob Bigelow, *Elements of Technology* (Boston: Hilliard, 1829), 4. This is, in fact, the first recorded use of the word "technology" in America.

42. Quoted in Harris, *The Artist in American Society*, 203.

43. Douglas, *The Feminization of American Culture*, 253.

44. Mary Ryan, *Cradle of the Middle Class: The Family in Oneida County, New York, 1790–1865* (Cambridge: Cambridge Univ. Press, 1981), 147, and Karen Haltunnen, *Confidence Men and Painted Women: A Study of Middle-Class Culture in America* (New Haven: Yale Univ. Press, 1982), 130.

45. In "Reification and the Consciousness of the Proletariat," Georg Lukács explains the relationship between these two natures: "On the one hand, men are constantly smashing, replacing and leaving behind them the 'natural,' irrational and actually existing bonds, while, on the other hand, they erect around themselves in the reality they have created and 'made,' a kind of second nature which evolves with exactly the same inexorable necessity as was the case earlier on with irrational forces of nature" (*History and Class Consciousness: Studies in Marxist Dialectics* [Cambridge: MIT Press, 1971], 128). Although Lukács nostalgically claims an ontological status for first nature, his formulation nevertheless remains useful for describing the function of the category of the "natural" with respect to the "made."

46. *Mount Auburn: Its Scenes, Its Beauties, Its Lessons*, ed. Wilson Flagg (1860; rpt. Boston: James Munroe, 1861), 56.

47. Blanche Linden-Ward, *Silent City on a Hill: Landscapes of Memory and Boston's Mount Auburn Cemetery* (Columbus: Ohio State Univ. Press, 1989), 206.

48. Charles Dearborn, *Dearborn's Guide Through Mount Auburn with Eighty-two Engravings, for the Benefit of Strangers, Desirous of Seeing the Clusters of Monuments with the Least Trouble*, 12th ed. (1852; rpt. Boston: No. 24 School Street, 1858), 10.

49. Mrs. C. W. Hunt adds more evidence to Haltunnen's already convincing claim that "even in mourning for the dead – in fact, especially in mourning for the dead – the bourgeois quest for genteel propriety was not to be abandoned" (*Confidence Men and Painted Women*, 134).

50. Bigelow's "hand of Taste" confirms Pierre Bourdieu's claim that articulations of taste depend upon a structure of negation: "Tastes (i.e., manifested preferences) are the practical affirmation of an inevitable difference. It is no accident that, when they have to be justified, they are asserted purely negatively, by the refusal of other tastes. . . . Tastes are perhaps first and foremost distastes" (*Distinction: A Social Critique of the Judgement of Taste*, trans. Richard Nice [Cambridge: Harvard Univ. Press, 1984], 56).

51. *The Journals of Bronson Alcott*, ed. Odell Shepard (Boston: Little, 1938), 82.

52. Quoted in Nina Baym, *Novels, Readers, and Reviewers: Responses to Fiction in Antebellum America* (Ithaca: Cornell Univ. Press, 1984), 135.

53. Quoted in ibid., 85.

54. Quoted in *Melville: The Critical Heritage*, ed. Watson G. Branch (London: Routledge & Kegan Paul, 1974), 234.

55. Quoted in Smith, *Harper's Ferry*, 80.

56. Melville, *White-Jacket; or, The World in a Man-of-War* (1850), ed. Harrison Hayford, Hershel Parker, and G. Thomas Tanselle (Evanston: Northwestern Univ. Press, 1970), 251.

57. William Charvat's *The Profession of Authorship in America, 1800–1870* (Columbus: Ohio State Univ. Press, 1968) is the definitive study of Melville's vexed relation to his audience.

58. *Uncle Tom's Cabin; or, Life Among the Lowly* (1852; rpt. New York: Penguin, 1981), 424. All further quotations will be from this edition and will be noted in the text.

59. Baym makes this point in her discussion of antebellum reviewers' attitudes toward narrative voice: "The healthy tone, then, implies first that the narrator-author's attention is directed away from himself and toward the beings he has created, and second that his attention to these beings is loving. Conversely, the unhealthy tone may come about either because the author's attention, directed toward himself, fails to encompass (and hence to realize) his characters, or because though directed at those characters it is not loving" (*Novels, Readers, and Reviewers*, 143).

60. Brown has noted how perilously close Stowe's "sentimental aesthetics" are to the "logic of fetishism often associated with commodities" (*Domestic Individualism*, 50). I think this image of ideal and invisible labor complicates her claim

that "far from concealing productive human relations in market relations, the fetishism of objects in Stowe's political economy projects the productive labor of housekeeping" (51). By adhering to a logic of erased labor, Stowe's sentimental aesthetics reproduces a cultural commitment to preserving the values of labor in the space of literature, thus aligning her with the values of the (literary) marketplace. My reading of Stowe is similar to that of Brook Thomas, who argues that "the success of *Uncle Tom's Cabin* in the marketplace was partially owing to its adherence to a value system that the northern public believed in. . . . Stowe's attack on the institution of slavery is [thus] strengthened by ideological assumptions supporting the social system of the North" (*Cross-Examinations of Law and Literature: Cooper, Hawthorne, Stowe, and Melville* [Cambridge: Cambridge Univ. Press, 1987], 148). On the relation between Stowe and the market, also see Walter Benn Michaels's chapter "Romance and Real Estate," in *The Gold Standard and the Logic of Naturalism* (Berkeley and Los Angeles: Univ. of California Press, 1987), and Lynn Wardley, "Relic, Fetish, Femmage: The Aesthetics of Sentiment in the Work of Stowe," *Yale Journal of Criticism*, 5 (1992), 165–91.

61. See Harriet Beecher Stowe and Catharine Beecher, *The American Woman's Home; or, Principles of Domestic Science* (1869; rpt. Hartford: Stowe–Day Foundation, 1987). On the invisibility of housework in the texts of Stowe and Beecher, see Brown and Kathryn Kish Sklar, *Catharine Beecher: A Study in American Domesticity* (New York: Norton, 1973). The physical ordeal of writing *Uncle Tom's Cabin* is discussed in Lora Romero's "Bio-Political Resistance in Domestic Ideology and *Uncle Tom's Cabin*," *American Literary History*, 1 (1989), 714–34.

62. "Introduction," *Uncle Tom's Cabin* (Boston: Houghton, Osgood, 1879), xiii–xiv. Also see Stowe's essay "Can the Immortality of the Soul Be Proved by the Light of Nature?," written when she was just twelve years old. In it she claims that man is "destined, after this earthly house of his tabernacle is dissolved, to an inheritance incorruptible, undefiled, and that fadeth not away, to a house not made with hands, eternal in the heavens" (quoted in the introduction by Eric J. Sundquist to *New Essays on Uncle Tom's Cabin*, ed. Eric J. Sundquist [Cambridge: Cambridge Univ. Press, 1986], 23). For a complete analysis of the composition of *Uncle Tom's Cabin*, see E. Bruce Kirkham, *The Building of Uncle Tom's Cabin* (Knoxville: Univ. of Tennessee Press, 1977).

63. Henry Ward Beecher, "Reading," in *Eyes and Ears* (Boston: Ticknor, 1862), 187.

64. Quoted in Baym, *Novels, Readers, and Reviewers*, 149.

65. Beecher, *Lectures*, 34.

66. Horace Bushnell, *Work and Play; or, Literary Varieties* (New York: Scribner, 1864), 22–3.

67. Bushnell's theory of literature and culture judges the moral and aesthetic value of a text according to its separation from the world of labor and material life. This attitude toward cultural production exemplifies what Herbert Marcuse has defined as "the affirmative character of culture": "The ontological cleavage of ideal from material values tranquilizes idealism in all that regards the material processes of life. In idealism, a specific historical form of the

division of labor and of social stratification takes on the eternal, metaphysical form of the relationship of necessity and beauty" (*Negations: Essays in Critical Theory* [Boston: Beacon, 1968], 93). By positing an unbridgeable gap between the ideal and the material processes of life, then, the affirmative character of culture functions to represent as transcendent historical forms which are, in fact, historically determined.

68. *Harper's*, 1 (1850), 860.

69. Quoted in Baym, *Novels, Readers, and Reviewers*, 91.

70. *Graham's*, 18 (1841), 199; quoted in Baym, *Novels, Readers, and Reviewers*, 93.

71. Baym, *Novels, Readers, and Reviewers*, 93.

72. Ibid., 92.

73. The complete title is *The Statesman's Manual; or, The Bible the Best Guide to Political Skill and Foresight: A Lay Sermon, Addressed to the Higher Class of Society, with an Appendix, Containing Comments and Essays Connected with the Study of the Inspired Writings* ("Lay Sermons" [1816], in *The Collected Works of Samuel Taylor Coleridge*, ed. R. J. White [London: Routledge & Kegan Paul, 1972], 3). Note 1 of this edition indicates that the sermon was not to be addressed "to a promiscuous audience" (3).

74. Catherine Gallagher, *The Industrial Reformation of English Fiction, 1832–1867* (Chicago: Univ. of Chicago Press, 1985), 194. On Coleridge and allegory, also see Steven Knapp, *Personification and the Sublime: Milton to Coleridge* (Cambridge: Harvard Univ. Press, 1985), and Jerome Christensen, *Coleridge's Blessed Machine of Language* (Ithaca: Cornell Univ. Press, 1981).

75. Emerson, *Essays*, 225.

76. Gallagher writes that in "The Statesman's Manual" "meaningless facts, such as the entire sphere of commerce and production, are sharply distinguished from those facts that represent a higher reality, such as the state itself. Consequently it is not surprising that Coleridge argued to exclude the majority of people from participation in government, for the majority are animated by the spirit of trade" (*The Industrial Reformation of English Fiction*, 192).

77. Rather than viewing Emerson as a Coleridgean symbolist par excellence, Julie Ellison claims that he is an aggressive allegorist ("Aggressive Allegory," *Raritan*, 4 [1984], 100–15). Although Ellison is correct to point out Emerson's use of allegory, I would argue that his commitment to "the great Order" and the "unalterable" "spiritual fact" is, ultimately, a commitment to the totalizing, dehistoricizing order of symbolism.

78. Angus Fletcher, *Allegory: The Theory of a Symbolic Mode* (Ithaca: Cornell Univ. Press), 23.

79. Henry Adams, *The Education of Henry Adams*, ed. Ernest Samuels (Boston: Houghton Mifflin, 1973), 466. All further quotations from this work will be from this edition and will be noted in the text.

80. Sharon Cameron has developed such a model in *The Corporeal Self: Allegories of the Body in Hawthorne and Melville* (Baltimore: Johns Hopkins Univ. Press, 1981). For a discussion of the relation between allegory and "the anatomization of a body," see Bainard Cowan, *Exiled Waters: Moby-Dick and the Crisis of Allegory* (Baton Rouge: Louisiana State Univ. Press, 1982), 29. Although

Cowan affirms the relevance of Benjamin for a reading of *Moby-Dick,* his analysis does not historicize allegory in the context of nineteenth-century American culture.

81. Richard Chase, *The American Novel and Its Tradition* (New York: Doubleday, 1957), 5–6.

82. Charles Feidelson, *Symbolism and American Literature* (Chicago: Univ. of Chicago Press, 1953), 15.

83. Jonathan Arac, *Critical Genealogies: Historical Situations for Postmodern Literary Studies* (New York: Columbia Univ. Press, 1987), 206–7.

84. Walter Benjamin, *The Origin of German Tragic Drama,* trans. John Osborne (London: New Left Books, 1977), 166.

85. The problematic reconfiguration of agency inherent in allegory pertains not only to the body but to the relation between author and text as well. Here is one place where Benjamin and Fletcher agree. In his discussion of agency in allegory, Fletcher claims: "Allegory . . . allows its creator a maximum of will and wish-fulfillment with a maximum of restraint" (69). The dialectic between will and restraint depicts the writer of allegory as much as the allegorical figure, whose restraints, we recall, are "muscle-bound." Benjamin has a very similar formulation: just as the object "is unconditionally in the power" (184) of the allegorist, those objects "secure power over him" (132). The allegorist, thus, occupies a highly contested space in which the relations between persons and objects, as well as the status of authorial agency, are being radically reconstructed.

86. Terry Eagleton, *Walter Benjamin or Towards a Revolutionary Criticism* (London: Verso, 1981), 20.

87. I say postmodern because Benjamin's idea of freedom resonates quite harmoniously with the following model proposed by Gilles Deleuze and Félix Guattari: "One can't really tell if submission doesn't finally conceal the greatest sort of revolt and if combat doesn't imply the worst of acceptances" (*On Kafka: Notes Toward a Minor Literature* [Minneapolis: Univ. of Minnesota Press, 1987], 82).

88. Paul de Man, "Semiology and Rhetoric," in *Allegories of Reading: Figural Language in Rousseau, Nietzsche, Rilke, and Proust* (New Haven: Yale Univ. Press, 1979), 29–30.

89. Paul de Man, *Blindness and Insight: Essays in the Rhetoric of Contemporary Criticism,* 2d ed. (Minneapolis: Univ. of Minnesota Press, 1983), 200.

90. Frank Lentricchia, *After the New Criticism* (Chicago: Univ. of Chicago Press, 1980), 290. Similarly, Stephen Melville argues, "although 'allegory' is supposed to point precisely toward the temporality of language, the very attempt to so name the essence of literature seems to preclude any recognition of its historicity" (*Philosophy Beside Itself: On Deconstruction and Modernism* [Minneapolis: Univ. of Minnesota Press, 1986], 128). It is also the case that de Man's turning away from history is a turning away from the body. Here would be another example of de Man's excluding an essential component of Benjamin's theory of allegory. De Man's reading of Rousseau is concerned with showing how "writing always includes the moment of dispossession in favor of the arbi-

trary power play of the signifier and from the point of view of the subject, this can only be experienced as a dismemberment, a beheading or a castration" (*Allegories of Reading*, 296). Thus, when he attends to "actual, bodily mutilations" (298) in Rousseau, he reads them as moments of textual allegory in which "the text as body . . . is displaced by the text as [deconstructive] machine" (298) – one that is "not unconscious but mechanical, systematic in its performance but arbitrary in its principle, like a grammar" (298). The mutilation of the body is always a "threat [that] remains sheltered behind its metaphoricity" (297). I agree with Lentricchia, who argues that it is possible for de Man to make this claim only by placing "literary discourse in a realm where it can have no responsibility to historical life" (*After the New Criticism*, 310) and by not "allowing the myriad discourses that *are* history to have some power" (310).

91. Barbara Foley, "The Politics of Deconstruction," in *Rhetoric and Form: Deconstruction at Yale*, ed. Robert Con Davis and Ronald Schleifer (Norman: Univ. of Oklahoma Press, 1985), in which she argues, "The fatal flaw of deconstruction – as it is practiced on both sides of the Atlantic, I would argue – is not that it is not so much ahistorical as it is antihistorical" (129).

CHAPTER 2. HAWTHORNE AND THE ECONOMICS OF ALLEGORY

1. Letter to James T. Fields, quoted in J. Donald Crowley, "Historical Commentary," in *The Centenary Edition of the Works of Nathaniel Hawthorne*, ed. William Charvat, Roy Harvey Pearce, and Claude M. Simpson, vol. 10: *Mosses from an Old Manse*, ed. Crowley, Fredson Bowers, et al. (Columbus: Ohio State Univ. Press, 1974), 522.

2. David S. Reynolds, *Beneath the American Renaissance: The Subversive Imagination in the Age of Emerson and Melville* (New York: Knopf, 1988), 39; Michael Davitt Bell, *The Development of American Romance: The Sacrifice of Relation* (Chicago: Univ. of Chicago Press, 1980), 134. While I am sympathetic to these readings, both fail to historicize the relation between Hawthorne and allegory. Whereas Bell's formalism explicitly disengages itself from historical concerns, Reynolds's argument, while addressing specific cultural issues, ultimately fails to be historical enough. This chapter aims to combine the rigors of Bell's close readings with the broad cultural analysis suggested by Reynolds. Most recently, Joel Pfister has read Hawthorne's career in terms of the production of the middle-class self in nineteenth-century America. Like Pfister, I find "The Birth-mark" to be a crucial text in Hawthorne's career and in the reconfiguration of allegory in nineteenth-century America. But rather than reading it as "an allegory about the way in which Hawthorne's own writing is complicit with and critical of a cultural process that discursively produces the female body as pathological (*The Production of Personal Life: Class, Gender, and the Psychological in Hawthorne's Fiction* [Stanford: Stanford Univ. Press, 1991], 38), I see an identification between Hawthorne and Georgiana against Aylmer, who is committed to making invisible the signs both of authorial and female labor. Whereas the burden of Pfister's task is to his-

toricize the psychological self in Hawthorne's time, my aim is to show the inextricable relation between constructions of the self and the development of the market economy in this period. In " 'The Bloody Hand' of Labor: Work, Class, and Gender in Three Stories by Hawthorne" (*American Quarterly*, 42 [1990], 542–64), Nicholas K. Bromell underscores the theme of work in "The Birth-mark" but does not consider the relation between allegory and work. Also see Donald E. Pease's work, in which he suggests that Hawthorne's allegory "transfigures actual persons, places, and things into exemplary forms, cultural resources whose mold can be recast for future cultural use" (*Visionary Compacts: American Renaissance Writings in Cultural Context* [Madison: Univ. of Wisconsin Press, 1987], 65), and Walter Benn Michaels's discussion of *The House of the Seven Gables,* in which he situates Hawthorne's experiments with the romance in the context of antebellum notions of property in order to argue that while "imagining the terms of a text that would escape republican fluctuation, Hawthorne imagined in fact the terms of the technology that made those fluctuations possible" (*The American Renaissance Reconsidered*, ed. Donald Pease and Walter Benn Michaels [Baltimore: Johns Hopkins Univ. Press, 1985], 177).

3. Analyses of Hawthorne's relation to Bunyan include David E. Smith, *John Bunyan in America* (Bloomington: Indiana Univ. Press, 1966), W. Stacy Johnston, "Hawthorne and *The Pilgrim's Progress,*" *Journal of English and Germanic Philology*, 50 (1951), 156–66, Robert Stanton, "Hawthorne, Bunyan, and the American Romances," *PMLA*, 71 (1956), 155–65, and John O. Rees, Jr., "Hawthorne's Conception of Allegory: A Reconsideration," *Philological Quarterly*, 54 (1975), 494–510. For a brief but insightful discussion of "The Celestial Rail-road," see John Limon, *The Place of Fiction in the Time of Science: A Disciplinary History of American Writing* (Cambridge: Cambridge Univ. Press, 1990), 185–7.

4. Lawrence Sargent Hall, *Hawthorne: Critic of Society* (New Haven: Yale Univ. Press, 1944), 10.

5. Fredric Jameson, *Postmodernism, or, The Cultural Logic of Late Capitalism* (Durham: Duke Univ. Press, 1991), 168.

6. Nathaniel Hawthorne, "The Birth-mark," in *Tales and Sketches*, ed. Roy Harvey Pearce (New York: Library of America, 1982), 766. All further quotations from "The Birth-mark" will be from this edition and will be noted in the text.

7. *The Scarlet Letter: A Romance* (1850; rpt. New York: Penguin, 1970), 136. All further quotations will be from this edition and will be noted in the text.

8. Quoted in *Hawthorne: The Critical Heritage*, ed. J. Donald Crowley (New York: Barnes & Noble, 1970), 305, 222.

9. Quoted in ibid., 137.

10. Quoted in Henry Nash Smith, *Democracy and the Novel: Popular Resistance to Classic American Writers* (Oxford: Oxford Univ. Press, 1978), 18.

11. *Hawthorne: The Critical Heritage*, 135–6.

12. Henry D. Bellows, *The Relation of Public Amusements to Public Morality, Especially of the Theatre to the Highest Interests of Humanity* (New York: C. S. Francis, 1857), 5.

13. References to Bunyan can be found throughout Hawthorne's texts ("The Hall of Fantasy" immediately comes to mind) and his journal entries. An 1836 entry reads, "What were the contents of the burden of Christian in the Pilgrim's Progress? He must have been taken for a pedler travelling with his pack" (*The Centenary Edition of the Works of Nathaniel Hawthorne*, ed. William Charvat, Roy Harvey Pearce, and Claude M. Simpson, vol. 8: *The American Notebooks*, ed. Claude M. Simpson [Columbus: Ohio State Univ. Press, 1974], 23), and the original idea for "The Celestial Rail-road" can be found in an 1842 entry which reads "An Auction (perhaps in Vanity Fair) of offices, honors, and all sorts of things considered desirable by mankind; together with things eternally valuable, which shall be considered by most people as worthless lumber" (238).

14. Nathaniel Hawthorne, "The Celestial Rail-road," in *Tales and Sketches*, ed. Roy Harvey Pearce (New York: Library of America, 1982), 808. All further quotations from "The Celestial Rail-road" will be from this edition.

15. F. O. Matthiessen, *The American Renaissance: Art and Expression in the Age of Emerson and Whitman* (New York: Oxford Univ. Press, 1941), 198.

16. John Bunyan, *The Pilgrim's Progress* (1678) (New York: Penguin, 1965), 39.

17. Quoted in *Hawthorne: The Critical Heritage*, 110.

18. Frederick Crews, *The Sins of the Fathers: Hawthorne's Psychological Themes* (New York: Oxford Univ. Press, 1966), 96. The extent to which Hawthorne's text undermines Bunyan's authority as a stable frame of reference for antebellum Americans is even more evident if we note Susan Warner's use of *The Pilgrim's Progress* in the 1850 bestseller *The Wide, Wide World*. Bunyan's allegory pervades the theme and tone of Warner's text, whether in the description of the heroine, Ellen Montgomery, as the "little pilgrim" or when Ellen's friend, Alice Humphreys, comments upon her impending death, "You remember, Ellie, in the Pilgrim's Progress, when Christiana and her companions were sent to go over the river? – I think the messenger has come for me" (*The Wide, Wide World* [1850; rpt. New York: Feminist Press, 1987], 354, 438). Bunyan's text makes its most dramatic appearance when John Humphreys gives Ellen a copy of *The Pilgrim's Progress*: "She saw to be sure that it was a fine copy, well bound, with beautiful cuts. But when she came to look further, she found all through the book, on the margin or at the bottom of the leaves, in John's beautiful handwriting, a great many notes – simple, short, plain, exactly what was needed to open the whole book to her and make it of the greatest possible use and pleasure" (370). Ellen first observes the external beauty of the text, but then, like a good Emersonian, she discovers the beauty and meaning of its interior. The repetition of the word beautiful, first used to describe the "cuts" and then John's handwriting, nicely intimates that the text's exterior and interior transparently mirror one another and that the move from outside to inside can be "exactly" accomplished by John's "simple" marginalia. In her moving from outside to inside, the book and its meaning are opened up to her. Warner makes Ellen's moral progress dependent upon her progress in learning how to read Bunyan's text. John's role as interpreter in no way undermines the transparency or stability of Bunyan's

text. His hermeneutic skills are required because Ellen's comparative unfamiliarity with the Bible prevents her from fully understanding Bunyan's meaning. It is clear throughout Ellen's journey that Bunyan's book functions as a
meaningful, accessible, and reliable concordance for her life. In contrast to the
ironic, urbane tone of "The Celestial Rail-road," which we have seen to be
significantly unlike Bunyan's text, the sentimental and emotive tone of *The
Wide, Wide World* is truer to its seventeenth-century predecessor. What is
culturally relevant for Warner, Hawthorne has deemed irrecoverable.

19. Quoted in George Rogers Taylor, *The Transportation Revolution, 1815–1860*
(Armonk, N.Y.: M. E. Sharpe, 1951), 75; *Graham's*, 16 (1840), 226.

20. One might even argue that the body of the locomotive is, in fact, a female
body. For a fascinating collection of essays on the relation between technology and the (female) body in contemporary science fiction, see *Alien Zone:
Cultural Theory and Contemporary Science Fiction Cinema*, ed. Annette Kuhn
(New York: Verso, 1990).

21. Karl Marx, *Capital: A Critique of Political Economy*, ed. Frederick Engels (New
York: International Publishers, 1967), vol. 1, 40.

22. This theme of the inarticulateness and incomprehensibility of language in
Vanity Fair runs throughout "The Celestial Rail-road." As the narrator journeys toward Vanity Fair, he hears "the awful murmurs, and shrieks, and deep
shuddering whispers of the blast, sometimes forming itself into words almost
articulate" (815), and again, when the Giant Transcendentalist "shout[s] after"
the narrator and the other passengers, it was "in so strange a phraseology that
we knew not what he meant" (817).

23. Fletcher, *Allegory*, 87.

24. Carolyn Porter, *Seeing and Being: The Plight of the Participant Observer in Emerson, James, Adams, and Faulkner* (Middletown, Conn.: Wesleyan Univ. Press,
1981), 33–4.

25. The dream is a conventional topos of allegorical texts from "The Dream of the
Rood" through *Piers Plowman* to *Pilgrim's Progress*. The dream in "The Celestial
Rail-road" reveals the homology between the narrator's imagination and the
market. Wai-chee Dimock makes a similar point about *The Confidence-Man*: "If
The Confidence-Man is animated by a market individualism, that individualism
works, we can now see, not only by putting the individual in the market but,
even more crucially, by putting the market in the individual" (*Empire for Liberty: Melville and the Poetics of Individualism* [Princeton: Princeton Univ. Press,
1989], 194). Also see Eric J. Sundquist's *Home as Found: Authority and Genealogy
in Nineteenth-Century American Literature* (Baltimore: Johns Hopkins Univ.
Press, 1979), in which he argues, "Hawthorne's commerce, whether with the
past or with his public, concerns itself as much with the intricacies of exchange
and barter as does Thoreau's assault on his 'Unappropriated Land' in the *Week*.
The bizarre edifice in which Hawthorne's narrator finds himself in 'The Hall of
Fantasy' . . . represents with the condensed economy of a dream the negotiations that Hawthorne's stories play out" (94). In claiming an inextricable relation between allegory and the market, I am suggesting that allegory and realism
are not as opposed as has been thought. Similarly, Kenneth Dauber suggests

that "allegory as Hawthorne writes it is the realism of a romantic age" (*The Idea of Authorship in America: Democratic Poetics from Franklin to Melville* [Madison: Univ. of Wisconsin Press, 1990], 185). In his discussion of "Lady Eleanore's Mantle," Michael Colacurcio makes a similar point by linking allegory with history: "If the allegory of 'Lady Eleanore's Mantle' stood alone, it might well lead interpretation out of the realm of the historic altogether, into the world of the moral, psychic, or grammatological a priori. But in fact the 'allegory' is here controlled by the 'legends' which surround it; it is really an allegory within a legend. The result of this deliberate mixing of modes is curious indeed, leaving us with an allegory that is yet somehow 'in history' " (*The Province of Piety: Moral History in Hawthorne's Early Tales* [Cambridge: Harvard Univ. Press, 1984], 425).

26. On the significance of compromise in Hawthorne's work, and in *The Scarlet Letter* in particular, see Sacvan Bercovitch's *The Office of the Scarlet Letter* (Baltimore: Johns Hopkins Univ. Press, 1991), esp. chap. 3, "The Red Badge of Compromise" (73–112). The language of compromise in "The Celestial Rail-road" is also the language of Melville's *The Confidence-Man: His Masquerade* (1857; rpt. Evanston: Northwestern Univ. Press, 1984), which was, after all, modeled upon Hawthorne's tale. Thus the confidence man says, "My Protean easy-chair is a chair so all over bejointed, behinged, and bepadded, everyway so elastic, springy, and docile to the airiest touch, that in some one of its endlessly-changeable accommodations of back, seat, footboard, and arms, the most restless body, the body most racked, nay, I had almost added the most tormented conscience must, somehow and somewhere, find rest" (38) and "If, confessedly, certain spiritual ends are to be gained but through the auxiliary agency of worldly means, then, to the surer gaining of such spiritual ends, the example of worldly policy in worldly projects should not by spiritual projectors be slighted" (40).

27. As in *The Confidence-Man,* where the instability of names enacts the instability of the market, the namelessness, the unnamed voice, of "The Celestial Rail-road" enacts the absent origin and ubiquitous presence of the market. My discussion of naming in Hawthorne is indebted to Dimock's brilliant discussion of naming in *Mardi* in *Empire for Liberty*.

28. There are, in fact, many similarities between "The Celestial Rail-road" and "Benito Cereno." Like Delano, the narrator often comes close to piercing the truth of his pilgrimage only to dismiss it by appeals to rationality and benevolence. As the narrator travels through the Valley of Death and sees "grim faces, that bore the aspect and expression of individual sins," which he "almost thought . . . were my own sins," he rationalizes them away by calling them "freaks of imagination – nothing more, certainly, – mere delusions" (816).

29. In *American Thought and Religious Typology*, Ursula Brumm correctly maintains that " 'The Celestial Rail-road' is an allegory based on another allegory" but incorrectly concludes that "the second allegory supplies the key to the correspondences" (New Brunswick, N.J.: Rutgers Univ. Press, 1970), 114.

30. David E. Smith claims, in no uncertain terms, that the absent narrator is "Bunyan's Ignorance, and he strides, or falters, in the later romances, along

the pathways of a wilderness he scarcely understands" (*John Bunyan in America*, 62). In urging us to consider Hawthorne's sketch less "for its originality" than "for the place it shared with similar Bunyan adaptations" (62), Smith fails to see an economic tradition of allegory that is being generated in "The Celestial Rail-road."

31. On the materiality of the body, see Elaine Scarry, *The Body in Pain* (Oxford: Oxford Univ. Press, 1985), and *Literature and the Body: Essays on Populations and Persons*, ed. Elaine Scarry (Baltimore: Johns Hopkins Univ. Press, 1988).

32. Whereas Brown argues for a "feminization of this disembodiment" (*Domestic Individualism*, 68), my reading of "The Birth-mark," as well as my analysis of the discourse of literary labor, claims that this disembodiment also applies to Hawthorne (and other male authors).

33. Maureen Quilligan, *The Language of Allegory: Defining the Genre* (Ithaca: Cornell Univ. Press, 1985), 25.

34. The classic formulation of the doctrine of separate spheres can be found in Nancy Cott, *The Bonds of Womanhood: "Woman's Sphere" in New England, 1780–1835* (New Haven: Yale Univ. Press, 1977). For recent challenges to Cott, see Mary Kelley, *Private Woman, Public Stage: Literary Domesticity in Nineteenth-Century America* (Oxford: Oxford Univ. Press, 1984), and Mary P. Ryan, *Women in Public: Between Banners and Ballots, 1825–1880* (Baltimore: Johns Hopkins Univ. Press, 1990).

35. Marx, *Capital*, vol. 1, 84.

36. *The Works of William Ellery Channing* (1882; rpt. New York: Burt Franklin, 1970), 14.

37. Henry Ward Beecher, *Lectures to Young Men on Various Important Subjects* (1844; rpt. Boston: Jewett, 1853), 26.

38. C. B. Macpherson has called this model of selfhood "possessive individualism," which he explains as follows: "Whatever the degree of state action, the possessive market model permits individuals who want more delights than they have, to seek to convert the natural powers of other men to their use. They do so through the market, in which everyone is necessarily involved. Since the market is continually competitive, those who would be content with the level of satisfactions they have are compelled to fresh exertions by every attempt of the others to increase theirs. Those who would be content with the level they have cannot keep it without seeking more power, that is, without seeking to transfer more powers of others to themselves, to compensate for the increasing amount that the competitive efforts of others are transferring from them" (*The Political Theory of Possessive Individualism: Hobbes to Locke* [Oxford: Oxford Univ. Press, 1962], 58–9).

39. Aminadab has very few identifiably human qualities, and this is most evident in his speech. He either "mutter[s]" (770) or "mumble[s]" (776), as in the following: "Hoh! Hoh!" mumbled Aminadab – "look, master, look!" (776).

40. King James Version. Another example is in Ruth 4:19–20: "Now these are the generations of Perez: Perez begat Hezron, and Hezron begat Ram, and Ram begat Amminadab, and Amminadab begat Nahshon, and Nahshon begat Salmon."

41. Although Aminadab's name functions as a sign of Hawthorne's labor, it is evident that Hawthorne also wishes to distance his own literary labors from the "earthiness" and "physical[ity]" that characterize Aminadab's labors. For another reading of Aminadab's name, see Thomas Pribek, "Hawthorne's Aminadab: Sources and Significance," *Studies in the American Renaissance*, 1987, 177–86.

42. Georgiana's blood spills onto the narrative in a variety of ways, the most important being the fact that the birthmark is often referred to as the "Crimson Hand" (766, 767, 768, 777) and even once as the "Bloody Hand" (765). It is very clear that Aylmer's aversion to Georgiana's birthmark stems from his anxiety about sexuality, especially since their problems begin "very soon after their marriage, [as] Aylmer sat gazing at his wife, with a trouble in his countenance that grew stronger" (764). This discussion of "The Birth-mark" seeks to link the highly visible and public circulations of Georgiana's sexuality with a system of economic circulation committed to invisibility and private property. For discussions of Hawthorne and feminism, see Nina Baym, "Thwarted Nature: Nathaniel Hawthorne as Feminist," in *American Novelists Revisited: Essays in Feminist Criticism*, ed. Fritz Fleischmann (Boston: G. K. Hall, 1982); Lauren Berlant's *The Anatomy of National Fantasy: Hawthorne, Utopia, and Everyday Life* (Chicago: Univ. of Chicago Press, 1991), which focuses almost exclusively on *The Scarlet Letter*; Brown, *Domestic Individualism*; Pfister, *The Production of Personal Life*; and, most recently, T. Walter Herbert, *Dearest Beloved: The Hawthornes and the Making of the Middle-Class Family* (Berkeley and Los Angeles: Univ. of California Press, 1993).

43. Michaels raises some of these same issues in "Romance and Real Estate," particularly in his discussion of Holgrave's daguerreotype of Judge Pyncheon: "The daguerreotype always sees through to the fixed truth behind the fluctuating movements of the 'public character'" (in *The American Renaissance Reconsidered*, 167). "The Birth-mark" also has a daguerreotype scene that would seem to concur with Michaels's reading. The results of Aylmer's daguerreotype are predictable: "The features of the portrait [were] blurred and indefinable; while the minute figure of a hand appeared where the cheek should have been" (772). As in *The House of the Seven Gables*, here the daguerreotype manages to expose the truth of the birthmark, but far from being fixed, its truth is the fact of its continual fluctuations.

44. Compelling arguments have been made based on similarities between Aylmer's science and Hawthorne's artistry, only to establish the difference between them or to rescue him from Aylmer's fate by pointing to Hawthorne's critical attitude towards Aylmer's violent, obsessive nature. Bell's *The Development of American Romance* and Limon's *The Place of Fiction in the Time of Science* most persuasively articulate this position.

45. *The American Notebooks*, 16.

46. The birthmark shares many of the allegorical qualities described by Fletcher in his chapter "The Cosmic Image" (*Allegory*, 70–146). Allegorical devices "often violate perspective (they are often out of proportion), and at the same time

they preserve their identities by being drawn with extremely sharp-etched outlines" (87).

47. Particularly influential texts that have dealt with *The Scarlet Letter* from one of these viewpoints include Sacvan Bercovitch, *The Puritan Origins of the American Self* (New Haven: Yale Univ. Press, 1975), Crews, *The Sins of the Fathers*, and Nina Baym, *The Shape of Hawthorne's Career* (Ithaca: Cornell Univ. Press, 1976).

48. Michael Gilmore, *American Romanticism and the Marketplace* (Chicago: Univ. of Chicago Press, 1982), 76. My reading of *The Scarlet Letter* is indebted to Gilmore's, but rather than emphasizing Hawthorne's capitulation to the literary marketplace and the ideology of authorial invisibility, I am interested in the ways in which *The Scarlet Letter* foregrounds Hawthorne's presence and, indeed, stages a drama not unlike "The Birth-mark" in which Hawthorne strives to keep visible the signs of his authorial labor. Similarly, Baym states that Hester "is an artist, Hawthorne leaves no doubt" (*The Shape of Hawthorne's Career*, 131) and that "in spite of himself, Dimmesdale has become an artist" (137).

49. Richard Brodhead has noted the connection between Dimmesdale and Aylmer: "[Aylmer] is the prototype for Hawthorne's idea-possessed men, who in the moment that they succumb to obsession also find an object – Reverend Hooper's black veil, Roderick Elliston's bosom serpent, Arthur Dimmesdale's scarlet letter – in which obsession lodges as an overdetermined meaning" (*The School of Hawthorne* [Oxford: Oxford Univ. Press, 1986], 35). I would add that Chillingworth descends from Aylmer in that Chillingworth is less committed to the erasure or visibility of Dimmesdale's mark than to the power that resides in his knowledge of the mark's presence.

50. Bushnell, *Work and Play,* 22–3.

51. Bell, "Arts of Deception: Hawthorne, 'Romance,' and *The Scarlet Letter*," in *New Essays on the Scarlet Letter*, ed. Michael J. Colacurcio (Cambridge: Cambridge Univ. Press, 1985), 40. The thorny issue of Hawthorne and the romance has been a staple of Hawthorne criticism from Mattheissen to Chase to Bell's earlier work, *The Development of American Romance*, to Edgar A. Dryden's more recent *The Form of American Romance* (Baltimore: Johns Hopkins Univ. Press, 1988). I am less interested in arriving at a definitive sense of what Hawthorne thought the romance actually was (I agree here with Bell, who argues that this is, in fact, an impossibility and that Hawthorne wanted it that way) and more interested in how this moment of seeming definition exemplifies Hawthorne's continual concealment and exposure of his literary labors.

52. Hawthorne laments that his labors in the Custom House lead to the kind of mental atrophy about which factory workers were also complaining: "It was not merely during the three hours and a half which Uncle Sam claimed as his share of my daily life, that this wretched numbness held possession of me" (65) or "I began to grow melancholy and restless; continually prying into my mind, to discover which of its poor properties were gone, and what degree of detriment had already accrued to the remainder" (69). He thus frames his return to literary life not only in terms of political necessity (the victory of the

Whigs) but also in terms of the salvific nature of literary labor as opposed to the labor of customs surveyor, in which one finds "one's intellect is dwindling away; or exhaling, without your consciousness, like ether out of a phial" (68). What Hawthorne discovers upon his return, however, is that literary labor effects an analogous "dwindling away" whereby authorial agency must remain invisible. Hawthorne's career both as "Surveyor of the Customs" (68) and as author of *The Scarlet Letter* would seem to end up in some version of decapitation.

53. Quoted in Matthiessen, *American Renaissance*, 241, 244. The best discussion of Hawthorne's conflicted attitude toward allegory can be found in Matthiessen's chapter "Allegory and Symbolism" (242–315). On the making of Hawthorne's reputation after *The Scarlet Letter*, see Brodhead, *The School of Hawthorne*, and Tompkins, *Sensational Designs*.

54. Quoted in *The Critical Response to Nathaniel Hawthorne's "The Scarlet Letter,"* ed. Gary Scharnhorst (New York: Greenwood Press, 1992), 24, 20.

55. Adam Smith, *An Inquiry into the Nature and Causes of the Wealth of Nations*, ed. James Rogers (Oxford: Clarendon Press, 1880), vol. 2, 28.

56. Although I emphasize Smith for the obvious reason that the figure of the hand so powerfully conjoins *The Wealth of Nations* and "The Birth-mark," the presence of Locke should also be noted. In *The Second Treatise of Government* (New York: Bobbs-Merrill, 1952), Locke notes that "a state of liberty . . . is not a state of license; though man in that state have an uncontrollable liberty to dispose of his person or possessions, yet he has not liberty to destroy himself, or so much as any creature in his possession" (5). The best discussion of Locke and antebellum configurations of the self can be found in Howard Horwitz's *By the Law of Nature: Form and Value in Nineteenth-Century America* (Oxford: Oxford Univ. Press, 1991).

57. Bercovitch, *The Office of The Scarlet Letter*, 41. For a brilliant discussion of Smith's thought, see Jean-Christophe Agnew, *Worlds Apart: The Market and the Theater in Anglo-American Thought, 1550–1750* (Cambridge: Cambridge Univ. Press, 1986), esp. 149–94. For a brief discussion of Smith's impact on American economic theory and the late-nineteenth-century novel, see Horwitz, *By the Law of Nature*, 126–8.

58. Whereas Aylmer depends upon the fluctuating meanings of the birthmark to exert his power, Ahab attempts to empower himself by hypostatizing the meanings of Moby Dick.

59. Macpherson, *Possessive Individualism*, 48.

CHAPTER 3. MELVILLE'S OPERATIVES

1. Melville, "The Paradise of Bachelors and the Tartarus of Maids," in *The Writings of Herman Melville: The Piazza Tales and Other Prose Pieces 1839–1860*, ed. Harrison Hayford et al. (Evanston: Northwestern Univ. Press, 1987), 328. All quotations from this short story will be from this edition and will be noted in the text.

2. Although *The Confidence-Man* and *Pierre* raise some of these issues, I have

chosen to focus on *Mardi*, *Moby-Dick*, and *Billy Budd* because these texts engage most fully the entire range of issues evoked by an economics of allegory: the aesthetic ideology of invisible labor, the destabilization of the work ethic, and the conjunction between literary and industrial labor.

3. Herman Melville, *Mardi: And a Voyage Thither* (1849), ed. Harrison Hayford, Hershel Parker, and G. Thomas Tanselle (Evanston: Northwestern Univ. Press, 1970), 116. All further quotations from *Mardi* will be noted in the text.

4. Quoted in Hugh W. Hetherington, *Melville's Reviewers: British and American, 1846–1891* (Chapel Hill: Univ. of North Carolina Press, 1961), 125.

5. Harold Beaver, for example, writes: "On and on he scribbled, piling chapter on chapter for his wife or sisters dutifully to copy and assemble. The result was a farrago, a mess" ("*Mardi*: A Sum of Inconsistencies," in *Herman Melville: Reassessments*, ed. A. Robert Lee [Totowa, N.J.: Barnes & Noble, 1984], 28).

6. Of course there are exceptions. Two of the finest analyses of *Mardi*, about which I shall have more to say, are Wai-chee Dimock, *Empire for Liberty: Melville and the Poetics of Individualism* (Princeton: Princeton Univ. Press, 1989), and Richard Brodhead, "*Mardi*: Creating the Creative," in *New Perspectives on Melville*, ed. Faith Pullin (Kent: Kent State Univ. Press, 1978). In addition, Michael Rogin offers some highly suggestive comments about *Mardi* in *Subversive Genealogy: The Politics and Art of Herman Melville* (New York: Knopf, 1983).

7. Quoted in *Melville: The Critical Heritage*, ed. Watson G. Branch (London: Routledge & Kegan Paul, 1974), 139.

8. Quoted in Jay Leyda, *The Melville Log: A Documentary Life of Herman Melville, 1819–1892* (New York: Gordian Press, 1969), vol. 1, 324.

9. Quoted in ibid., 299.

10. Quoted in *Melville: The Critical Heritage*, 157–8.

11. The opening of *Typee* is similar: "Six months at sea! Yes, reader, as I live, six months out of sight of land; cruising after the sperm-whale beneath the scorching sun of the Line, and tossed on the billows of the wide-rolling Pacific" (*Typee: A Peep at Polynesian Life* [1846], ed. Harrison Hayford, Hershel Parker, and G. Thomas Tanselle [Evanston: Northwestern Univ. Press, 1968], 3).

12. The narrator in the passage uses the allegorical character in Sheridan's play (and Priestley's philosophy) as a way to anchor himself to a stable authority from the eighteenth century. Allegorical characters in *Mardi*, however, possess an authority that derives from quite a different source – the instabilities of America's nineteenth-century market economy.

13. Alexander de Tocqueville, *Democracy in America*, ed. Phillips Bradley (New York: Random House, 1948), vol. 1, 305.

14. Karl Marx, *Capital*, ed. Frederick Engels (New York: International Publishers, 1967), vol. 1, 71.

15. Quoted in Baym, *Novels, Readers, and Reviewers*, 93.

16. E. M. Forster, *Aspects of the Novel* (New York: Harcourt Brace & World, 1927), 78. The names Jiji and Oh-Oh, and many others in *Mardi*, such as Vee-Vee, Donjalolo, and Babbalanja, also embody the repetitions within language

itself. Similarly, words are often repeated in *Mardi*. The narrator claims that the tobacco leaves in Mardi were "almost as broad as the broad fans of the broad-bladed banana" (372). One of the most striking instances concludes the chapter "They Visit the Extreme South of Vivenza": "'Amen! amen! amen!' cried echoes echoing echoes" (535).

17. The problem, of course, was that in calling attention to his fictional work as work, he also brought upon himself the wrath of literary critics who urged writers to erase the signs of their labor.

18. Brodhead, "*Mardi*: Creating the Creative," 39.

19. Henry Ward Beecher, *Eyes and Ears* (Boston: Ticknor & Fields, 1862), 188.

20. Dimock, *Empire for Liberty*, 68.

21. Quoted in Baym, *Novels, Readers, and Reviewers*, 252.

22. Quoted in *Moby-Dick as Doubloon: Essays and Extracts (1851–1970)*, ed. Hershel Parker and Harrison Hayford (New York: Norton, 1970), 28.

23. Quoted in ibid., 41, 24, 18.

24. Quoted in ibid., 13–14.

25. *Harper's*, 1 (1850), 550.

26. Walter Benjamin describes the *Trauerspiel* as "not so much plays which cause mourning, as plays through which mournfulness finds satisfaction: plays for the mournful" (*The Origin of German Tragic Drama*, trans. John Osborne [London: New Left Books, 1977], 119).

27. Quoted in *Moby-Dick as Doubloon*, 50. Duyckinck had been one of Melville's most ardent and powerful supporters (even of *Mardi*). Melville never forgave him for this review and wrote a vicious satire of Duyckinck in *Pierre*.

28. Quoted in Leyda, *The Melville Log*, vol. 1, 340.

29. Leonard Levy, *The Law of the Commonwealth and Chief Justice Shaw* (Cambridge: Harvard Univ. Press, 1957), 172.

30. Quoted in ibid., 176, 169.

31. Beecher, *Eyes and Ears*, 70, 71.

32. Levy, *The Law of the Commonwealth*, 182.

33. Quoted in Leyda, *The Melville Log*, vol. 1, 316.

34. Herman Melville, *Moby-Dick; or, The Whale* (1851), ed. Harrison Hayford, Hershel Parker, and G. Thomas Tanselle (Evanston: Northwestern Univ. Press, 1988), 71. All further quotations from *Moby-Dick* will be from this edition and will be noted in the text.

35. Dimock, *Empire for Liberty*, 114. Dimock's dazzling reading of *Moby-Dick* is convincing except for the fact that it does not take into account Ishmael, a fact which she herself acknowledges. Dimock's "skeptical view of Ishmael" (236) extends, I think, to a skepticism of Melville that implicates Melville in the process of Ahab's victimization while neglecting the history of victimization experienced by Melville himself. Dimock does not need to talk about Ishmael, because her critique of Melville also functions as a critique of Ishmael. This reading of Dimock would seem to be confirmed by her allusion to Pease's analysis of *Moby-Dick*, which asks the question "Is [Ishmael's] will any less totalitarian, however indeterminate its local exertions, than a will to convert all the world into a single struggle?" (271) Skepticism toward

Ishmael does not, I think, require one to collapse the differences between Ishmael and Ahab. Their distinctive approaches to the problem of accountability, for instance, provide us with a means to distinguish between them. Carolyn Porter's "Call Me Ishmael, or How to Make Double-Talk Speak" (in *New Essays on Moby-Dick,* ed. Richard Brodhead [Cambridge: Cambridge Univ. Press, 1986], 73–108) convincingly argues that Ishmael's strategy of parody provides Ishmael with a means of subverting authority, particularly Ahab's.

36. R. P. Blackmur, "The Craft of Herman Melville: A Putative Statement," in *The Lion and the Honeycomb: Essays in Solicitude and Critique* (New York: Harcourt Brace & World, 1955), 131.

37. Tompkins makes this point in her reading of *The Last of the Mohicans*: "I am convinced that it is unnecessary to set aside or apologize for the surface characteristics of Cooper's fiction for any reason whatever. Cooper need not be found wanting because his characters are not psychologically profound, or because his settings lack the dense texture of society novels. . . . It is possible to dispense with these concessions by reading the Leatherstocking tales neither as modernist fiction manqué, nor as ahistorical romance, nor as inartistic social commentary, but as social criticism written in an allegorical mode" (*Sensational Designs,* 103).

38. The fragility of the body is a continual theme in *Moby-Dick.* Not only do we see people maimed, but the possibility of mutilation is omnipresent. For example, in the chapter "The Line," the narrator writes: "The least tangle or kink in the coiling would, in running out, infallibly take somebody's arm, leg, or entire body off" (279). Also, while describing the monkey rope, the narrator reminds us that "[Queequeg] and the sharks were at times half hidden by the blood-muddied water, [and] those indiscreet spades of [the other harpooners] would come nearer amputating a leg than a tail" (321).

39. This discussion of *Moby-Dick* is deeply indebted to Michael Gilmore, who argues: "[Ahab] is as much involved in an exchange process as his former shipmates, the *Pequod*'s owners, only in his case he converts objects not into money but into meaning" (*American Romanticism,* 117).

40. My reading of antebellum mournfulness is informed by Benjamin's discussion of the introduction of Lutheranism: "The rigorous morality of its teaching in respect of civic conduct stood in sharp contrast to its renunciation of 'good works.' By denying the latter any special miraculous spiritual effect, making the soul dependent on grace through faith, and making the secular-political sphere a testing ground for a life which was only indirectly religious, being intended for the demonstration of civic virtues, it did, it is true, instil into the people a strict sense of obedience to duty, but in its great men it produced melancholy. . . . Human actions were deprived of all value. Something new arose: an empty world. . . . For those who looked deeper saw the scene of their existence as a rubbish heap of partial, inauthentic actions" (*The Origin,* 138–9). The historical context of Melville's allegory is, of course, significantly different from that of the *Trauerspiel,* although I do think that Benjamin's notion of melancholy is useful for understanding the experiences

of corporeal and psychic pain articulated by workers in antebellum America and registered in the frequent scenes of pain in *Moby-Dick*.

41. It is important to note that the crew are "like machines." Unlike machines, they remain "ever conscious that the old man's despot eye was on them." Appearing like a machine is not the same as being one. With Babo in "Benito Cereno" and Billy in *Billy Budd*, Melville explores the subversive potential in appearing like a machine.

42. Benjamin's theory of mourning is especially relevant: "Mourning is the state of mind in which feeling revives the empty world in the form of a mask, and derives an enigmatic satisfaction in contemplating it" (*The Origin*, 139). Also see Neal L. Tolchin's discussion of mourning customs during Melville's time, in which he claims that "in his heightened, transgressive sense of bereavement, Ahab provides deep insight into the experience of mourning" (*Mourning, Gender, and Creativity in the Art of Herman Melville* [New Haven: Yale Univ. Press, 1988], 130). Tolchin goes on to argue that Ahab's mournfulness combines Allan Melville's deathbed madness and Maria Melville's experience of his death.

43. Donald E. Pease links Ahab's corporeal loss to a loss of rhetorical certitude: "Unlike the spokesmen for the American jeremiad, Ahab cannot depend on Divine Writ to sanction his words. Consequently, a dual recognition accompanies his every act of persuasion: the terrible doubt that it may be without foundation, and the 'experience' of his separation from another. Both recognitions remind him of the loss of his leg. And it is Ahab's need to justify this sense of loss – to make it his, rather than God's or fate's – that leads him to turn his will, which in each act of persuasion repeats that separation of his body from his leg, into the ground for his existence" (*Visionary Compacts*, 270).

44. Ishmael, to the contrary, foregrounds his own labor at the very moment that he calls attention to the labor of others. His labors as reader of whales and worker on the *Pequod* are inextricably connected to the labors of previous readers and fellow workers. The presence of Ishmael's labor has been thoroughly discussed by Gilmore: "[Ishmael] makes no effort to conceal the mechanics of literary production. As he busily goes about assembling his material, he constantly reminds his readers of the man-madeness of the object before them" (*American Romanticism*, 119).

45. In their reading of Kafka, Gilles Deleuze and Félix Guattari make a similar point: "[Kafka] knows that all the lines link him to a literary machine of expression for which he is simultaneously the gears, the mechanic, the operator, and the victim" (*Kafka: Toward a Minor Literature*, trans. Dana Polan [Minneapolis: Univ. of Minnesota Press, 1986], 58).

46. When Ishmael asks in the opening chapter of *Moby-Dick*, "Why did the old Persians hold the sea holy? Why did the Greeks give it a separate deity, and make him the own brother of Jove?" and replies, "Surely all this is not without meaning" (5) and in the next sentence wonders, "And still deeper the meaning of that story of Narcissus," it is clear that his acknowledgment of meaning differs radically from Ahab's imperious demand for meaning.

47. Dimock, *Empire for Liberty*, 131.
48. See Gilmore's excellent discussion in *American Romanticism*, 113–31. Whereas Gilmore understands Ishmael's disappearance to signify the presence of the commodity structure in *Moby-Dick*'s narrative form, I am arguing that the disappearance of Ishmael's individual voice and its replacement with a cacophonous community of voices is a strategy to avoid the market-based notion of individual accountability that makes so many problems for Ahab.
49. For some, this is its strength. Melville has transcended the limits of history. For others, its weakness. Melville excludes history and has become the very figure of authority he had spent his whole career critiquing. New critics tend toward the first reading, more contemporary critics toward the latter. Thus Newton Arvin in *Herman Melville* (New York: Viking, 1950) acknowledges certain historical features about the text (the Nore Mutiny in particular), only to dismiss them as "matters of the surface; they have a genuine interest, but they say little about the real feeling of *Billy Budd*" (294). Similarly, Werner Berthoff in *The Example of Melville* (Princeton: Princeton Univ. Press, 1962) claims that "the historical circumstances touch on the story at every crisis but do not essentially determine it" (185) and that Melville "had swung clear of his tormenting search for belief, so that he was free to rise at the climax of his story to a different and surer theme: the conjunction of the two magnanimities, making sacrifice to the military necessity" (201). In contrast, Rowland A. Sherrill argues that Melville had become "so anxious about the efficacy of fiction that his narrator strips and reduces the very vision of life he wished to accredit for his readers" (*The Prophetic Melville: Experience, Transcendence, and Tragedy* [Athens: Univ. of Georgia Press, 1979], 236–7). Rogin most powerfully argues for Melville's conservative politics. He argues that Melville "purified complex, novelistic, historical material, splintering a potential novel into a spare, spectral, dualistic, historical fiction" (296) and "performed on the potentially novelistic material of *Billy Budd* the sort of operation which Vere performed in his court" (*Subversive Genealogy*, 301). Interestingly, both Sherrill and Rogin critique the politics of *Billy Budd* on the ground of its allegorical characters: "The asides function to tear away the complex concretions which might have accrued to Claggart and Billy as genuine symbols, to rob them of what Ishmael would have recognized as the necessary opaqueness which belongs to the mysterious agency of symbols, and to convert them, instead, into the less-textured, but clearer, stuff of allegory. In his *strenuous efforts* to clarify the reality of the wonder-world in human experience, then, the narrator drives his objects of wonder away from experience into the realm of abstractions about experience" (*The Prophetic Melville*, 229; emphasis mine). Similarly, Rogin argues, "Lacking history, interiority, or complex social location, Billy gains vividness from allegorical association more than human interaction" (*Subversive Genealogy*, 301). Earlier discussions of the relation between *Billy Budd* and Haymarket include Robert K. Wallace, "*Billy Budd* and the Haymarket Hangings," *American Literature*, 47 (1945), 108–13; H. Bruce Franklin, "From Empire to Empire: *Billy Budd, Sailor*," in *Herman Melville: Reassessments*, ed. A. Robert Lee (Totowa, N.J.: Barnes & Noble, 1984), 199–214; and Alan Trachtenberg, *The*

Incorporation of America: Culture and Society in the Gilded Age (New York: Hill & Wang, 1982), esp. 201–7.

50. Herman Melville, *Billy Budd, Sailor (An Inside Narrative)*, ed. Harrison Hayford and Merton M. Sealts, Jr. (Chicago: Univ. of Chicago Press, 1962), 43. All further quotations from *Billy Budd* will be from this edition and will be noted in the text.

51. In her brilliant piece "Melville's Fist: The Execution of *Billy Budd*," in *The Critical Difference* (Baltimore: Johns Hopkins Univ. Press, 1980), Barbara Johnson explains that this scene "can have no other purpose than to dramatize the central importance for the story of the question of arbitrary accident versus determinable motivation" (91). In contrast to her rigorous analysis of the scene in which Billy spills soup on Claggart and the moment when Billy hits and kills Claggart, Johnson has surprisingly little to say about this image of two people reading Billy's suspended body. By deflecting attention away from a discussion of Billy's body, Johnson misses an opportunity to explore the cultural politics of the body in late-nineteenth-century America – a politics that is intimately concerned with "getting inside." Interestingly, like de Man in his reading of Rousseau, Johnson foreshortens her analysis of a scene which addresses issues of the body in order to continue her analysis of language in *Billy Budd*. This erasure of the body is also evident in her explanation of how the category of nature, like the category of the king, is constructed by textual authority. Johnson's reading certainly enables us to see that "nature is authority whose textual origins have been forgotten" (104), but her theoretical strategy leads her to ignore the fact that nature as represented in the bodies of the text must also be subjected to a rigorous analysis of the "natural."

52. Eve Kosofsky Sedgwick offers a somewhat different reading of bodies in *Epistemology of the Closet* (Berkeley and Los Angeles: Univ. of California Press, 1990). Whereas she explores what she sees as "the ineradicable double entendre between the mutiny question and the homosexuality question" (103), I focus more on how the threat of mutiny resonates with anxieties about class conflict in late-nineteenth-century America.

53. For a similar reading of the narrator's position, see Susan Mizruchi's stunning essay "Cataloging the Creatures of the Deep: 'Billy Budd, Sailor' and the Rise of Sociology," *boundary 2*, 17 (1990), 272–304.

54. This account of the Haymarket affair can be found in Philip S. Foner, *History of the Labor Movement in the United States: From the Founding of the A.F. of L. to the Emergence of American Realism*, vol. 2 (New York: International Publishers, 1955), 105–14.

55. Paul Avrich, *The Haymarket Tragedy* (Princeton: Princeton Univ. Press, 1984), 276.

56. Quoted in Foner, *History of the Labor Movement*, 107.

57. Henry David, *The History of the Haymarket Affair: A Study in the American Social-Revolutionary and Labor Movements* (New York: Russell & Russell, 1936), 222–3.

58. Avrich, *The Haymarket Tragedy*, 277.

59. Quoted in ibid., 277.

60. Melville begins his *Battle-Pieces* with the poem "The Portent": "Hanging from the beam, / Slowly swaying (such the law), / Gaunt the shadow on your green, / Shenandoah! / The cut is on the crown / (Lo, John Brown), / And the stabs shall heal no more. / Hidden in the cap / Is the anguish none can draw; / So your future veils its face, / Shenandoah! / But the streaming beard is shown / (Weird John Brown), / The meteor of the war" (*Battle-Pieces and Aspects of the War*, ed. Sidney Kaplan [Amherst: Univ. of Massachusetts Press, 1972], 11). On the anarchists and John Brown, see *Haymarket Scrapbook*, ed. Dave Roediger and Franklin Rosemont (Chicago: Charles H. Kerr, 1986), 93.

61. *Famous Speeches of the Eight Chicago Anarchists* (1910), ed. Robert M. Fogelson and Richard E. Rubenstein (New York: Arno, 1969), 42.

62. *The Mind and Spirit of John Peter Altgeld: Selected Writings and Addresses*, ed. Henry M. Christman (Urbana: Univ. of Illinois Press, 1960), 98.

63. Quoted in Avrich, *The Haymarket Tragedy*, 266, 264.

64. Quoted in Foner, *History of the Labor Movement*, 108.

65. Herman Melville, "Benito Cereno," in *The Piazza Tales and Other Prose Pieces*, ed. Harrison Hayford, Alma A. MacDougall, and G. Thomas Tanselle (Evanston: Northwestern Univ. Press, 1987), 51. All further quotations from "Benito Cereno" will be from this edition and will be noted in the text.

66. Eric J. Sundquist convincingly argues that in staging an ironic performance of his own, the narrator is engaged in a kind of "rhetorical mimicry" ("Benito Cereno and New World Slavery," in *Reconstructing American Literary History*, ed. Sacvan Bercovitch [Cambridge: Cambridge Univ. Press, 1986], 112). Also see Sundquist's "Suspense and Tautology in 'Benito Cereno,'" *Glyph*, 8 (1981), 103–26, and Carolyn Karcher, *Shadow over the Promised Land: Slavery, Race, and Violence in Melville's America* (Baton Rouge: Louisiana State Univ. Press, 1980).

67. The language of the passage also suggests the opposite; that is, Delano's language could be read as registering the fact that he (or the narrator or both) knows exactly what's going on. First, the similes in the passage work to undermine the certainty of Delano's reading of the action. Being "like a mute" and "like a brave prisoner" allows for the possibility that one is neither a mute nor a brave prisoner. Second, the word "mute" carries with it a number of conflicting significations: it could be someone who is incapable of speech, someone who murmurs discontentedly, or an actor in a dumb show. When Babo describes Atufal's muteness, he most likely means that Atufal is like an actor on a stage (the way all the slaves are actors in the story). The last two sentences, which include the words "muteness" and "mutineer," come from the cacophonous, mimicking voice of the narrator (and/or Delano). For Delano, on the other hand, Atufal's "muteness" presumably refers to his speechlessness. The final sentence, in which Delano refers to Atufal as a "mulish mutineer," suggests that on the level of language, at least, Delano understands Atufal to be capable of mutiny, or perhaps once again the narrator is playing with us (and Delano) and giving us one more clue as to the true state of affairs. In this passage, the mute have become mutinous.

68. Rogin, *Subversive Genealogy*, 211.

69. Robert Levine, *Conspiracy and Romance: Studies in Brockden Brown, Cooper, Hawthorne, and Melville* (Cambridge: Cambridge Univ. Press, 1989), 199.

70. Quoted in Sander Gilman, *Difference and Pathology: Stereotypes of Sexuality, Race, and Madness* (Ithaca: Cornell Univ. Press, 1985), 137.

71. Quoted in Ronald Walters, *The Antislavery Appeal: American Abolitionism After 1830* (New York: Norton, 1978), 82.

72. Quoted in Rogin, *Subversive Genealogy*, 211.

73. Sundquist, "Suspense and Tautology," 106.

74. Examples of this difficult prose abound. Here is one: "Habitually living with the elements and knowing little more of the land than as a beach, or, rather, that portion of the terraqueous globe providentially set apart for dance-houses, doxies, and tapsters, in short what sailors call a 'fiddler's green,' his simple nature remained unsophisticated by those moral obliquities which are not in every case incompatible with that manufacturable theory known as respectability" (52).

75. Whereas Rogin and Thomas are especially strong on Vere's "liberal" deployment of specific legal practices, Sedgwick and Mizruchi are more interested in Vere's staging of the trial in order to achieve the desired result. Thus Sedgwick claims that Vere "entirely *creates* the fatality of the paranoid knot of Claggart and Billy Budd" (*Epistemology of the Closet*, 106), and Mizruchi argues that "Vere's power is based on a strategy of heightening and manipulating others' uncertainties while denying his own" ("Cataloging the Creatures of the Deep," 292).

76. Quoted in the notes and commentary of Hayford and Sealts's edition of *Billy Budd*, 178.

77. Quoted in Foner, *The History of the Labor Movement*, 109.

78. Michel Foucault, *Discipline and Punish*, trans. Alan Sheridan (New York: Random House, 1975), 138.

79. Ibid.

80. Lewis Mumford, *Herman Melville* (New York: Literary Guild, 1929), 354; John Seelye, *Melville: The Ironic Diagram* (Evanston: Northwestern Univ. Press, 1970), 163.

81. Henry George, *Social Problems* (1883; rpt. New York: Doubleday, 1912), 35.

82. Henry D. Lloyd, *Men, the Workers* (New York: Doubleday, 1909), 30.

83. Carroll Wright, *Some Ethical Phases of the Labor Question* (Boston: American Unitarian, 1902), 151.

84. Washington Gladden, *Working People and Their Employers* (New York: Funk, 1894), 20. Gladden's career reveals an increasing skepticism about the virtues of machinery. Three years after *Working People*, he wrote: "[When] children toil in the mills and the factories . . . the health of many of them is injured, the minds are dwarfed, their lives are blasted" (*Social Facts and Forces* [New York: Putnam, 1897], 41).

85. In *Social Problems*, for instance, George focuses on the ubiquity of the machine, whether it be on the level of state and federal politics, in which "the power of the machine is increasing" (16), or the "newspaper, [which] has become an immense machine" (46). George's convincing analysis of the accu-

mulation of societal machines, though, exposes the naiveté of his plan for the public ownership of land. He claims, "The laws of nature are the decrees of the Creator. There is written in them no recognition of any right save that of labor" (*Progress and Poverty: An Inquiry into the Cause of Industrial Depressions and the Increase of Want with Increase of Wealth – The Remedy* [1880] [New York: Robert Schalkenbach, 1951], 38). This religiously inspired appeal to nature not only fails to challenge the potential problems with industrialization but in fact mirrors his opponent's strategy of claiming the category of the natural for the machine itself.

86. Brook Thomas, *Cross-Examinations of Law and Literature*, 250.
87. Walter Benjamin, "Theses on the Philosophy of History," in *Illuminations*, ed. Hannah Arendt (New York: Schocken, 1973), 256.

CHAPTER 4. TWAIN IN THE MAN-FACTORY

1. This is an unfortunate result of periodization, which has not only separated antebellum from postbellum literature but has also made it more difficult to use terms traditionally ascribed to one period as a way to illuminate the other. Thus Twain's representative status as a realist would preclude a serious consideration of allegory, and Hawthorne's representative status as an allegorist (or symbolist) would make irrelevant a consideration of his realism. There are, of course, exceptions. See Richard Brodhead, *The School of Hawthorne* (Oxford: Oxford Univ. Press, 1986), Gillian Brown, *Domestic Individualism: Imagining Self in Nineteenth-Century America* (Berkeley and Los Angeles: Univ. of California Press, 1990), and Howard Horwitz, *By the Law of Nature: Form and Value in Nineteenth-Century America* (Oxford: Oxford Univ. Press, 1991).
2. See Amy Kaplan's excellent discussion of Howells's literary criticism, in which she writes: "True life – reality – is here equated with work, which is viewed not simply as an occupation but more importantly as a system of value which privileges industriousness and self-discipline as the basis of communal life. As a cultural force, realism turns reading into work, an act which unites its practitioners not through the worship of high art or the transport to imaginary worlds but through the mutual recognition of a common identity rooted in the productive sphere" (*The Social Construction of American Realism* [Chicago: Univ. of Chicago Press, 1989], 17).
3. This differs from Horwitz's interpretation of *Life on the Mississippi,* in which he argues, "Twain's romance denies the labor of piloting; because when labor is visible, the self's involvement with institutions is all too evident, and its independence, the inalienability of its labor and property, too obviously contingent" (*By the Law of Nature,* 104). Although Horwitz convincingly accounts for the relation between labor and piloting, his analysis shortchanges the complex relation between labor and writing in the text.
4. On the development of engineering, see David Noble, *America by Design: Science, Technology, and the Rise of Corporate Capitalism* (Oxford: Oxford Univ. Press, 1977).
5. Mark Twain, *Life on the Mississippi* (1883; rpt. New York: Penguin, 1984), 95.

All further quotations from *Life on the Mississippi* will be from this edition and will be noted in the text.

6. Leo Marx, "Landscape Conventions and *Huckleberry Finn*," in *The Pilot and the Passenger: Essays on Literature, Technology, and Culture in the United States* (Oxford: Oxford Univ. Press, 1988), 24.

7. Henry Nash Smith, *Mark Twain: The Development of a Writer* (New York: Atheneum, 1967), 80. One of the problems with these readings is that they elide the narrator with Mark Twain, thereby simplifying the complex shadings of the narrator's sometimes ironic, sometimes romantic voice.

8. Twain's relation to Hawthorne is unsurprisingly ambiguous. In 1879, for example, he claims that "nobody writes a finer & purer English than Motley[,] Howells, Hawthorne & Holmes," and in 1885 he writes, "I can't stand George Eliot, & Hawthorne & those people; I see what they are at, a hundred years before they get to it, & they just tire me to death" (quoted in Alan Gribben, *Mark Twain's Library* [Boston: G. K. Hall, 1980], 301).

9. Although the engineers do not overtly conceive of the river as a female body, the language of the narrator analogizes their (re)construction of the Mississippi to the "original job of creating it" (205). Whereas the romantic conceptualizes the river's body as female in order to safeguard nature, the engineer attempts to appropriate the reproductive power of the female river in order to create a new river. Whether from the romantic's or the engineer's perspective, one of the objectives in the restructuring of the Mississippi is definition and control of the female body.

10. See Louis Althusser, "Ideology and Ideological State Apparatuses," in *Lenin and Philosophy* (New York: Monthly Review Press, 1971). By establishing a system of "beacons" and "signals," the West Pointers "interpellate" the Mississippi River (and the pilots), thereby transforming them into subjects.

11. *Selected Mark Twain–Howells Letters, 1872–1910*, ed. Frederick Anderson, William M. Gibson, and Henry Nash Smith (New York: Atheneum, 1968), 200. The best account of the composition of *Life on the Mississippi* can be found in Horst H. Kruse's *Mark Twain and "Life on the Mississippi"* (Amherst: Univ. of Massachusetts Press, 1981).

12. *Twain–Howells Letters*, 202–3.

13. Cecilia Tichi, *Shifting Gears: Technology, Literature, Culture in Modernist America* (Chapel Hill: Univ. of North Carolina Press, 1987), 99. Although the narrator of *Life on the Mississippi* starts out by celebrating the engineer in contrast to the scientist, who "gets such wholesale returns of conjecture out of such a trifling investment of fact" (147), the engineer quickly becomes guilty of trying to "fetter and handcuff that river and boss him" (205). The word "boss" clearly predicts Hank Morgan, the "boss of Camelot," and his complex relation to medieval England.

14. Twain's process of composition is notoriously problematic (one need only think of *The Adventures of Huckleberry Finn* and *Pudd'nhead Wilson*), and some of the finest criticism has dealt with the relation between plot and ideology. See Horwitz, *By the Law of Nature*; Edgar J. Burde, "Mark Twain: The Writer as Pilot," *PMLA*, 93 (1978), 878–92; and Lawrence Howe, "Transcending the

Limits of Experience: Mark Twain's *Life on the Mississippi*," *American Literature*, 63 (1991), 420–39.

15. In the manuscript, Uncle Mumford's question "*where* in blazes are you going with that barrel now?" originally appeared as "where in the hell are you going with that barrel now?" (447 n.35). This editorial "reform" seems ironic given the fact that the narrator takes on the task of editing and omitting certain elements in Mumford's text. In this case, the narrator's editing must in turn be edited.

16. Another example of this narrative detouring occurs in the following passage: "Upon that text I desire to depart from the direct line of my subject, and make a little excursion" (360).

17. *Life on the Mississippi* was not one of Twain's more successful books, and the reviews were mixed. A *Harper's* review described it as "a graphic account teeming with solid information, occasionally alleviated by mirth-provoking oddities of thought and expression" (quoted in Everett Emerson, *The Authentic Mark Twain: A Literary Biography of Samuel L. Clemens* [Philadelphia: Univ. of Pennsylvania Press, 1984], 126). Most critics have found the second half deficient, beginning with an English reviewer who dismissed it as "mere reportage" (quoted in ibid., 126). Leo Marx mourns the second half of *Life on the Mississippi* as "mark[ing] the passing of a way of life, a mode of apprehending nature, and by inference, a literary style" (*The Pilot and the Passenger*, 26).

18. Quoted in Kruse, *Mark Twain and "Life on the Mississippi,"* xvi.

19. Here Mark Seltzer's discussion of statistical persons in Crane is relevant. Whereas "Crane's stories are populated if not quite peopled by statistical persons," according to Seltzer, *Life on the Mississippi* includes statistical persons and what we might call more traditional fictional characters (*Bodies and Machines* [New York: Routledge, 1992], 106).

20. Reprinted in *Discussions in Economics and Statistics*, ed. Davis R. Dewey, vol. 2 (New York: Holt, 1899), 51. An excellent bibliographical source of material on demography and social science is Daniel Horowitz's "Genteel Observers: New England Economic Writers and Industrialization," *New England Quarterly*, 48 (1975), 65–83.

21. This article appeared in *Atlantic Monthly*, 24 (1869), 689–701, and is reprinted in *Discussions in Economics and Statistics*, 4.

22. The production of names but not "real" (as real as persons can be in a fiction) persons occurs in "A Burning Brand," in which Jack Hunt, a burglar having finished his jail sentence, writes a sentimental letter to his friend and cellmate Charlie Williams detailing his adventures outside prison and the moral successes he has after encountering a certain Mr. Brown. The letter turns out to be a scam, written by Williams himself to himself in order to secure his own release from prison. The story is an exercise in the invention of names sans persons: in the letter allegedly written by Jack Hunt, Hunt has taken Williams's name; Jack Hunt turns out to be "an imaginary person" (369), as does "the benevolent Brown," who "was not a real person" (369); and last, the narrator was given permission to print the story only if he agreed to "suppress

names and places" (368). For another reading of this story, see Horwitz, *By the Law of Nature*, 114–19.

23. The narrator, in typical Twain fashion, does not rest easy with the statistical model of personhood. As comfortable as he may be with recording demo graphic statistics as if they were the absolute truth about persons, he includes the following: "One Monday, near the time of our visit to St. Louis, the 'Globe-Democrat' came out with a couple of pages of Sunday statistics, whereby it appeared that 119,448 St. Louis people attended the morning and evening church services the day before, and 23,102 children attended Sunday-school. Thus 142,550 persons, out of the city's total of 400,000 population, respected the day religious-wise. I found these statistics, in a condensed form, in a telegram of the Associated Press, and preserved them. They made it apparent that St. Louis was in a higher state of grace than she could have claimed to be in my time. But now that I canvass the figures narrowly, I suspect that the telegraph mutilated them. It cannot be that there are more than 150,000 Catholics in the town; the other 250,000 must be classified as Protestants. Out of these 250,000, according to this questionable telegram, only 26,362 attended church and Sunday-school, while out of the 150,000 Catholics, 116,118 went to church and Sunday-school" (359).

24. For a fine discussion of the systematic response to suffering, see George M. Fredrickson, *The Inner Civil War: Modern Intellectuals and the Crisis of the Union* (New York: Harper & Row, 1965), 92–112. Also see Ann Douglas, *The Feminization of American Culture*, 240–72, and Karen Haltunnen, *Confidence Men and Painted Women*, 124–52.

25. *Mark Twain's Notebooks and Journals*, vol. 3, *1883–1891*, ed. Robert Pack Browning, Michael B. Frank, and Lin Salamo (Berkeley and Los Angeles: Univ. of California Press, 1979), 230.

26. Horace Greeley et al., *The Great Industries of the United States: Being an Historical Summary of the Origin, Growth, and Perfection of the Chief Industrial Arts of This Country* (Hartford: Burr & Hyde, 1873), v, 71.

27. Norman J. Ware, *The Labor Movement in the United States, 1860–1895* (Chicago: Quadrangle Books, 1929), 55.

28. 1885 Documents. "It Took In Millions" [.] undated, unidentified newspaper article in Mark Twain Papers, Bancroft Library, University of California, Berkeley (hereafter abbreviated as MTP).

29. John S. Thompson, *History of Composing Machines: A Complete Record of the Art of Composing Type by Machinery* (Chicago: Inland, 1904), 25.

30. Richard Huss, *The Development of Printers' Mechanical Typesetting Methods, 1822–1925* (Charlottesville: Univ. Press of Virginia, n.d.), 80, 25. On July 26, 1887, Twain wrote to Paige, "You are required to prosecute the work on the machine as fast as tracings may be furnished, and instead of doing so, you have unnecessarily protracted the work and caused a serious delay in building the machine. This delay is a great damage to me" (MTP).

31. Justin Kaplan, *Mr. Clemens and Mark Twain* (New York: Pocket Books, 1968), 355.

32. Ibid., 335.

33. 1885 Documents. "It Took In Millions" [.] undated, unidentified newspaper article in MTP.
34. JWP to SLC, August 20, 1885; JWP to SLC, November 18, 1885; JWP to SLC, July 5, 1887 (MTP). This pattern continued throughout the 1890s until Twain's friend and financial guardian angel, Henry Huttleston Rogers, helped Twain abrogate his connection with Paige.
35. Quoted in Kaplan, *Mr. Clemens and Mark Twain,* 360.
36. Only one typesetter remains. It is on display at Twain's house in Hartford, Connecticut.
37. Huss, *Printers' Mechanical Typesetting Methods,* 381.
38. Huss does admit that "a grave error was made. . . . Many parts of the first combined machine were used in the construction of the new machine, with the result that when the machine was completed and in operation it contained features which prevented its use as a model upon which to base a plant for manufacturing" (380).
39. Thompson, *History of Composing Machines,* 26. Kaplan notes, "The machine was so obsessively tinkered with and 'improved' that it was rarely in working order" (*Mr. Clemens and Mark Twain,* 356).
40. *A Connecticut Yankee in King Arthur's Court* (1889), ed. Allison R. Ensor (New York: Norton, 1982), 173. All further quotations from *A Connecticut Yankee* will be from this edition and will be noted in the text.
41. Although scientific management did not officially appear on the American scene until the turn of the century, its program of hard work, efficient output, and routinized labor were well in place before 1895, when Taylor gave his lecture "A Piece Rate System: Being a Step Toward Partial Solution of the Labor Problem" to the American Society of Mechanical Engineers. In the discussion of Melville, we noted the powerful presence of the work ethic in antebellum America. In fact, one need only recall that Henry Ward Beecher chose "Industry and Idleness" as the first topic in his *Lectures to Young Men on Various Important Subjects* (1844; rpt. Boston: Jewett, 1853), in which he describes "the wiles of idleness – how it creeps upon men, how secretly it mingles with their pursuits, how much time it purloins from the scholar, from the professional man, and from the artisan" (23). Jeremiads like this represented one attempt to get the most out of workers by warning them of the sins of idleness. Taylor's system wholeheartedly accepted this basic suspicion of idleness, but, rather than relying on workers' moral strength to combat this "wile," scientific management offered workers a technological program to prevent idleness from "secretly mingl[ing] with their pursuits."
42. FJH to SLC, August 5, 1889, MTP.
43. 1885 Documents. Paige Machine Notes, late 1880s–1890. No. 199 "The Paige Compositor," MTP.
44. Quoted in Leon Litwack, *The American Labor Movement* (Englewood Cliffs, N.J.: Prentice-Hall, 1962), 16.
45. Quoted in *Popular Culture and Industrialism, 1865-1890,* ed. Henry Nash Smith (New York: New York Univ. Press, 1967), 293.
46. *Mark Twain's Notebooks and Journals,* vol. 3, 147.

47. FJH to SLC, August 19, 1889, MTP.
48. March 22, 1886. Manuscript unpublished speech delivered as: "The Knights of Labor – The New Dynasty" before the Monday Evening Club on March 22, 1886, MTP.
49. SLC to HHR, December 22, 1894, in *Mark Twain's Correspondence with Henry Huttleston Rogers, 1893–1909*, ed. Lewis Leary (Berkeley and Los Angeles: Univ. of California Press, 1969), 108. Twain was not the only one to anthropomorphize the Paige typesetter. An advertisement raves, "It is not a mere type-setting machine. It is a compositor in the truest sense of the word, as it performs simultaneously all the work of a human compositor" (*The Paige Compositor* [New York: Connecticut Co., 1892], 13). Even Henry Huttleston Rogers, Twain's voice of reason, writes: "I am sure the Paige Compositor will have an opportunity of speaking for itself at a later time. If it speaks correctly, that is all we desire" (HHR to SLC, March 13, 1894, in *Mark Twain's Correspondence*, 45).
50. Quoted in *Popular Culture and Industrialism*, 342.
51. Henry George, *Social Problems* (New York: Doubleday, 1912), 49.
52. Quoted in *Popular Culture and Industrialism*, 366.
53. Quoted in ibid., 360.
54. Henry Nash Smith, *Mark Twain's Fable of Progress: Political and Economic Ideas in "A Connecticut Yankee"* (New Brunswick, N.J.: Rutgers Univ. Press, 1964), 85. Similarly, Bernard DeVoto has the following complaint about Twain's later characters: "They are just puppets, unreal creatures moving in a shadow-play, and they are seen with the detachment of an immortal spirit, passionless and untouched" (*Mark Twain at Work* [Cambridge: Harvard Univ. Press, 1942], 128). Also see James M. Cox, *Mark Twain: The Fate of Humor* (Princeton: Princeton Univ. Press, 1966), 198–221, and Kenneth S. Lynn, *Mark Twain and Southwestern Humor* (1960) (Westport, Conn.: Greenwood Press, 1976), 249–58.
55. Walter Benjamin, *The Origin of German Tragic Drama*, trans. John Osborne (London: New Left Books, 1977), 187.
56. James M. Cox, "*A Connecticut Yankee in King Arthur's Court*: The Machinery of Self-Preservation," in *A Connecticut Yankee in King Arthur's Court*, 396.
57. Mark Twain, *The Mysterious Stranger, #44*, ed. William M. Gibson (Berkeley and Los Angeles: Univ. of California Press, 1982), 63–4. All further quotations will be from this edition and will be noted in the text.
58. Quoted in Daniel Rodgers, *The Work Ethic in Industrial America, 1850–1920* (Chicago: Univ. of Chicago Press, 1974), 53.
59. In *The American Claimant* (1891; rpt. New York: Doubleday, n.d.), Colonel Sellers plans to "materialize the dead" and thereby solve the labor problem. Speaking to an unbeliever, Sellers declares, "Let the world stand aghast, for it shall see marvels . . . you shall see me call the dead of any century, and they will arise and walk . . . I shall have a monopoly; they'll all belong to me, won't they? Two thousand policemen in the city of New York. Wages, four dollars a day. I'll replace them with dead ones at half the money" (30). The answer to labor agitation is not the improvement of conditions in the workplace but rather the resurrection of an endless supply of laborers – whether they be scabs or dead people.

60. Taylor's ideal workforce is, in fact, not unlike Bernard DeVoto's description of Twain's later characters.

61. Frederick Winslow Taylor, *The Principles of Scientific Management* (New York: Norton, 1967), 6–7, 43.

62. Samuel Haber, *Efficiency and Uplift: Scientific Management in the Progressive Era, 1890–1920* (Chicago: Midway, 1975), 5.

63. Quoted in Rodgers, *The Work Ethic*, 178.

64. Henry George, *Progress and Poverty: An Inquiry into the Cause of Industrial Depressions and the Increase of Want with Increase of Wealth – The Remedy* (1880; rpt. New York: Robert Schalkenbach, 1951), 285; Henry D. Lloyd, *Men, the Workers* (New York: Doubleday, 1909), 29.

65. Josephine Goldmark, *Fatigue and Efficiency: A Study in Industry* (New York: Charities Publication Committee, 1912), 79–80.

66. Washington Gladden, *Social Facts and Forces* (New York: Putnam, 1897), 3; Starr Hoyt Nichols, "Men and Machinery," *North American Review*, 166 (1898), 603.

67. Quoted in Smith, *Popular Culture*, 274; William C. Redfield, "The Moral Value of Scientific Management," *Atlantic Monthly*, 110 (1912), 415, 412.

68. Sigmund Freud, "The Uncanny," in *The Standard Edition of the Complete Psychological Works of Sigmund Freud*, vol. 17, ed. James Strachey (London: Hogarth, 1955), 235. Interestingly, Freud refers to Twain's comedic use of the uncanny in *A Tramp Abroad*: "One may wander about in a dark, strange room, looking for the door or the electric switch, and collide time after time with the same piece of furniture – though it is true that Mark Twain succeeded by wild exaggeration in turning this latter situation into something irresistibly comic" (237).

69. Ibid., 234.

70. The manuscripts of *The Mysterious Stranger, #44* have been the subject of much debate. See John S. Tuckey, *Mark Twain and Little Satan: The Writing of "The Mysterious Stranger,"* Purdue Univ. Studies (West Lafayette, 1963), and Sholom J. Kahn, *Mark Twain's Mysterious Stranger: A Study of the Manuscript Texts* (Columbia: Univ. of Missouri Press, 1978).

71. Henry Wood, *The Political Economy of Natural Law* (Boston: Lee & Shepard, 1894), 6.

72. Washington Gladden, *Working People and Their Employers* (New York: Funk, 1894), 43. James Dodge, a Philadelphia manufacturer, also calculates this symbiotic understanding of the relations between workers and employers: "[The worker] must appreciate that his interests and those of his employer are mutual, and that their happiness and success depend upon mutual trust and consideration." (Quoted in *Scientific Management: A Collection of the More Significant Articles Describing the Taylor System of Management*, ed. Clarence Bertrand Thompson [Harvard Business Studies, 1; Cambridge, Mass.: Harvard Univ. Press, 1914], 295.)

73. Susan Gillman, *Dark Twins: Imposture and Identity in Mark Twain's America* (Chicago: Univ. of Chicago Press, 1989), 167.

74. The duplicates of *The Mysterious Stranger, #44* support Walter Benn Michaels's

claims about the conception of character in *A Connecticut Yankee* "as mechanical and as thus susceptible only (but absolutely) to external change . . . To put it another way, the Yankee doesn't exactly *have* a character, he *is* the character he can be described as having; he is incapable of behaving 'out of character' because his character is defined by nothing but his behavior" ("An American Tragedy, or the Promise of American Life," *Representations*, 25 [1989], 79).

75. Fussell, "The Structural Problem of *The Mysterious Stranger*," *Studies in Philology*, 49 (1952), 96; Michelson, "Deus Ludens: The Shaping of Mark Twain's Mysterious Stranger," *Novel*, 14 (1980), 56. In his reading of the "Eseldorf" version of *The Mysterious Stranger*, Henry Nash Smith links Eseldorf to Hannibal and argues that Twain "is destroying the image which had served him for thirty years as a metaphor for all human society. . . . He performs this desperate action because man is literally beneath contempt and the Deity who could make such a creature is too absurd to be taken seriously" ("Mark Twain's Images of Hannibal: From St. Petersburg to Eseldorf," *Texas Studies in English*, 37 [1958], 22).

CHAPTER 5. THE MANIKIN, THE MACHINE, AND THE VIRGIN MARY

1. In the introduction to *Renaissance Self-Fashioning: From More to Shakespeare* (Chicago: Univ. of Chicago Press, 1980), Greenblatt offers the following explanation of self-fashioning: "Self-fashioning derives its interest precisely from the fact that it functions without regard for a sharp distinction between literature and social life. It invariably crosses the boundaries between the creation of literary characters, the shaping of one's identity, the experience of being molded by forces outside one's control, the attempt to fashion other selves" (3).

2. Henry Adams, *The Education of Henry Adams*, ed. Ernest Samuels (Boston: Houghton Mifflin, 1973), xxx. All further quotations from *The Education* will be from this edition and will be noted in the text.

3. Carolyn Porter argues that through the figure of the manikin "Adams objectifies himself, and the figure so objectified functions . . . as an observer" (*Seeing and Being: The Plight of the Participant Observer in Emerson, James, Adams and Faulkner* [Middletown, Conn.: Wesleyan Univ. Press, 1981], 168). Like Porter's my discussion of Adams's personae reveals the ways in which Adams's manikin pose allows him to be both subject and object, tailor and manikin.

4. Ralph M. Hower, *History of Macy's of New York, 1858–1919* (Cambridge: Harvard Univ. Press, 1943), 163. See also 114–16.

5. Lloyd Wendt and Herman Kogan, *Give the Lady What She Wants! The Story of Marshall Field and Company* (Chicago: Rand McNally, 1952), 307, 291. Also see Alan Trachtenberg, *The Incorporation of America: Culture & Society in the Gilded Age* (New York: Hill & Wang, 1982), esp. 130–6, Rachel Bowlby, *Just Looking: Consumer Culture in Dreiser, Gissing, and Zola* (London: Methuen, 1983), and Susan Porter Benson, *Counter Cultures: Saleswomen, Managers, and Customers in American Department Stores, 1890–1940* (Urbana: Univ. of Illinois Press, 1988).

6. Quoted in Neil Harris, "Museums, Merchandising, and Popular Taste," in *Material Culture and the Study of American Life*, ed. Ian M. G. Quimby (New York: Norton, 1978), 151.

7. Stuart Culver, "What Manikins Want: *The Wonderful World of Oz* and *The Art of Decorating Dry Goods Windows*," *Representations*, 21 (1988), 110.

8. On the use of manikins in the department stores of Great Britain during this time, see Alison Adburgham, *Shops and Shopping, 1800–1914: Where, and in What Manner the Well-Dressed Englishwoman Bought Her Clothes* (London: Allen, 1964), 201–3.

9. Quoted in Benson, *Counter Cultures*, 43.

10. *Scientific Management: A Collection of the More Significant Articles Describing the Taylor System of Management*, ed. Clarence Bertrand Thompson (Harvard Business Studies, 1; Cambridge: Harvard Univ. Press, 1914), 545, 549.

11. HA to EC, October 8, 1893, in *The Letters of Henry Adams*, ed. J. C. Levenson, Ernest Samuels, Charles Vandersee, and Viola Hopkins Winner (Cambridge: Harvard Univ. Press, 1982–8), vol. 4 (*1892–1899*), 132. The organizers of the fair had divided the exhibits into two distinct areas, White City and the Midway. The buildings of White City, such as Machinery Hall and Agricultural Hall, showcased the newest technological inventions which would demonstrate America's "conquest of nature in the industrial world" (*The Historical World's Columbian Exposition and Chicago Guide* [St. Louis: Pacific Publishing, 1892], 4).

12. William E. Cameron, Thomas W. Palmer, and Frances E. Willard, *The Chicago World's Fair: Being a Pictorial History of the Columbian Exposition* (Philadelphia: National Publishing, 1893), 657.

13. For examples of Adams as the displaced artist, see Tony Tanner, "The Lost America – The Despair of Henry Adams and Mark Twain," *Modern Age*, 5 (1961), 299–310, and William Wasserstrom, *The Ironies of Progress: Henry Adams and the American Dream* (Carbondale: Southern Illinois Univ. Press, 1984). On Adams's relation to science, see William Jordy, *Henry Adams: Scientific History* (New Haven: Yale Univ. Press, 1952), and Ronald Martin, *American Literature and the Universe of Force* (Durham: Duke Univ. Press, 1981). On Adams's use of language, see Melvin Lyon, *Symbol and Idea in Henry Adams* (Lincoln: Univ. of Nebraska Press, 1970), and John Carlos Rowe, *Henry James and Henry Adams* (Ithaca: Cornell Univ. Press, 1985).

14. T. J. Jackson Lears, *No Place of Grace: Antimodernism and the Transformation of American Culture, 1880–1920* (New York: Pantheon, 1981), 276. My understanding of Adams's relation to the work ethic is indebted to Lears's brilliant revisionary reading of this period in American culture, in which he argues, "[Adams's] scientific speculation was driven by a desire to turn science against itself, to discredit positivist certainties" (263). Lears's notion of Adams as an "antimodern modernist" (297) anticipates the function of allegory in *The Education*, which, in its temporal duality, signifies the presence of an archaic and a modern worldview at one and the same time. This reading of *The Education* differs, however, in that whereas Lears uses a psychoanalytic paradigm that analogizes Adams's relation to his father and attitude toward sci-

ence, my analysis stresses how Adams's appropriation of discourses, whether work, science, or religion, undoes the authority of those very discourses.

15. Thorstein Veblen, *The Theory of the Leisure Class* (1899; rpt. New York: Penguin, 1967), 57. Critics have had little to say about the relation between Adams and Veblen. Ernest Samuels quotes Adams as saying, "Throughout all the thought of Germany, France, and England, – for there is no thought in America – runs a growing stream of pessimism which comes in a continuous current from Malthus and Karl Marx and Schopenhauer" and then adds, "[Adams] thus cavalierly dismissed as mere pretenders William James, John Dewey, Josiah Royce, Arthur Lovejoy, Thorstein Veblen, and all their fellows" (*Henry Adams: The Major Phase* [Cambridge: Harvard Univ. Press, 1964], 472).

16. Walter Benn Michaels, "An American Tragedy, or the Promise of American Life," *Representations*, 25 (1989), 84.

17. Washington Irving opens *The Sketch Book of Geoffrey Crayon, Gent.* with the following confession: "My whole course of life . . . has been desultory, and I am unfitted for any periodically recurring task, or any stipulated labor of body or mind" ([1820; rpt. New York: New American Library, 1961], x). Similarly, "Song of Myself" begins with Whitman's famous celebration of laziness: "I loafe and invite my soul, / I lean and loafe at my ease observing a spear of summer grass" (*Leaves of Grass* [1855], ed. Sculley Bradley and Harold W. Blodgett [New York: Norton, 1973], 28).

18. Michael Denning, *Mechanic Accents: Dime Novels and Working-Class Culture in America* (New York: Verso, 1987), 149.

19. Orlando F. Lewis, "The American Tramp," *Atlantic Monthly*, 1 (1908), 748.

20. Ibid., 744.

21. Washington Gladden, *Working People and Their Employers* (New York: Funk, 1894), 62–3.

22. Detailed discussions of the unemployment problem at this time can be found in Paul T. Ringenbach, *Tramps and Reformers, 1873–1916: The Discovery of Unemployment in New York* (Westport, Conn.: Greenwood, 1973), and Alexander Keyssar, *Out of Work: The First Century of Unemployment in Massachusetts* (Cambridge: Cambridge Univ. Press, 1986).

23. A latter-day version of Beecher was Josiah Strong, who admonished America about its rapidly developing "unemployed class, which furnishes ready recruits to the criminal, intemperate, socialistic and revolutionary classes" and then blamed the needy when their "enforced idleness . . . soon brings want" (*Our Country: Its Possible Future and Its Present Crisis* [New York: Baker & Taylor, 1880], 98, 106). Henry George claimed that tramps "are surely the marks of 'material progress' as are costly dwellings, rich warehouses, and magnificent churches" but went on to defend tramps on the basis that they wished to work but could not find employment (*Progress and Poverty: An Inquiry into the Cause of Industrial Depressions and the Increase of Want with Increase of Wealth – The Remedy* [1880; rpt. New York: Robert Schalkenbach, 1951], 3–4). For George, it was the idleness of the rich that produced the idleness of the poor.

24. For an exhaustive analysis of America's preoccupation with efficiency and waste during this time, see Cecilia Tichi, *Shifting Gears: Technology, Literature, Culture in Modernist America* (Chapel Hill: Univ. of North Carolina Press, 1987).

25. Frederick Winslow Taylor, *The Principles of Scientific Management* (1911; rpt. New York: Norton, 1967), 13.

26. Ibid., 6, 79, 78.

27. Haber, *Efficiency and Uplift*, x, 24.

28. Although she approaches these issues of leisure and labor through the lens of both a different country and a different genre, Kristin Ross's analysis of Rimbaud provides an enlightening account of Rimbaud's attempts through poetry to revise his culture's traditional definitions of work. By challenging the conventional reading of Rimbaud's laziness as an "art for art's sake" avoidance of social issues in nineteenth-century France, she argues for the subversiveness of Rimbaud's laziness: "The true threat to existing order comes not from some untainted working class but from a challenge to the boundaries *between* labor and leisure, producer and consumer, worker and bourgeois, worker and intellectual" (*The Emergence of Social Space: Rimbaud and the Paris Commune* [Minneapolis: Univ. of Minnesota Press, 1988], 61).

29. For one of the few attempts to explain the effects of Marian and Henry's childlessness, see Katherine Simonds, "The Tragedy of Mrs. Henry Adams," *New England Quarterly*, 9 (1936), 564–82.

30. Quoted in ibid., 577.

31. HA to CMG, November 25, 1877, in *The Letters*, vol. 2 (*1868–1885*), 327.

32. Ernest Samuels, *The Middle Years* (Cambridge, Mass.: Harvard Univ. Press, 1958), 39. We do know, however, that Mrs. Adams was eager to cultivate her friendship with Mitchell, "whom [she] long wished to know . . . and [who] was very bright and full of talk" (MA to Robert Hooper, March 11, 1883, in *The Letters of Mrs. Henry Adams*, ed. Ward Thoron [Boston: Little, 1937], 428).

33. Samuels, *The Middle Years*, 430 n. 24.

34. James Marion Sims, *Clinical Notes on Uterine Surgery – With Special Reference to the Management of Sterile Conditions* (New York: J. H. Vail, 1886), 13.

35. Ibid., 18.

36. Taylor, *Principles of Scientific Management*, 83.

37. For a thorough discussion of Sims's mechanical approach to female sexuality and sexual intercourse, see G. J. Barker-Benfield, *The Horrors of the Half-Known Life: Male Attitudes Toward Women and Sexuality in Nineteenth-Century America* (New York: Harper & Row, 1976), 91–119.

38. Seale Harris, *Woman's Surgeon: The Life Story of J. Marion Sims* (New York: Macmillan, 1950), 176. Carroll Smith-Rosenberg views Sims's invention and use of surgical instruments as an attempt "through the development of virtuoso surgical skills to raise the status of gynecology as a surgical specialty" (*Disorderly Conduct: Visions of Gender in Victorian America* [Oxford: Oxford Univ. Press, 1985], 4).

39. Horace Bushnell, *Women's Suffrage; The Reform Against Nature* (New York: Scribner, 1869), 136.

40. George M. Beard, *American Nervousness and Its Consequences* (1881; rpt. New York: Arno, 1972), 76–7.

41. About Marian's death, Porter writes, "It is impossible to overestimate Marian Adams' suicide as a force in Adams' subsequent life and thought" (*Seeing and Being*, 180).

42. In "The Dynamo and the Virgin," Adams says about Edward Gibbon: "One would have paid largely for a photograph of the fat little historian, on the background of Notre Dame of Amiens" (386).

43. Adams, *Mont-Saint-Michel and Chartres* (Princeton: Princeton Univ. Press, 1981), xiv. All quotations from *Mont-Saint-Michel and Chartres* will be from this edition and will be noted in the text.

44. Walter Benjamin, "The Work of Art in the Age of Mechanical Reproduction," in *Illuminations*, ed. Hannah Arendt (New York: Schocken, 1969), 221.

45. "The Dynamo and the Virgin" is the chapter in *The Education* that has received the most attention. For examples of criticism solely about this chapter, see Lynn White, "Dynamo and Virgin Reconsidered," *American Scholar*, 27 (1958), 183–94, and Leo Marx, *The Machine in the Garden*. For more recent readings of these images, see Mark Seltzer, *Bodies and Machines*, and Tichi, *Shifting Gears*.

46. Ralph Maud, "Henry Adams: Irony and Impasse," *Essays in Criticism*, 8 (1958), 383.

47. Lyon, *Symbol and Idea in Henry Adams*, 8, 10.

48. Similarly, Tichi argues that "Adams' own ambivalence [about technology] impaired him. His respect for technology had its well-known negative side, which undermined his efforts at symbolism" (*Shifting Gears*, 158). "Undermining symbolism," far from impairing Adams, is precisely what generates allegory in *The Education*. Indeed, Adams's understanding of the modern world has very little to do with the process of symbolism as formulated by Coleridge.

49. Samuel Taylor Coleridge, "Lay Sermons," in *The Collected Works of Samuel Taylor Coleridge*, ed. R. J. White (London: Routledge & Kegan Paul, 1972), 30.

50. Tichi, *Shifting Gears*, 164.

51. Like the window decorator of Frank Baum's *The Art of Decorating Dry Goods Windows* (Chicago: Show Window Publishing Co., 1900), who must direct attention "toward the carrying out of the small details, without which there can be no perfect specimen of the window trimmer's art" (14), Adams's Virgin is "extremely sensitive to neglect, to disagreeable impressions, [and] to want of intelligence in her surroundings" (90).

52. Benson, *Counter Cultures*, 17. For more on the relation between neurasthenia and the work ethic, see Anson Rabinbach, *The Human Motor: Energy, Fatigue, and the Origins of Modernity* (New York: Basic, 1990).

53. HA to EC, July 13, 1899, in *The Letters*, vol. 4, 735.

54. Max Weber's analysis of the work ethic sheds light on Adams's interest in and exploration of Catholicism: "The God of Calvinism demanded of his believers not single good works, but a life of good works combined into a unified system. There was no place for the very human Catholic cycle of sin, repen-

tance, atonement, release, followed by renewed sin. Nor was there any balance of merit for a life as a whole which could be adjusted by temporal
punishments or the Churches' means of grace" (*The Protestant Ethic and the
Spirit of Capitalism* [New York: Scribner, 1958], 117).

55. Gregory Jay offers an excellent deconstructive reading of the Virgin in *America the Scrivener: Deconstruction and the Subject of Literary History* (Ithaca: Cornell
Univ. Press, 1990), 220. William Merrill Decker similarly claims that "the
problematizing of the author is relentless. We must keep in view all the more
the fact that these multiples of Henry Adams resolved sufficiently to materialize in acts of publication: the two first editions of the *Education*, which in time
became a singular, if in interpretation ever a multiple, bequest" (*The Literary
Vocation of Henry Adams* [Chapel Hill: Univ. of North Carolina Press, 1990],
272). On the complex relation between signature and presence–absence, see
Jacques Derrida, "Signature Event Context," in *Limited Inc* (Evanston: Northwestern Univ. Press, 1990).

56. Although one might be tempted to make the argument that Adams's glorifica-
tion of medieval guilds and the lack of individual agency that characterizes
them is a thirteenth-century version of Taylor's twentieth-century attack on
agency, it seems clear that the kind of labor represented by these guilds had little
to do with the standardizing and isolating techniques of scientific management
which Walter Benn Michaels has delineated in "An American Tragedy."

57. *Summa Theologiae*, vol. 52 (New York: McGraw-Hill, 1972), 101. Adams's
letters of 1900 indicate that he read widely in Aquinas. He writes to John Hay,
"I study scholastic dialectics and St Thomas Aquinas in a darkened room on
the fifth story of a house which has one hundred and twenty seven stairs and
an occasional lift" (*The Letters*, vol. 5 [*1899–1905*], 139). He writes to his
brother Brooks, "As for me, I have been absorbed in St Thomas Aquinas, and
have hardly looked at anything else" (ibid., 134). Adams's special interest in
Aquinas's views on the Virgin is evident in a 1904 letter to Charles Milnes
Gaskell: "The Virgin and St Thomas are my vehicles of anarchism. Nobody
knows enough to see what they mean, so the Judges will probably not be able
to burn me according to law" (ibid., 618).

58. Walter Benjamin, *The Origin of German Tragic Drama*, trans. John Osborne
(London: New Left Books, 1977), 119.

59. HA to EC, February 8, 1903, in *The Letters*, vol. 5, 452.

60. HA to Ward Thoron, June 10, 1910, in *The Letters*, vol. 6 (*1906–1918*), 343.

61. HA to EC, January 24, 1910, in ibid., 301.

62. HA to BW, May 18, 1910, in ibid., 337.

63. For example, Jordy in *Henry Adams: Scientific History* emphasizes the correct-
ness or incorrectness of Adams's use of science and does not consider that his
appropriation of scientific language might be ironic.

AFTERWORD

1. Roosevelt's speech is quoted in *The Muckrakers*, ed. Arthur Weinberg and Lila
Weinberg (New York: Capricorn Books, 1964), 59. As I have indicated, he

gave an early version of the speech at the Gridiron Club and shortly thereafter gave it again at a political ceremony that marked the laying of the cornerstone of the United States House of Representatives office building in Washington, D.C. The speech was reprinted in the April 15, 1906, issue of the *New York Tribune*.

2. On the question of corporate agency and its relation to individual agency, see Howard Horwitz, *By the Law of Nature: Form and Value in Nineteenth-Century America* (Oxford: Oxford Univ. Press, 1991), in particular his brilliant chapter "Transcendent Agency: Emerson, the Standard Trust, and the Virtues of De-corporation" (171–91), which argues for a line of continuity between the ideology of agency illustrated by Emerson's transparent eyeball and the corporate agency of the Standard Oil Trust. Also see Walter Benn Michaels's chapter "Corporate Fiction" (183–213) in *The Gold Standard and the Logic of Naturalism: American Literature at the Turn of the Century* (Berkeley and Los Angeles: Univ. of California Press, 1987). Convincing as these arguments are, they focus exclusively on Ida Tarbell's *The History of the Standard Oil Company* and do not consider her work in the context of other muckraking efforts. If we examine other texts in the muckraking tradition, the situation takes on greater complexity. Horwitz is correct to argue that "the scandal of the trust for Tarbell is not just that it was immoral, but that the agent (and hence evidence) of its immorality was obscured in the shadow of the institution he spawned" (173), but this is not the case for all of the muckrakers. Much of their work suggests that the agent of immorality can be exposed if one gets deep enough in the muck.

3. "Making Steel and Killing Men" originally appeared in *Everybody's Magazine*, November 1907, and is reprinted in *The Muckrakers* (358).

4. This article originally appeared in *McClure's Magazine*, January 1903, and is reprinted in *The Muckrakers* (6).

5. This article originally appeared in *Cosmopolitan*, March 1906, and is reprinted in *The Muckrakers* (71).

6. This article originally appeared in *Harper's Magazine*, December 1909, and is reprinted in *The Muckrakers* (160).

7. Lincoln Steffens's "The Shame of Minneapolis" concludes with "Minneapolis should be clean and sweet for a little while at least, and the new administration should begin with a clear deck" (quoted in ibid., 21).

Index

accountability (issue), 89, 102–4, 113–14, 233n35

Adams, Charles Francis, 180–1

Adams, Henry, 4, 5, 11, 60, 173–206; childlessness, 190, 192; family life, 189–95; manikin in, 173–8; master of disguise, 178–89; private secretary to father, 180–1, 183, 188

Adams, John, 179

Adams, John Quincy, 179

Adams, Marian, 190, 192

Addams, Jane, 190

Address to the Members of Trade Societies and the Working Classes (Heighton), 19

Adventures of Huckleberry Finn, The (Twain), 240n14

aesthetic ideology, 36, 57, 88, 106; antebellum, 38, 98, 215n4; and economics, 9; erasure of labor in, 199; invisible labor in, 79, 80, 82, 90, 231n2; in literary labors of Twain, 131

aesthetics: of allegory and symbol, 44; of literary marketplace, 40–3

agency, 3, 4–5, 6, 9, 21, 50, 79; absence of, 29–30, 42, 200–1; and accountability, 102, 114; of allegorical characters, 35–6, 96, 109; characterological, 9, 78; of corporations, 207, 252n2; and discipline, 114; erasure of, 41; of Hawthorne, 78; in law, 89; in literary text, 40; loss of, 50;

machine and, 111; of mechanical bodies, 10; in *Moby-Dick,* 103–4; and muckrakers, 207, 208–11; name and, 112; of poet, 45; in possession/dispossession, 54, 109; problematic status of, 42, 43; reconfiguration of, in allegory, 221n85; relationship to labor and bodies, 10, 12; revealed as myth, in Melville, 100, 103; undermining of, 52; work and, 87, 95–7; work ethic and, 35; *see also* authorial agency

Ahab (character), 4, 24, 89, 93, 103, 106, 203; body of, 106–7; dismemberment of, 189–90; machine and mechanic, 107–14

Albro v. Agawam Canal Company, 102, 113, 114

Alcott, Bronson, 32

Aldrich, Nelson W., 209

allegorical characters, 4–6, 7, 14, 173, 196; in Adams, 190; agency in, 35–6, 96, 109; corporeal element of, 48; correlation with what they stand for, 2–3; in cultural context, 9–12; cultural disease with, 3–4; discomfort with, 42; flatness of, 6–7 (*see also* flat characters); Fletcher's explanation of, 212n5; in Hawthorne, 53–4, 67, 73–4; in Melville, 88–9, 95–8, 101, 104–5, 106, 114, 115, 120, 121, 124, 125; muckrakers as,

253

Bercovitch, Sacvan, 83

Bigelow, Jacob, 27–8, 30; "hand of
taste," 27–8, 31–2, 40

Billy Budd (character), 89, 114–23,
124, 127; body of, 115–16, 117,
122–3, 127–8

*Billy Budd, Sailor (An Inside Narra-
tive)* (Melville), 89, 153, 161, 164,
165, 234n41; function of allegory
in, 12; inside narratives from outside, 114–22

birthmark, allegorical, 55, 69–78; as
invisible hand made visible, 82–6,
87; as sign of Hawthorne's literary
labors, 70–8

"Birth-mark, The" (Hawthorne), 11,
53–4, 55, 69–79, 82–6, 115, 116,
128; parallels with *Life on the Mississippi,* 133; theme of work in, 223n2

Blackmur, R. P., 104, 105

Blacksmith (character) (Perth), 89,
104, 105–6, 111

bodily mutilation, 222n90; in *Moby-
Dick,* 106–7, 108

body(ies), 5, 7, 11; accountability for
injury to, 102–3; in Adams, 175,
190; of Ahab, 89, 106–7, 111; in allegorical characters, 104–6; and/as allegory, 1, 2–5, 8, 9, 10, 11, 47–8;
author's, 42; of Billy Budd, 115–16,
117, 122–3, 127–8; in "The Birthmark," 69; black, 120–1; in "The
Celestial Rail-road," 60; of characters, 7; consumer, 177; contextualized, 122–8; convergence of domesticity and laboratory in, 70–1;
cultural politics of, 236n51; disciplining of, 115; economics of allegory
and, 69–82; in factory labor, 104;
fragility of, 233n38; ideal, 3–4; and
identity, 11; labor and, 36; logic of
market and, 55; manikin, 174, 177,
178, 189–90; maternal, 167, 169,
171; mechanical, 4, 10, 174, 203;
mechanization and manikinization
of, 187; model, 177; reconstruction
of, 42; relation to itself, 50; relation-

ship with labor and agency, 10, 12;
relationship with work and writing,
87–8; as site of competitive market
economy, 85–6; technological, 60,
69; *see also* female body(ies)

body(ies) of workers, 33, 95, 120,
125, 164, 165, 177; allegory of labor
inscribed on, 48; machinery and,
20–3

body parts, 4, 35; as commodities, 8;
machinery and, 150; in *Moby Dick,*
106, 107; loss of, 89, 106

Bomford, George, 33–4

Bonfield, John, 117

Boston Post, 33

Bourdieu, Pierre, 218n50

Brodhead, Richard, 97, 229n49

Bromell, Nicholas K., 213n9, 223n2

Brown, Gillian, 216n29, 218n60

Brown, John, 118, 128

Bruce, Edward, 24

Bulwer-Lytton, William Henry, 7, 42

Bunyan, John, 7, 9, 10, 43, 53, 55, 56,
58–9, 207; Hawthorne's debt to, 54,
61–2, 68–9; names in, 67; personhood in, 64

Bushnell, Horace, 41, 80, 192, 219n67

Butler, Ed, 208

Calhoun, John C., 120

"Call to the Members of the Legislature and the Mechanics and the Laborers of this Commonwealth, A"
(Whitney), 17–18

Cameron, Elizabeth, 203–4

Cameron, Sharon, 220n80

capital: relationship to labor, 167–8

Carpenter (character), 47, 89, 104–5,
108, 111, 145, 188

Catholicism, 250n54

"Celestial Rail-road, The" (Hawthorne), 11, 53, 54–61, 86; idea for,
224n13; names of characters in, 61–
9; similarities to "Benito Cereno,"
226n28

cemetery reform movement, 27, 28, 32

censuses, 141

CAMBRIDGE STUDIES IN AMERICAN LITERATURE AND CULTURE

PS 374 .W64 W45 1995

Weinstein, Cindy.

The literature of labor and
 the labors of literature

GAYLORD S